This book, written by one of the most distinguished of contemporary philosophers of mathematics, is a fully rewritten and updated successor to the author's earlier *The Unprovability of Consistency* (1979). Its subject is the relation between provability and modal logic, a branch of logic invented by Aristotle but much disparaged by philosophers and virtually ignored by mathematicians. Here it receives its first scientific application since its invention.

Modal logic is concerned with the notions of necessity and possibility. What George Boolos does is to show how the concepts, techniques, and methods of modal logic shed brillant light on the most important logical discovery of the twentieth century: the incompleteness theorems of Kurt Gödel and the "self-referential" sentences constructed in their proof. The book explores the effects of reinterpreting the notions of necessity and possibility to mean provability and consistency. It describes the first application of quantified modal logic to formal provability as well as the results of applying modal logic to well-known formal systems of mathematics.

This book will be of critical importance to all logicians and philosophers of logic and mathematics and to many mathematicians.

"I found it lively, lucid, and informative... Boolos' style of writing is unusually kind to the reader. When an argument becomes tricky, he breaks it down into a lot of small steps, showing the reader in detail just how to proceed. A result is that the book is remarkably easy to read."

Vann McGee
Rutgers University

THE LOGIC OF PROVABILITY

THE LOGIC OF PROVABILITY

GEORGE BOOLOS

Massachusetts Institute of Technology

CAMBRIDGE
UNIVERSITY PRESS

Published by the Press Syndicate of the University of Cambridge
The Pitt Building, Trumpington Street, Cambridge CB2 1RP
40 West 20th Street, New York, NY 10011-4211, USA
10 Stamford Road, Oakleigh, Melbourne 3166, Australia

First published 1993

Printed in the United States of America

Library of Congress Cataloging-in-Publication Data

Boolos, George.

The logic of provability / George Boolos.

p. cm.

Includes bibliographical references and index.

ISBN 0-521-43342-8

1. Modality (Logic) 2. Proof theory. I. Title.
BC199.M6B65 1993 92-43610
160 – dc20 CIP

A catalog record for this book is available from the British Library.

ISBN 0-521-43342-8 hardback

This book is for Ruth, Saul, Vann, Warren, Van, Charles, Hilary, Burt, Tim, ⟨Jim⟩, David, Paul, David, Rohit, Raymond, Harvey, Bob, Craig, Sol, Dana, Kit, Lisa, Bob, Harold, Giovanni, Franco, Claudio, Roberto, Sergei, Lena, Valery, Gogi, Kostya, Volodya, Leva, Larisa, Dick, Albert, Johan, Henk, Dirk, Max, Rob, Krister, Angus, Alex, *without whom not.*

Contents

Preface

When modal logic is applied to the study of provability, it becomes provability logic. This book is an essay on provability logic.

In the preface to the precursor to this work, after expressing regret at not being able to include a treatment of the application of quantified modal logic to proof theory, I mentioned that one major question then (1979) open was whether quantified provability logic could be axiomatized. It was a natural enough problem to pose in a work on the application of modal logic to proof theory, and I hoped that the solver, whoever it might be, would send me the answer. I imagined that one morning I would go to the office, get my mail, and find in it an envelope from an unfamilar source, which would turn out to contain a preprint of the long-desired solution.

Well, it happened exactly that way, but the blessed thing turned out to be in Russian. In August 1985, Valery Vardanyan sent me his proof that there is no axiomatization of quantified provability logic. It was contained in a $5\frac{1}{2}$-by-$8\frac{1}{2}$-in. pamphlet, the cover of which read:

В. А. ВАРДАНЯН

О ПРЕДИКАТНОЙ ЛОГИКЕ ДОКАЗУЕМОСТИ

(препринт)

Knowing the Greek alphabet, I deciphered "*predikatnoj*", "*logike*", and "*preprint*" quickly enough, and on noticing inside the telltale: Π_2 as well as formulas like

$$\forall x \forall y \forall z(x + y = z \rightarrow \Box(x + y = z))$$

I sped out the door and bought the only plausible Russian–English dictionary I could then find.

I spent the next week deciphering the pamphlet; and as soon as I became convinced that Vardanyan had indeed proved that quantified provability logic could not be axiomatized, plans for this book began to form.

After exchanges of letters, personal contacts with Soviet logicians, as they were once called, began at the Eighth International Congress of Logic, Methodology and the Philosophy of Science, which was held in Moscow in 1987. ("Have you seen the front page of Pravda today?" "Ssh, not over the telephone," was the current joke.) There I made the acquaintance of Vardanyan and of Sergei Artemov and his remarkable group of students and junior associates, who then included Giorgie Dzhaparidze (from Tbilisi), Lev Beklemishev, and Vladimir Shavrukov; Konstantin Ignatiev would later join their number. Without the results of Vardanyan, Artemov, Dzhaparidze, and Ignatiev, there would have been no call for this book.

"Is it a new book or [just] a second edition of your other book?" my colleagues have asked me.

New book.

All right, there are borderline cases, aren't there? (Hmm, maybe books don't exist since we lack strict criteria of book identity.) And cases over the border, but near it, too. That's what I think the situation is with *The Logic of Provability*: there's enough new material in it for it to be a new book. Of course, when I thought I couldn't do better than I had done in *The Unprovability of Consistency*, I unashamedly copied sections from it. But I think I may call this work the "successor" to that.

What is entirely new is the material in the last six chapters. Chapters 13 and 14 contain proofs of theorems due to Robert Solovay. The theorems were announced in his fundamental 1976 paper, "Provability interpretations of modal logic", and concern set-theoretical interpretations of the box ($\Box$) of modal logic and the modal properties of the notion "provable in second-order arithmetic with the aid of the ω-rule". Proofs of the theorems appear here, for the first time, I believe. Chapter 15 contains completeness theorems due to Dzhaparidze for systems of "bi"-modal logic with two boxes ($\Box$ and $\boxed{1}$) intended to represent ordinary provability and the dual of ω-consistency. Chapter 16 contains, among other things, the fixed point theorem, due to Ignatiev, for the system discussed in Chapter 15.

The basic theorems on quantified provability logic are contained in Chapter 17. The first result in this area was obtained in 1984 by Artemov: the set of formulas of quantified modal logic that are true under all substitutions of formulas of arithmetic is not arithmetical, i.e., not definable by a formula of the language of arithmetic. The other theorems are Vardanyan's result mentioned above and a theorem refining Artemov's theorem that is due to Vann McGee, Vardanyan, and the author. These last two results state that the class of formulas provable under all substitutions from arithmetic and the class of formulas true under all such substitutions are as undecidable as it is a priori possible for them to be. Explanations and precise definitions are supplied in the chapter, but for those who know, the classes are Π^0_2-complete and Π^0_1-complete in the truth set for arithmetic, respectively.

Without Chapter 18, this book would be prettier and easier to read. Found in that final chapter are proofs of the remarkable results of Vardanyan that the theorems of Chapter 17 hold for the fragmentary language of quantified modal logic containing only one one-place predicate letter and forbidding nesting of boxes. The proofs there are intricate; perhaps simpler ones will be found. I hope so. Significant stretches of argumentation in that chapter are due to McGee, Warren Goldfarb, Shavrukov, and the author.

Two other quite major differences between this book and *The Unprovability of Consistency* are the simplification of the semantical (Kripke model) completeness theorem for the books' main system of modal logic – it's now only very slightly less easy than the completeness proof for K, the modal system with the simplest completeness proof of all – and the expansion of the chapter on provability in Peano Arithmetic, now about four times as long as its counterpart.

I've also decided to change the name of the main system, from 'G' to 'GL'. 'GL' slights neither M. H. Löb nor Peter Geach. The system G* has also become GLS, the 'S' for Solovay.

My hope in expanding the chapter on provability in arithmetic was to make it plain how syntax could be developed in a system of arithmetic that explicitly quantifies only over the natural numbers and whose primitive symbols are **0**, **s**, **+**, and **×**. What is problematical is not so much the technique of Gödel numbering as the development in arithmetic of the theory of the "cut-and-paste" operations used to construct new formulas and proofs from old. Via Gödel numbering, formulas and proofs can be construed as finite sequences, or finite sequences of finite sequences, of natural numbers. But how to do the theory of finite sequences and the cut-and-paste operations on *them*? As a student I was perplexed by the fact that although the β-function is introduced to do the work of finite sequences in defining in arithmetic such primitive recursive functions as ! (factorial), the standard proof that the β-function works as desired appeals to the existence of $n!$. So how to formalize that proof if one is to prove the second incompleteness theorem for arithmetic in arithmetic? I hope those who read Chapter 2 on arithmetic will cease to be troubled by such perplexities and will have the sense that they are taking nothing on faith. (By the way, the solution is to make a minor change in the standard proof. The only property of $n!$ that is used in that proof is that $n!$ is a number divisible by all positive integers between 1 and n; but the existence of such a number can easily be proved, by the obvious induction on n. One need *not* appeal to the existence of $n!$.)

Other chapters of the book are meatier and (I hope) neater than their analogues in the earlier book. The chapter on the fixed point theorem, in particular, now contains three quite different proofs of that theorem. And I hope that the exposition of Solovay's theorem now lets one see exactly where the rabbit is at all times.

An annotated list of the contents of the book is found at the end of the introduction.

Some important topics not discussed in the body of the book are the modal logic of relative interpretability (a *very* significant application of modal logic to the study of provability in formal systems); Rosser sentences and the modal logics that have been developed to treat the notion: S has a proof with a smaller Gödel number than S'; the bimodal logic of provability in systems like ZF and PA, where one system is much stronger than the other (these two topics are well covered in Craig Smorynski's *Self-Reference and Modal Logic*); the Sienese algebraic treatment of provability; modal logics that treat the notion: conservative extension; theorems on the classification of the kinds of propositional provability logics there are; and diagonalizable algebras.

The *diagonalizable algebra* of a theory T, with a provability predicate $P(y)$, is the Boolean algebra of T-equivalence classes $[S]$ of sentences S, augmented with a one-place operator $\Box$ such that for all S, $\Box[S] = [P(\ulcorner S \urcorner)]$. A recent remarkable theorem of Shavrukov's is that the diagonalizable algebras of ZF and PA are not isomorphic.

The major open question in provability logic now is whether the first-order theory of the diagonalizable algebra of PA, with Bew(x), is decidable. [Added July 1993; Shavrukov has just announced that it is *not* decidable.]

I wish to thank the National Science Foundation for grant SES-8808755: a monograph on the logic of provability and the incompleteness theorems. Here it is.

I am also grateful to Josep Macia-Fabrega, Joana Roselló-Asensi, and Andrew Sutherland for helpful comments on a draft of Chapter 2 as well as to David Auerbach and an anonymous Cambridge University Press referee for useful comments on the whole.

Vann McGee wrote a long, careful, and detailed commentary on a draft of this book. Moreover, he rescued the book's final chapter from a fatal error, one he had detected some months before finding the remedy for it.

Ideas of Warren Goldfarb seem to have found their way onto almost every other page of this book. I hope, but doubt, that I've managed to acknowledge them all. I have been greatly encouraged over the years by his support and that of several of his colleagues. It is they who have made Cambridge, Massachusetts, so stimulating a location in which to work on this material.

Finally, I am also grateful to Giovanni Sambin, Giorgie Dzhaparidze, and Sergei Artemov for incredible hospitality, both scientific and personal, some of it provided in rather unusual circumstances.

Introduction

The theme of the present work is the way in which *modal logic*, a branch of logic first studied by Aristotle, has been found to shed light on the mathematical study of mathematical reasoning, a study begun by David Hilbert and brought to fruition by Kurt Gödel.

Modal logic

The basic concepts of modal logic are those of necessity and possibility: A statement is called "possible" if it *might* be true (or might have been true) and "necessary" if it *must* be true (or could not have been untrue). E.g., since there might be a war in the year 2000, the statement that there will be a war then is possible; but the statement is not necessary, for there might not be one. On the other hand, the statement that there will or won't be a war in 2000 *is* necessary.

Necessity and possibility are interdefinable: a statement is necessary iff (if and only if) its negation is not possible, and, therefore, a statement is possible iff its negation is not necessary.

The customary sign for necessity in modal logic is the box, '$\Box$', read 'necessarily', or 'it is necessary that...'; the sign for possibility is the diamond '$\Diamond$', read 'possibly,' or 'it is possible that...'. Thus like $\wedge$ and $\vee$ and $\forall$ and $\exists$, either one of $\Box$ and $\Diamond$ can be regarded as defined from the other, $\Box$ as $\neg\Diamond\neg$ and $\Diamond$ as $\neg\Box\neg$. We shall usually take $\Box$ as primitive and $\Diamond$ as defined: '$\Diamond A$' will abbreviate: '$\neg\Box\neg A$'.

Because of the metaphysical character of the notions of necessity and possibility, their remoteness from sensory experience, and the uncertain application of the terms "necessary" and "possible", modal logic has always been a subject more or less on the periphery of logic. Aristotle himself, who developed the theory of the syllogism in almost perfect form, also worked on a theory of modal syllogisms, in which premisses and conclusions may contain the terms "necessary" and "possible". Sympathetic commentators have found the theory defective. According to Jan Lukasiewicz, "Aristotle's modal syllogistic is almost incomprehensible because of its many faults and inconsistencies".[1] William and Martha Kneale write that his theory of modal syllogisms "is generally recognized to be confused and unsatisfactory".[2]

Medieval logicians such as Abelard continued to study modal notions, which also figured importantly in the writings of Leibniz. In our century, the most important contributors to modal logic have been C. I. Lewis and Saul Kripke. Despite the work of these authors, the subject has not been considered to be of central interest to contemporary logic.

Moreover, although the term "logic" (in one of its main uses) has come to refer to the one system known as classical first-order predicate calculus and "set theory" likewise to Zermelo–Fraenkel set theory (ZF), "modal logic" still stands for a *family* of systems, of a bewildering profusion. Most systems of modal logic agree on what counts as a (well-formed) formula or sentence of the logic: One almost always adds to the formation rules of ordinary logic, whether propositional or quantificational, just one clause stating that if A is a formula, then so is $\Box A$. It is with with respect to the notion of *asserted* sentence, or *theorem*, that the systems of modal logic differ from one another. It is difficult to avoid the suspicion that the diversity of modal systems is to be explained by the absence of any intelligible or clear notion of necessity whose properties it is the task of modal logic to codify.

We are going to use modal logic to study not the notion of necessity but that of formal provability, a concept at the heart of the subject of logic, and the fundamental notion studied in Kurt Gödel's famous paper of 1931, "On formally undecidable propositions of *Principia Mathematica* and related systems I". We shall be interested in the effects of construing the box to mean "it is provable that..." rather than "it is necessary that..." and, dually, of taking the diamond to mean "it is consistent that..." rather than "it is possible that...". Here provability and consistency are taken with respect to some one formal system, usually classical first-order arithmetic ["Peano arithmetic" (PA)]. In our study of formal provability we shall pay particular attention to a system of propositional modal logic that we call *GL*, for Gödel and M. H. Löb.

The same expressions count as well-formed sentences in GL as in the more common systems of propositional modal logic; these are set out in Chapter 1. Moreover, as with the other usual systems, all tautologies and all sentences $\Box(A \to B) \to (\Box A \to \Box B)$ are axioms of GL, and modus ponens and necessitation (if a sentence A is a theorem, so is $\Box A$) are its rules of inference. Substitution is also a derived rule of inference of GL. And all sentences $\Box A \to \Box\Box A$ turn out to be theorems of GL.

But familiarity ends here. For:

(1) The sentence $\Box p \to p$ is not a theorem of GL
(2) The sentences $\Box(\Box p \to p) \to \Box p$, $((\Box p \to p) \wedge \Box(\Box p \to p)) \to p$, and $\Box(\Box\bot \to \bot) \to \Box\bot$ are theorems of GL, as are $\Diamond p \to \Diamond(p \wedge \Box\neg p)$ and $\Diamond\top \to \neg\Box\Diamond\top$.
(3) Indeed, all sentences of the form $\Box(\Box A \to A) \to \Box A$ are axioms of GL; these are the only axioms of GL that have not yet been mentioned.
(4) No sentence of the form $\Diamond A$, not even $\Diamond(p \to p)$ or $\Diamond\top$, is a theorem of GL; nor is $\neg\Box\bot$ a theorem of GL.
(5) $\Box\Diamond\top$ is not a theorem of GL.
(6) Whenever a sentence of the form $\Box A \to A$ is a theorem of GL, so is the sentence A.
(7) $\Box\bot \leftrightarrow \Box\Diamond\top$ is a theorem of GL.

Here $\top$ and $\bot$ are the two 0-place propositional connectives: $\top$ counts as a tautology and $\bot$ as a contradiction. Negation may be defined from $\to$ and $\bot$ in ordinary propositional logic: $\neg A$ is equivalent to $A \to \bot$. And of course $\top$ itself is equivalent to $\neg\bot$.

To recapitulate: the sentences of GL are $\bot$, the sentence letters $p, q, r, \ldots$, and $(A \to B)$ and $\Box A$, where A and B are themselves sentences; the axioms of GL are all tautologies and all sentences $\Box(A \to B) \to (\Box A \to \Box B)$ and $\Box(\Box A \to A) \to \Box A$; and the rules of inference are modus ponens and necessitation.

The odd properties of GL described in (1)–(7) reflect the strange properties enjoyed by provability and consistency in formal systems: For example, as $\neg\Box\bot$ is not a theorem of GL, so the statement that $2+2=5$ is not a theorem of ZF is not a theorem of ZF (if, as we suppose, ZF is consistent). Indeed, although for *every* theorem S of ZF, there is also a theorem of ZF to the effect that S is a theorem of ZF, for *no* non-theorem S' of ZF is there a theorem of ZF to the effect that S' is a non-theorem of ZF (again, if ZF is consistent).

C. I. Lewis, who began the modern study of modal logic, conceived of the subject as the relation that holds between propositions p and

q when p can be correctly said to *imply* q. (Lewis, reasonably enough, held that more is needed for p to imply q than that p should be false or q true.) In early formulations of modal logic the fishhook "$\prec$" was used as the sign for implication, and either "$A \prec B$" was defined as: $\Box(A \rightarrow B)$, or "$\prec$" was taken as primitive and "$\Box A$" defined as: $(A \rightarrow A) \prec A$. Lewis claimed that one proposition implies another when the latter is *deducible* from the former.

Exactly what Lewis had in mind by "implies" or "deducible" is uncertain. Some passages in his and Langford's *Symbolic Logic*, a work published almost twenty years after he first published a paper on modal logic, suggest that he was thinking of deducibility in formal systems, like that of *Principia Mathematica*:

> 17.32 $p \prec r \cdot q \prec s \cdot p \circ q : \prec \cdot r \circ s$ ... For example, if a postulate p implies a theorem r, and a postulate q implies a theorem s, and the two postulates are consistent, then the theorems will be consistent. A system deduced from consistent postulates will be consistent throughout.[3]
>
> [With reference to *Principia Mathematica*]: When mathematical ideas have been defined – defined in terms of logical ideas – the postulates for arithmetic, such as Peano's postulates for arithmetic... can all be *deduced* [Lewis's italics].[4]

Other passages indicate that he meant to be treating a notion of necessity now commonly called logical, mathematical, or metaphysical necessity. For example:

> It should also be noted that the words "possible," "impossible," and "necessary" are highly ambiguous in ordinary discourse. The meaning here assigned to $\Diamond p$ is a *wide* meaning of "possibility" – namely, logical conceivability or the absence of self-contradiction.[5]

However unclear Lewis may have been about the nature of the subject matter of the systems of modal logic he himself created, he was certainly right to think that deducibility can and should be studied with the aid of formal systems of modal logic similar to his own. Despite the striking differences between the metaphysical notions of necessity and implication and the logical notions of provability and deducibility, the symbolism of modal logic turns out to be an exceedingly useful notation for representing the forms of sentences of formal theories that have to do with these fundamental logical notions, and the techniques originally devised to study systems of modal logic disclose facts of great interest about these notions and their strange properties.

The development of modal logic was greatly advanced with the introduction, by Saul Kripke and others, of mathematical models (now called Kripke models) of Leibniz's fantasy of the actual world as one "possible world" among others. In Kripkean semantics, sentences are true or false *at* various possible worlds, but, typically, not all worlds are possible relative to, or "accessible from", others. A Kripke model is a triple $\langle W, R, V\rangle$, consisting of a domain W, the set of (possible) worlds, a binary relation R on W, the accessibility relation, and a relation V between worlds and sentence letters specifying which sentence letters are true at which worlds. The truth-value of a truth-functional compound at a world w is computed in the familiar manner from the truth-values of its components at w. And a sentence $\Box A$ is true at w iff A is true at all worlds x such that wRx. (Thus the box acts like a universal quantifier over possible worlds.) A sentence is *valid* in a model $\langle W, R, V\rangle$ iff it is true at all worlds in W.

Kripke proved a number of adequacy (= soundness + completeness) theorems of the form: a sentence A is provable in the system ... if and only if A is valid in all models $\langle W, R, V\rangle$, where R is ___. For example, A is provable in the system S4 iff A is valid in all $\langle W, R, V\rangle$, where R is transitive and reflexive on W.

A similar adequacy theorem holds for GL. A relation R is called *wellfounded* if and only if there is no infinite sequence $w_0, w_1, w_2, \ldots$ such that $\ldots w_2 R w_1 R w_0$. Krister Segerberg proved that the theorems of GL are precisely the sentences valid in all models $\langle W, R, V\rangle$, *where R is transitive and the converse of R is wellfounded.* (If the converse of R is wellfounded, then R is irreflexive; otherwise for some w, $\ldots wRwRw$. Thus in Kripke models for GL, no world is accessible from itself!) The adequacy theorem for GL can be strengthened: W can be taken to be *finite*.

There are two central theorems concerning GL. One is the fixed point theorem, due to Dick de Jongh and Giovanni Sambin. The fixed point theorem yields highly interesting information about the truth-conditions of "self-referential sentences" of arithmetic and other formal theories. We give three different proofs of the fixed point theorem in Chapter 8. Although all of these proofs use the techniques of modal semantics, the theorem can in fact be proved purely syntactically and without Kripke semantics.

The other theorem is the arithmetical completeness theorem for GL, due to Robert Solovay. Solovay's theorem states that the theorems of GL are precisely the sentences of modal logic that are provable in arithmetic under all substitutions of sentences of arithmetic for sentence letters. We prove Solovay's theorem in Chapter 9; the proof involves a kind of "embedding" of Kripke models into formal systems. Solovay's theorem is a deep theorem about provability in formal systems; many interesting generalizations have been found and the technique of its proof has become a fundamental method in the investigation of provability and related notions. But unlike the fixed point theorem, all known proofs of Solovay's theorem make use of Kripke semantics. If ever scientific justification were needed for the study of modal logic or the semantical notions developed for its investigation, Solovay's theorem and its proof provide it.

Formal arithmetic

In "On formally undecidable propositions...", Gödel introduced a formal system of arithmetic, which he called "P", and proved two celebrated incompleteness theorems concerning P and other systems related to it.

P can be described as the result of adding three Dedekind–Peano axioms for the natural numbers to a version of the (simple) theory of types. For each positive integer n, P contains (infinitely many) variables $x_n, y_n, z_n, \ldots$. In the intended interpretation of P the variables $x_1, y_1, z_1, \ldots$ range over the natural numbers, $x_2, y_2, z_2, \ldots$ over the classes of natural numbers, $x_3, y_3, z_3, \ldots$ over the classes of classes of natural numbers, and so forth. Besides the usual logical apparatus, there are signs for the number zero, the successor function, and the relation that holds between the members of a class and that class. (We shall depart from Gödel's notation and write these: $\mathbf{0}$, s, $\in$.) The *numeral* $\mathbf{n}$ for the natural number n is the term $\mathbf{ss}\ldots\mathbf{s0}$ (n occurrences of $\mathbf{s}$); under the intended interpretation of P, the numeral $\mathbf{n}$ does indeed denote n.

The rules of inference of P are modus ponens and universal generalization. In addition to standard logical axioms, P also has axioms of extensionality:

$$\forall x_{n+1} \forall y_{n+1} (\forall z_n [z \in x \leftrightarrow z \in y] \rightarrow x = y)$$

asserting that classes with the same members are identical, and axioms of comprehension

$$\exists x_{n+1} \forall y_n (y \in x \leftrightarrow A)$$

asserting, for each variable x of type $n+1$ and each formula A (in which x is not free), the existence of the class, of type $n+1$, of items of type n satisfying A.

The remaining three axioms of P are the Dedekind–Peano axioms,

$$\forall x_1 \neg \mathbf{0} = \mathbf{s}x$$

$$\forall x_1 \forall y_1 (\mathbf{s}x = \mathbf{s}y \rightarrow x = y)$$

$$\forall z_2 (\mathbf{0} \in z \wedge \forall x_1 (x \in z \rightarrow \mathbf{s}x \in z) \rightarrow \forall x_1 x \in z)$$

which say, respectively, that 0 is not the successor of any natural number, that different natural numbers have different successors, and that mathematical induction holds for natural numbers.

A formal system is said to be *incomplete* if there are statements that can be formulated in the language of the system but neither proved nor disproved by the means of proof available in the system; such statements are called *undecidable* propositions of the system.

A formal system is called *ω-inconsistent* if for some formula $A(x)$, $\exists x \neg A(x)$ and all of $A(\mathbf{0})$, $A(\mathbf{1})$, $A(\mathbf{2})$, ... are provable. Here we assume that x is a variable whose intended range is the set of natural numbers, and for each natural number n, $\mathbf{n}$ is the numeral for n in the language of the system. (So if the system in question is P or one of its extensions, x would be one of $x_1, y_1, z_1, \ldots$.) And of course a system is ω-consistent if it is not ω-inconsistent.

If a system is ω-consistent, then not everything is provable in the system, and therefore it is (simply) consistent. Gödel was the first to construct examples of consistent but ω-inconsistent systems. Thus the condition of ω-consistency is stronger than that of "simple" (i.e., ordinary) consistency.

A *primitive recursive extension* of a system is one obtained from the system by the addition of a primitive recursive set of axioms. A set is primitive recursive if the set of Gödel numbers of its members is. We give the definition of "primitive recursive" in Chapter 2. For now it will suffice to say that the primitive recursive sets form a proper subclass of the recursive sets and that by the Church–Turing thesis, a set is recursive if and only if it is decidable (a different usage of the term from that of "undecidable proposition"), that is, if and only if there exists an algorithm for deciding membership in the set. (One should be aware that in "On formally undecidable propositions..." Gödel defined the term "*rekursiv*" to apply only to those sets now called "primitive recursive".) At the time of writing "On formally undecidable propositions...", Gödel did not know of a satisfactory definition of *decidable set*. Suitable definitions were provided later, notably by Church and Turing.

Gödel gave what has come to be called the first incompleteness theorem as Theorem VI of "On formally undecidable propositions...". It runs: any ω-consistent primitive recursive extension of P is incomplete. Later in the article Gödel noted that the condition that the set of new axioms be "primitive recursive" can be replaced by the weaker condition that the set be "numeralwise expressible"[6]; only after Church and Turing provided their definitions of a decidable set was it proved that the numeralwise expressible sets are precisely the recursive ones.

It was J. B. Rosser who, in 1936, showed that the condition of ω-consistency could be replaced by that of simple consistency in the statement of the first incompleteness theorem. It is noteworthy that Rosser did not show (and could not have shown) the undecidability of the statements described by Gödel to follow from the simple consistency of the relevant systems; instead he found *different* statements whose undecidability so follows.

The second incompleteness theorem, given as Theorem XI of "On formally undecidable propositions...", states that if P is consistent, then the proposition asserting that P is consistent is not a theorem of P; moreover, the same holds for each consistent primitive recursive extension P' of P: the proposition asserting the consistency of P'[7] is not provable in P'.

Gödel only outlined the proof of the second theorem, announcing at the very end of his paper that a detailed proof would be given in a sequel. The sequel, alas, never appeared. The crucial sentence of Gödel's sketch reads,

> We now observe the following: all notions defined (or statements proved) in Section 2, and in Section 4 up to this point, are also expressible (or provable) in P. For throughout we have used only the methods of definition and proof that are customary in classical mathematics, as they are formalized in the system P.

In Section 3 of his paper Gödel shows that the arithmetical relations, those definable from addition and multiplication with the aid of quantifiers ranging over the natural numbers, propositional connectives, and identity, are closed under the operation of primitive recursion; thus all primitive recursive relations are arithmetical. But it is uncertain whether Gödel realized at the time of writing "On formally undecidable propositions..." that the *argumentation* leading to the first incompleteness theorem could be formalized not just in P but in first-order arithmetic as well, so that the second theorem could be proved for systems whose means of expression and proof were far weaker than those of P. One may speculate that the detailed proof in the projected sequel might have also proved the second theorem for first-order systems of arithmetic, which contain variables only for natural numbers and not for classes of natural numbers.

In any event, the proof for a system of first-order arithmetic was carried out fairly soon afterwards, in the second volume of Hilbert and Bernays's *Grundlagen der Mathematik*, published in 1939.

Henceforth it is first-order arithmetic with which we shall mainly be concerned, in particular with the first-order theory called *Peano arithmetic*[8] (PA), or *arithmetic*. Arithmetic is classical first-order arithmetic with induction and the usual axioms concerning zero, successor, addition, and multiplication, symbolized in PA by $\mathbf{0}$, $\mathbf{s}$, $+$, and $\times$. We describe this theory at length in Chapter 2. To explain the connection between modal logic and arithmetic that is of interest to us, we need to recall the idea of a Gödel numbering: a mechanical (effective, algorithmic, computational) one–one assignment of numbers to the expressions and sequences of expressions of a language. We suppose the expressions of PA (and sequence of them) to have been assigned Gödel numbers in some reasonable way.

If F is an expression, we shall let '$\ulcorner F \urcorner$' denote the numeral for the Gödel number of F. Thus if n is the Gödel number of F, $\ulcorner F \urcorner$ is identical with the expression $\mathbf{n}$, which, it will be recalled, is $\mathbf{0}$ preceded by $\mathbf{n}$ occurrences of $\mathbf{s}$.

We write '$\vdash F$' to indicate that F is a theorem of PA.

Following Gödel's procedure in "On formally undecidable propositions...", we can construct a formula Bew(x) (from *beweisbar*, "provable") that expresses that (the value of the variable x) is the Gödel number of a sentence that is provable in PA.[9] The construction of Bew(x) is described in Chapter 2, where we also show that for all sentences S, S' of PA, Bew(x) satisfies the following three conditions:

(i) If $\vdash S$, then $\vdash \mathrm{Bew}(\ulcorner S \urcorner)$;
(ii) $\vdash \mathrm{Bew}(\ulcorner (S \to S') \urcorner) \to (\mathrm{Bew}(\ulcorner S \urcorner) \to \mathrm{Bew}(\ulcorner S' \urcorner))$;
(iii) $\vdash \mathrm{Bew}(\ulcorner S \urcorner) \to \mathrm{Bew}(\ulcorner \mathrm{Bew}(\ulcorner S \urcorner) \urcorner)$.

It is important to be clear about the distinction between '$\vdash$' and 'Bew(x)'. '$\vdash$' is a *verb* of our language, one that means "is provable in PA". It is a verb that happens to be written *before* certain noun phrases, such as 'Bew(⌜S⌝)', that refer to formulas of PA. 'Bew(x)' is a *noun* phrase of *our* language; it refers to a certain formula of PA, one that, *in the language of PA*, plays the role of a verb phrase and can be said to mean "is provable in PA".

Conditions (i), (ii), and (iii) are an attractive modification, due to Löb, of three rather more cumbersome conditions that Hilbert and Bernays showed to be satisfied by the analogue of Bew(x) in the system "(Z_μ)" for which they were concerned to give a proof of the second incompleteness theorem. They are now known as the (Hilbert–Bernays–Löb) *derivability conditions.*

We shall refer to Bew(⌜S⌝) as the sentence that asserts, or says, that S is provable (in PA), or as the sentence that expresses the provability of S, etc. According to (i), if S is provable, so is the sentence that says that S is provable. According to (ii), it is always provable that if a conditional and its antecedent are provable, so is its consequent. According to (iii), it is always provable that if S is provable, then it is provable that S is provable, i.e., always provable that any sentence S satisfies (i).

Perhaps the most striking aspect of "On formally undecidable propositions..." was the technique Gödel used to produce a sentence that is equivalent in P to the assertion that it itself is unprovable in P. In Chapter 3 we shall see how to construct an analogous sentence for PA, which would be a sentence G such that

$$\vdash G \leftrightarrow \neg \mathrm{Bew}(\ulcorner G \urcorner)$$

It is clear from condition (i) alone that if PA proves no falsehoods, then any such sentence G must be undecidable in PA: For if $\vdash G$, then $\vdash \neg \mathrm{Bew}(\ulcorner G \urcorner)$, and by (i), also $\vdash \mathrm{Bew}(\ulcorner G \urcorner)$; and so G proves at least one falsehood. Thus $\nvdash G$; i.e., G is unprovable, and therefore $\mathrm{Bew}(\ulcorner G \urcorner)$ is false. And then if $\vdash \neg G$, then since $\vdash G \leftrightarrow \neg \mathrm{Bew}(\ulcorner G \urcorner)$, the falsehood $\mathrm{Bew}(\ulcorner G \urcorner)$ is provable. So neither $\vdash G$ nor $\vdash \neg G$.

A sentence S is called a *fixed point*[10] of a formula $P(x)$ in a theory T if $S \leftrightarrow P(\ulcorner S \urcorner)$ is a theorem of T. So a sentence G such that $\vdash G \leftrightarrow \neg \mathrm{Bew}(\ulcorner G \urcorner)$ is a fixed point of $\neg \mathrm{Bew}(x)$ (in PA). A fixed point of $P(x)$ may be said to assert that it itself has whatever property is expressed by $P(x)$. In Section 35 of his *Logical Syntax of Language*, Rudolf Carnap observed that in systems like PA, any formula $P(x)$ whatsoever has a fixed point: a noteworthy observation.

Following Gödel, we can show that

(*) If PA is consistent, then no fixed point of $\neg$Bew(x) is provable in PA; and
if PA is ω-consistent, then no fixed point of $\neg$Bew(x) is *disprovable* in PA

Thus, since fixed points of $\neg$Bew(x) exist, we have Gödel's first incompleteness theorem for PA: if PA is ω-consistent, PA is incomplete.
We can also show that

(**) Every conditional whose antecedent is the sentence of PA that expresses the consistency of PA and whose consequent is a fixed point of $\neg$Bew(x) is provable in PA

Gödel's second incompleteness theorem for PA then follows: if PA is consistent, then the sentence that expresses the consistency of PA is not provable in PA.

For if the sentence that expresses the consistency of PA is provable in PA, then, by (**) so is some, indeed every, fixed point of $\neg$Bew(x), and then PA is inconsistent, by (*).

Exactly which sentence is meant by "the sentence of PA that expresses the consistency of PA"? Although there are several different, but coextensive, definitions of consistency that can be given (not all sentences provable, no contradiction provable, no conjunction of theorems disprovable, no sentence and its negation provable, some absurd sentence, e.g., $\mathbf{0} = \mathbf{1}$, unprovable), for a theory in which the 0-place connective $\bot$ is one of the primitive symbols, one definition of consistency seems salient: $\bot$ is not a theorem of the theory. $\bot$ will be a primitive symbol in our formulation of PA, and we therefore take the sentence expressing the consistency of PA to be:

$$\neg \mathrm{Bew}(\ulcorner \bot \urcorner)$$

The second incompleteness theorem for PA may then be crisply put:

$$\nvdash \neg \mathrm{Bew}(\ulcorner \bot \urcorner) \text{ if } \nvdash \bot$$

In 1952 Leon Henkin raised the question whether fixed points of Bew(x), sentences S such that $\vdash S \leftrightarrow \mathrm{Bew}(\ulcorner S \urcorner)$, are provable or not. A fixed point of Bew(x) thus asserts that it itself is provable. Unlike fixed points of $\neg$Bew(x), it was not at all evident what the answer to Henkin's question was, or even that it must be the same for all fixed points of Bew(x): perhaps some are provable and hence true, while others are unprovable and hence false. In advance of the solution and remembering the "truth-teller" sentence "This very sentence is true",[11] one might well guess that all fixed points of Bew(x) are false. (Liars are not known for denying that they are telling the truth.)

The surprising answer to Henkin's question, that all such fixed points are in fact *provable* and hence true, was discovered by Löb in 1954. Henkin observed that Löb's original proof that these fixed points are all provable actually proved that if $\vdash \mathrm{Bew}(\ulcorner S \urcorner) \rightarrow S$, then $\vdash S$; the result, in this improved formulation, is now called Löb's theorem. We prove Löb's theorem in Chapter 3.

Around 1966, Kripke realized that Löb's theorem is a direct consequence of Gödel's second incompleteness theorem for single-sentence extensions of PA. Here is the argument:

Let PA^+ be the result of adjoining $\neg S$ as a new axiom to PA. PA^+ is consistent iff S is not provable in PA, and the sentence expressing the consistency of PA^+ is equivalent even in PA, and hence in PA^+, to $\neg \mathrm{Bew}(\ulcorner S \urcorner)$. Thus $\mathrm{Bew}(\ulcorner S \urcorner) \rightarrow S$ is provable in PA iff $\neg S \rightarrow \neg \mathrm{Bew}(\ulcorner S \urcorner)$ is provable in PA; iff $\neg \mathrm{Bew}(\ulcorner S \urcorner)$ is provable in PA^+; iff the sentence expressing the consistency of PA^+ is provable in PA^+; iff, by the second incompleteness theorem for PA^+, PA^+ is inconsistent; iff S is provable in PA.

Conversely, as Kreisel had observed in 1965, the second incompleteness theorem for PA follows instantaneously from Löb's theorem: if $\nvdash \bot$, then $\nvdash \mathrm{Bew}(\ulcorner \bot \urcorner) \rightarrow \bot$, and so $\nvdash \neg \mathrm{Bew}(\ulcorner \bot \urcorner)$, since $\neg p$ and $p \rightarrow \bot$ are equivalent.

Modal logic and arithmetic

We now turn to the link between modal logic and PA, the interpretation of the box $\Box$ of modal logic as the formula Bew(x) of PA. We want to capture the idea that, e.g., if the sentence letters p and q are assigned the sentences S and S' of PA, then the modal sentence $(\Box p \wedge p) \rightarrow \Box \Box q$ should be assigned the sentence $(\mathrm{Bew}(\ulcorner S \urcorner) \wedge S) \rightarrow \mathrm{Bew}(\ulcorner \mathrm{Bew}(\ulcorner S' \urcorner) \urcorner)$ of PA.

We thus define a *realization* to be a function that assigns to each sentence letter of modal logic a sentence of the language of arithmetic. We shall use the asterisk ($*$) as a variable over realizations.

We define the translation A^* of the sentence A of modal logic under $*$ as follows:

$p^* = *(p)$ for any sentence letter p;
$\bot^* = \bot$;

$(A \to B)^* = (A^* \to B^*)$;
if $A = \Box B$, then $A^* = \mathrm{Bew}(\ulcorner B^* \urcorner)$.

A^* is thus always a sentence of arithmetic.

We suppose that truth-functional connectives are defined from $\to$ and $\bot$; so $(\neg A)^* = \neg(A^*)$, $(A \wedge B)^* = (A^* \wedge B^*)$, etc., and: $\Diamond A$ is taken to abbreviate: $\neg \Box \neg A$.

Thus, for example, if $*(p)$ is $\mathbf{ss0} + \mathbf{ss0} = \mathbf{ssss0}$ and $*(q)$ is $\mathbf{sss0} = \mathbf{ss0} \times \mathbf{0}$, then $(\Box p \wedge p \to \Box \Box q)^*$ is

$$(\mathrm{Bew}(\ulcorner \mathbf{ss0} + \mathbf{ss0} = \mathbf{ssss0} \urcorner) \wedge \mathbf{ss0} + \mathbf{ss0} = \mathbf{ssss0}) \to \mathrm{Bew}(\ulcorner \mathrm{Bew}(\ulcorner \mathbf{sss0} = \mathbf{ss0} \times \mathbf{0} \urcorner) \urcorner)$$

And no matter what $*$ may be, $(\neg \Box \bot \to \neg \Box \neg \Box \bot)^*$ is

$$\neg \mathrm{Bew}(\ulcorner \bot \urcorner) \to \neg \mathrm{Bew}(\ulcorner \neg \mathrm{Bew}(\ulcorner \bot \urcorner) \urcorner)$$

which is the sentence of PA that expresses the second incompleteness theorem for PA.

We call a sentence A of modal logic *always provable* if for every realization $*$, A^* is provable in PA. In Chapter 3 we shall see that *every theorem of* GL *is always provable*, a result that may be called the arithmetical soundness theorem for *GL*. In Chapter 9 we shall prove the converse, Solovay's arithmetical completeness theorem: *Every modal sentence that is always provable is a theorem of GL.* Thus the theorems of GL are precisely the sentences of modal logic that are always provable.

The sentence $\Box(\Box p \to p) \to \Box p$ is an axiom of GL; every sentence of arithmetic is p^* for some $*$. The arithmetical soundness of GL thus implies that, for every sentence S of arithmetic, the sentence

$$\mathrm{Bew}(\ulcorner (\mathrm{Bew}(\ulcorner S \urcorner) \to S) \urcorner) \to \mathrm{Bew}(\ulcorner S \urcorner)$$

is provable in arithmetic. That is to say, every instance of Löb's theorem is provable (not merely in informal mathematics or in set theory but) *in arithmetic*.

A sentence of PA is true (without qualification) if it is true when its variables range over the natural numbers and $\mathbf{0}$, $\mathbf{s}$, $+$, and $\times$ denote zero, successor, addition, and multiplication. Every theorem of PA is of course true (or we are very badly mistaken!), and therefore every sentence $\mathrm{Bew}(\ulcorner S \urcorner) \to S$ of arithmetic is true.

We may call a sentence A of modal logic *always true* if for every realization $*$, A^* is true. Which sentences are always true? We know that every sentence that is always provable is always true, we have just seen that every sentence $\Box A \to A$ is always true, and it is obvious enough that if $(A \to B)$ and A are always true, then so is B. Are any other sentences always true other than those required to be by these obvious constraints?

The answer is no, as another theorem of Solovay tells us. Let GLS be the system whose axioms are all theorems of GL and all sentences $\Box A \to A$ and whose sole rule of inference is modus ponens. Then, as we have just noticed, *every theorem of GLS is always true* (the soundness theorem for GLS). Solovay's completeness theorem for GLS is that the converse holds: *every sentence that is always true is a theorem of GLS.*

Not only is necessitation not one of the primitive rules of inference of GLS, it is not a derived rule either: there are theorems A of GLS such that $\Box A$ is not a theorem. $\Box \bot \to \bot$ is one example. It is an axiom and hence a theorem, but if $\Box(\Box \bot \to \bot)$ is a theorem, then by soundness $\mathrm{Bew}(\ulcorner(\mathrm{Bew}(\ulcorner\bot\urcorner) \to \bot)\urcorner)$ is true, and so $\mathrm{Bew}(\ulcorner\bot\urcorner) \to \bot$ is provable in PA, and therefore so is $\neg\mathrm{Bew}(\ulcorner\bot\urcorner)$, contra the second incompleteness theorem.

The set of axioms of GLS was given as the set of all theorems of GL and all sentences $\Box A \to A$. In fact, this set of axioms is decidable, since as we shall prove in Chapter 5, GL is decidable. However, a more transparent axiomatization of GLS is given in Chapter 3.

It is clear that A is always provable iff $\Box A$ is always true. The proof of Solovay's completeness theorem for GLS supplies a reduction in the opposite direction: A is always true iff $(\bigwedge\{\Box B \to B\colon \Box B$ is a subsentence of $A\} \to A)$ is always provable. It follows that GLS, like GL, is decidable.

Constant sentences and fixed points

There is a natural class of sentences of PA[12] of which GL provides us with an excellent understanding: those built up from $\bot$ with the aid of truth-functional connectives and $\mathrm{Bew}(\ulcorner\cdot\urcorner)$. We call these the *constant* sentences. Among the constant sentences are

$\neg\mathrm{Bew}(\ulcorner\bot\urcorner)$,

$\mathrm{Bew}(\ulcorner\neg\mathrm{Bew}(\ulcorner\bot\urcorner)\urcorner)$,

$\neg\mathrm{Bew}(\ulcorner\bot\urcorner) \to \neg\mathrm{Bew}(\ulcorner\neg\mathrm{Bew}(\ulcorner\bot\urcorner)\urcorner)$, and

$\mathrm{Bew}(\ulcorner\neg\mathrm{Bew}(\ulcorner\bot\urcorner) \to \neg\mathrm{Bew}(\ulcorner\neg\mathrm{Bew}(\ulcorner\bot\urcorner)\urcorner)\urcorner)$.

The first of these asserts that PA is consistent; it is true but unprovable. The second asserts that the consistency of PA is provable; it is false. The third expresses the second incompleteness theorem for PA; it is true and provable. The fourth says that the second incompleteness theorem for PA is provable; it too is true and provable. Which constant sentences are true? which provable? It would be nice to be able to tell.

Since a constant sentence S is provable iff the sentence $\mathrm{Bew}(\ulcorner S \urcorner)$, which is also a constant sentence, is true, an algorithm for calculating the truth-value of any constant sentence can also be used to tell whether a constant sentence is provable or not.

A *letterless* sentence is a sentence of modal logic, such as $\neg \Box \bot \rightarrow \neg \Box \neg \Box \bot$, that contains no sentence letters at all. The constant sentences are precisely the sentences A^* for some letterless sentence A. (A is letterless, and therefore the identity of A^* does not depend on the choice of $*$.) In Chapter 7 we shall show how to find from any letterless sentence A a truth-functional combination B of the sentences $\Box \bot$, $\Box \Box \bot$, $\Box \Box \Box \bot, \ldots$ such that GL proves $A \leftrightarrow B$, whence A^* is true iff B^* is true. But since we know that $\Box \bot^*$, $\Box \Box \bot^*$, $\Box \Box \Box \bot^*, \ldots$ are all false (PA proves nothing false), we do have our desired algorithm for telling whether a constant sentence is true or false.

Above, we called the fixed point theorem of de Jongh and Sambin one of the two central results concerning GL. We state a version of it now.

A modal sentence A is called *modalized in* the sentence letter p if every ocurrence of p in A lies in the scope of an occurrence of $\Box$. Thus, e.g., $\Box \neg p$, q, $\Box p \rightarrow \Box \neg p$, $\neg \Box \bot$, and $\Box p \rightarrow \bot$ are modalized in p, but p and $\Box p \rightarrow p$ are not.

Then the fixed point theorem asserts that for any sentence A that is modalized in p, there is a sentence H containing only sentence letters contained in A that are distinct from p and such that

$$\Box (p \leftrightarrow A) \leftrightarrow \Box (p \leftrightarrow H)$$

is a theorem of GL. Two of the three proofs of the fixed point theorem found in Chapter 8 explicitly provide explicit algorithms for constructing H from A.

For example, if A is $\Box p$, $\neg \Box p$, $\Box \neg p$, $\neg \Box \neg p$, $\Box p \rightarrow \Box \neg p$, or $\Box p \rightarrow q$, then, as we shall later see, H may be chosen to be $\top$, $\neg \Box \bot$, $\Box \bot$, $\bot$, $\Box \Box \bot \rightarrow \Box \bot$, or $\Box q \rightarrow q$, respectively.

The fixed point theorem may be used to demystify certain "self-referential" characterizations of sentences of PA. Let us consider the second case, where A is $\neg\Box p$ and, according to the algorithm provided by one of the proofs of the theorem, H is $\neg\Box\bot$.

Let S be an arbitrary sentence and let $*$ be some realization such that $p^* = S$. Since $\Box(p\leftrightarrow\neg\Box p)\leftrightarrow\Box(p\leftrightarrow\neg\Box\bot)$ is a theorem of GL, by the soundness of GL, we have that

$$\vdash(\Box(p\leftrightarrow\neg\Box p)\leftrightarrow\Box(p\leftrightarrow\neg\Box\bot))^*, \text{ i.e.}$$
$$\vdash \mathrm{Bew}(\ulcorner(S\leftrightarrow\neg\mathrm{Bew}(\ulcorner S\urcorner))\urcorner)\leftrightarrow\mathrm{Bew}(\ulcorner(S\leftrightarrow\neg\mathrm{Bew}(\ulcorner\bot\urcorner))\urcorner)$$

Since anything provable in PA is true,

$$\vdash S\leftrightarrow\neg\mathrm{Bew}(\ulcorner S\urcorner) \quad \text{iff} \vdash S\leftrightarrow\neg\mathrm{Bew}(\ulcorner\bot\urcorner)$$

Thus we see that a sentence is equivalent in PA to the assertion of its own unprovability iff it is equivalent to the assertion that PA is consistent.

We can likewise show that

$$\vdash S\leftrightarrow\mathrm{Bew}(\ulcorner S\urcorner) \text{ iff} \vdash S\leftrightarrow\top,$$
$$\vdash S\leftrightarrow\mathrm{Bew}(\ulcorner\neg S\urcorner) \text{ iff} \vdash S\leftrightarrow\mathrm{Bew}(\ulcorner\bot\urcorner),$$
$$\vdash S\leftrightarrow\neg\mathrm{Bew}(\ulcorner\neg S\urcorner) \text{ iff} \vdash S\leftrightarrow\bot$$

and (a more complex example)

$$\vdash S\leftrightarrow(\mathrm{Bew}(\ulcorner S\urcorner)\rightarrow\mathrm{Bew}(\ulcorner\neg S\urcorner)) \text{ iff}$$
$$\vdash S\leftrightarrow(\mathrm{Bew}(\ulcorner\mathrm{Bew}(\ulcorner\bot\urcorner)\urcorner)\rightarrow\mathrm{Bew}(\ulcorner\bot\urcorner))$$

The last example shows that a sentence is equivalent to the assertion that it itself is disprovable if provable iff it is equivalent to the assertion that arithmetic is inconsistent if the inconsistency of arithmetic is provable.

Thus with the aid of the fixed point theorem we can see how to replace certain "self-referential" characterizations of sentences of arithmetic, e.g. "sentence that is equivalent to the assertion that it itself is disprovable", with equivalent descriptions, such as "sentence that is equivalent to the assertion that PA is inconsistent", that involve no such self-reference. If a sentence is characterized in such a self-referential manner, it may be far from clear that unique conditions have been specified under which it is true, and farther still what those conditions might be; but in a vast variety of cases of interest, the fixed point theorem shows that unique truth-conditions have indeed been given and tells us what those conditions are. Thus a theorem of pure modal logic sheds brilliant light upon the concept of provability in formal systems.

ω-consistency, set theory, second-order arithmetic

A sentence S is consistent with a theory T iff $T+S$, the theory that results when S is added to T as a new axiom, is consistent. Similarly, S is ω-consistent with T iff $T+S$ is ω-consistent.

The second incompleteness theorem may be formulated: if PA is consistent, then the negation of the sentence expressing that PA is consistent with PA is consistent with PA. Suppose that to each occurrence of "consistent" in this formulation of the theorem we prefix an 'ω-'. Is the resulting statement provable?

In 1937, in a paper entitled "Gödel theorems for non-constructive logics", Rosser gave the answer "yes" for the system P of "On formally undecidable propositions...".[13] Rosser proved analogues of both incompleteness theorems for each of a series of extensions P_k of P, where P_0 is P and P_{k+1} is the theory obtained from P_k by taking as new axioms all sentences $\forall x F(x)$ such that for all n, $F(\mathbf{n})$ is a theorem of P_k. It is not hard to see that P_{k+1} is simply consistent iff P_k is ω-consistent, and that that fact can be proved in P_0. Rosser's argumentation certainly carries over to PA.

One might wonder what the properties of ω-consistency are that can be expressed in the language of propositional modal logic.

It is easy to see that $S \vee S'$ is ω-consistent (with PA) iff either S or S' is ω-consistent, and it can be shown without too much difficulty that if a statement to the effect that a certain statement S is ω-consistent is itself ω-consistent, then S is ω-consistent. Both of these facts, moreover, can be proved in PA.

It turns out to be a routine matter to modify the proofs of Solovay's completeness theorems in order to prove[14] that GL is the modal logic of ω-consistency, in the same sense in which it is the modal logic of (simple) consistency. That is, let ω-Con(x) be the formula of PA expressing ω-consistency and redefine the translation scheme for modal sentences so that if $A = \Box B$, then $A^* = \neg\,\omega\text{-Con}(\ulcorner \neg B^* \urcorner)$. Then the sentences A of modal logic such that $\vdash A^*$ for all $*$ are precisely the theorems of GL, and the sentences A such that A^* is true for all $*$ are precisely the theorems of GLS.

Another result in Rosser's paper is that the consistency of P_0 can be proved in P_1. The analogous result for PA is that the negation of the consistency assertion is ω-inconsistent with PA. (Since the undecidable statement constructed by Gödel is equivalent to the consistency assertion, this result follows immediately from the second part of the first incompleteness theorem for PA.)

Thus we are led to study *bimodal* propositional logic, whose language contains a second pair of operators $\langle 1\rangle$ and $\boxed{1}$, intended to represent ω-consistency and its dual.

The principles concerning consistency and ω-consistency that we have mentioned are codified in the following system, GLB (B for "bimodal"):

The axioms of GLB are all tautologies and all sentences:

$\Box(A \to B) \to (\Box A \to \Box B)$,
$\boxed{1}(A \to B) \to (\boxed{1} A \to \boxed{1} B)$,
$\Box(\Box A \to A) \to \Box A$,
$\boxed{1}(\boxed{1} A \to A) \to \boxed{1} A$,
$\Box A \to \boxed{1} A$, and
$\neg \Box A \to \boxed{1} \neg \Box A$.

The rules of inference of GLB are modus ponens and $\Box$-necessitation (from A, infer $\Box A$). Of course $\boxed{1}$-necessitation is a derived rule of GLB.

The scheme of translation for sentences of GLB is then the obvious one: if $A = \Box B$, then $A^* = \mathrm{Bew}(\ulcorner B^* \urcorner)$ (as before), and if $A = \boxed{1} B$, then $A^* = \neg\,\omega\text{-Con}(\ulcorner \neg B^* \urcorner)$.

It is easy to show GLB arithmetically sound. Since consistency follows from ω-consistency, any bimodal sentence $\Box A \to \boxed{1} A$ is always provable; $\neg \Box A \to \boxed{1} \neg \Box A$ is also always provable: if S is consistent, then the assertion that S is inconsistent is ω-inconsistent.

In 1985, Giorgie Dzhaparidze proved the arithmetical completeness of GLB. He also proved the arithmetical completeness of a system GLSB related to GLB as GLS is to GL. Both of his theorems are proved in Chapter 15.

Dzhaparidze's proof was a *tour de force* and anything but a routine modification of Solovay's original argument. Insurmountable difficulties arise when one attempts to formulate a Kripke-style semantics for the whole of GLB. In 1990, Konstantin Ignatiev gave simpler proofs of Dzhaparidze's theorems for GLS and GLSB. Ignatiev's main idea was to isolate a subsystem of GLB for which a reasonable Kripke-style completeness theorem could be proved. Ignatiev also succeeded in proving the fixed point theorem for GLB by proving a closely related version for his subsystem and then readily deducing the theorem for GLB. These results are all proved in Chapters 15 and 16.

In Chapters 13 and 14 we prove two theorems of Solovay's on set-theoretical interpretations of $\Box$ and a third on the connections between modal logic and the ω-rule. [The ω-rule is the "infinitary" rule of inference that permits a divine mathematician to infer $\forall x A(x)$ once she has proved the infinitely many particular statements $A(\mathbf{n})$, n a natural number.] These two chapters are, unfortunately, not self-contained – all others are – and we shall be brief about the theorems here. Those having to do with set theory give modal completeness theorems for the notions "true in all transitive models of set theory" and "true in all universes". (A set is transitive if every member of a member of it is a member of it; a universe is a set V_κ, κ inaccessible.) The theorem on the ω-rule states that GL is also the modal logic of provability in analysis (alias second-order arithmetic) under unrestricted application of the ω-rule.

Necessity, quantification

It seems appropriate here to mention one philosophical misunderstanding that must be obviated, which has to do with W.V. Quine's well-known critique of the notions of necessity and possibility. Quine has argued that we have no reason to believe that there are any statements with the properties that necessary truths are commonly supposed to have. If $\Box$ is read "it is (logically, metaphysically, mathematically) necessary that...", then it would be irrational of us to suppose that there are *any* truths of the form $\Box p$. According to Quine, for all anyone has been told, the box is a "falsum" operator. We do not wish to argue either that logical necessity is a viable, respectable, intelligible, legitimate, or otherwise useful notion, or that it is not, but it is part of the purpose of this work to show that the mathematical ideas that have been invented to study this notion are of interest and use in the investigation of fundamental questions of logic. It may be *odd* that mathematical techniques devised to study notions of no philosophical or mathematical value should turn out to be of great logical interest – but then they have that interest.

Far from undermining Quine's critique of modality, provability logic provides an example of the interpretation of the box whose intelligibility is beyond question. Quine has never published an opinion on the matter, but it would be entirely consonant with the views he has expressed for him to hold that provability logic is what modal logicians should have been doing all along.

In a number of publications, Quine has also questioned the intelligibility of "quantifying in", constructing sentences such as $\forall x \Box \exists y\, x = y$, in which at least one modal operator occurs within the scope of at least one quantifier. However, if quantifiers are taken as ranging over the natural numbers and the box as referring to some formal system of arithmetic (e.g., PA), then all such "in" quantifications may be interpreted readily and without problems. One need only explain under what conditions a formula $\Box A(x_1, \ldots, x_n)$ is true with respect to the assignment of natural numbers $i_1, \ldots, i_n$ to the variables $x_1, \ldots, x_n$. And this can easily be done: $\Box A(x_1, \ldots, x_n)$ is true with respect to this assignment iff $A(\mathbf{i}_1, \ldots, \mathbf{i}_n)$, the sentence that results from the formula $A(x_1, \ldots, x_n)$ when the numerals $\mathbf{i}_1, \ldots, \mathbf{i}_n$ for the numbers $i_1, \ldots, i_n$ are respectively substituted for the variables $x_1, \ldots, x_n$, is provable. So, for example, $\forall x \Box \exists y\, y = x$ will make the (true, indeed provable) assertion that for every number i, the sentence $\exists y\, y = \mathbf{i}$ is provable. A sort of quantified modal logic is thus available to the Quinean.

Under such a treatment of quantified modal logic, which may be called *quantified provability logic*, the Barcan formula $\forall x \Box Fx \rightarrow \Box \forall x Fx$, named for Ruth Barcan Marcus, does not turn out to be always true: substitute for Fx the formula of PA expressing that the value of x is not the Gödel number of a proof of $\bot$. Then the antecedent is true, for it asserts that every number is such that it can be proved not to be a proof of $\bot$; but the consequent is false, for it says that consistency is provable. The converse Barcan formula $\Box \forall x Fx \rightarrow \forall x \Box Fx$ is, however, always provable, for if a universally quantified sentence is provable, then so are all its instances.

In view of the undecidability of quantificational logic, we cannot hope that quantified provability logic is decidable, but we might hope that it could be axiomatized.

There are two questions that one might ask: Is there an axiomatization of the formulas F of quantified modal logic that are provable (in PA) under all substitutions of formulas of arithmetic for the predicate letters in F? *and ditto*, but with "true" in place of "provable (in PA)".

In the spring of 1985, Sergei Artemov answered the second question negatively; shortly afterwards Valery Vardanyan answered the first, also negatively. The main new idea in both proofs is the use of Stanley Tennenbaum's theorem that there are no nonstandard recursive models of PA. In 1984 Franco Montagna had shown that there are formulas provable under all arithmetical substitutions that are not theorems of the result of adding quantificational logic to GL. Vardanyan showed that the set of always provable formulas of quantified modal logic was as undecidable as it was a priori possible for it to be "Π^0_2-complete". Later McGee, Vardanyan, and the author extended Artemov's result to show that the set of always true formulas was also as undecidable as it could, a priori, be: "Π^0_1-complete" in the set of Gödel numbers of true sentences of arithmetic. (The notions of Π^0_2-completeness and of Π^0_1-completeness in a set are explained in Chapter 17.) These perhaps disappointing results concerning quantified provability logic settled natural and long-standing questions. Proofs and further elaboration are found in Chapter 17.

A stunning extension of these two results was proved by Vardanyan: they hold even for formulas containing *only one one-place predicate letter and in which no box occurs nested within the scope of another.* Vardanyan's extensions, which require much trickery and are as yet little understood, are proved in Chapter 18.

Let us close our introduction with a description of the contents of the rest of the book:

1. GL and other systems of propositional modal logic (K, K4, T, S4, B, and S5).
2. Peano arithmetic, Bew(x), and the Hilbert–Bernays–Löb derivability conditions.
3. The diagonal lemma, Löb's theorem, the second incompleteness theorem, and the arithmetical soundness of GL and GLS.
4. Kripke semantics for GL and other systems of modal logic.
5. Soundness and completeness theorems for GL and other modal logics.
6. Canonical models for systems of modal logic.
7. The normal-form theorem for letterless sentences of GL, reflection principles and iterated consistency assertions, the rarity of reasonable normal forms in GL, and the incompactness of GL.
8. Three proofs of the fixed point theorem for GL and the Craig and Beth theorems for GL.
9. Solovay's completeness theorems for GL and GLS and extensions of them.

10. The method of trees for GL.
11. The incompleteness of the system $K + \{\Box(A \leftrightarrow \Box A) \rightarrow \Box A\}$, a simplest possible incomplete modal logic.
12. The system Grz(egorczyk), which extends S4, and its completeness under the interpretation of $\Box$ as meaning "true and provable".
13. Modal logics for three set-theoretical interpretations of $\Box$, under which it is read as "provable in ZF", "true in all transitive models", and "true in all models V_κ, κ inaccessible".
14. The analytical completeness of GL (for provability) and GLS (for truth) with respect to ordinary provability and, more interestingly, provability under unrestricted use of the ω-rule. (Analysis is second-order arithmetic.)
15. The arithmetical completeness of GLB and GLSB.
16. The fixed point theorem for GLB, a normal form theorem for letterless sentences of GLB, and a short discussion of the "analytical" completeness of GLB and GLSB with respect to ordinary provability in analysis and provability in analysis under unrestricted use of the ω-rule.
17. The set of always provable formulas of quantified modal logic and the set of always true formulas are as undecidable as it is possible, a priori, for them to be: Π^0_2-complete and Π^0_1-complete in the set of Gödel numbers of true sentences of arithmetic.
18. The results of Chapter 17 are extended to the case in which modal formulas contain only one one-place predicate letter and nested boxes are forbidden.

1

GL and other systems of propositional modal logic

We are going to investigate a system of propositional modal logic, which we call 'GL', for Gödel and Löb.[1] GL is also sometimes called *provability logic*, but the term is also used to mean modal logic, as applied to the study of provability. By studying GL, we can learn new and interesting facts about *provability* and *consistency*, concepts studied by Gödel in "On formally undecidable propositions of *Principia Mathematica* and related systems I", and about the phenomenon of self-reference.

Like the systems T (sometimes called 'M'), S4, B, and S5, which are four of the best-known systems of modal logic, GL is a *normal* system of propositional modal logic. That is to say, the theorems of GL contain all tautologies of the propositional calculus (including, of course, those that contain the special symbols of modal logic); contain all distribution axioms, i.e., all sentences of the form $\Box(A \to B) \to (\Box A \to \Box B)$; and are closed under the rules of modus ponens, substitution, and necessitation, according to which $\Box A$ is a theorem provided that A is. Nor does GL differ from those other systems in the syntax of its sentences: exactly the same sequences of symbols count as well-formed sentences in all five systems.

GL differs greatly from T, S4, B, and S5, however, with respect to basic questions of theoremhood. All sentences $\Box(\Box A \to A) \to \Box A$ are axioms of GL. In particular, then, $\Box(\Box p \to p) \to \Box p$ and $\Box(\Box(p \wedge \neg p) \to (p \wedge \neg p)) \to \Box(p \wedge \neg p)$ are axioms of GL. The other axioms of GL are the tautologies and distribution axioms; its rules of inference are, like those of the other systems, just modus ponens and necessitation.

It follows that either GL is inconsistent or some sentence $\Box A \to A$ is not a theorem of GL or some sentence $\Box(\Box A \to A)$ is not a theorem of GL. For if $\Box(\Box A \to A) \to \Box A$, $\Box(\Box A \to A)$, and $\Box A \to A$ are always theorems of G, then for any sentence A whatsoever, e.g. $(p \wedge \neg p)$, two applications of modus ponens show A to be a theorem of GL, and GL is inconsistent.

It will turn out that GL is perfectly consistent; we shall see quite soon that neither $\Box p \to p$ nor its substitution instance $\Box(p \wedge \neg p) \to (p \wedge \neg p)$ is a theorem of GL and, later, that $\Box(\Box p \to p)$ is also not a theorem.

In order to contrast GL with its better-known relatives, we shall take a general look at systems of propositional modal logic. Much of the material in this chapter may be quite familiar, but it will be important to reverify certain elementary facts in order to establish that they hold in the absence of $\Box p \to p$, which we shall be living without in most of the rest of this book. The material of this chapter will be of a purely syntactic or "proof-theoretical" character. We take up the semantics of modal logic in Chapter 4.

We begin our general look at modal logic by defining the notion of a sentence of propositional modal logic, or "modal sentence" or "sentence" for short.

Modal sentences. Fix a countably infinite sequence of distinct objects, of which the first five are $\bot$, $\to$, $\Box$, (, and) and the others are the sentence letters; 'p', 'q', ... will be used as variables over sentence letters. Modal sentences will be certain finite sequences of these objects. We shall use 'A', 'B', ... as variables over modal sentences. Here is the inductive definition of *modal sentence*:

(1) $\bot$ is a modal sentence;
(2) each sentence letter is a modal sentence;
(3) if A and B are modal sentences, so is $(A \to B)$; and
(4) if A is a modal sentence, so is $\Box(A)$.

[We shall very often write: $(A \to B)$ and: $\Box(A)$ as: $A \to B$ and: $\Box A$.]

Sentences that do not contain sentence letters are *letterless*. For example, $\bot$, $\Box\bot$, and $\Box\bot \to \bot$ are letterless sentences.

Since a handy, perfectly general, and non-arbitrary way to say that a system is consistent is simply to say that $\bot$ is not one of its theorems, taking the 0-ary propositional connective $\bot$ to be one of our primitive symbols provides a direct way to represent in the notation of modal logic many interesting propositions expressible in the language of arithmetic concerning consistency and provability. Thus, e.g., the letterless sentence $\neg\Box\bot$ will turn out to represent the proposition that arithmetic is consistent; $\Box\neg\Box\bot$, the proposition that the consistency of arithmetic is provable in arithmetic;

and $\neg\Box\bot\to\neg\Box\neg\Box\bot$, the second incompleteness theorem of Gödel.

Of course, with the aid of $\bot$ and $\to$, all connectives of ordinary propositional logic are definable: $\neg p$ may be defined as $(p\to\bot)$, and as is well known, all propositional connectives are definable from $\neg$ and $\to$.

$\wedge$ (and), $\vee$ (or), and $\leftrightarrow$ (iff) are defined in any one of the usual ways. The 0-ary propositional connective $\top$ has the definition $\bot\to\bot$. $\Diamond A$ is defined as $\neg\Box\neg A$, i.e., as $\Box(A\to\bot)\to\bot$.

The inductive definition of *subsentence* of A runs: A is a subsentence of A; if $B\to C$ is a subsentence of A, so is B and so is C; and if $\Box B$ is a subsentence of A, so is B. A sentence letter p *occurs*, or *is contained*, in a sentence A if it is a subsentence of A.

We shall take a system of propositional modal logic to be a set of sentences, the axioms of the system, together with a set of relations on the set of sentences, called the rules of inference of the system. As usual, a proof in a system is a finite sequence of sentences, each of which is either an axiom of the system or deducible from earlier sentences in the sequence by one of the rules of inference of the system. (B is said to be deducible from $A_1,\ldots,A_n$ by the rule of inference R if $\langle A_1,\ldots,A_n,B\rangle$ is in R.) A proof $A,B,\ldots,Z$ is a proof *of* Z, and a sentence is called a theorem of, or provable in, the system if there is a proof of it in the system. We write: $\mathrm{L}\vdash A$ to mean that A is a theorem of the system L.

A set of sentences is said to be *closed* under a rule of inference if it contains all sentences deducible by the rule from members of the set.

Modus ponens is the relation containing all triples $\langle(A\to B),A,B\rangle$.

Necessitation is the relation containing all pairs $\langle A,\Box A\rangle$.

Let F be a sentence. The result $(F_p(A))$ – $F_p(A)$ for short, or even $F(A)$, if the identity of p is clear from context – of substituting A for p in F may be inductively defined as follows:

If $F=p$, then $F_p(A)$ is A;
if F is a sentence letter $q\neq p$, then $F_p(A)$ is q;
if $F=\bot$, then $F_p(A)$ is $\bot$;
$(F\to G)_p(A)=(F_p(A)\to G_p(A))$; and
$\Box(F)_p(A)=\Box(F_p(A))$.

Thus $F_p(A)$ is the result of substituting an occurrence of A for each occurrence of p in F.

A sentence $F_p(A)$ is called a *substitution instance of F*.

Substitution is the relation containing all pairs $\langle F, F_p(A)\rangle$.

Simultaneous substitution. Let $p_1, \ldots, p_n$ be a list of distinct sentence letters, $F, A_1, \ldots, A_n$ a list of sentences. We define the simultaneous substitution $F_{p_1,\ldots,p_n}(A_1, \ldots, A_n)$ analogously:

If $F = p_i$ $(1 \leqslant i \leqslant n)$, then $F_{p_1,\ldots,p_n}(A_1, \ldots, A_n)$ is A_i;
if F is a sentence letter $q \neq p_1, \ldots, p_n$, then $F_{p_1,\ldots,p_n}(A_1, \ldots, A_n)$ is q;
the other cases are as in the previous definition.

Note that $F_p(A)_q(B)$ need not be identical with $F_{p,q}(A, B)$. For example, let $F = (p \wedge q)$, $A = (p \vee q)$, $B = (p \rightarrow q)$. Then $F_p(A) = ((p \vee q) \wedge q)$, and $F_p(A)_q(B) = ((p \vee (p \rightarrow q)) \wedge (p \rightarrow q))$. But $F_{p,q}(A, B) = ((p \vee q) \wedge (p \rightarrow q))$. However, a set of sentences that is closed under (ordinary) substitution is closed under simultaneous substitution. For let $q_1, \ldots, q_n$ be a list of distinct *new* sentence letters, i.e., sentence letters none of which is identical with any of $p_1, \ldots, p_n$ and that occur nowhere in $F, A_1, \ldots, A_n$. Then $F_{p_1,\ldots,p_n}(A_1, \ldots, A_n)$ is identical with

$$F_{p_1}(q_1)_{p_2}(q_2)\ldots_{p_n}(q_n)_{q_1}(A_1)_{q_2}(A_2)\ldots_{q_n}(A_n)$$

any so any set containing F and closed under substitution will contain $F_{p_1}(q_1)$, $F_{p_1}(q_1)_{p_2}(q_2), \ldots$, and $F_{p_1,\ldots,p_n}(A_1, \ldots, A_n)$

A *distribution axiom* is a sentence of the form

$(\Box(A \rightarrow B) \rightarrow (\Box A \rightarrow \Box B))$, i.e., a sentence that *is*
$(\Box(A \rightarrow B) \rightarrow (\Box A \rightarrow \Box B))$, for some sentences A, B.

A system is called *normal* if the set of its theorems contains all tautologies and all distribution axioms and is closed under modus ponens, necessitation, and substitution. (According to Kripke's original definition,[2] the axioms of a normal system had also to include all sentences $\Box A \rightarrow A$. The definition we have given, which does not impose this further requirement, is now the standard one, however.)

We now present seven systems of modal logic. In each system, all tautologies and all distribution axioms are axioms and the rules of inference are just modus ponens and necessitation.

The system K, which is named after Kripke, has no other axioms.
The other axioms of the system K4 are the sentences $\Box A \rightarrow \Box\Box A$.
The other axioms of the system T are the sentences $\Box A \rightarrow A$.
The other axioms of the system S4 are the sentences $\Box A \rightarrow A$ and $\Box A \rightarrow \Box\Box A$.
The other axioms of the system B are the sentences $\Box A \rightarrow A$ and $A \rightarrow \Box\Diamond A$.[3]
The other axioms of the system S5 are the sentences $\Box A \rightarrow A$ and $\Diamond A \rightarrow \Box\Diamond A$.
The other axioms of the system GL are the sentences $\Box(\Box A \rightarrow A) \rightarrow \Box A$.

A system L′ *extends* a system L if every theorem of L is a theorem of L′. If we write '$\supseteq$' and '$\subseteq$' to mean "extends" and "is extended by", then it is evident that we have:

$$\begin{array}{ccccc} & & \mathrm{GL} & & \\ & & \text{\rotatebox{90}{$\supseteq$}} & & \\ & & \mathrm{K} & \subseteq & \mathrm{K4} \\ & & \text{\rotatebox{90}{$\subseteq$}} & & \text{\rotatebox{90}{$\subseteq$}} \\ \mathrm{S5} & \supseteq & \mathrm{T} & \subseteq & \mathrm{S4} \\ & & \text{\rotatebox{90}{$\subseteq$}} & & \\ & & \mathrm{B} & & \end{array}$$

By the end of the chapter we shall have shown that in fact:

$$\begin{array}{ccccc} \mathrm{K} & \subseteq & \mathrm{K4} & \subseteq & \mathrm{GL} \\ \text{\rotatebox{90}{$\subseteq$}} & & \text{\rotatebox{90}{$\subseteq$}} & & \\ \mathrm{T} & \subseteq & \mathrm{S4} & & \\ \text{\rotatebox{90}{$\subseteq$}} & & \text{\rotatebox{90}{$\subseteq$}} & & \\ \mathrm{B} & \subseteq & \mathrm{S5} & & \end{array}$$

But our first task will be to verify that these systems are normal. To see that they are, it is necessary only to verify that any substitution instance of a theorem is itself a theorem. Thus suppose that $F^1, \ldots, F^n$ is a proof in one of the systems – call it L. We want to see that $F^1_p(A), \ldots, F^n_p(A)$ is also a proof in L. But it is clear that it *is* a proof, since if F^i is an axiom of L, so is its substitution instance $F^i_p(A)$, and if F^i is immediately deducible from F^j and F^k by modus ponens or from F^j by necessitation, then the same goes for $F^i_p(A)$, $F^j_p(A)$, and $F^k_p(A)$, by the definitions of $(F \to G)_p(A)$ and $\Box(F)_p(A)$. Thus if F^n has a proof in L, so does its substitution instance $F^n_p(A)$.

Normal systems are also closed under truth-functional consequence, for if B follows truth-functionally from the theorems $A_1, \ldots, A_n$ of a normal system, then the tautology $A_1 \to (\cdots \to (A_n \to B) \cdots)$ is also a theorem of the system, and therefore so is B, which can be inferred from these theorems by n applications of modus ponens.

Until further notice, assume that L is a normal system.

Theorem 1. *Suppose* $\mathrm{L} \vdash A \to B$. *Then* $\mathrm{L} \vdash \Box A \to \Box B$.

Proof. Applying necessitation gives us that $\mathrm{L} \vdash \Box(A \to B)$. Since $\mathrm{L} \vdash \Box(A \to B) \to (\Box A \to \Box B)$, $\mathrm{L} \vdash \Box A \to \Box B$, by modus ponens. ⊣

Theorem 2. *Suppose* $\mathrm{L} \vdash A \leftrightarrow B$. *Then* $\mathrm{L} \vdash \Box A \leftrightarrow \Box B$.

Proof. By truth-functional logic, $\mathrm{L} \vdash A \to B$ and $\mathrm{L} \vdash B \to A$. By Theorem 1, $\mathrm{L} \vdash \Box A \to \Box B$ and $\mathrm{L} \vdash \Box B \to \Box A$. The conclusion follows truth-functionally from these. ⊣

Theorem 3. $\mathrm{L} \vdash \Box(A \wedge B) \leftrightarrow (\Box A \wedge \Box B)$.

Proof. We have $\mathrm{L} \vdash (A \wedge B) \to A$ and $\mathrm{L} \vdash (A \wedge B) \to B$, whence by Theorem 1,

(1) $\mathrm{L} \vdash \Box(A \wedge B) \to \Box A$ and

(2) $\mathrm{L} \vdash \Box(A \wedge B) \to \Box B$.

We also have $\mathrm{L} \vdash A \to (B \to (A \wedge B))$, whence by Theorem 1,

(3) $\mathrm{L} \vdash \Box A \to \Box(B \to (A \wedge B))$, and

(4) $\mathrm{L} \vdash \Box(B \to (A \wedge B)) \to (\Box B \to \Box(A \wedge B))$ (distribution).

The theorem follows truth-functionally from (1), (2), (3), and (4). ⊣

Theorem 4. $\mathrm{L} \vdash \Box(A_1 \wedge \cdots \wedge A_n) \leftrightarrow (\Box A_1 \wedge \cdots \wedge \Box A_n)$.

Proof. The theorem holds if $n = 0$, for the empty conjunction is identified with $\top$, and $\mathrm{L} \vdash \Box \top$. The theorem is trivial if $n = 1$ and has just been proved if $n = 2$. If $n > 2$, then

$$\begin{aligned} \mathrm{L} \vdash \Box(A_1 \wedge A_2 \wedge \cdots \wedge A_n) &\leftrightarrow \Box(A_1 \wedge (A_2 \wedge \cdots \wedge A_n)) \\ &\leftrightarrow \Box A_1 \wedge \Box(A_2 \wedge \cdots \wedge A_n) \\ &\leftrightarrow (\Box A_1 \wedge \Box A_2 \cdots \wedge \Box A_n) \end{aligned}$$

The first of these equivalences holds by Theorem 2, the second by Theorem 3, and the third by the induction hypothesis. ⊣

We write: $A \leftrightarrow B, \leftrightarrow C$, etc. to mean: $(A \leftrightarrow B) \wedge (B \leftrightarrow C)$, etc.

Theorem 5. *Suppose* $\mathrm{L} \vdash A_1 \wedge \cdots \wedge A_n \to B$. *Then* $\mathrm{L} \vdash \Box A_1 \wedge \cdots \wedge \Box A_n \to \Box B$.

Proof. By the supposition and Theorem 1, $\mathrm{L} \vdash \Box(A_1 \wedge \cdots \wedge A_n) \to \Box B$. The conclusion then follows by Theorem 4. ⊣

Theorem 6. *Suppose* $\mathrm{L} \vdash A \to B$. *Then* $\mathrm{L} \vdash \Diamond A \to \Diamond B$.

Proof. Truth-functionally, we have
$\mathrm{L} \vdash \neg B \to \neg A$, whence
$\mathrm{L} \vdash \Box \neg B \to \Box \neg A$ by Theorem 1, and then truth-functionally
$\mathrm{L} \vdash \neg \Box \neg A \to \neg \Box \neg B$, i.e., $\mathrm{L} \vdash \Diamond A \to \Diamond B$. ⊣

Theorem 7. *Suppose* $\mathrm{L} \vdash A \leftrightarrow B$. *Then* $\mathrm{L} \vdash \Diamond A \leftrightarrow \Diamond B$.

Proof. The theorem follows from Theorem 6 via truth-functional logic and definitions. ⊣

Theorem 8. $\mathrm{L} \vdash \Diamond A \wedge \Box B \to \Diamond(A \wedge B)$.

Proof. By the definition of $\Diamond$, it is enough to show that
$\mathrm{L} \vdash \Box \neg(A \wedge B) \wedge \Box B \to \Box \neg A$. But this is clear, since
$\mathrm{L} \vdash \Box \neg(A \wedge B) \to \Box(B \to \neg A)$. ⊣

Henceforth we shall refer to the facts stated in Theorems 1–8, together with obvious consequences of these, as *normality*.

The first substitution theorem. *Suppose* $\mathrm{L} \vdash A \leftrightarrow B$. *Then* $\mathrm{L} \vdash F_p(A) \leftrightarrow F_p(B)$.

Proof. Induction on the complexity of F. If $F = p$, the sentence asserted in the conclusion to be a theorem of L is just $A \leftrightarrow B$; if $F = q$, it is $q \leftrightarrow q$, and if $F = \bot$, it is $\bot \leftrightarrow \bot$, both theorems of L. If $F = (G \to H)$ and the conclusion of the theorem holds for G and H, then it holds for F by propositional logic and the definition of substitution. Finally, if $F = \Box(G)$ and $\mathrm{L} \vdash G_p(A) \leftrightarrow G_p(B)$, then by Theorem 2,
$\mathrm{L} \vdash \Box(G_p(A)) \leftrightarrow \Box(G_p(B))$, i.e.,
$\mathrm{L} \vdash \Box(G)_p(A) \leftrightarrow \Box(G)_p(B)$, i.e.,
$\mathrm{L} \vdash F_p(A) \leftrightarrow F_p(B)$. ⊣

Definition. For any modal sentence A, $\boxdot A$ is the sentence $(\Box A \wedge A)$.

The definition has a point since $\Box A \to A$ is not, in general, a theorem of K, K4, or GL. The notation $\boxdot$ is most useful when one is considering K4 or one of its extensions, e.g., GL.

Theorem 9. $\mathrm{K4} \vdash \boxdot \Box A \leftrightarrow \Box A, \leftrightarrow \Box \boxdot A$; $\mathrm{K4} \vdash \boxdot A \leftrightarrow \boxdot \boxdot A$.

Proof. $\mathrm{K4} \vdash \Box A \to \Box \Box A$, and so by normality we have $\mathrm{K4} \vdash (\Box \Box A \wedge \Box A) \leftrightarrow \Box A, \leftrightarrow \Box(\Box A \wedge A)$. That $\mathrm{K4} \vdash \boxdot A \leftrightarrow \boxdot \boxdot A$ is proved similarly. ⊣

Theorem 10. *Suppose* L *extends* K4 *and* $\mathrm{L} \vdash \boxdot A \to B$. *Then* $\mathrm{L} \vdash \Box A \to \Box B$ *and* $\mathrm{L} \vdash \boxdot A \to \boxdot B$.

Proof. We have $\mathrm{L} \vdash \Box \boxdot A \to \Box B$, whence by Theorem 9, $\mathrm{L} \vdash \Box A \to \Box B$, and then by the definition of $\boxdot$, $\mathrm{L} \vdash \boxdot A \to \boxdot B$. ⊣

The second substitution theorem. $\mathrm{K4} \vdash \boxdot(A \leftrightarrow B) \to (F_p(A) \leftrightarrow F_p(B))$.

Proof. The proof is a formalization in K4 of the first substitution theorem and proceeds by induction on the complexity of F. If F is p, q $(\neq p)$, or $\bot$, then the sentence asserted to be a theorem of K4 is the tautology $\boxdot(A \leftrightarrow B) \to (A \leftrightarrow B)$, the tautology $\boxdot(A \leftrightarrow B) \to (q \leftrightarrow q)$, or the tautology $\boxdot(A \leftrightarrow B) \to (\bot \leftrightarrow \bot)$, respectively. If $F = (G \to H)$ and the theorem holds for G and H, then, truth-functionally it holds for F. Finally suppose that $F = \Box(G)$ and
$\mathrm{K4} \vdash \boxdot(A \leftrightarrow B) \to (G_p(A) \leftrightarrow G_p(B))$. Then
$\mathrm{K4} \vdash \Box \boxdot(A \leftrightarrow B) \to \Box(G_p(A) \leftrightarrow G_p(B))$, whence
$\mathrm{K4} \vdash \Box \boxdot(A \leftrightarrow B) \to (\Box(G_p(A)) \leftrightarrow \Box(G_p(B)))$, and then by the definition of substitution,
$\mathrm{K4} \vdash \Box \boxdot(A \leftrightarrow B) \to (\Box(G)_p(A) \leftrightarrow \Box(G)_p(B))$, i.e.,
$\mathrm{K4} \vdash \Box \boxdot(A \leftrightarrow B) \to (F_p(A) \leftrightarrow F_p(B))$. By Theorem 9,
$\mathrm{K4} \vdash \boxdot(A \leftrightarrow B) \to \Box \boxdot(A \leftrightarrow B)$, and we are done. ⊣

Corollary. $\mathrm{K4} \vdash \Box(A \leftrightarrow B) \to \Box(F_p(A) \leftrightarrow F_p(B))$; $\mathrm{K4} \vdash \boxdot(A \leftrightarrow B) \to \boxdot(F_p(A) \leftrightarrow F_p(B))$.

Proof. By the theorem and Theorem 10. ⊣

The next theorem is a somewhat surprising result about K4.[4]

Theorem 11. $K4 \vdash \Box\Diamond\Box\Diamond A \leftrightarrow \Box\Diamond A$.

Proof. We begin by observing that $K \vdash \Box(\Diamond B \wedge \Box C \to \Diamond D)$ whenever
$K \vdash \Box(B \wedge C \to D)$, for then $K \vdash \Box(C \wedge \neg D \to \neg B)$,
$K \vdash \Box\Box(C \wedge \neg D \to \neg B)$,
$K \vdash \Box(\Box C \wedge \Box\neg D \to \Box\neg B)$, whence
$K \vdash \Box(\Diamond B \wedge \Box C \to \Diamond D)$. Similarly, $K \vdash \Box(\Box B \wedge \Diamond C \to \Diamond D)$ whenever
$K \vdash \Box(B \wedge C \to D)$.

Since, evidently,
$K \vdash \Box(A \wedge \Diamond A \to \Diamond A)$, we have
$K \vdash \Box(\Diamond A \wedge \Box\Diamond A \to \Diamond\Diamond A)$,
$K \vdash \Box(\Box\Diamond A \wedge \Diamond\Box\Diamond A \to \Diamond\Diamond\Diamond A)$, and
$K \vdash \Box(\Diamond\Box\Diamond A \wedge \Box\Diamond\Box\Diamond A \to \Diamond\Diamond\Diamond\Diamond A)$. But
$K4 \vdash \Diamond\Diamond\Diamond\Diamond A \to \Diamond A$, whence
$K4 \vdash \Box(\Diamond\Diamond\Diamond\Diamond A \to \Diamond A)$, and so
$K4 \vdash \Box(\Diamond\Box\Diamond A \wedge \Box\Diamond\Box\Diamond A \to \Diamond A)$ and
$K4 \vdash \Box\Diamond\Box\Diamond A \wedge \Box\Box\Diamond\Box\Diamond A \to \Box\Diamond A$. But
$K4 \vdash \Box\Diamond\Box\Diamond A \to \Box\Box\Diamond\Box\Diamond A$. Thus
$K4 \vdash \Box\Diamond\Box\Diamond A \to \Box\Diamond A$.

Conversely,
$K \vdash \Diamond A \wedge \Box\Box\Diamond A \to \Diamond(A \wedge \Box\Diamond A)$, and so
$K \vdash \Diamond A \wedge \Box\Box\Diamond A \to \Diamond\Box\Diamond A$, whence
$K \vdash \Box(\Diamond A \wedge \Box\Box\Diamond A) \to \Box\Diamond\Box\Diamond A$. But
$K4 \vdash \Box\Diamond A \to \Box\Box\Box\Diamond A$,
$K4 \vdash \Box\Diamond A \to \Box\Diamond A \wedge \Box\Box\Box\Diamond A$, and so
$K4 \vdash \Box\Diamond A \to \Box(\Diamond A \wedge \Box\Box\Diamond A)$. Thus
$K4 \vdash \Box\Diamond A \to \Box\Diamond\Box\Diamond A$. $\dashv$

We emphasize that no use of $\Box p \to p$ has been made thus far; the two substitution theorems and their corollary are results about K4 and hence about all extensions of K4.

Theorem 12. $T \vdash A \to \Diamond A$; $T \vdash \Box A \to \Diamond A$.

Proof. $T \vdash \Box\neg A \to \neg A$; contraposing, we obtain $T \vdash A \to \Diamond A$. Since $T \vdash \Box A \to A$, $T \vdash \Box A \to \Diamond A$ also. $\dashv$

Theorem 13. $S4 \vdash \Diamond\Diamond A \to \Diamond A$.

Proof. By contraposition, from $S4 \vdash \Box\neg A \to \Box\Box\neg A$. $\dashv$

Theorem 14. $S4 \vdash \Box A \leftrightarrow \Box\Box A$; $\Diamond A \leftrightarrow \Diamond\Diamond A$.

Theorem 15. $\mathrm{S4} \vdash$

$$\begin{array}{ccccc} \Box p & \rightarrow & \Box\Diamond\Box p & \rightarrow & \Diamond\Box p \\ \Big| & & \downarrow & & \downarrow \\ \Big| & & \Box\Diamond p & \rightarrow & \Diamond\Box\Diamond p \\ \downarrow & & & & \downarrow \\ p & & \longrightarrow & & \Diamond p \end{array}$$

A *modality* is a sequence of $\Box$*s* and $\neg$*s*. It follows from Theorems 11, 14, and 15 that there are at most 14 inequivalent modalities σ in S4, i.e., at most 14 inequivalent sentences of the form σp, namely the 7 mentioned in Theorem 15 and their negations. The completeness theorem for S4 given in Chapter 5 will enable us to see that these 14 modalities are in fact inequivalent. The completeness theorems for B and GL also found there can be used to show that no two of the modalities [empty], $\Box$, $\Box\Box$,... are equivalent in either of those logics.

We now examine S5. We first show that S5 has an alternative axiomatization. Let S5* be the system of modal logic whose axioms are all the sentences that are either axioms of S4 or B and whose rules of inference are modus ponens and necessitation.

Theorem 16. $\mathrm{S5}^* \vdash A$ *iff* $\mathrm{S5} \vdash A$.

Proof. It is enough to show that for every A, $\mathrm{S5} \vdash \Box A \rightarrow \Box\Box A$, $\mathrm{S5} \vdash A \rightarrow \Box\Diamond A$, and $\mathrm{S5}^* \vdash \Diamond A \rightarrow \Box\Diamond A$.
$\mathrm{S5} \vdash \Box A \rightarrow \Box\Box A$: Since S5 extends T,
$\mathrm{S5} \vdash \Box A \rightarrow \Diamond\Box A$; also
$\mathrm{S5} \vdash \Diamond\Box A \rightarrow \Box\Diamond\Box A$ (because $\mathrm{S5} \vdash \Diamond B \rightarrow \Box\Diamond B$), and therefore
$\mathrm{S5} \vdash \Box A \rightarrow \Box\Diamond\Box A$. But also
$\mathrm{S5} \vdash \Diamond\Box A \rightarrow \Box A$ (because $\mathrm{S5} \vdash \Diamond\neg A \rightarrow \Box\Diamond\neg A$), whence by normality
$\mathrm{S5} \vdash \Box\Diamond\Box A \rightarrow \Box\Box A$. Thus
$\mathrm{S5} \vdash \Box A \rightarrow \Box\Box A$.
$\mathrm{S5} \vdash A \rightarrow \Box\Diamond A$: This is immediate from
$\mathrm{S5} \vdash A \rightarrow \Diamond A$ and $\mathrm{S5} \vdash \Diamond A \rightarrow \Box\Diamond A$. Finally,
$\mathrm{S5}^* \vdash \Diamond A \rightarrow \Box\Diamond A$: For since
$\mathrm{S5}^* \vdash \Diamond\Diamond A \rightarrow \Diamond A$ (S5* extends S4), by normality,
$\mathrm{S5}^* \vdash \Box\Diamond\Diamond A \rightarrow \Box\Diamond A$. But also
$\mathrm{S5}^* \vdash \Diamond A \rightarrow \Box\Diamond\Diamond A$ (S5* extends B), and so we have what we want. $\dashv$

Theorem 17. $\mathrm{S5} \vdash (\Diamond\Diamond A \leftrightarrow \Diamond A) \wedge (\Box\Diamond A \leftrightarrow \Diamond A) \wedge (\Box\Box A \leftrightarrow \Box A) \wedge (\Diamond\Box A \leftrightarrow \Box A)$.

According to Theorem 17, if σ is a string containing a positive number of $\Box$s and $\Diamond$s ending in $\Box$ or in $\Diamond$ but not $\neg$, then σp is equivalent to $\Box p$ or to $\Diamond p$, respectively. Thus there are at most six inequivalent modalities in S5: $\Box$, [empty], $\Diamond$, and their negations. The completeness theorem for S5 given in Chapter 5 will enable us to see that no two of these six modalities are in fact equivalent in S5.

We shall now show that $\Box p \to p$ is not a theorem of GL and that GL is consistent: Define A^* by $\bot^* = \bot$, $p^* = p$ (for all sentence letters p), $(A \to B)^* = (A^* \to B^*)$, and $\Box(A)^* = \top$. (Then A^* is the result of taking $\Box$ to be a *verum* operator in A.) If A is a tautology, so is A^*; if A is a distribution axiom, then A^* is $\top \to (\top \to \top)$; and if A is a sentence $\Box(\Box B \to B) \to \Box B$, then $A^* = \top \to \top$. Moreover if A^* and $(A \to B)^*$ are tautologies, so is B^*, and if A^* is a tautology, then so is $\Box(A)^* = \top$. Thus if A is a theorem of GL, A^* is a tautology. But $(\Box p \to p)^* = (\top \to p)$, which is not a tautology. Thus $\Box p \to p$ is not a theorem of GL, hence not one of K4 or K.

Similarly, $\Box(\Box p \to p) \to \Box p$ is not a theorem of S5, hence not one of B, S4, T, K4, or K. Define $\bot^*$, p^*, and $(A \to B)^*$ as before, but now let $\Box(A)^* = A^*$. (A^* is now the result of taking $\Box$ to be *decoration* in A.) Again if A is a theorem of S5, A^* is a tautology. But $(\Box(\Box p \to p) \to \Box p)^*$ is now $((p \to p) \to p)$, which is not a tautology. Therefore $(\Box(\Box p \to p) \to \Box p)$ is not a theorem of S5.

GL and T are thus consistent normal systems of modal logic, but there is no consistent normal system that extends both of them.

A remarkable fact about GL, the proof of which was independently discovered by de Jongh, Kripke, and Sambin, is that $\Box p \to \Box\Box p$ is a theorem of GL and thus that for all sentences A, $\Box A \to \Box\Box A$ is a theorem of GL. ("Had" $\Box p \to \Box\Box p$ not been a theorem of GL, we should have been interested in the smallest normal extension of GL in which it was one!) In practice, sentences $\Box A \to \Box\Box A$ are treated rather as if they were axioms of GL.

Theorem 18. $\mathrm{GL} \vdash \Box A \to \Box\Box A$.

Proof. Truth-functionally, we have
$\mathrm{GL} \vdash A \to ((\Box\Box A \wedge \Box A) \to (\Box A \wedge A))$, whence by normality,
$\mathrm{GL} \vdash A \to (\Box(\Box A \wedge A) \to (\Box A \wedge A))$. By normality again,
$\mathrm{GL} \vdash \Box A \to \Box(\Box(\Box A \wedge A) \to (\Box A \wedge A))$. But where $B = (\Box A \wedge A)$,
$\Box(\Box B \to B) \to \Box B$ is an axiom of GL, i.e.,

$\mathrm{GL} \vdash \Box(\Box(\Box A \wedge A) \rightarrow (\Box A \wedge A)) \rightarrow \Box(\Box A \wedge A)$. Truth-functionally, $\mathrm{GL} \vdash \Box A \rightarrow \Box(\Box A \wedge A)$. But by normality, $\mathrm{GL} \vdash \Box(\Box A \wedge A) \rightarrow \Box\Box A$. From these last two, we have $\mathrm{GL} \vdash \Box A \rightarrow \Box\Box A$. $\dashv$

It follows that GL extends K4; it is worth mentioning that the substitution theorems therefore hold when 'K4' is replaced by 'GL'.

Theorem 19. $\mathrm{GL} \vdash \Box(\Box A \rightarrow A) \leftrightarrow \Box A, \leftrightarrow \Box(\Box A \wedge A)$.

Proof. Immediate by normality and Theorem 18. $\dashv$

Theorem 20. *If* $\mathrm{GL} \vdash (\Box A_1 \wedge A_1 \wedge \cdots \wedge \Box A_n \wedge A_n \wedge \Box B) \rightarrow B$, *then* $\mathrm{GL} \vdash (\Box A_1 \wedge \cdots \wedge \Box A_n) \rightarrow \Box B$.

Proof. Suppose that $\mathrm{GL} \vdash (\Box A_1 \wedge A_1 \wedge \cdots \wedge \Box A_n \wedge A_n \wedge \Box B) \rightarrow B$. Then $\mathrm{GL} \vdash \Box A_1 \wedge A_1 \wedge \cdots \wedge \Box A_n \wedge A_n \rightarrow (\Box B \rightarrow B)$. By normality, $\mathrm{GL} \vdash \Box(\Box A_1 \wedge A_1) \wedge \cdots \wedge \Box(\Box A_n \wedge A_n) \rightarrow \Box(\Box B \rightarrow B)$. By both equivalences of Theorem 19, $\mathrm{GL} \vdash (\Box A_1 \wedge \cdots \wedge \Box A_n) \rightarrow \Box B$. $\dashv$

Theorem 21. $\mathrm{GL} \vdash \Box\bot \leftrightarrow \Box\Diamond p$.

Proof. $\mathrm{GL} \vdash \bot \rightarrow \Diamond p$. Thus by normality, $\mathrm{GL} \vdash \Box\bot \rightarrow \Box\Diamond p$. Conversely, $\mathrm{GL} \vdash \Diamond p \rightarrow \Diamond\top$, and by the definition of $\Diamond$, $\mathrm{GL} \vdash \Diamond\top \rightarrow (\Box\bot \rightarrow \bot)$. Thus $\mathrm{GL} \vdash \Diamond p \rightarrow (\Box\bot \rightarrow \bot)$, and by normality, $\mathrm{GL} \vdash \Box\Diamond p \rightarrow \Box(\Box\bot \rightarrow \bot)$. Since $\mathrm{GL} \vdash \Box(\Box\bot \rightarrow \bot) \rightarrow \Box\bot$, we also have that $\mathrm{GL} \vdash \Box\Diamond p \rightarrow \Box\bot$. $\dashv$

Theorem 22. $\mathrm{GL} \vdash \Box\Diamond\bot \rightarrow \Box\bot$.

Proof. Substitute $\bot$ for p in Theorem 21 and weaken. $\dashv$

In Chapter 3 we shall see how Theorem 21 can be regarded as telling us that (PA) asserts of each sentence S that PA is inconsistent if and only if it is provable (in PA) that S is consistent (with PA). Theorem 22, we shall also see there, will similarly tell us that the second incompleteness theorem is a theorem of PA.

Our proof that $\Box p \rightarrow p$ is not a theorem of GL cannot be used to show that $p \rightarrow \Box\Diamond p$ and $\Diamond p \rightarrow \Box\Diamond p$ are not theorems of GL. In Chapter 3 we shall see that $\Box\bot$ is not a theorem of GL. It follows from Theorem 21 that $\top \to \Box \Diamond \top$ and $\Diamond \top \to \Box \Diamond \top$ are both equivalent to $\Box \Diamond \top$. Thus neither is provable in GL, and therefore $p \to \Box \Diamond p$ and $\Diamond p \to \Box \Diamond p$ are also unprovable in GL.

The proof of the next theorem formalizes the argument used in the proof of Löb's theorem. As we shall see in Chapter 3, the theorem may be used in a variant proof of a basic fact about GL: every theorem of GL is provable in PA under every translation.

Theorem 23. K4 $\vdash \Box(q \leftrightarrow (\Box q \to p)) \to (\Box(\Box p \to p) \to \Box p)$.

Proof.

(1) K4 $\vdash \Box(q \leftrightarrow (\Box q \to p)) \to (\Box q \to \Box(\Box q \to p))$, since K4 is normal.

(2) K4 $\vdash \Box(\Box q \to p) \to (\Box \Box q \to \Box p)$ – a distribution axiom.

(3) K4 $\vdash \Box q \to \Box \Box q$.

(4) K4 $\vdash \Box(q \leftrightarrow (\Box q \to p)) \to (\Box q \to \Box p)$ – (4) follows truth-functionally from (1), (2), and (3).

(5) K4 $\vdash \Box \Box(q \leftrightarrow (\Box q \to p)) \to \Box(\Box q \to \Box p)$ – (5) follows from (4) by normality.

(6) K4 $\vdash \Box(q \leftrightarrow (\Box q \to p)) \to \Box \Box(q \leftrightarrow (\Box q \to p))$ – (6) is of the form $\Box A \to \Box \Box A$.

(7) K4 $\vdash \Box(\Box p \to p) \to (\Box(\Box q \to \Box p) \to \Box(\Box q \to p))$, by normality.

(8) K4 $\vdash \Box(q \leftrightarrow (\Box q \to p)) \to (\Box(\Box q \to p) \to \Box q)$, by normality. ⊣

Theorem 23 then follows truth-functionally from (6), (5), (7), (8), and (4).

Theorem 24

(a) GL $\vdash \Box(p \leftrightarrow \neg \Box p) \leftrightarrow \Box(p \leftrightarrow \neg \Box \bot)$,

(b) GL $\vdash \Box(p \leftrightarrow \Box p) \leftrightarrow \Box(p \leftrightarrow \top)$,

(c) GL $\vdash \Box(p \leftrightarrow \Box \neg p) \leftrightarrow \Box(p \leftrightarrow \Box \bot)$, *and*

(d) GL $\vdash \Box(p \leftrightarrow \neg \Box \neg p) \leftrightarrow \Box(p \leftrightarrow \bot)$.

Proof. (a) K4 $\vdash \Box(p \leftrightarrow \neg \Box p) \to \Box(p \to \neg \Box p)$. Since
K4 $\vdash \Box(p \to \neg \Box p) \to \Box \Box(p \to \neg \Box p)$,
K4 $\vdash \Box(p \leftrightarrow \neg \Box p) \to \Box(\Box p \to \Box \neg \Box p)$ by normality. But
K4 $\vdash \Box p \to \Box \Box p$ and
K4 $\vdash \Box \Box p \wedge \Box \neg \Box p \to \Box \bot$. Thus
K4 $\vdash \Box(p \leftrightarrow \neg \Box p) \to \Box(\Box p \to \Box \bot)$. Since
K4 $\vdash \Box \bot \to \Box p$,

$K4 \vdash \Box(p \leftrightarrow \neg\Box p) \rightarrow \Box(\Box p \leftrightarrow \Box\bot)$, and so
$K4 \vdash \Box(p \leftrightarrow \neg\Box p) \rightarrow \Box(\neg\Box p \leftrightarrow \neg\Box\bot)$. But
$K4 \vdash \Box(p \leftrightarrow \neg\Box p) \wedge \Box(\neg\Box p \leftrightarrow \neg\Box\bot) \rightarrow \Box(p \leftrightarrow \neg\Box\bot)$. Thus
$K4 \vdash \Box(p \leftrightarrow \neg\Box p) \rightarrow \Box(p \leftrightarrow \neg\Box\bot)$, whence
$GL \vdash \Box(p \leftrightarrow \neg\Box p) \rightarrow \Box(p \leftrightarrow \neg\Box\bot)$.
Conversely, by Theorem 21 (with $\bot$ for p),
$GL \vdash \Box(p \leftrightarrow \neg\Box\bot) \rightarrow \Box\Box(p \leftrightarrow \neg\Box p)$, and so
$GL \vdash \Box(p \leftrightarrow \neg\Box\bot) \rightarrow \Box(\Box p \leftrightarrow \Box\neg\Box p)$. By Theorem 21 (with $\neg p$ for p)
$GL \vdash \Box\neg\Box p \leftrightarrow \Box\bot$. Thus
$GL \vdash \Box(p \leftrightarrow \neg\Box\bot) \rightarrow \Box(\Box p \leftrightarrow \Box\bot)$ and
$GL \vdash \Box(p \leftrightarrow \neg\Box\bot) \rightarrow \Box(\neg\Box\bot \leftrightarrow \neg\Box p)$. Since
$GL \vdash \Box(p \leftrightarrow \neg\Box\bot) \wedge \Box(\neg\Box\bot \leftrightarrow \neg\Box p) \rightarrow \Box(p \leftrightarrow \neg\Box p)$,
$GL \vdash \Box(p \leftrightarrow \neg\Box\bot) \rightarrow \Box(p \leftrightarrow \neg\Box p)$.
(b) Since $GL \vdash \top \leftrightarrow \Box\top$,
$GL \vdash \Box(p \leftrightarrow \Box p) \rightarrow \Box(\Box p \rightarrow p), \rightarrow \Box p, \rightarrow \Box(p \leftrightarrow \top), \rightarrow \Box p,$
$\rightarrow (\Box p \wedge \Box\Box p), \rightarrow \Box(p \wedge \Box p), \rightarrow \Box(p \leftrightarrow \Box p)$.
Substituting $\neg p$ for p in (a) yields
$GL \vdash \Box(\neg p \leftrightarrow \neg\Box\neg p) \leftrightarrow \Box(\neg p \leftrightarrow \neg\Box\bot)$. Simplifying, we obtain
$GL \vdash \Box(p \leftrightarrow \Box\neg p) \leftrightarrow \Box(p \leftrightarrow \Box\bot)$, i.e., (c).

We can obtain (d) by similarly substituting $\neg p$ for p in (b). $\dashv$

As we shall see, Theorem 24 will tell us that it is a theorem of PA that a sentence *S* is equivalent (in PA) to the assertion that *S* is unprovable/provable/disprovable/consistent if and only if *S* is respectively equivalent to the assertion that PA is consistent/that $0 = 0$/that PA is inconsistent/that $0 = 1$. Many other interesting facts about PA can be learned from a study of GL.

2

Peano arithmetic

Peano arithmetic (*PA*, or *arithmetic*, for short) is classical first-order arithmetic with induction. The aim of this chapter is to define the concepts mentioned in, and describe the proofs of, five important theorems about Bew(x), the standard "provability" or "theoremhood" predicate of PA:

(i) If $\vdash S$, then $\vdash \mathrm{Bew}(\ulcorner S \urcorner)$,
(ii) $\vdash \mathrm{Bew}(\ulcorner (S \to T) \urcorner) \to (\mathrm{Bew}(\ulcorner S \urcorner) \to \mathrm{Bew}(\ulcorner T \urcorner))$,
(iii) $\vdash \mathrm{Bew}(\ulcorner S \urcorner) \to \mathrm{Bew}(\ulcorner \mathrm{Bew}(\ulcorner S \urcorner) \urcorner)$,
(iv) $\mathrm{Bew}(\ulcorner S \urcorner)$ is a Σ sentence, and
(v) if S is a Σ sentence, then $\vdash S \to \mathrm{Bew}(\ulcorner S \urcorner)$

(for all sentences S, T of Peano arithmetic).

'$\vdash$' is, as usual, the sign for theoremhood; in this chapter we write '$\vdash S$' to mean that S is a theorem of PA. $\ulcorner S \urcorner$ is the numeral in PA for the Gödel number of sentence S, that is, if n is the Gödel number of S, then $\ulcorner S \urcorner$ is $\mathbf{0}$ preceded by n occurrences of the successor sign **s**. $\mathrm{Bew}(\ulcorner S \urcorner)$ is therefore the result of substituting $\ulcorner S \urcorner$ for the variable x in Bew(x), and (iii) immediately follows from (iv) and (v). $\mathrm{Bew}(\ulcorner S \urcorner)$ may be regarded as a sentence asserting that S is a theorem of PA. Σ sentences (often called Σ_1 sentences) are, roughly speaking, sentences constructed from atomic formulas and negations of atomic formulas by means of conjunction, disjunction, existential quantification, and bounded universal quantification ("for all x less than y"), but not negation or universal quantification. A precise definition is given below.

Notice the distinction between 'Bew(x)' and '$\vdash$'. 'Bew(x)' denotes a certain formula of the language of PA and thus Bew(x) *is* that formula; it is a formula that is true of (the Gödel numbers of) those formulas of PA that are provable in PA. '$\vdash$', on the other hand, is a (pre-posed) predicate of *our* language (logicians' English, a mixture of English, mathematical terminology, and symbolism) and has the meaning "is a theorem of PA". Thus when we write

$$\text{If } \vdash S, \text{ then } \vdash \text{Bew}(\ulcorner S \urcorner)$$

we are claiming that if S is a theorem of PA, then so is the sentence that results when $\ulcorner S \urcorner$ is substituted for the variable x in the formula $\text{Bew}(x)$.

(i), (ii), and (iii) are known as the (Hilbert–Bernays–Löb) *derivability conditions* [for $\text{Bew}(x)$ and PA]. They are called derivability conditions because they are sufficient conditions on an arbitrary formula $B(x)$ and an arbitrary theory Z for the second incompleteness theorem, with $B(x)$ playing the role of $\text{Bew}(x)$, to be derivable in Z. That is, if Z is a theory in which a few simple facts about the natural numbers (namely, the first six axioms of PA and $\forall x(x \neq \mathbf{0} \rightarrow \exists y\, x = \mathbf{s}y)$) are provable, and for all sentences S, T of Peano arithmetic,

$$\text{if } Z \vdash S, \text{ then } Z \vdash B(\ulcorner S \urcorner),$$
$$Z \vdash B(\ulcorner (S \rightarrow T) \urcorner) \rightarrow (B(\ulcorner S \urcorner) \rightarrow B(\ulcorner T \urcorner)), \text{ and}$$
$$Z \vdash B(\ulcorner S \urcorner) \rightarrow B(\ulcorner B(\ulcorner S \urcorner) \urcorner),$$

then if Z is consistent, $Z \nvdash \neg B(\ulcorner \bot \urcorner)$.

In their proof of the second incompleteness theorem for a system related to PA called Z_μ, Hilbert and Bernays had listed three somewhat ungainly conditions,[1] from whose satisfaction they showed the second incompleteness theorem for Z_μ to follow. The isolation of (the attractive) (i), (ii), and (iii) is due to Löb.[2]

(v) and the notion of a Σ sentence are used only in later chapters; by the time we reach these, we shall have established a number of striking results about the notions of provability, consistency, relative consistency, and diagonal sentences (fixed points). The reader who does not like incomplete and (apparently) irremediably messy proofs of syntactic facts may wish to skim over the rest of this chapter and take it for granted that $\text{Bew}(x)$ satisfies the three derivability conditions. Many of the details of the proofs of (i)–(v) have been explicitly included, however, with a view to reducing the number of propositions that have to be taken on faith.

We begin with a (partial) characterization of PA.

$v_0, v_1, \ldots$ is a countably infinite sequence of distinct (individual) *variables*. In addition to the variables, there are four other logical symbols of PA, $\bot$ (the 0-place truth-functional connective for logical falsity), the conditional sign $\rightarrow$, the universal quantifier $\forall$, and the sign = of identity. The remaining four primitive symbols of PA are the non-logical symbols of PA, the individual constant **0**, the 1-place function symbol **s** ("successor"), and two 2-place function symbols **+** and **×**. (Since zero can be proved in PA to be the unique number k such that $j+k=j$ for all j and the successor of i can be proved to be the unique k such that $j \times k = j \times i + j$ for all j, **0** and **s** could have been dispensed with, but it simplifies matters considerably for them to be taken as primitives.)

Caution! $\perp$ (e.g.) is a symbol. What sort of thing the symbol $\perp$ is, whether it is a shape with a stem and a base, or whether it is a set or a number, or something else entirely, we have not said (and need not say). '$\perp$', in contrast, is the name of $\perp$ (and is itself also a symbol, maybe the same one as $\perp$, maybe not); '$\perp$' definitely does have a stem and a base.

We want now to make explicit some of our "background" assumptions concerning the existence of objects of various sorts.

We assume that for any objects a and b, there is an object $\langle a, b \rangle$, the *ordered pair* of a and b. The law of ordered pairs is: if $\langle a, b \rangle = \langle c, d \rangle$, then $a = c$ and $b = d$.

The *ordered triple* $\langle a, b, c \rangle$ *of* a, b, and c is the ordered pair $\langle a, \langle b, c \rangle \rangle$. Thus if $\langle a, b, c \rangle = \langle d, e, f \rangle$, then $a = d$, $b = e$, and $c = f$.

A *finite* sequence is an object s with a *length* k (a natural number) and, for each $i < k$, an object s_i that is its *value* at i. We assume that there are a finite sequence of length 0 and, for each finite sequence s of length k and each object a, a finite sequence s' of length $k+1$ such that for each $i < k$, $s'_i = s_i$ and $s'_k = a$. If s is a finite sequence of length k, then s_0 is the *first* value of s; s_{k-1} is the *last*; and s_i is an *earlier* value of s than s_j for $i < j$. The law of finite sequences is: Finite sequences are identical if they have the same length k and the same values at all $i < k$. (Sometimes the values of a finite sequence are called its "terms", but we shall use the word "term" with another meaning.) We write: $[s_0, \ldots, s_{k-1}]$ for the finite sequence s of length k whose value at each $i < k$ is s_i; thus $[]$ is the finite sequence of length 0. When referring to a finite sequence of positive length, we often omit the brackets.

The terms and formulas of PA are constructed from the four non-logical constants in the standard way. Here is a definition of *term of PA*:

Every variable is a term;
0 is a term;

if t is a term, then $\mathbf{s}t$ is a term; and
if t and t' are terms, then $(t + t')$ and $(t \times t')$ are terms.

We shall follow Smullyan[3] in supposing that $\mathbf{s}t$ is the ordered pair of $\mathbf{s}$ and t and that $(t + t')$ and $(t \times t')$ are the ordered triples of $+$, t, and t' and of $\times$, t, and t'.

The definition of *term* just given was an inductive one. Using the notion of a finite sequence, we recast this inductive definition as an explicit one, which we regard as the "official" definition of term:

Explicitly, then, an object t is a term of PA if and only if there is a finite sequence whose last value is t, each value of which is either $\mathbf{0}$, a variable, the ordered pair of $\mathbf{s}$ and an earlier value of the sequence, the ordered triple of $+$ and two earlier values of the sequence, or the ordered triple of $\times$ and two earlier values of the sequence.

$t = t'$ is the ordered triple of $=$, t, and t'.

F is an *atomic formula* if either F is the symbol $\perp$ or for some terms t, t', F is $t = t'$.

$(F \to F')$ is the ordered triple of $\to$, F, and F'; $\forall vF$ is the ordered triple of $\forall$, v, and F. The advantage of taking terms and formulas to be ordered pairs and triples instead of finite sequences of primitive symbols is that the unique readability of terms and formulas is immediate: it follows directly from the law of ordered pairs that each term or formula can be parsed in exactly one way.

An object F is defined to be a *formula of PA* if and only if there is a finite sequence whose last value is F, each value of which is either an atomic formula, the ordered triple of $\to$ and two earlier values of the sequence, or the ordered triple of $\forall$, a variable, and an earlier value of the sequence.

$\neg F$, the negation of F, is defined as $(F \to \perp)$. $t \neq t'$ abbreviates $\neg t = t'$, as usual. We suppose that the other familiar logical symbols, $\wedge$, $\vee$, $\to$, $\leftrightarrow$, and $\exists$, are defined in any one of the usual ways, and we often omit parentheses and the multiplication sign when it is reasonable to do so.

G is said to be a *consequence by modus ponens of* $(F \to G)$ and F and $\forall vF$ is said to be a *consequence by generalization of* F. We shall assume given some standard axiomatic formulation of logic in which the rules of inference are modus ponens and generalization,[4] but we leave it open exactly which formulas in the language of PA we take as logical axioms.

The (non-logical axioms) of PA are the *recursion axioms for successor, sum, and product*, which are the six formulas

(1) $\mathbf{0} \neq \mathbf{s}x$,
(2) $\mathbf{s}x = \mathbf{s}y \rightarrow x = y$,
(3) $x + \mathbf{0} = x$,
(4) $x + \mathbf{s}y = \mathbf{s}(x + y)$,
(5) $x \times \mathbf{0} = \mathbf{0}$, and
(6) $x \times \mathbf{s}y = (x \times y) + x$,

(Here we suppose that x is the variable v_0 and y is the variable v_1.)

and the *induction axioms*, which are the (infinitely) many formulas of PA:

$$(\forall x(x = \mathbf{0} \rightarrow F) \wedge \forall y[\forall x(x = y \rightarrow F) \rightarrow \forall x(x = \mathbf{s}y \rightarrow F)]) \rightarrow F$$

where F is any formula, x is any variable, and y is any variable not in F and different from x. Each induction axiom expresses a statement to the effect that any number at all has a property (expressed by F) provided that zero has it and the successor of every number with the property also has it.

Thus the *axioms* of PA are the logical axioms, the recursion axioms for successor, sum, and product, and the induction axioms.

As one would expect, a *proof* in PA of the formula F is a finite sequence of formulas, each value of which is either an axiom of PA or a consequence by modus ponens or generalization of earlier formulas in the sequence and whose last value is F. The formula F is *provable in* or a *theorem of* PA if there is a proof of F in PA.

Other definitions pertaining to the syntax of PA:

A term is *closed* if no variable occurs in it.

The variable v is free in the formula F has the following explicit definition: there is a finite sequence $h_0, \ldots, h_r$ such that h_0 is an atomic formula $t = t'$ and v occurs in either t or t', h_r is F, and for all $i < r$, either for some formula F', $h_{i+1} = (h_i \rightarrow F')$ or $(F' \rightarrow h_i)$, or for some variable u different from v, $h_{i+1} = \forall u h_i$.

A formula is a *sentence*, or *closed*, if no variable is free in it.

The result $t'_v(t)$ of substituting the term t for the variable v in the term t' can be explicitly defined by saying that there are two sequences of the same length, one constructing t' and its subterms from the ground up, the other substituting t into subterms of t' *pari passu.*[5] There is a similar definition of *the result $F_v(t)$ of substituting the term t for the variable v in the formula F*, but we shall omit it.

These definitions having been made, each induction axiom is then logically equivalent to a formula

$$F_x(\mathbf{0}) \rightarrow (\forall x(F \rightarrow F_x(\mathbf{s}x)) \rightarrow F)$$

The semantics of PA requires only brief discussion: A sentence of PA is called *true* if it is true when its variables range over the natural numbers $0, 1, 2, \ldots$, and $\mathbf{0}$ and $\mathbf{s}$, $+$, and $\times$ denote zero and the successor, addition, and multiplication functions. Each closed term t *denotes* a unique natural number: $\mathbf{0}$ denotes 0, and if t and t' denote i and i', then $\mathbf{s}t$, $t + t'$, and $t \times t'$ denote $i + 1$, $i + i'$, and $i \times i'$. The *numeral* $\mathbf{i}$ *for* the number i is the closed term that is the result of attaching i occurrences of the successor sign $\mathbf{s}$ to $\mathbf{0}$. Thus $\mathbf{3}$ is $\mathbf{sss0}$, $\mathbf{1}$ is $\mathbf{s0}$ (and $\mathbf{0}$ is $\mathbf{0}$). $\mathbf{i}$ denotes i and a sentence $\exists xF$ is true if and only if for some number i, the result $F_x(\mathbf{i})$ of substituting $\mathbf{i}$ for x in F is true. A formula F with x its sole free variable *defines* the class of numbers i such that $F_x(\mathbf{i})$ is true. More generally, a formula F, together with a sequence $x_1, \ldots, x_n$ of distinct variables among which are all variables free in F, *defines* the n-place relation that holds among exactly those numbers $i_1, \ldots, i_n$ such that $F_{x_1}(\mathbf{i_1})_{x_2}(\mathbf{i_2})_{\ldots x_n}(\mathbf{i_n})$ is true. We sometimes say that F (together with a sequence of variables) is *true of* numbers $i_1, \ldots, i_n$ if and only if the relation defined by F (together with the sequence) holds among $i_1, \ldots, i_n$.

Before discussing (i)–(v) and their proofs, we shall need to discuss the capacity of PA to prove various facts about the natural numbers. Since the language of PA contains only the non-logical symbols $\mathbf{0}, \mathbf{s}, +$, and $\times$, it is not immediately apparent that much interesting mathematics can be formulated, let alone proved, in PA. It may not even be apparent whether formulas in the language of PA like $x + y = y + x$, which express elementary generalizations about the natural numbers, can actually be proved in PA. In fact, PA's capacity to express and to prove facts about the natural numbers is quite strong, and we shall need to see how to utilize that capacity. Let us begin by showing that certain familiar laws of numbers are provable in PA.

(1) $\vdash x = \mathbf{0} \lor \exists y\, x = \mathbf{s}y$

Proof. Let F be the formula $(x = \mathbf{0} \lor \exists y\, x = \mathbf{s}y)$. Then $\forall x(x = 0 \rightarrow F)$ and $\forall x(x = \mathbf{s}y \rightarrow F)$ are logical truths. Thus $\vdash \forall x(x = 0 \rightarrow F)$ and $\vdash \forall y(\forall x(x = y \rightarrow F) \rightarrow \forall x(x = \mathbf{s}y \rightarrow F))$. By an induction axiom, $\vdash F$, i.e., $\vdash x = \mathbf{0} \lor \exists y\, x = \mathbf{s}y$. $\dashv$

(2) $\vdash x + y = y + x$

Proof. $\vdash \mathbf{0} + \mathbf{0} =_3 \mathbf{0}$;
$\vdash \mathbf{0} + x = x \rightarrow \mathbf{0} + \mathrm{s}x =_4 \mathrm{s}(\mathbf{0} + x) =_{\text{ant.}} \mathrm{s}x$; thus by an induction axiom,
$\vdash \mathbf{0} + x = x$; since
$\vdash x =_3 x + \mathbf{0}$,
$\vdash \mathbf{0} + x = x + \mathbf{0}$;
$\vdash y + \mathrm{s}\mathbf{0} =_4 \mathrm{s}(y + \mathbf{0}) =_3 \mathrm{s}y =_3 \mathrm{s}y + \mathbf{0}$;
$\vdash y + \mathrm{s}x = \mathrm{s}y + x \rightarrow y + \mathrm{ss}x =_4 \mathrm{s}(y + \mathrm{s}x) =_{\text{ant.}} \mathrm{s}(\mathrm{s}y + x) =_4 \mathrm{s}y + \mathrm{s}x$;
thus by an induction axiom, $y + \mathrm{s}x = \mathrm{s}y + x$.
$\vdash x + y = y + x \rightarrow x + \mathrm{s}y =_4 \mathrm{s}(x + y) =_{\text{ant.}} \mathrm{s}(y + x) =_4 y + \mathrm{s}x =$ (by the foregoing) $\mathrm{s}y + x$. Thus by an induction axiom,
$\vdash x + y = y + x$. ⊣

(The subscripts "3" and "4" indicate which axiom of PA justifies the identity, "ant." means that the identity is justified by the antecedent of the conditional.)

(3) $\vdash x + (y + z) = (x + y) + z$

(4) $\vdash x \times (y + z) = (x \times y) + (x \times z)$

(5) $x \times (y \times z) = (x \times y) \times z$

(6) $\vdash x \times y = y \times x$

(7) If $i + j = k$, then $\vdash \mathbf{i} + \mathbf{j} = \mathbf{k}$

Notice that here we are claiming that if the sum of the numbers i and j is the number k, then the formula $\mathbf{i} + \mathbf{j} = \mathbf{k}$ of PA is provable in PA.

Proof. If $i + j = k$ and $j = 0$, then $i = k$ and the numeral $\mathbf{j}$ is $\mathbf{0}$, and $\vdash \mathbf{i} + \mathbf{j} = \mathbf{i} + \mathbf{0} = \mathbf{i} = \mathbf{k}$. And if for all k, $\vdash \mathbf{i} + \mathbf{j} = \mathbf{k}$ whenever $i + j = k$, then the same holds for $j + 1$: If $i + (j + 1) = k$, then for some m, $i + j = m$, $k = m + 1$ and $\mathbf{k}$ is $\mathbf{sm}$. Thus $\vdash \mathbf{i} + \mathbf{j} = \mathbf{m}$, whence $\vdash \mathbf{i} + \mathbf{s}\,\mathbf{j} = \mathbf{s}(\mathbf{i} + \mathbf{j}) = \mathbf{sm} = \mathbf{k}$. ⊣

(8) If $i \times j = k$, then $\vdash \mathbf{i} \times \mathbf{j} = \mathbf{k}$

(9) If t is a closed term and t denotes i, then $\vdash t = \mathbf{i}$

Proof. Induction on the construction of t: If t is $\mathbf{0}$, then t denotes 0. If t denotes i and t' denotes j, then $t + t'$ denotes $i + j$. Let $k = i + j$. By the induction hypothesis, $\vdash t = \mathbf{i}$ and $\vdash t' = \mathbf{j}$. By (7), $\vdash \mathbf{i} + \mathbf{j} = \mathbf{k}$.

Thus $\vdash t + t' = \mathbf{i} + \mathbf{j} = \mathbf{k}$. Similarly for successor and multiplication. $\dashv$

(10) If t and t' are closed and $t = t'$ is true, then $\vdash t = t'$

Proof. Let t and t' denote i and i'. By (9), $\vdash t = \mathbf{i}$ and $\vdash t' = \mathbf{i}'$. If $t = t'$ is true, then $i = i'$ and $\mathbf{i}$ is the same numeral as $\mathbf{i}'$. Thus $\vdash t = t'$. $\dashv$

Definition. $x < y$ is the formula $\exists z\, x + \mathbf{s}z = y$.

Definition. $x > y$ is the formula $y < x$; $x \leqslant y$ is the formula $(x < y \vee x = y)$; and $x \geqslant y$ is the formula $y \leqslant x$.

(11) $\vdash \neg x < \mathbf{0}$

Proof. $\vdash x + \mathbf{s}z = \mathbf{s}(x + z) \neq \mathbf{0}$. $\dashv$

(12) $\vdash x < \mathbf{s}y \leftrightarrow x < y \vee x = y$

Proof. $\vdash x < \mathbf{s}y \leftrightarrow \exists z\, x + \mathbf{s}z = \mathbf{s}y$, $\leftrightarrow \exists z\, \mathbf{s}(x + z) = \mathbf{s}y$, $\leftrightarrow \exists z\, x + z = y$, $\leftrightarrow$[by (1)] $(x + \mathbf{0} = y \vee \exists w\, x + \mathbf{s}w = y)$, $\leftrightarrow x = y \vee x < y$. $\dashv$

Definition. $\bigvee\{x = \mathbf{j} : j < i\}$ is the disjunction of all sentences $x = \mathbf{j}$ for $j < i$ and is $\bot$ if $i = 0$.

(13) $\vdash x < \mathbf{i} \leftrightarrow \bigvee\{x = \mathbf{j} : j < i\}$

Proof. Induction on i. If $i = 0$, $\vdash \neg x < \mathbf{0}$, whence $\vdash x < \mathbf{0} \leftrightarrow \bot$. Suppose $\vdash x < \mathbf{i} \leftrightarrow \bigvee\{x = \mathbf{j} : j < i\}$. Then by (12) and the induction hypothesis, $\vdash x < \mathbf{si} \leftrightarrow (x < \mathbf{i} \vee x = \mathbf{i})$, $\leftrightarrow (\bigvee\{x = \mathbf{j} : j < i\} \vee x = \mathbf{i})$, $\leftrightarrow \bigvee\{x = \mathbf{j} : j < i + 1\}$. $\dashv$

(14) (Strong induction) For any formula $F(x)$,

$$\vdash \forall x(\forall y(y < x \rightarrow F(y)) \rightarrow F(x)) \rightarrow F(x)$$

Proof. Assume

$$(*) \quad \forall x(\forall y(y < x \rightarrow F(y)) \rightarrow F(x))$$

Define $G(x)$ as $(\forall y(y < x \rightarrow F(y)) \wedge F(x))$. We shall show $G(x)$, whence $F(x)$ follows. By induction, it is enough to show $G(\mathbf{0})$ and $\forall x(G(x) \rightarrow$

$G(\mathbf{s}x))$. $G(\mathbf{0})$: By (11), $\forall y \neg y < \mathbf{0}$, whence by logic, $\forall y(y < \mathbf{0} \rightarrow F(y))$, and then by $(*)$, $F(\mathbf{0})$, and thus $G(\mathbf{0})$. $\forall x(G(x) \rightarrow G(\mathbf{s}x))$: Assume $G(x)$, i.e., $\forall y(y < x \rightarrow F(y))$ and $F(x)$. By (12), $\forall y(y < \mathbf{s}x \rightarrow F(y))$, whence by $(*)$, $F(\mathbf{s}x)$, and thus $G(\mathbf{s}x)$. $\dashv$

The least number principle: $\vdash F(x) \rightarrow \exists x(Fx \wedge \forall y(y < x \rightarrow \neg F(y)))$ follows directly from strong induction: substitute $\neg F(x)$ for $F(x)$.

(15) $\vdash \neg x < x$; $x < y < z \rightarrow x < z$; $x < y \vee x = y \vee y < x$;

$x < y \rightarrow x + z < y + z$; $x < y \wedge \mathbf{0} < z \rightarrow x \times z < y \times z$

(16) If $i < j$, then $\vdash \mathbf{i} < \mathbf{j}$

If $i \neq j$, then $\vdash \mathbf{i} \neq \mathbf{j}$

If $i \geqslant j$, then $\vdash \neg \mathbf{i} < \mathbf{j}$

Proof. If $i < j$, then for some k, $i + (k + 1) = j$, and $\vdash \mathbf{i} + \mathbf{sk} = \mathbf{j}$ by (7); thus $\vdash \mathbf{i} < \mathbf{j}$. If $i \neq j$, then $i < j$ or $j < i$ and $\vdash \mathbf{i} < \mathbf{j}$ or $\vdash \mathbf{j} < \mathbf{i}$, whence $\vdash \mathbf{i} \neq \mathbf{j}$ by the first conjunct of (15). If $i \geqslant j$, then $j < i$ or $j = i$, whence $\vdash \mathbf{j} < \mathbf{i}$ or $\vdash \mathbf{j} = \mathbf{i}$ and thus $\vdash \neg \mathbf{i} < \mathbf{j}$ by the second or first conjunct of (15). $\dashv$

As will soon become apparent, it is not our intention to give a thorough axiomatization of even the most elementary portions of arithmetic or to supply full proofs in PA (!) of theorems like (v) above or the second incompleteness theorem of Gödel. Our interest, rather, lies in showing that, and how, such theorems can be proved in PA and in showing how to prove the metatheory of PA in PA itself. We want to show that certain notions and statements can be defined and proved in PA; to do so, it is not necessary to exhibit formal derivations in PA. We shall rely heavily on the reader's good sense and knowledge of logic and (very) elementary arithmetic, which will enable us to omit sufficiently many details of proofs to make our development (in PA) of the theory of PA's own syntax comprehensible; but, as we have said, we will take pains to exhibit all necessary details where particular difficulties arise, e.g., in the definitions of "finite sequence" and "term of PA". Our intention is to omit only those proofs that are, in our view, thoroughly routine, e.g., that of the associativity of multiplication. One example of a theorem whose proof is not routine is the statement that a prime that divides *ab* divides *a* or *b*; we need to know that this (ancient) theorem is actually provable in PA; below we give enough detail to enable the reader to see that it is.

Hoping to improve readability, we shall frequently use English expressions instead of their symbolic counterparts in our claims that certain sentences of PA are theorems of PA; where we do so, we shall sometimes also use lightface instead of boldface type, which we avoid altogether in proofs. Thus we shall write "$\vdash$ If $x > 1$, then some prime divides x" to mean that the formula of PA,

$$(x > \mathbf{1} \rightarrow \exists p(\mathrm{Prime}(p) \wedge p|x))$$

is a theorem of PA ("Prime" and "|" being suitably defined). We use English in this manner, of course, only where it is plain which formulas of PA are the counterparts of the English expressions. Typically, a proof of ours that a certain formula is provable in PA will constitute an outline of a formal derivation in PA of that formula.

In what follows, we shall use sans serif 'x', here exemplified, to abbreviate '$x_1, \ldots, x_n$'. Notice the difference between 'x' and 'x'.

Pterms and Σ formulas

Since the only non-logical symbols of PA are the constant $\mathbf{0}$, the 1-place function symbol $\mathbf{s}$, and the 2-place function symbols $+$ and $\times$, it might appear that the class of functions that PA is capable of treating is quite limited. Indeed, it is quite easy to see that no term of PA denotes the function 2^x: if a term of PA were to denote 2^x, then it could be assumed to contain only the variable x (0 could be substituted for any other variables); but any term of PA containing only x is provably identical to a polynomial in x; and all polynomials in x denote functions that are eventually majorized by 2^x.

Nevertheless, PA can quite often discuss functions that are not denoted by any terms of its language. Call a formula $F(\mathsf{x}, y)$ of the language of PA a *pterm* (with respect to the variable y) if the formula $\exists!\, yF(\mathsf{x}, y)$, i.e., the formula

$$\exists y(F(\mathsf{x}, y) \wedge \forall z(F(\mathsf{x}, z) \rightarrow y = z))$$

is provable in PA ("p" is for "pseudo"). Any pterm $F(\mathsf{x}, y)$ defines an n-place function, and many functions, among them exponentiation and 2^x, not denoted by terms of PA can be discussed in PA by means of pterms that define them. If $F(\mathsf{x}, y)$ is a pterm, we shall often refer to it as: $f(\mathsf{x})$ instead of as: $F(\mathsf{x}, y)$, omitting the variable y and changing upper case to lower. And where $A(y)$ is a formula of PA and $F(\mathsf{x}, y)$ a pterm, we write: $A(f(\mathsf{x}))$ to denote the PA formula $\exists y(F(\mathsf{x}, y) \wedge A(y))$. In view of the provability of relevant formulas of the form $\exists!\, yF(\mathsf{x}, y)$, expressions such as $B(h(g(\mathsf{x}))\ g(\mathsf{x}))$, with $B(w, z)$ a formula and $G(\mathsf{x}, y)$ and $H(\mathsf{x}, y)$ pterms, are unambiguous: all "disabbreviations" of such formulas are provably equivalent in PA. Let us observe that since $\exists!\, yF(\mathsf{x}, y)$ is provable, $A(f(\mathsf{x}))$, i.e., $\exists y(F(\mathsf{x}, y) \wedge A(y))$, is equivalent to $\forall y(F(\mathsf{x}, y) \rightarrow A(y))$.

We use $\forall y < xF$ and $\exists y < xF$ to abbreviate $\forall y(y < x \rightarrow F)$ and $\exists y(y < x \wedge F)$.

We now define two important classes of formula: the Σ formulas and the Δ formulas.

We call a formula a *strict Σ formula* if it is a member of the smallest class that contains all formulas $u = v$, $\mathbf{0} = u$, $\mathbf{s}u = v$, $u + v = w$, and $u \times v = w$, and contains $(F \wedge G)$, $(F \vee G)$, $\exists xF$, and $\forall x < yF$ whenever it contains F and G. A Σ *formula* is one that is equivalent, i.e., provably equivalent in PA, to a strict Σ formula. (Σ formulas are usually called Σ_1 formulas; but we shall not now need to consider the classes of $\Sigma_2, \Sigma_3, \ldots$ formulas and have accordingly dropped the subscript.)

All atomic formulas are Σ formulas, for any atomic formula whatsoever is equivalent to a formula constructed by conjunction and existential quantification from formulas of the five forms: $u = v$, $\mathbf{0} = u$, $\mathbf{s}u = v$, $u + v = w$, and $u \times v = w$. E.g., $x + \mathbf{s}y = \mathbf{s0}$ is equivalent to $\exists u \exists v \exists w(\mathbf{s}y = u \wedge x + u = v \wedge \mathbf{0} = w \wedge \mathbf{s}w = v)$. It follows that $x < y$, i.e., $\exists z(x + \mathbf{s}z = y)$, is also a Σ formula. Thus if F is a Σ formula, so is $\exists x < yF$ and the Σ formulas are closed under both bounded universal and bounded existential quantification. It also follows that the negation of any atomic formula is a Σ formula, since by (15), $\neg x = y$ is equivalent to $x < y \vee y < x$. The adjective "atomic" was indispensable just then; it is *not* the case that the negation of a Σ formula is always Σ.

A Σ sentence is just a Σ formula that is a sentence. If F is a Σ formula and S is a sentence obtained from F by the substitution of closed terms, such as numerals, for free variables in F, then S is a Σ sentence. The following theorem gives a key fact about Σ sentences.

(17) If S is a true Σ sentence, then $\vdash S$

Proof. If S is a true atomic formula, then $\vdash S$, by (10). If $(S \wedge S')$ is true, then S and S' are true, whence $\vdash S$ and $\vdash S'$, and so $\vdash (S \wedge S')$. If $(S \vee S')$ is true, then S or S' are true, whence $\vdash S$ or $\vdash S'$, and so

$\vdash (S \vee S')$. If $\exists x F$ is true, then for some i, $F(\mathbf{i})$, the result of substituting $\mathbf{i}$ for x in F is true; thus $\vdash F(\mathbf{i})$, and so $\vdash \exists x F$. If $\forall x < \mathbf{i} F$ is true, then for every $j < i$, $F(\mathbf{j})$ is true, and thus for every $j < i$, $\vdash F(\mathbf{j})$ and $\vdash x = \mathbf{j} \to F$. But $\vdash x < \mathbf{i} \leftrightarrow \bigvee \{x = \mathbf{j}: j < i\}$ by (13). So $\vdash x < \mathbf{i} \to F$ and $\vdash \forall x < \mathbf{i} F$. Finally, if S is equivalent to a provable sentence, S is provable. $\dashv$

In due course the wide scope of the class of Σ sentences will become apparent: it will turn out that, e.g., the negation of the Goldbach conjecture can be expressed by a Σ sentence. Thus if Goldbach's conjecture is undecidable in PA, i.e., neither provable nor disprovable in PA, then it is true (!); for if Goldbach's conjecture is false, then its negation is expressed by a true Σ sentence, which by (17) is provable, and Goldbach's conjecture itself is therefore disprovable, not undecidable.

PA will be seen to fail to prove some truths, and indeed truths whose *negations* are Σ sentences (so-called true Π, or Π_1, sentences.) But (17) tells us that PA proves all truths to the effect that a certain sentence is provable (in some particular formal system) or that a certain computational device eventually halts, for these can all be expressed as Σ sentences of the language of arithmetic, as will be evident by the end of this chapter. The provability of all true Σ sentences can therefore be considered as a significant partial (non-in)completeness theorem for PA.

A formula A is called a Δ *formula* if A and $\neg A$, the negation of A, are both Σ formulas. We note some closure properties of the class of Δ formulas.

Each atomic formula $t = t'$ is Δ, for, as we have noted, atomic formulas and their negations are both Σ.

$t < t'$ is Δ: $t < t'$ is equivalent to $\exists x \exists y(t = x \wedge t' = y \wedge x < y)$, which is Σ, and $\neg t < t'$ is equivalent to $t = t' \vee t' < t$.

The negation of a Δ formula is obviously Δ. If A and B are Δ, so is their conjunction, for then $A, B, \neg A$, and $\neg B$ are all Σ, and therefore so are $A \wedge B$ and $\neg A \vee \neg B$. Thus the Δ formulas are closed under all Boolean operations. Since the Σ formulas are closed under both bounded universal and bounded existential quantification, the Δ formulas are also closed under both kinds of bounded quantification: If A and $\neg A$ are Σ, so is $\forall x < yA$, and $\neg \forall x < yA$ is equivalent to the Σ formula $\exists x < y \neg A$. Similarly for bounded existential quantification.

If $F(\mathsf{x}, y)$ is Σ and a pterm, then it is Δ, for by the provability of $\exists!\, yF(\mathsf{x}, y)$, $\neg F(\mathsf{x}, y)$ is equivalent to the Σ formula $\exists z(F(\mathsf{x}, z) \wedge \neg z = y)$.

If $A(y)$ is Δ and $F(\mathsf{x}, y)$ is a Σ pterm, then $A(f(\mathsf{x}))$ is Δ: For $A(f(\mathsf{x}))$ is the Σ formula $\exists y(F(\mathsf{x}, y) \wedge A(y))$, and since this formula is equivalent to $\forall y(F(\mathsf{x}, y) \rightarrow A(y))$, $\neg A(f(\mathsf{x}))$ is equivalent to the Σ formula $\exists y(F(\mathsf{x}, y) \wedge \neg A(y))$.

In brief, the Δ formulas contain all atomic formulas and all formulas $t < t'$ and are closed under boolean operations, bounded quantification, and substitution of Σ pterms.

We shall often write: $\exists x \leqslant yF$ and: $\forall x \leqslant yF$ instead of: $\exists x < \mathbf{s}yF$ and: $\forall x < \mathbf{s}yF$. Clearly these are Σ or Δ if F is.

It follows from (17) that if $F(\mathsf{x})$ is a Δ formula and i an n-tuple of natural numbers, then either $\vdash F(\mathbf{i})$ or $\vdash \neg F(\mathbf{i})$. For since $F(\mathsf{x})$ is Δ, $F(\mathbf{i})$ and $\neg F(\mathbf{i})$ are both Σ. By (17), whichever of these is true is a theorem of PA. Thus all instances of Δ formulas are decidable, and therefore Δ formulas are, to use Gödel's term, *entscheidungsdefinit* ("numeralwise expressible").

We now resume our consideration of the more arithmetical aspects of PA.

Division, quotient, and remainder

> **Definition.** $d|x$ is the formula $\exists q\, q \times d = x$. ("|" is read "divides"; we are assuming that 0 divides n iff $n = 0$.)

$d|x$ is visibly a Σ formula. The next theorem shows that the formula $d|x$ is actually Δ, since it is equivalent to one built up from atomic formulas by boolean operations, bounded quantification, and substitution of Σ pterms:

(18) $\vdash \exists q\, q \times d = x \rightarrow \exists q(q \leqslant x \wedge q \times d = x)$

(19) $\vdash d|d$

(20) $\vdash d|x \wedge x|y \rightarrow d|y$

(21) $\vdash d|x \rightarrow (d|(x + y) \leftrightarrow d|y)$

(22) $\vdash d \neq 0 \rightarrow \exists q \exists r(x = q \times d + r \wedge r < d \wedge$
$\forall q' \forall r'(x = q' \times d + r' \wedge r' < d \rightarrow q = q' \wedge r = r'))$

We now define rm ("remainder"). We shall take the remainder on dividing a number x by 0 to be x:

Definition. $\mathrm{Rm}(x, d, r)$ is the formula
$((r < d \wedge \exists q\, x = q \times d + r) \vee (d = 0 \wedge r = x))$.

$\mathrm{Rm}(x, d, r)$ is Σ and, in virtue of (22), a pterm.

(23) $\vdash \mathrm{rm}(x, 0) = x$

(24) $\vdash d | x \leftrightarrow \mathrm{rm}(x, d) = 0$

(25) $\vdash \mathrm{rm}(x + yd, d) = \mathrm{rm}(x, d)$

Subtraction is not a total function on the natural numbers. We introduce a pterm for a variant, sometimes called "cut-off subtraction" or "monus", that is total: x monus y is x minus y if $y \leqslant x$ and is 0 if $y > x$. Since we do not deal with negative integers, we use the usual subtraction sign "$-$" to mean "monus".

(26) $\vdash y \leqslant x \rightarrow \exists!\, z\, x = y + z$

Definition. $\mathrm{Monus}(x, y, z)$ is $(x = y + z \vee (x < y \wedge z = 0))$.

$\mathrm{Monus}(x, y, z)$ is clearly a Σ pterm; we write: $x - y$ instead of: $\mathrm{monus}(x, y)$.

Definition. $\mathrm{Prime}(p)$ is $(p \neq \mathbf{1} \wedge \forall d(d | p \rightarrow d = \mathbf{1} \vee d = p))$.

$\mathrm{Prime}(p)$ is not visibly Δ; but notice that since $\vdash d | p \rightarrow d \leqslant p$, $\mathrm{Prime}(p)$ is equivalent to $p \neq \mathbf{1} \wedge \forall d \leqslant p(d | p \rightarrow d = \mathbf{1} \vee d = p)$, which is Δ, for it is constructed from Δ formulas by truth-functional operations and bounded quantification.

(27) $\vdash$ 2 is the least prime

(28) $\vdash$ If $x > 1$, then some prime divides x

Proof. Consult Euclid's *Elements*, Book VII, theorem 31. The proof given there may be formalized in PA with the aid of the least number principle. ⊣

Definition. $\mathrm{RelativelyPrime}(a, b)$ is $\forall d(d | a \wedge d | b \rightarrow d = \mathbf{1})$.

$\mathrm{RelativelyPrime}(a, b)$ is Δ, since it is equivalent to
$\forall d \leqslant a(d | a \wedge d | b \rightarrow d = \mathbf{1})$.

(29) $\vdash$ a and b are relatively prime iff no prime divides both a and b

Proof. By (20) and (28). $\dashv$

The following proposition states an important fact about relatively prime numbers.

(30) $\vdash$ If a and b are greater than 1 and relatively prime, then for some x, y, $ax + 1 = by$.

Proof. Call a number i *good* iff $\exists x \exists y\, ax + i = by$. We must show that 1 is good, on the supposition that a and b are greater than 1 and relatively prime. a is good: take $x = b - 1$ and $y = a$; and b is also good: take $x = 0$ and $y = 1$. If i is good, then so is qi. And if i and i' are good and $i \geqslant i'$, then $i - i'$ is also good. For if $ax + i = by$ and $ax' + i' = by'$, let $x'' = x + by' + (b-1)x'$ and let $y'' = y + ax' + (a-1)y'$. Then, as is readily checked, $ax'' + (i - i') = by''$. Let d be the least positive good number. Then if i is good, $d|i$: for some q, r, $i = qd + r$ and $r < d$; so qd is good and $i \geqslant qd$; since $i - qd = r$, r is good, $r = 0$ (by leastness of d), $i = qd$, and $d|i$. Since a and b are good, $d|a$, $d|b$, $d = 1$, and 1 is good. $\dashv$

(31) $\vdash$ If p is prime and divides ab, then p divides a or p divides b

Proof. Suppose p divides ab. If p does not divide a, then a and p are relatively prime; by (30), for some x, y, $ax + 1 = py$ and then $abx + b = pby$. Since $p|ab$, $p|abx$ and $p|pby$; whence by (21), $p|b$. $\dashv$

Least common multiple

In what follows $M(x, y)$ and $H(x, y)$ are arbitrary pterms of PA. (Notice that "m" and "h" are lower case "M" and "H".)

(32) $\vdash$ If for all $i < k$, $m(i) > 0$, then there is a (unique) least positive l such that for all $i < k$, $m(i)|l$.

Proof. By induction on k, if for all $i < k$, $m(i) > 0$, then there is a positive l such that for all $i < k$, $m(i)|l$: 1 is an l that works for $k = 0$, and multiply any l that works for k by $m(k)$ to get an l that works for $k + 1$. Then apply the least number principle. $\dashv$

Definition. $\mathrm{Lcm}[m(i): i < k](l)$ is the formula

$$(\forall i < k\, m(i) > \mathbf{0} \wedge l > \mathbf{0} \wedge \forall i < k\, m(i)|l$$
$$\wedge \forall j < l \neg [j > \mathbf{0} \wedge \forall i < k\, m(i)|j]) \vee (\exists i < k\, m(i) = \mathbf{0} \wedge l = \mathbf{0})$$

This definition is a definition-schema, yielding from any pterm $M(x, y)$ the definition of a formula $\mathrm{Lcm}[m(i){:}\, i < k](l)$ with the free variables k and l. By (32), $\mathrm{Lcm}[m(i){:}\, i < k](l)$ is a pterm. If $M(x, y)$ is a Σ pterm, then so is $\mathrm{Lcm}[m(i){:}\, i < k](l)$ (with respect to the variable l).

Here "lcm" is short for "least common multiple". The contrast between the least common multiple and the product of the values of a sequence of numbers is noteworthy: the former, but apparently not the latter, can be easily defined in the language of PA and easily proved in PA to exist.

(33) $\vdash j < k \rightarrow m(j) \mid \mathrm{lcm}[m(i){:}\, i < k]$

(34) $\vdash$ Any multiple of all $m(i)$, $i < k$, is a multiple of $\mathrm{lcm}[m(i){:}\, i < k]$

Proof. Suppose $m(i) \mid x$ for all $i < k$. Let $l = \mathrm{lcm}[m(i){:}\, i < k]$. We may suppose that $l > 0$. For some q, r, $x = ql + r$ and $r < l$. Since $m(i) \mid l, x$, $m(i) \mid r$ for all $i < k$, contra leastness of l if $r > 0$. Thus $r = 0$ and $l \mid x$. $\dashv$

(35) $\vdash$ If p is prime and $p \mid \mathrm{lcm}[m(i){:}\, i < k]$, then $p \mid m(i)$ for some $i < k$

Proof. An induction on k: If $k = 0$, $\mathrm{lcm}[m(i){:}\, i < 0] = 1$ and p does not divide $\mathrm{lcm}[m(i){:}\, i < 0]$. Suppose $p \mid \mathrm{lcm}[m(i){:}\, i < k + 1]$. $\mathrm{lcm}[m(i){:}\, i < k + 1] \mid \mathrm{lcm}[m(i){:}\, i < k] \times m(k)$ by (34) since every $m(i)$, $i < k + 1$, divides $\mathrm{lcm}[m(i){:}\, i < k] \times m(k)$. By (31) either $p \mid \mathrm{lcm}[m(i){:}\, i < k]$, whence by the induction hypothesis p divides some $m(i)$, $i < k$, or $p \mid m(k)$. $\dashv$

(36) (***The Chinese remainder theorem***)
$\vdash [\forall i < k(1, h(i) < m(i)) \wedge \forall i, j(i < j < k \rightarrow m(i)$ and $m(j)$ are relatively prime$)] \rightarrow \exists a < \mathrm{lcm}[m(i){:}\, i < k] \forall i < k\, \mathrm{rm}(a, m(i)) = h(i)$

The Chinese remainder theorem is a standard theorem of number theory, proved in nearly every textbook on the subject. The proof we shall give is somewhat more complicated than usual because we are working with the natural numbers (which, unlike the integers, are not closed under subtraction), we must avoid the concept of a finite sequence of natural numbers, we will later need the bound "$a < \mathrm{lcm}[m(i){:}\, i < k]$", and we wish to make it clear that the entire argument can be carried out in PA.

Proof of the Chinese remainder theorem. Assume the antecedent. Use induction on $n \leqslant k$. If $n = 0$, let $a = 0$. $a < 1 = \mathrm{lcm}[m(i){:}\, i < 0]$.

Suppose $n<k$, $a<\text{lcm}[m(i): i<n]$, and $\text{rm}(a, m(i))=h(i)$ for all $i<n$. Let $l=\text{lcm}[m(i): i<n]$, $m=m(n)$. l and m are relatively prime: if $p|l$, then by (35) for some $i<n$, $p|m(i)$, and since $m(i)$ and m are relatively prime, p does not divide m.

Since l and m are relatively prime, by (30) for some x, y, $lx+1=my$. Multiplying both sides by $a+(l-1)h(n)$ shows that for some (other) x, y, $lx+a+(l-1)h(n)=my$. Let $a^*=l(x+h(n))+a$. Then $a^*=my+h(n)$. If $i<n$, then since $m(i)|l$, $\text{rm}(a^*, m(i))=\text{rm}(a, m(i))=h(i)$, and $\text{rm}(a^*, m(n))=\text{rm}(a^*, m)=h(n)$, since $h(n)<m(n)=m$. Let $l'=\text{lcm}[m(i): i<n+1]$. If $a^*<l'$, we are done. If $a^*\geqslant l'$, then let b be the greatest multiple of l' that is $\leqslant a^*$, and let $a^{**}=a^*-b$. Then $a^{**}<l'$, and since $m(i)|l'|b$ for all $i<n+1$, $\text{rm}(a^{**}, m(i))=\text{rm}(a^*-b, m(i))=\text{rm}(a^*, m(i))=h(i)$. $\dashv$

(37) $\vdash$ For every k there is a unique greatest value of $m(i)$, $i<k$.

Definition. $\text{Max}[m(i): i<k](l)$ is $[\exists i<k\, m(i)=l \wedge \forall i<k\, m(i)\leqslant l]$.

$\text{Max}[m(i): i<k](l)$ is a Σ pterm.

Definition. $\text{Max}(x, y, z)$ is $[(x\geqslant y \wedge z=x) \vee (x<y \wedge z=y)]$.

$\text{Max}(x, y, z)$ is a Σ pterm.

The ternary function β is defined as follows: $\beta(a, b, i)=$ the remainder on dividing a by $1+(i+1)b$.

Gödel introduced the function β in order to code finite sequences of natural numbers as pairs of numbers; the main result concerning β is the β-function lemma, whose provability in PA in recorded as proposition (38):

Definition. $\text{Beta}(a, b, i, r)$ is $\text{rm}(a, \mathbf{1}+(\mathbf{i}+\mathbf{1})\times b)=r$.

$\text{Beta}(a, b, i, r)$ is a Σ pterm.

As was stated above, $H(x, y)$ is an arbitrary pterm.

(38) (Gödel's β-function lemma)
$\vdash$ For every k, there are a, b such that for all $i<k$, $\text{beta}(a, b, i)=h(i)$; moreover, where $s=\max(k, \max[h(i): i<k])+1$, a and b can be so chosen that $b<\text{lcm}[i+1: i<s]+1$ and $a<\text{lcm}[1+(i+1)b: i<k]$

Proof. Let s be as in the statement of the lemma. Then $s > k$ and for all $i < k$, $s > h(i)$. Let $b = \text{lcm}[i+1 : i < s]$. Suppose $i < j < k$. We shall show $1 + (i+1)b$ and $1 + (j+1)b$ relatively prime. Assume $p | 1 + (i+1)b$ and $p | 1 + (j+1)b$. Then p divides their difference $(j-i)b$, and so either $p | j-i$ or $p | b$. Since $1 \leqslant j - i < k < s$, $j - i | b$. In either case, $p | b$, and so $p | (i+1)b$. Since $p | 1 + (i+1)b$, p divides their difference 1, contradiction. Thus if $i < j < k$, $1 + (i+1)b$ and $1 + (j+1)b$ are relatively prime. Moreover, for all $i < k$, $h(i) < s \leqslant b < 1 + (i+1)b$ and $1 < 1 + (i+1)b$. By (36), now taking $m(i) = 1 + (i+1)b$, for some $a < \text{lcm}[1 + (i+1)b : i < k]$, $\text{beta}(a, b, i) = h(i)$ for all $i < k$. ⊣

Note that the pterms that provide bounds on a and b in the β-function lemma are Σ provided that $H(x, y)$ is. These pterms will enable us to see that certain notions concerning the syntax of PA, such as "Gödel number of a term of PA" and "Gödel number of a formula of PA" are defined by Δ formulas.

(39) $\vdash$ For any c, d, k, n there exist a, b such that $\text{beta}(a, b, k) = n$ and for all $i < k$, $\text{beta}(a, b, i) = \text{beta}(c, d, i)$

Proof. Define $H(i, y)$ by $y = \text{beta}(c, d, i)$ if $i < k$ and $= n$ otherwise, and let a, b be as in the β-function lemma (with "$k + 1$" instantiating "for every k"), ⊣

We now begin to develop the syntax of PA within PA itself. The development within a theory of that theory's own syntax has been called "pulling the metalanguage into the object language" but might more informatively be termed "proving the metatheory in the object theory."

The way in which PA proves the statements about its own syntax that constitute its metatheory is rather different from the way in which it proves statements about the natural numbers.

For PA to prove a statement about the natural numbers is simply for a sentence or formula of the language of PA expressing that statement to be a theorem of PA. For example, let S be the sentence $\forall x \forall y\, x + y = y + x$. S is a theorem of PA and expresses the commutativity of addition, i.e., the statement that for any natural numbers i and j, i plus j equals j plus i. S expresses the commutativity of addition because it is, as we suppose, interpreted in accordance with the usual interpretation N of PA, *as we standardly give that interpretation*. We standardly define, or "give", N by saying: Under N the variables $x, y, \ldots$ range over the natural numbers $0, 1, 2, \ldots$, and the nonlogical symbols have their usual meanings ($+$ denotes plus etc.). Having *so* described N, we are entitled to say, not only that S is true if and only if addition is commutative, but also that it *expresses* the commutativity of addition. What sentences of the language of PA express depends upon *how* the range of their variables and the denotations of their non-logical symbols are characterized, as well as upon what the range is and what the non-logical symbols denote. When we say that $+$ denotes plus in N, using "plus" or a synonym to say so, we allow it to be understood that $+$ is to have the sense of "plus", whatever that might be (and not, say, that of "plus the cube root of the square root of the cube of the square of"). Similarly for the other symbols of the language, including the variables, the manner of specification of whose range, i.e., *as* over the natural numbers, contributes in large measure to the determination of the meanings of quantified sentences of PA.

Under N, given in the standard way, sentences of PA can express statements only about the natural numbers and relations and operations on them definable in N in the language of PA. Thus it is not to be expected that PA could, in the same way in which it can prove the commutativity of addition, prove even so simple a truth about its own syntax as that the universal quantifier $\forall$ is not a variable, let alone the significant statement to the effect that if $\bot$ is not provable in PA, then neither is $\neg \mathrm{Bew}(\ulcorner \bot \urcorner)$.

Nevertheless, it seems entirely justifiable to regard PA as capable of proving facts about its own syntax for the following reason.

Let us give the name "Syntax" to the informal mathematical theory of the syntax of PA, whose rudiments we developed when we gave our description of PA. Syntax is an informal theory, and we leave it vague exactly what it contains. The language of Syntax, as we have presented it, is (a portion of) logicians' English, containing names such as "$\forall$" and predicates such as "is a formula". The objects of Syntax, those with which Syntax deals, are the primitive symbols of PA and various ordered pairs and finite sequences of objects.

There is a double correspondence between Syntax and PA: first, between the objects of Syntax and the objects of PA, which are the natural numbers, and secondly, between the names and predicates of the language of Syntax and the terms and formulas of the language of PA. The numbers that correspond to the objects of Syntax are called the Gödel numbers, or code numbers, of those objects; we shall shortly present a system of Gödel numbering. A term of (the language of) PA that corresponds to a name in (the language of) Syntax denotes the Gödel number of the object denoted by that name (e.g., if the symbol ∀ has the Gödel number 5, then the name "∀" of the language of Syntax, which denotes the symbol ∀, corresponds to the term **sssss0** of the language of arithmetic, which denotes the number 5); a formula of PA that corresponds to a predicate of Syntax is true of exactly those numbers that are the Gödel numbers of the objects of Syntax of which the predicate holds. Furthermore, various proof-theoretical and definitional connections hold among terms, formulas, and sentences of, and proofs in, PA that resemble, more or less roughly, those that hold among names, predicates, and sentences of, and (informal mathematical) proofs in, Syntax: the correspondence between names and predicates of Syntax and terms and formulas of PA naturally extends itself to one between sentences of Syntax and sentences of PA built up from terms and formulas corresponding to the names and predicates from which the sentences of Syntax are formed; under the correspondence, sentences of PA are provable in PA only if their counterparts are demonstrable in Syntax. (We cannot say "if and only if", for in Syntax we can, for example, prove that $\bot$ is not a theorem of PA, by means not available to us in PA.[6]) However, the sentences of Syntax that express the familiar and elementary (and some not so elementary) syntactic truths will be counterparts of provable sentences of PA. Moreover, the correspondence extends to the definition of complex notions: definitions of complex correlated formulas of PA from simpler ones frequently resemble the informal definitions by means of which their counterpart predicates in Syntax are defined from one another. Finally, the correspondence also extends, significantly more roughly, to one between informal proofs in Syntax and proofs in PA: to the sequences of (open and closed) sentences expressing informal proofs in Syntax of syntactic facts there will often correspond (portions of) proofs in PA of sentences whose counterparts in the language of Syntax formulate those facts.

This double correspondence between a major portion of Syntax and PA thus supplies a sufficiently clear sense to the assertion that elementary parts of the syntax of PA can be *replicated, mirrored, copied, reproduced, treated, developed, executed, carried out, formalized, encoded, interpreted, proved, given,* or *done,* in PA; it will be in virtue of our having established such a far-reaching *general* correspondence that we shall consider ourselves entitled to say that various particular statements about the syntax of PA are provable in PA, including both the triviality that the universal quantifier is not a variable and the significant result that $\bot$ is provable in PA if $\neg \mathrm{Bew}(\ulcorner \bot \urcorner)$ is. Recognition of the way in which PA contains a copy of a part of Syntax can be facilitated by the use of names for the terms and formulas of PA that are orthographically similar to their counterpart names and predicates. If this part is replicated in PA in this manner, the formal development resembles the informal one so strikingly that it becomes entirely natural to regard the terms, formulas, and sentences mentioned in the development as concerned with syntactic, rather than arithmetical, matters.

We now associate with each primitive symbol of PA a natural number, called its Gödel number, or code. To the eight symbols $\bot, \rightarrow, \forall, =, \mathbf{0}, \mathbf{s}, +,$ and $\times$, we assign the numbers 1, 3, 5, 7, 9, 11, 13, and 15. To the variable v_i, we assign the number $2i + 17$. Thus every primitive symbol of PA has an odd Gödel number.

Let $\pi(i,j) = 2((i+j)(i+j) + i + 1)$. We now stipulate that if the objects x and y (whether symbols or ordered pairs) have Gödel numbers i and j, then the ordered pair $\langle x, y \rangle$ shall have the Gödel number $\pi(i,j)$. $\pi(i,j)$ is even and therefore not the Gödel number of a primitive symbol of PA.

All terms and formulas of PA have now acquired Gödel numbers, for each term or formula either is a variable, the symbol $\mathbf{0}$, or the symbol $\bot$, all of which have expressly been assigned Gödel numbers, or is an ordered pair (or an ordered triple, which is itself an ordered pair) of items with Gödel numbers.

Before we begin to prove the syntax of PA in PA, we shall develop the rudiments of the theory of finite sequences of natural numbers in PA; to do so we must first give a development in PA of the theory of ordered pairs of natural numbers. For this we need only supply a Σ pterm $\mathrm{Pair}(x, y, z)$ for which we can prove in PA the law of ordered pairs; if $\langle i, j \rangle = \langle i', j' \rangle$, then $i = i'$ and $j = j'$. Shoenfield has observed that the number $(i+j)(i+j) + i + 1$ can be used as the code of $\langle i, j \rangle$; we follow his pretty treatment, except that since we want all Gödel numbers of ordered pairs to be even, we multiply by two.

Definition. $\mathrm{Pair}(x, y, z)$ is the formula $2((x+y)(x+y) + x + 1) = z$. $\mathrm{Pair}(x, y, z)$ is a Σ pterm. We write (x, y) instead of pair (x, y).

Where we can, we shall henceforth give explicit definitions of pterms by means of definitional identities, writing them, e.g.,

Definition. $(x, y) = 2((x+y)(x+y)+x+1)$.

and avoiding the rigmarole of introducing predicates that will never be seen again.

(40) $\vdash$ If $(x, y) = (x', y')$, then $x = x'$ and $y = y'$

Proof. Assume the antecedent. Then $(x+y)(x+y)+x+1 = (x'+y')(x'+y')+x'+1$. If $x+y < x'+y'$, then $(x+y)(x+y)+x+1 \leqslant (x+y+1)(x+y+1) \leqslant (x'+y')(x'+y') < (x'+y')(x'+y')+x'+1$, impossible. Similarly, if $x'+y' < x+y$, then $(x', y') < (x, y)$, impossible. Thus $x+y = x'+y'$, $x = x'$, and $y = y'$. $\dashv$

PA thus tells us that the function π adequately codes pairs of natural numbers as single numbers. We note that every term or formula of PA either has an odd Gödel number or has a Gödel number of the form $\pi(i, j)$, with i odd.

Further useful features of Shoenfield's definition are given in the next theorems.

(41) $\vdash x, y < (x, y)$

Notice that the Gödel number of a term is larger than that of each of its proper subterms, that the Gödel number of an atomic formula $t = t'$ is larger than that of t or t', that the Gödel number of a formula is larger than that of each of its proper subformulas, and that the Gödel number of a formula $\forall vF$ is larger than that of the variable v.

(42) $\vdash x < x' \rightarrow (x, y) < (x', y)$, $\quad y < y' \rightarrow (x, y) < (x, y')$

Definition. $\mathrm{Fst}(z, w)$ is the formula
$(\exists y < z\,(w, y) = z \vee (\neg \exists x, y < z\,(x, y) = z \wedge w = \mathbf{0}))$.

Definition. $\mathrm{Snd}(z, w)$ is the formula
$(\exists x < z\,(x, w) = z \vee (\neg \exists x, y < z\,(x, y) = z \wedge w = \mathbf{0}))$.

As usual, $\mathrm{Fst}(z, w)$ and $\mathrm{Snd}(z, w)$ are Σ pterms.

(43) $\vdash \mathrm{fst}((x, y)) = x$, $\quad \mathrm{snd}((x, y)) = y$

We define a pterm for the ordered triple $\langle i, j, k \rangle$:

Definition. $(x, y, z) = (x, (y, z))$.

Definition. $\mathrm{ft}(w) = \mathrm{fst}(w)$; $\mathrm{sd}(w) = \mathrm{fst}(\mathrm{snd}(w))$; $\mathrm{td}(w) = \mathrm{snd}(\mathrm{snd}(w))$.

(44) $\vdash \mathrm{ft}((x, y, z)) = x$; $\mathrm{sd}((x, y, z)) = y$; $\mathrm{td}((x, y, z)) = z$

(45) $\vdash x, y, z < (x, y, z)$

Coding finite sequences

An ordered pair is determined by its first and second components. Similarly, a finite sequence $h_0, \ldots, h_{k-1}$ is determined by its *length* k, and its *values* h_i at integers i less than k: different finite sequences with the same length have different values for some integer less than their common length.

We now define "finite sequence". We have already arranged matters so that no formula of PA other than $\bot$ has the same Gödel number as any primitive symbol of PA. Because proofs will be defined as finite sequences of a certain sort, we shall wish to assign them Gödel numbers that are different from those of primitive symbols or formulas. Since every primitive symbol has an odd Gödel number, every formula of PA other than $\bot$ has a Gödel number of the form $\pi(i, \pi(a, b))$, with i odd, and $\pi(a, b)$ is even, we can achieve this aim by taking the Gödel numbers of finite sequences to be certain numbers of the form $\pi(\pi(a, b), k)$, namely those such that for every c, d for which $\pi(c, d) < \pi(a, b)$, there is some $i < k$ such that $\beta(c, d, i) \neq \beta(a, b, i)$.

Definition. $\mathrm{FinSeq}(s)$ is the formula
$\exists a < s \exists b < s \exists k < s (s = ((a, b), k) \wedge$
$\forall c < s \forall d < s ((c, d) < (a, b) \rightarrow \exists i < k\, \mathrm{beta}(c, d, i) \neq \mathrm{beta}(a, b, i)).$

Definition. $\mathrm{lh}(s) = \mathrm{snd}(s)$.

Definition. $\mathrm{val}(s, i) = \mathrm{beta}(\mathrm{fst}(\mathrm{fst}(s)), \mathrm{snd}(\mathrm{fst}(s)), i)$.

$\mathrm{FinSeq}(s)$ is a Δ formula and $\mathrm{lh}(s)$ and $\mathrm{val}(s, i)$ are Σ pterms. We write: s_i instead of: $\mathrm{val}(s, i)$.

It is now immediate that the law of finite sequences is provable in PA:

(46) $\vdash(\text{FinSeq}(s) \wedge \text{FinSeq}(s') \wedge \text{lh}(s)=\text{lh}(s') \wedge \forall i<\text{lh}(s)\, s_i=s'_i)\rightarrow s=s'$

(47) $\vdash \exists!s\ (\text{FinSeq}(s) \wedge \text{lh}(s)=\mathbf{0})$

Proof. $((0,0),0)$ is a finite sequence whose length is 0. Uniqueness follows from (46).

Definition. $[\,] = ((\mathbf{0},\mathbf{0}),\mathbf{0})$.

(48) $\vdash \text{lh}(s)=k \rightarrow \exists! s'(\text{FinSeq}(s') \wedge \text{lh}(s')=\mathbf{s}k \wedge \forall i<k\, s'_i=s_i \wedge s'_k=n)$

Proof. Suppose $\text{lh}(s)=k$. Let $c=\text{fst}(\text{fst}(s))$, $d=\text{snd}(\text{fst}(s))$. By (39), there exist a, b such that $\text{beta}(a,b,k)=n$ and for all $i<k$, $\text{beta}(a,b,i)=\text{beta}(c,d,i)$. Let $s'=((a,b),sk)$. Then $\text{lh}(s')=sk$, $s'_i=\text{beta}(a,b,i)=\text{beta}(c,d,i)=s_i$, for all $i<k$, and $s'_k=\text{beta}(a,b,k)$. By the least number principle we may suppose (a,b) minimal. $\dashv$

(49) For any pterm $H(i, y)$, we have $\vdash\exists!s(\text{FinSeq}(s) \wedge \text{lh}(s)=k \wedge \forall i<k\, s_i=h(i))$

Proof. An induction on k, using (47) when $k=0$ and appealing to (48) with $n=h(k)$ when k is positive. $\dashv$

To treat the "scissors-and-paste" operations of *truncation* and *concatenation*, which enable us to define new terms, formulas, and proofs from old, we need the next two theorems.

(50) $\vdash e\leqslant j<k \wedge \text{lh}(s)=k\rightarrow$
$$\exists! s'(\text{FinSeq}(s) \wedge \text{lh}(s')=j-e \wedge \forall i<j-e\, s'_i=s_{e+i}).$$

Proof. Induction on $j-e$. If $j=e$, $[\,]$ works. And if $e<j+1<k$ and s' works for j, then by (48), let s'' be such that $\text{lh}(s'')=j-e+1$, $s''_i=s'_i$ for $i<j-e$ and $s''_{j-e}=s_j$. Then s'' works for $j+1$. $\dashv$

(51) $\vdash \text{lh}(s)=k \wedge \text{lh}(s')=k' \wedge j\leqslant k+k'$
$$\rightarrow \exists s''(\text{FinSeq}(s'') \wedge \text{lh}(s'')=j \wedge$$
$$\forall i<j(i<k\rightarrow s''_i=s_i \wedge k\leqslant i<j\rightarrow s''_i=s'_{i-k})$$

Proof. A similar induction on j, starting with $[\,]$, and using (48) to tack on appropriate values to longer and longer sequences. $\dashv$

(52) $\vdash \mathrm{lh}(s) = k \wedge \mathrm{lh}(s') = k'$
$\rightarrow \exists s''(\mathrm{FinSeq}(s'') \wedge \mathrm{lh}(s'') = k + k' \wedge$
$\forall i < k\, s''_i = s_i \wedge \forall i < k'\, s''_{k+i} = s'_i)$

Proof. By (51). ⊣

The *truncation* of the finite sequence $h_0, \ldots, h_e, \ldots, h_j, \ldots$ *from e to j* is the sequence $h_e, \ldots, h_{j-1}$. It is the null sequence in case $j \leqslant e$. The result of *concatenating* a finite sequence $a, \ldots, b$ of length k with a finite sequence $c, \ldots, d$ of length k' is the finite sequence $a, \ldots, b, c, \ldots, d$ of length $k + k'$. $[n]$ is the finite sequence of length 1 whose value at 0 is n.

Definition. $\mathrm{Trunc}(s, e, j, s')$ is the formula $(\neg e \leqslant j < \mathrm{lh}(s) \wedge s' = [\,]) \vee (e \leqslant j < \mathrm{lh}(s) \wedge \mathrm{FinSeq}(s') \wedge \mathrm{lh}(s') = j - e \wedge \forall i < j - e\; s'_i = s_{e+i})$. $\mathrm{Trunc}(s, e, j, s')$ is a Σ pterm. Write: $s_{[e,j)}$ instead of: $\mathrm{trunc}(s, e, j)$.

Definition. $\mathrm{Concat}(s, s', s'')$ is the formula $(\mathrm{FinSeq}(s'') \wedge \mathrm{lh}(s'') = \mathrm{lh}(s) + \mathrm{lh}(s') \wedge \forall i < \mathrm{lh}(s)\, s''_i = s_i \wedge \forall i < \mathrm{lh}(s')\, s''_{\mathrm{lh}(s)+i} = s'_i)$. $\mathrm{Concat}(s, s', s'')$ is a Σ pterm. Write: $s * s'$ instead of: $\mathrm{concat}(s, s')$.

Definition. $\mathrm{Seq}(n, s)$ is the formula $\mathrm{FinSeq}(s) \wedge \mathrm{lh}(s) = 1 \wedge s_0 = n$. $\mathrm{Seq}(n, s)$ is a Σ pterm. Write: $[n]$ instead of: $\mathrm{seq}(n)$.

(53) $\vdash$ If s is a finite sequence, then $[\,] * s = s = s * [\,]$

(54) $\vdash$ If s, s', and s'' are finite sequences, then $s*(s'*s'') = (s*s')*s''$

Proof. Let the lengths of s, s', and s'' be k, k', and k''. Let $u = s'*s''$, $u' = s*s'$, $v = s*u$, and $v' = u'*s''$. Then, as an easy argument using the associativity of addition shows, v and v' are finite sequences of length $k + k' + k''$, and for all $i < k + k' + k''$, $v_i = v'_i$. The conclusion follows by the law of finite sequences. ⊣

A digression: With the aid of the notions we have just introduced, we can construct many pterms defining functions not denoted by terms of PA: for example, let $\mathrm{Exp}(x, y, z)$ be the formula

$$\exists s(\mathrm{lh}(s) = y + \mathbf{1} \wedge s_0 = \mathbf{1} \wedge \forall i < y\, s_{i+1} = s_i \times x \wedge s_y = z)$$

Then $\mathrm{Exp}(x, y, z)$ is visibly Σ and defines exponentiation, x^y. It is also a pterm, as a routine induction on y shows.

Many other functions can be similarly shown to be defined by Σ pterms. Among these are the primitive recursive functions, which are defined as follows: The *zero function* is the 1-place function whose value is 0 for every natural number. The *successor function* is the 1-place function whose value is $i+1$ for every natural number i. If $1 \leqslant m \leqslant n$, there is an n-place *identity function* whose value for all n-tuples $i_1, \ldots, i_n$ of natural numbers is i_m. If f is an m-place function and $g_1, \ldots, g_m$ are all n-place functions, then the n-place function h *comes from* f *and* $g_1, \ldots, g_m$ by *composition* if for all $i_1, \ldots, i_n$, $h(i_1, \ldots, i_n) = f(g_1(i_1, \ldots, i_n), \ldots, g_m(i_1, \ldots, i_n))$. And if f is an n-place and h an $(n+2)$-place function, then the $(n+1)$-place function h *comes from* f and g by *primitive recursion* if $h(i_1, \ldots, i_n, 0) = f(i_1, \ldots, i_n)$ and for all j, $h(i_1, \ldots, i_n, j+1) = g(i_1, \ldots, i_n, j, h(i_1, \ldots, i_n, j))$. The *primitive recursive functions* are the members of the smallest class that contains the zero, successor, and identity functions and contains all functions that come from members of the class by composition and primitive recursion.

The only difficulty in seeing that all primitive recursive functions are defined by Σ pterms is in the case of primitive recursion. Suppose that $F(x_1, \ldots, x_n, y)$ and $G(x_1, \ldots, x_n, x_{n+1}, x_{n+2}, y)$ are Σ pterms that define an n-place and an $(n+2)$-place function. Then the function that comes from these by primitive recursion is defined by the Σ pterm $H(x_1, \ldots, x_n, x_{n+1}, y)$:

$$\exists s(\mathrm{lh}(s) = x_{n+1} + \mathbf{1} \wedge F(x_1, \ldots, x_n, s_0) \\ \wedge \forall w < x_{n+1} G(x_1, \ldots, x_n, w, s_w, s_{w+1}) \wedge s_{x_{n+1}} = y)$$

This formula is visibly Σ; it may be shown to be a pterm by induction on x_{n+1}. Moreover,

$$\vdash h(x_1, \ldots, x_n, \mathbf{0}) = f(x_1, \ldots, x_n) \text{ and} \\ \vdash h(x_1, \ldots, x_n, w+1) = g(x_1, \ldots, x_n, w, h(x_1, \ldots, x_n, w))$$

However, it is not only primitive recursive functions that are defined by Σ pterms. The Ackermann function ack, defined by

$$\mathrm{ack}(i, 0) = 2 \\ \mathrm{ack}(0, j+1) = \mathrm{ack}(0, j) + 2 \\ \mathrm{ack}(i+1, j+1) = \mathrm{ack}(i, \mathrm{ack}(i+1, j))$$

is not primitive recursive[7] but is defined by the Σ pterm $H(x, y, z)$,

$$\exists s(\mathrm{lh}(s) = x + \mathbf{1} \wedge \forall i \leqslant x(\mathrm{lh}(s_i) \geqslant \mathbf{1} \wedge s_{i,0} = \mathbf{2}) \wedge \mathrm{lh}(s_x) = y + \mathbf{1} \wedge$$
$$s_{x,y} = z \wedge \forall j < \mathrm{lh}(s_0)\, s_{0,j+1} = s_{0,j} + \mathbf{2} \wedge$$
$$\forall i < x \forall j < \mathrm{lh}(s_{i+1}) - \mathbf{1}(s_{i+1,j} < \mathrm{lh}(s_i) \wedge s_{i+1,j+1} = s_{i,s_{i+1,j}}))$$

where we have written, e.g., "$s_{x,y}$" instead of "s_{x_y}". End of digression.

Terms and formulas of PA in PA

We can now treat the terms and formulas of PA.

If σ is a term or formula of PA or one of the symbols $\bot, \rightarrow, \forall, =, \mathbf{0}$, $\mathbf{s}$, $+$, $\times$, and i is its Gödel number, then we write: $\ulcorner\sigma\urcorner$ instead of: $\mathbf{i}$.

Definitions. $\ulcorner\bot\urcorner, \ulcorner\rightarrow\urcorner, \ulcorner\forall\urcorner, \ulcorner=\urcorner, \ulcorner\mathbf{0}\urcorner, \ulcorner\mathbf{s}\urcorner, \ulcorner+\urcorner$, and $\ulcorner\times\urcorner$ are, respectively, the terms $\mathbf{1}, \mathbf{3}, \mathbf{5}, \mathbf{7}, \mathbf{9}, \mathbf{11}, \mathbf{13}$, and $\mathbf{15}$.

The Gödel number of $\mathbf{0}$ is 9; but that of $\ulcorner\mathbf{0}\urcorner$, i.e., $\mathbf{9}$, i.e., $\mathbf{sssssssss0}$, is very large.

Definition. Variable(v) is the Δ formula $\exists i < v\, v = \mathbf{2} \times i + \mathbf{17}$.

(55) $\vdash \neg$ Variable$(\ulcorner\forall\urcorner)$

Thus it is provable in PA that $\forall$ is not a variable.

We earlier gave the definition of *term of PA*: t is a term if and only if there is a finite sequence whose last value is t, each value of which is either $\mathbf{0}$, a variable, the ordered pair of $\mathbf{s}$ and an earlier value of the sequence, the ordered triple of $+$ and two earlier values of the sequence, or the ordered triple of $\times$ and two earlier values of the sequence.

Definition. Term(t) is the formula

$$\exists s[\mathrm{FinSeq}(s) \wedge \mathrm{lh}(s) > \mathbf{0} \wedge s_{\mathrm{lh}(s)-1} = t \wedge$$
$$\forall i < \mathrm{lh}(s)(s_i = \ulcorner\mathbf{0}\urcorner \vee \mathrm{Variable}(s_i) \vee \exists j, k < i[s_i = (\ulcorner\mathbf{s}\urcorner, s_j) \vee$$
$$s_i = (\ulcorner+\urcorner, s_j, s_k) \vee s_i = (\ulcorner\times\urcorner, s_j, s_k)])]$$

Let "$A(s,t)$" abbreviate "[FinSeq$(s) \wedge \cdots)])]$" in the definition of Term(t). $A(s,t)$ is clearly a Δ formula and so Term(t) is clearly a Σ formula. But because of the unbounded quantifier "$\exists s$", further argument is needed to show that Term(t) is Δ. (Cf. Definition 23 of "On formally undecidable propositions...." and the accompanying footnote.) The following theorem, whose (grisly) proof provides that argument, shows that Term(t) is indeed Δ:

(56) $\vdash \exists s A(s,t) \leftrightarrow \exists b < \mathrm{lcm}[i+1: i<t+2]+1$
$\exists a < \mathrm{lcm}[1+(i+1)b: i<t+1] \exists s \leqslant ((a,b),t+1) A(s,t)$

Proof. In outline: If s is a finite sequence that shows t to be a term, then there is an irredundant finite sequence s' of which each value is $\leqslant t$. By an application of the pigeonhole principle, the length of s' is $t+1$. By the β-function lemma, there is such a sequence $\leqslant ((a,b),t+1)$ for some a,b bounded as in the statement of the theorem by functions defined by Σ pterms.

In full detail: The $\leftarrow$ direction is obvious. For the converse, suppose that $A(s,t)$. Then there is a sequence s' such that $A(s',t)$ and $(*)$ for all $i<\mathrm{lh}(s')$, $s'_i \leqslant t$. (Intuitively, we obtain s' from s by inductively deleting values larger than t from right to left.)

For: by induction on j, there is a sequence s' such that $A(s',t)$ and ($*j$) if $j \leqslant \mathrm{lh}(s') = k'$, then for all i, if $k'-j \leqslant i < k'$, then $s'_i \leqslant t$.

For if $j=0$, s is a suitable s'. Suppose that $A(s',t)$, ($*j$) holds for s', and $j+1 \leqslant \mathrm{lh}(s') = k'$. Let $c = k'-(j+1)$. If $s'_c > t$, let s'' be the result of deleting s'_c from s', i.e., the sequence $s'_{[0,c)} * s'_{[c+1,k)}$; otherwise let $s'' = s'$. Then ($*j+1$) holds for s''. Moreover, $A(s'',t)$: if $s'_c > t$, $l > c$, and $s'_l = $ (say) $(\mathrm{gn}(+), s_{l'}, s_{l''})$, then $s'_{l'}, s'_{l''} < s'_l \leqslant t$, and $s'_{l'}, s'_{l''} \neq s'_c$.

Setting $j = \mathrm{lh}(s')$ in ($*j$) gives an s' such that $A(s',t)$ and for which $(*)$ holds. A similar argument shows that we may also assume that for all i,j, if $i<j<\mathrm{lh}(s')$, then $s'_i \neq s'_j$.

Relettering: s' as: s, we may assume that for all $i<\mathrm{lh}(s)$, $s_i \leqslant t$, and for all $i<j<\mathrm{lh}(s)$, $s_i \neq s_j$.

It follows by a version of the pigeonhole principle (which states that if m pigeonholes contain among them n letters and $n>m$, then some pigeonhole contains at least two letters) that $\mathrm{lh}(s) \leqslant t+1$.

For: for all finite sequences s, if for all $i \leqslant t+1$, $s_i \leqslant t$, then for some i,j, $i<j \leqslant t+1$ and $s_i = s_j$. The proof is by induction on t: The statement is trivial for $t=0$. Suppose it true for t. Assume that for all $i \leqslant t+2$, $s_i \leqslant t+1$. We must show that for some $i<j \leqslant t+2$, $s_i = s_j$. Clearly, we may assume that for at most one $i \leqslant t+2$, $s_i = 0$. Let s' be a sequence such that for all $i \leqslant t+1$, $s'_i = s_i - 1$. (The existence of such an s' can be proved by induction as above.) Then for all $i \leqslant t+1$, $s'_i \leqslant t$, and by the induction hypothesis, for some i,j, $i<j \leqslant t+1$, $s'_i = s'_j$. If for no $i \leqslant t+1$, $s_i = 0$, then $s_i = s'_i + 1 = s'_j + 1 = s_j$, and we are done. Thus we may assume that there is exactly one $l \leqslant t+1$ such that $s_l = 0$ and hence that $s_{t+2} \neq 0$. Let

s'' be such that $s''_i = s_i - 1$ if $i < l$ and $= s_{i+1} - 1$ if $l + 1 \leqslant i \leqslant t + 2$. Then for all $i \leqslant t + 1$, $s''_i \leqslant t$; by the induction hypothesis for some i, j, $i < j \leqslant t + 1$, $s''_i = s''_j$, and thus for some i, j, $i < j \leqslant t + 2$, $s_i = s_j$.

We conclude that for some finite sequence s, $A(s, t)$, $\mathrm{lh}(s) \leqslant t + 1$, and for every $i < \mathrm{lh}(s)$, $s_i \leqslant t$. By the β-function lemma, there are a, b such that for all $i < t + 1$, $\beta(a, b, i) = s_i$, $b < \mathrm{lcm}[i + 1{:}\ i < \max(t + 1, \max[s_i{:}\ i < t + 1]) + 1] + 1 = \mathrm{lcm}[i + 1{:}\ i < t + 2] + 1$, and $a < \mathrm{lcm}[1 + (i + 1)b{:}\ i < t + 1]$. So for some finite sequence $s' \leqslant ((a, b), t + 1)$, $A(s', t)$. $\dashv$

The atomic formulas of PA are identities and $\bot$.

AtForm(x) is the formula

$$(\exists t < x \exists t' < x[\mathrm{Term}(t) \wedge \mathrm{Term}(t') \wedge x = (\ulcorner = \urcorner, t, t')] \vee x = \ulcorner \bot \urcorner)$$

AtForm(x) is a Δ formula, since Term(t) is Δ.

Since the formulas of PA are built up in the usual manner from atomic formulas by means of truth-functional connectives and quantifiers, the definition of Formula(x) is similar to that of Term(t).

Formula(x) is the formula

$$\begin{aligned}&\exists s[\mathrm{FinSeq}(s) \wedge \mathrm{lh}(s) > \mathbf{0} \wedge s_{\mathrm{lh}(s)-1} = x \wedge \\ &\forall i < \mathrm{lh}(s)(\mathrm{AtForm}(s_i) \vee \exists j, k < i\, s_i = (\ulcorner \rightarrow \urcorner, s_j, s_k) \vee \\ &\qquad\qquad \exists j < i \exists v[\mathrm{Variable}(v) \wedge s_i = (\ulcorner \forall \urcorner, v, s_k)])]\end{aligned}$$

There are unbounded quantifiers $\exists s$ and $\exists v$ in the definition of Formula(x). The proof that these can be bounded by "$\leqslant x$" is quite similar to that of (56) and we omit it.

Of course, it is now possible to prove in PA the sentence $\forall x(\mathrm{Formula}(x) \rightarrow \mathrm{Formula}((\ulcorner \rightarrow \urcorner, x, \ulcorner \bot \urcorner))$, asserting the existence of the negation of any formula, as well as many other sentences of PA stating syntactic facts of a similarly elementary and familiar character. We shall not undertake any systematic exposition of the elementary syntactic facts of this kind that can be proved in PA.

Under any standard formulation of logic, e.g., that of Tarski and Monk,[8] "axiom of PA" turns out to be defined by some Δ formula Ax(x) of PA. We suppose such a definition given. We also suppose given a Σ pterm sub(t, i, x) for the operation of substituting the term that is the value of t for (all free occurrences of) the ith variable in the formula that is the value of x.[9]

We now complete the sequence of our definitions of the main concepts of Syntax.

ConseqByModPon(x, y, z) and ConseqByGen(x, y) are the Δ formulas

$(\text{Formula}(x) \wedge \text{Formula}(z) \wedge y = (\ulcorner\rightarrow\urcorner, z, x))$ and
$\exists v < x(\text{Formula}(y) \wedge \text{Variable}(v) \wedge x = (\ulcorner\forall\urcorner, v, y))$, respectively.

The last Δ formula in our series is Pf(y, x),

$$\begin{aligned}&(\text{FinSeq}(y) \wedge s_{\text{lh}(y)-1} = x \wedge \forall i < \text{lh}(y) - 1[\text{Ax}(y_i) \vee \\ &\exists j < i \exists k < i\, \text{ConseqByModPon}(y_i, y_j, y_k) \vee \\ &\exists j < i\, \text{ConseqByGen}(y_i, y_j)])\end{aligned}$$

The formula Bew(x), which expresses provability in PA, is simply

$$\exists y\, \text{Pf}(y, x)$$

It is evident that Bew(x) is Σ; but Bew(x) is not Δ (unless PA is inconsistent). We may now begin to investigate what PA proves about provability in PA.

The basic properties of Bew(x)

Since Bew(x) is a Σ formula, for any sentence S of PA, Bew$(\ulcorner S\urcorner)$ is a Σ sentence; i.e., (iv), found at the beginning of this chapter, holds. Thus if S is a sentence and $\vdash S$, then Bew$(\ulcorner S\urcorner)$ is a true Σ sentence, and by (17), $\vdash$ Bew$(\ulcorner S\urcorner)$; i.e., (i) holds.

We now show that (ii) also holds.

(57) Let S and T be sentences of PA
Then $\vdash \text{Bew}(\ulcorner(S \rightarrow T)\urcorner) \rightarrow (\text{Bew}(\ulcorner S\urcorner) \rightarrow \text{Bew}(\ulcorner T\urcorner))$

Proof. It is sufficient to observe that

$$\vdash \text{Pf}(y, \ulcorner(S \rightarrow T)\urcorner) \wedge \text{Pf}(y', \ulcorner S\urcorner) \rightarrow \text{Pf}(y^* y'^*[\ulcorner T\urcorner], \ulcorner T\urcorner)$$

(Intuitively, since modus ponens is one of the two rules of inference of PA, the finite sequence whose values are those of a proof of $S \rightarrow T$, followed by those of a proof of S, followed by the sentence T, is a proof of T.) $\dashv$

(v) remains: we must show that $\vdash S \rightarrow \text{Bew}(\ulcorner S\urcorner)$ for any Σ sentence S. We first need to show that the function that assigns to every number i the Gödel number of the numeral **i** is defined by a Σ pterm.

Definition. Num(x, y) is the formula

$$\exists s(\mathrm{lh}(s) = x + \mathbf{1} \wedge s_0 = \ulcorner \mathbf{0} \urcorner \wedge \forall i < x\, s_{i+1} = (\ulcorner \mathbf{s} \urcorner, s_i) \wedge s_x = y)$$

Num(x, y) clearly works as desired.

We also need a Σ pterm for the function that assigns to each i the Gödel number of the ith variable.

Definition. $\mathrm{var}(x) = \mathbf{2} \times x + \mathbf{17}$.

Definition. $\mathrm{su}(x, y, z) = \mathrm{sub}(\mathrm{num}(x), \mathrm{var}(y), z)$.

The value of the function defined by the Σ pterm su(x, y, z) for any i, j, k is (the Gödel number of) the result, $F_{v_j}(\mathbf{i})$, of substituting $\mathbf{i}$ for the jth variable v_j in the formula with Gödel number k. So, e.g.,

(58) $\vdash \mathrm{su}(\mathbf{3}, \mathbf{4}, \ulcorner v_4 = v_1 \urcorner) = \ulcorner \mathbf{3} = v_1 \urcorner$

We must now explain a piece of notation: 'Bew$[F]$'.

Suppose that F is a formula of PA in which exactly m variables are free and that these are $v_{k_1}, \ldots, v_{k_m}$, with $k_1 < \cdots < k_m$. Then Bew$[F]$ is the formula

$$\mathrm{Bew}(\mathrm{su}(v_{k_m}, \mathbf{k}_m, \ldots, \mathrm{su}(v_{k_2}, \mathbf{k}_2, \mathrm{su}(v_{k_1}, \mathbf{k}_1, \ulcorner F \urcorner)) \cdots))$$

Notice that Bew$[F]$ has the same variables free as F, namely, $v_{k_1}, \ldots, v_{k_m}$. Bew$[F]$ is true of the numbers $i_1, \ldots, i_m$ (when these are assigned to $v_{k_1}, \ldots, v_{k_m}$, respectively) if and only if the result

$$F_{v_{k_1}}(\mathbf{i}_1) \ldots {}_{v_{k_m}}(\mathbf{i}_m)$$

of respectively substituting the numerals $\mathbf{i}_1, \ldots, \mathbf{i}_m$ denoting those numbers for the variables $v_{k_1}, \ldots, v_{k_m}$ in F is a theorem of PA. If F has no free variables, i.e., if F is a sentence, then Bew$[F]$ is to be Bew$(\ulcorner F \urcorner)$.

(59) ("provable modus ponens")
For any formulas F, G of the language of PA,
$\vdash \mathrm{Bew}[(F \to G)] \to (\mathrm{Bew}[F] \to \mathrm{Bew}[G])$

Proof. To reduce clutter, let us suppose that the free variables of F are v_2 and v_3, and that those of G are v_1 and v_3. Then
Bew$[F]$ is $\mathrm{Bew}(\mathrm{su}(v_3, \mathbf{3}, (\mathrm{su}(v_2, \mathbf{2}, \ulcorner F \urcorner))))$,
Bew$[G]$ is $\mathrm{Bew}(\mathrm{su}(v_3, \mathbf{3}, (\mathrm{su}(v_1, \mathbf{1}, \ulcorner G \urcorner))))$, and
Bew$[(F \to G)]$ is $\mathrm{Bew}(\mathrm{su}(v_3, \mathbf{3}, \mathrm{su}(v_2, \mathbf{2}, \mathrm{su}(v_1, \mathbf{1}, \ulcorner (F \to G) \urcorner))))$.

Observe now that

$$\vdash \mathrm{su}(v_3, \mathbf{3}, \mathrm{su}(v_2, \mathbf{2}, \mathrm{su}(v_1, \mathbf{1}, \ulcorner(F \to G)\urcorner)))$$
$$= (\ulcorner\to\urcorner, \mathrm{su}(v_3, \mathbf{3}(\mathrm{su}(v_2, \mathbf{2}, \ulcorner F\urcorner))), \mathrm{su}(v_3, \mathbf{3}, (\mathrm{su}(v_1, \mathbf{1}, \ulcorner G\urcorner))))$$

(Intuitively: substitution of numerals in two formulas commutes with forming their conditional.) Then, as in the proof of (57),

$$\vdash \mathrm{Pf}(y, \mathrm{su}(v_3, \mathbf{3}, \mathrm{su}(v_2, \mathbf{2}, \mathrm{su}(v_1, \mathbf{1}, \ulcorner(F \to G)\urcorner))))$$
$$\wedge\ \mathrm{Pf}(y', \mathrm{su}(v_3, \mathbf{3}, (\mathrm{su}(v_2, \mathbf{2}, \ulcorner F\urcorner))))$$
$$\to \mathrm{Pf}(y^* y'^* [\mathrm{su}(v_3, \mathbf{3}, (\mathrm{su}(v_1, \mathbf{1}, \ulcorner G\urcorner)))], \mathrm{su}(v_3, \mathbf{3}, (\mathrm{su}(v_1, \mathbf{1}, \ulcorner G\urcorner)))) \quad \dashv$$

An analogue of (i) also holds:

(60) For any formula F of PA, if $\vdash F$, then $\vdash \mathrm{Bew}[F]$

Proof. Suppose, again for the sake of simplicity, that $m = 2$ and the two free variables of F are v_3 and v_5. Then $\mathrm{Bew}[F]$ is the formula $\mathrm{Bew}(\mathrm{su}(v_5, \mathbf{5}, \mathrm{su}(v_3, \mathbf{3}, \ulcorner F\urcorner)))$. Let G be $\forall v_3 \forall v_5 F$. Then G is a sentence, and by (i), $\vdash \mathrm{Bew}(\ulcorner G\urcorner)$. Let H be $\forall v_5 F$. We want to see that $\vdash \mathrm{Bew}(\ulcorner G\urcorner) \to \mathrm{Bew}[H]$. [Intuitively: $(G \to H_{v_3}(\mathbf{i}))$ is provable by logic alone and is indeed an axiom of many formulations of logic; thus to obtain a proof of $H_{v_3}(\mathbf{i})$, append a proof of $(G \to H_{v_3}(\mathbf{i}))$ to a proof of G, and apply modus ponens.]

Thus, since
$\vdash \exists y\, \mathrm{Pf}(y, (\ulcorner\to\urcorner, \ulcorner G\urcorner, \mathrm{su}(v_3, \mathbf{3}, \ulcorner H\urcorner)))$ and
$\vdash \mathrm{Pf}(y, (\ulcorner\to\urcorner, \ulcorner G\urcorner, \mathrm{su}(v_3, \mathbf{3}, \ulcorner H\urcorner))) \wedge \mathrm{Pf}(y', \ulcorner G\urcorner)$
$\to \mathrm{Pf}(y'^* y^* [\mathrm{su}(v_3, \mathbf{3}, \ulcorner H\urcorner)], \mathrm{su}(v_3, \mathbf{3}, \ulcorner H\urcorner))$,
existentially quantifying, we have that
$\vdash \mathrm{Bew}(\ulcorner G\urcorner) \to \mathrm{Bew}(\mathrm{su}(v_3, \mathbf{3}, \ulcorner H\urcorner))$, i.e.,
$\vdash \mathrm{Bew}(\ulcorner G\urcorner) \to \mathrm{Bew}[H]$. Similarly,
$\vdash \mathrm{Bew}[H] \to \mathrm{Bew}[F]$, and therefore $\vdash \mathrm{Bew}[F]$. $\dashv$

We will now prove that for any Σ formula F, $\vdash F \to \mathrm{Bew}[F]$. (v) is the special case of this result in which F is a sentence. In particular, since $\mathrm{Bew}(\ulcorner S\urcorner)$ is a Σ sentence, $\vdash \mathrm{Bew}(\ulcorner S\urcorner) \to \mathrm{Bew}(\ulcorner \mathrm{Bew}(\ulcorner S\urcorner)\urcorner)$, i.e., (iii) holds.

(61) ("Provable Σ_1-completeness")
For any Σ formula, $\vdash F \to \mathrm{Bew}[F]$

Proof. We begin by observing that we may suppose F to be a *strict* Σ formula, for if F is Σ, then for some strict Σ formula G, F is equivalent to G, i.e., $\vdash F \rightarrow G$ and $\vdash G \rightarrow F$, whence by (60), $\vdash \text{Bew}[G \rightarrow F]$. But then by (59), $\vdash \text{Bew}[G] \rightarrow \text{Bew}[F]$. And then if $\vdash G \rightarrow \text{Bew}[G]$, $\vdash F \rightarrow \text{Bew}[F]$.

We first consider the case in which F is some formula $u + v = w$. Suppose that F is the formula $v_5 + v_2 = v_3$. We want to see that $\vdash v_5 + v_2 = v_3 \rightarrow \text{Bew}[v_5 + v_2 = v_3]$.

Here is an argument, formalizable in PA, that shows this. The argument is nothing but an elaboration of the proof of (7)

Let i_5 be arbitrary. (In the formalization, the variable v_5 plays the role of i_5 in the present argument.)

Suppose that for an arbitrary $i_3, i_5 + 0 = i_3$. (In the formalization, axiom (3) is written down at about this point.) Then $i_5 = i_3$, and $\mathbf{i}_5$ is $\mathbf{i}_3$. (Here identity axioms from logic would be used.) $v_0 \mathbf{+} \mathbf{0} = v_0$ is an axiom of PA, hence provable. Then by generalization, $\forall v_0\, v_0 \mathbf{+} \mathbf{0} = v_0$ is provable. $\forall v_0\, v_0 \mathbf{+} \mathbf{0} = v_0 \rightarrow \mathbf{i}_5 \mathbf{+} \mathbf{0} = \mathbf{i}_5$ is a logical axiom. Thus $\mathbf{i}_5 \mathbf{+} \mathbf{0} = \mathbf{i}_5$, i.e., $\mathbf{i}_5 \mathbf{+} \mathbf{0} = \mathbf{i}_3$ is provable. Thus for all i_3, $\mathbf{i}_5 \mathbf{+} \mathbf{0} = \mathbf{i}_3$ is provable if $i_5 + 0 = i_3$.

Let i_2 be arbitrary. Suppose that for all $\mathbf{i}_3, \mathbf{i}_5 + \mathbf{i}_2 = \mathbf{i}_3$ is provable if $i_5 + i_2 = i_3$. Let $i_4 = i_2 + 1$. We shall show that for all $\mathbf{i}_3, \mathbf{i}_5 + \mathbf{i}_4 = \mathbf{i}_3$ is provable if $i_5 + i_4 = i_3$. Now let i_3 be arbitrary and assume that $i_5 + i_4 = i_3$. Then $i_5 + (i_2 + 1) = (i_5 + i_2) + 1 = i_3$. Since 0 is not a successor, $i_3 \neq 0$, and thus for some number i_1, $i_3 = i_1 + 1$. So $(i_5 + i_2) + 1 = i_1 + 1$ and $i_5 + i_2 = i_1$. By the supposition, $\mathbf{i}_5 + \mathbf{i}_2 = \mathbf{i}_1$ is provable. By the axiomhood of (4), $\forall v_0 \forall v_1\, v_0 \mathbf{+} \mathbf{s} v_1 = \mathbf{s}(v_0 \mathbf{+} v_1)$ is provable, and therefore so is $\mathbf{i}_5 + \mathbf{s}\mathbf{i}_2 = \mathbf{s}\mathbf{i}_1$. But $\mathbf{s}\mathbf{i}_2$ is $\mathbf{i}_4$ and $\mathbf{s}\mathbf{i}_1$ is $\mathbf{i}_3$. Thus $\mathbf{i}_5 + \mathbf{i}_4 = \mathbf{i}_3$ is provable. Therefore for all i_3, $\mathbf{i}_5 + \mathbf{i}_4 = \mathbf{i}_3$ is provable if $i_5 + i_4 = i_3$. Thus for all i_2, if for all i_3, $\mathbf{i}_5 + \mathbf{i}_2 = \mathbf{i}_3$ is provable if $i_5 + i_2 = i_3$, then, where $i_4 = i_2 + 1$, for all i_3, $\mathbf{i}_5 + \mathbf{i}_4 = \mathbf{i}_3$ is provable if $i_5 + i_4 = i_3$.

By induction (at this point in the formalization, an induction axiom occurs), for all i_3, $\mathbf{i}_5 + \mathbf{i}_2 = \mathbf{i}_3$ is provable if $i_5 + i_2 = i_3$. Thus if $i_5 + i_2 = i_3$, then the result $\mathbf{i}_5 + \mathbf{i}_2 = \mathbf{i}_3$ of respectively substituting $\mathbf{i}_2, \mathbf{i}_3$, and $\mathbf{i}_5$ for the 2nd, 3rd, and 5th variables in $v_5 + v_2 = v_3$ is provable.

Similarly for other choices of variables, and similarly if F is a formula $u = v$, $\mathbf{0} = u$, $\mathbf{s}u = v$, or $u \times v = w$.

To prove the theorem, it suffices to show that $\vdash F \rightarrow \text{Bew}[F]$, if F is a formula that comes from formulas G such that $\vdash G \rightarrow \text{Bew}[G]$ by conjunction, disjunction, existential quantification, or bounded universal quantification.

Conjunction: Suppose that F is $(G \wedge H)$,
$\vdash G \to \text{Bew}[G]$ and
$\vdash H \to \text{Bew}[H]$. Then
$\vdash F \to (\text{Bew}[G] \wedge \text{Bew}[H])$. Now
$\vdash G \to (H \to F)$. By (60),
$\vdash \text{Bew}[(G \to (H \to F))]$. But by (59),
$\vdash \text{Bew}[(G \to (H \to F)] \to (\text{Bew}[G] \to \text{Bew}[(H \to F)])$ and
$\vdash \text{Bew}[(H \to F)] \to (\text{Bew}[H] \to \text{Bew}[F])$. By the propositional calculus,
$\vdash F \to \text{Bew}[F]$.

The argument for disjunction is similar but somewhat easier.

Existential quantification: Suppose that F is $\exists xG$ and
$\vdash G \to \text{Bew}[G]$. By logic,
$\vdash G \to F$. By (59) and (60),
$\vdash \text{Bew}[G] \to \text{Bew}[F]$. Thus
$\vdash G \to \text{Bew}[F]$. The variable x is not free in F, hence not free in Bew$[F]$, which has the same free variables as F. By logic,
$\vdash \exists xG \to \text{Bew}[F]$, i.e.,
$\vdash F \to \text{Bew}[F]$.

Bounded quantification is delicate: Let H be an arbitrary formula. We wish to see that $\text{Bew}[H_y(\mathbf{s}y)]$ and $\text{Bew}[H]_y(\mathbf{s}y)$ are equivalent. Suppose that y is v_k, the kth variable, and suppress mention of variables other than y and numbers other than the one whose numeral is substituted for y. Then by a formalization of the proof of the claim that for any number i, the result of substituting **si** for y in H is the result of substituting **i** for y in $H_y(\mathbf{s}y)$,
$\vdash \text{su}(y, \mathbf{k}, \ulcorner H_y(\mathbf{s}y)\urcorner) = \text{su}(\mathbf{s}y, \mathbf{k}, \ulcorner H\urcorner)$. Now
$\text{Bew}[H_y(\mathbf{s}y)]$ is $\text{Bew}(\text{su}(y, \mathbf{k}, \ulcorner H_y(\mathbf{s}y)\urcorner))$ and
$\text{Bew}[H]_y(\mathbf{s}y)$ is $\text{Bew}(\text{su}(\mathbf{s}y, \mathbf{k}, \ulcorner H\urcorner))$; thus
$\vdash \text{Bew}[H_y(\mathbf{s}y)] \leftrightarrow \text{Bew}[H]_y(\mathbf{s}y)$.
Similarly, since y is not free in $H_y(\mathbf{0})$,
$\vdash \text{su}(y, \mathbf{k}, \ulcorner H_y(\mathbf{0})\urcorner) = \ulcorner H_y(\mathbf{0})\urcorner = \text{su}(\mathbf{0}, \mathbf{k}, \ulcorner H\urcorner)$, and
$\vdash \text{Bew}[H_y(\mathbf{0})] \leftrightarrow \text{Bew}[H_y](\mathbf{0})$.

Now suppose that F is $\forall x < yG$ and
$\vdash G \to \text{Bew}[G]$. Thus $F_y(\mathbf{0})$ is $\forall x(x < \mathbf{0} \to G_y(\mathbf{0}))$. Since
$\vdash \neg x < \mathbf{0}$,
$\vdash F_y(\mathbf{0})$,
$\vdash \text{Bew}[F_y(\mathbf{0})]$ by (60),
$\vdash \text{Bew}[F]_y(\mathbf{0})$ by the foregoing, and
$\vdash F_y(\mathbf{0}) \to \text{Bew}[F]_y(\mathbf{0})$, i.e.,
$\vdash (F \to \text{Bew}[F])_y(\mathbf{0})$. Then since

$\vdash x < \mathbf{s}y \leftrightarrow x < y \vee x = y$,
$\vdash F_y(\mathbf{s}y) \leftrightarrow (F \wedge G)$, whence by (59) and (60),
$\vdash \text{Bew}[F] \wedge \text{Bew}[G] \rightarrow \text{Bew}[F_y(\mathbf{s}y)]$. Since
$\vdash G \rightarrow \text{Bew}[G]$,
$\vdash (F \rightarrow \text{Bew}[F]) \rightarrow (F_y(\mathbf{s}y) \rightarrow \text{Bew}[F] \wedge \text{Bew}[G])$. And since
$\vdash \text{Bew}[F_y(\mathbf{s}y)] \leftrightarrow \text{Bew}[F]_y(\mathbf{s}y)$,
$\vdash (F \rightarrow \text{Bew}[F]) \rightarrow (F_y(\mathbf{s}y) \rightarrow \text{Bew}[F]_y(\mathbf{s}y))$, i.e.,
$\vdash (F \rightarrow \text{Bew}[F]) \rightarrow (F \rightarrow \text{Bew}[F])_y(\mathbf{s}y)$, and therefore
$\vdash \forall y((F \rightarrow \text{Bew}[F]) \rightarrow (F \rightarrow \text{Bew}[F])_y(\mathbf{s}y))$. By an induction axiom,
$\vdash F \rightarrow \text{Bew}[F]$.

Thus for every Σ formula F, $\vdash F \rightarrow \text{Bew}[F]$. $\dashv$

Afterword on the choice of PA

In the next chapter we are going to show how to construct from any formula $P(y)$, a sentence S for which the biconditional sentence $S \leftrightarrow P(\ulcorner S \urcorner)$ is a theorem of PA; S is then equivalent in PA to the assertion that S has the property expressed by $P(y)$. To carry out the construction, which is given in the proof of the generalized diagonal lemma, the full power of PA is not needed; in fact, the subtheory Q of PA, whose axioms are axioms (1)–(6) and the theorem $x = \mathbf{0} \vee \exists y\, x = \mathbf{s}y$ of PA, suffices.

Q is an extremely weak theory, incapable even of proving the commutativity of addition, and is certainly not a sufficient theory in which to develop a theory of the syntax of PA or of any other system. But the full power of PA is also not needed to obtain the theorems about the syntax of PA and the concept of provability in PA that we have been concerned to establish in the present chapter. Certain appreciably weaker systems, whose axioms do not include all of the induction axioms, suffice for the theory of finite sequences and the proofs of the derivability conditions (for PA and for those weaker systems themselves). In those weaker theories, it should also be noted, stronger theorems about the syntax of PA than those we have stated can also be proved. One example is the single sentence of the language of PA that generalizes condition (ii) and asserts that all provable conditionals with provable antecedents have provable consequents; another is a similar generalization of condition (iii).

The phenomenon of a theory able to prove facts about its own syntax is as much an example of "self-reference" as is that of a sentence asserting its own unprovability (say); but PA, as we have said, is by no means the weakest theory wherein this phenomenon is displayed.

PA does, however, have a noteworthy trait: among standard arithmetical theories capable of proving the diagonal lemma and results about their own syntax like the derivability conditions, PA is distinguished as the simplest, i.e., simplest to describe, now known. For this reason it will be the theory we primarily use and examine in the pages that follow.

3

The box as Bew(x)

One of the principal aims of this study is to investigate the effects of interpreting the box of modal logic to mean "it is provable (in a certain formal theory) that...". When modal logic is viewed in this way, a question immediately comes to mind: Which principles of modal logic are correct when the box is interpreted in this way? The answer is not evident; near the end of this chapter we shall say what the answer is, and in Chapter 9, when we prove the arithmetical completeness theorems of Solovay, we shall show that it is the answer.

In order to express our question precisely, we make two definitions:

A *realization*[1] is a function that assigns to each sentence letter a sentence of the language of Peano arithmetic. It is standard practice to use "*" as a variable over interpretations; we shall use "#" as well.

The *translation* A^* of a modal sentence A under a realization $*$ is defined inductively:

(1) $\bot = \bot$
(2) $p^* = {*}(p)$ (p a sentence letter)
(3) $(A \to B)^* = (A^* \to B^*)$
(4) $\Box(A)^* = \mathrm{Bew}[A^*]$

($\mathrm{Bew}[A^*] = \mathrm{Bew}(\ulcorner A^* \urcorner)$, as A^* is a sentence.)

We have taken $\bot$ and $\to$ to be among the primitive logical symbols of PA, and therefore the translation of any modal sentence under any realization is a sentence of the language of PA. Clauses (1) and (3) guarantee that the translation (under $*$) of a truth-functional combination of sentences is that same truth-functional combination of the translations of those sentences. Clause (4) ensures that if the translation of A is S, then the translation of $\Box A$ is $\mathrm{Bew}(\ulcorner S \urcorner)$, the result of substituting the numeral for the Gödel number of S for the free variable x in $\mathrm{Bew}(x)$, which is a sentence of Peano arithmetic that may be regarded as expressing the assertion that S is provable.

If $*$ and $\#$ are realizations that assign the same sentences of arithmetic to all sentence letters occurring in A, then $A^* = A^\#$. Thus if A is a letterless sentence, $A^* = A^\#$ for all realizations $*$ and $\#$, and the identity of the sentence A^* of arithmetic does not depend on $*$.

Our original question – Which principles of modal logic are correct if the box is taken to mean "it is provable that..."? – now gives way to two precisely formulated questions: Which modal sentences A are such that, for all realizations $*$, A^* is true (in the standard model N)? Which modal sentences A are such that, for all realizations $*$, A^* is provable in PA? Since A^* is provable in PA iff $\Box A^*$ is true, an answer to the first of these questions, which seems a more likely explication of our original question, immediately supplies one to the second. Both, however, are interesting questions with interesting answers, and we shall be able to give a satisfactory answer to the first only by using techniques devised to answer the second.

Recall the system K4 from Chapter 1. Its axioms are all tautologies, all distribution axioms, and all sentences $\Box A \to \Box\Box A$, and its rules of inference are modus ponens and necessitation. We shall show below that if A is a theorem of GL, then for every realization $*$, A^* is a theorem of PA. In order to do so, we first show that the same holds for the subsystem K4 of GL.

Theorem 1. *If* K4$\vdash A$, *then for every realization* $*$, PA$\vdash A^*$.

Proof. If A is a tautological combination of modal sentences, then A^* is the same tautological combination of sentences of the language of PA, and therefore PA$\vdash A^*$.

In Chapter 2 we saw that for every pair S, T of sentences of the language of PA, PA$\vdash \mathrm{Bew}(\ulcorner(S \to T)\urcorner) \to (\mathrm{Bew}(\ulcorner S\urcorner) \to \mathrm{Bew}(\ulcorner T\urcorner))$. Thus for every realization $*$ and every pair A, B of modal sentences, PA$\vdash \mathrm{Bew}(\ulcorner(A^* \to B^*)\urcorner) \to (\mathrm{Bew}(\ulcorner A^*\urcorner) \to \mathrm{Bew}(\ulcorner B^*\urcorner))$. Since

$$\begin{aligned}&\mathrm{Bew}(\ulcorner(A^* \to B^*)\urcorner) \to (\mathrm{Bew}(\ulcorner A^*\urcorner) \to \mathrm{Bew}(\ulcorner B^*\urcorner))\\ &\quad = (\Box(A \to B) \to (\Box A \to \Box B))^*,\end{aligned}$$

we have that for every pair A, B of modal sentences, PA$\vdash (\Box(A \to B) \to (\Box A \to \Box B))^*$.

In Chapter 2 we also saw that for every sentence S of the language of PA, PA$\vdash \mathrm{Bew}(\ulcorner S\urcorner) \to (\mathrm{Bew}(\ulcorner \mathrm{Bew}(\ulcorner S\urcorner)\urcorner))$. Thus for every realization $*$

and every modal sentence A, $\mathrm{PA} \vdash \mathrm{Bew}(\ulcorner A^* \urcorner) \to \mathrm{Bew}(\ulcorner \mathrm{Bew}(\ulcorner A^* \urcorner) \urcorner)$. Since $\mathrm{Bew}(\ulcorner A^* \urcorner) \to \mathrm{Bew}(\ulcorner \mathrm{Bew}(\ulcorner A^* \urcorner) \urcorner) = (\Box A \to \Box\Box A)^*$, we have that for every modal sentence A, $\mathrm{PA} \vdash (\Box A \to \Box\Box A)^*$.

If $\mathrm{PA} \vdash (A \to B)^*$ and $\mathrm{PA} \vdash A^*$, then $\vdash B^*$, since $(A \to B)^* = (A^* \to B^*)$.

Lastly, if $\mathrm{PA} \vdash A^*$, then, as we also saw in Chapter 2, $\mathrm{PA} \vdash \mathrm{Bew}(\ulcorner A^* \urcorner)$, and thus $\mathrm{PA} \vdash \Box A^*$, since $\mathrm{Bew}(\ulcorner A^* \urcorner) = \Box A^*$.

It follows that if A is a theorem of K4, then A^* is a theorem of PA. ⊣

In order to prove that every translation of every theorem of GL is a theorem of PA, we prove a fundamental theorem about PA and other formalized theories, the (generalized) *diagonal lemma.*

The generalized diagonal lemma. *Suppose that* $y_0, \ldots, y_n$, $z_1, \ldots, z_m$ *are distinct variables and that* $P_0(y_0, \ldots, y_n, \mathrm{z}), \ldots$, $P_n(y_0, \ldots, y_n, \mathrm{z})$ *are formulas of the language of* PA *in which all free variables are among* $y_0, \ldots, y_n, \mathrm{z}$. *('*$\mathrm{z}$*' abbreviates '*$z_1, \ldots, z_m$*'.) Then there exist formulas* $S_0(\mathrm{z}), \ldots, S_n(\mathrm{z})$ *of the language of* PA *in which all free variables are among* z, *such that*

$\mathrm{PA} \vdash S_0(\mathrm{z}) \leftrightarrow P_0(\ulcorner S_0(\mathrm{z}) \urcorner, \ldots, \ulcorner S_n(\mathrm{z}) \urcorner, \mathrm{z}), \ldots,$ *and*
$\mathrm{PA} \vdash S_n(\mathrm{z}) \leftrightarrow P_n(\ulcorner S_0(\mathrm{z}) \urcorner, \ldots, \ulcorner S_n(\mathrm{z}) \urcorner, \mathrm{z})$.

Proof. Let $\mathrm{Su}(w, x_0, \ldots, x_n, y)$ be a Σ pterm for the $(n+2)$-place function subst whose value at $a, b_0, \ldots, b_n$ is the Gödel number of the result of respectively substituting the numerals $\mathbf{b}_0, \ldots, \mathbf{b}_n$ for the variables $x_0, \ldots, x_n$ in the formula with Gödel number a.

For each $i \leqslant n$, let k_i be the Gödel number of

$$P_i(\mathrm{su}(x_0, x_0, \ldots, x_n), \ldots, \mathrm{su}(x_n, x_0, \ldots, x_n), \mathrm{z})$$

and let $S_i(\mathrm{z})$ be the formula

$$P_i(\mathrm{su}(\mathbf{k}_0, \mathbf{k}_0, \ldots, \mathbf{k}_n), \ldots, \mathrm{su}(\mathbf{k}_n, \mathbf{k}_0, \ldots, \mathbf{k}_n), \mathrm{z})$$

We need only show that

$$\mathrm{PA} \vdash \mathrm{su}(\mathbf{k}_i, \mathbf{k}_0, \ldots, \mathbf{k}_n) = \ulcorner S_i(\mathrm{z}) \urcorner$$

But the result of respectively substituting the numerals $\mathbf{k}_0, \ldots., \mathbf{k}_n$ for the variables $x_0, \ldots, x_n$ in the formula with Gödel number k_i, i.e., in the formula

$$P_i(\mathrm{su}(x_0, x_0, \ldots, x_n), \ldots., \mathrm{su}(x_n, x_0, \ldots, x_n), \mathrm{z})$$

is the formula $S_i(\mathrm{z})$ and therefore $\mathrm{subst}(k_i, k_0, \ldots, k_n) =$ the Gödel number of $S_i(\mathrm{z})$. Therefore the Σ sentence

$$\mathrm{su}(\mathbf{k}_i, \mathbf{k}_0, \ldots, \mathbf{k}_n) = \ulcorner S_i(\mathrm{z}) \urcorner$$

is true, and by the provability of true Σ sentences,

$$\mathrm{PA} \vdash \mathrm{su}(\mathbf{k}_i, \mathbf{k}_0, \ldots, \mathbf{k}_n) = \ulcorner S_i(\mathrm{z}) \urcorner \quad \dashv$$

Let us observe that if the formulas $P_0(y_0, \ldots, y_n, \mathrm{z}), \ldots, P_n(y_0, \ldots, y_n, \mathrm{z})$ are all Σ or all Δ, then the formulas $S_0(\mathrm{z}), \ldots, S_n(\mathrm{z})$ are also all Σ or all Δ, respectively.

Corollary 1. *Suppose that* $P_0(y_0, \ldots, y_n), \ldots, P_n(y_0, \ldots, y_n)$ *are formulas of the language of* PA *in which all free variables are among* $y_0, \ldots, y_n$. *Then there exist sentences* $S_0, \ldots, S_n$ *of the language of* PA *such that*

$\mathrm{PA} \vdash S_0 \leftrightarrow P_0(\ulcorner S_0 \urcorner, \ldots, \ulcorner S_n \urcorner), \ldots,$ *and*
$\mathrm{PA} \vdash S_n \leftrightarrow P_n(\ulcorner S_0 \urcorner, \ldots, \ulcorner S_n \urcorner)$.

Proof. This is just the case of the generalized diagonal lemma in which $m = 0$. $\dashv$

Corollary 2 (the diagonal lemma). *Suppose that $P(y)$ is a formula of the language of* PA *in which no variable other than y is free. Then there exists a sentence S of the language of* PA *such that* $\mathrm{PA} \vdash S \leftrightarrow P(\ulcorner S \urcorner)$.

Proof. This is just the case of Corollary 1 in which $n = 0$. $\dashv$

In 1952, Leon Henkin raised the question[2] whether the sentence S constructed as in the diagonal lemma by taking $P(x)$ to be $\mathrm{Bew}(x)$ is provable or not; for such S, $\mathrm{PA} \vdash S \leftrightarrow \mathrm{Bew}(\ulcorner S \urcorner)$. The question was answered in 1954 by M. H. Löb, who showed that for all sentences S, if $\mathrm{PA} \vdash \mathrm{Bew}(\ulcorner S \urcorner) \to S$, then $\mathrm{PA} \vdash S$.[3] This result is now known as Löb's theorem. Löb's theorem, of course, immediately settles Henkin's question, for if $\mathrm{PA} \vdash S \leftrightarrow \mathrm{Bew}(\ulcorner S \urcorner)$, then $\mathrm{PA} \vdash \mathrm{Bew}(\ulcorner S \urcorner) \to S$, and therefore $\mathrm{PA} \vdash S$.

Löb's theorem is utterly astonishing for at least five reasons. In the first place, it is often hard to understand how vast the mathematical gap is between truth and provability. And to one who lacks that understanding and does not distinguish between truth and provability, $\mathrm{Bew}(\ulcorner S \urcorner) \to S$, which the hypothesis of Löb's theorem asserts to be provable, might appear to be trivially true in *all* cases, whether S is true or false, provable or unprovable. But if S is false, S had better not be provable. Thus it would seem that S ought not always to be provable provided merely that (the possibly trivial-seeming) $\mathrm{Bew}(\ulcorner S \urcorner) \rightarrow S$ is provable.

Secondly, Bew seems here to be working like negation. After all, if $\neg S \rightarrow S$ is provable, then so is S; proving S by proving $\neg S \rightarrow S$ is called *reductio ad absurdum* (or, sometimes, the law of Clavius). Moreover, inferring S solely on the ground that $(S \rightarrow S)$ is demonstrable is known as begging the question, or reasoning in a circle. To one who conflates truth and provability, it may then seem that Löb's theorem asserts that begging the question is an admissible form of reasoning in PA.

Thirdly, one might have thought that *at least on occasion*, PA would claim to be sound with regard to an unprovable sentence S, i.e., claim that *if* it proves S, then S holds. But Löb's theorem tells us that it never does so: PA makes the claim $\mathrm{Bew}(\ulcorner S \urcorner) \rightarrow S$ that it is sound with regard to S only when it obviously must, when the consequent S is actually provable. As Rohit Parikh once put it, "PA couldn't be more modest about its own veracity".

Fourthly, one might very naturally suppose that provability is a kind of necessity, and therefore, just as $\Box(\Box p \rightarrow p)$ always expresses a truth if the box is interpreted as "it is necessary that" – for then $\Box(\Box p \rightarrow p)$ says that it is necessarily true that if a statement is necessarily true, it is true – $\mathrm{Bew}(\ulcorner(\mathrm{Bew}(\ulcorner S \urcorner) \rightarrow S)\urcorner)$ would also always be true or at least true in some cases in which S is false and not true only in the rather exceptional cases in which S is actually provable.

Finally, it seems wholly bizarre that the statement that if S is provable, then S is true is not itself provable, in general. For isn't it perfectly obvious, for any S, that S is true if provable? Why are we bothering with PA if its theorems are false? And how could any such (apparently) obvious truth not be provable?

The proof of Löb's theorem we are about to present is reminiscent of Curry's paradox, which is a negation-free version of Russell's paradox:

Let "SC" abbreviate "Santa Claus exists". Let $c = \{x\text{: if } x \in x, \text{SC}\}$. Assume that $c \in c$; then c meets the defining condition of c, and thus if $c \in c$, SC; thus, on the assumption that $c \in c$, SC. We have now shown *outright*, i.e., on no assumptions at all, that if $c \in c$, SC. Thus c does after all meet the defining condition of c, and so $c \in c$, whence SC.

On reading Löb's proof, Henkin devised the following paradoxical "proof" that SC:

Let Sam be the sentence "if Sam is true, SC". Assume that Sam is true; then "if Sam is true, SC" is true; thus if Sam is true, SC; and so SC by modus ponens. Thus we have shown that SC on the assumption that Sam is true and have therefore shown outright that if Sam is true, SC. But then "If Sam is true, SC" is true, i.e., Sam is true, and by modus ponens again, SC.

Henkin's paradox appeals to the Tarski truth scheme:

'——' is true if and only if ——

in place of the unrestricted comprehension principle of naive set theory,

$$\exists y \forall x (x \in y \leftrightarrow \cdots x \cdots)$$

by which the existence of c was inferred in Curry's paradox.

Löb's theorem. *If* $\mathrm{PA} \vdash \mathrm{Bew}(\ulcorner S \urcorner) \rightarrow S$, *then* $\mathrm{PA} \vdash S$.

Proof. Let $Q(x)$ be $(\mathrm{Bew}(x) \rightarrow S)$. By the diagonal lemma, there is a sentence I such that

$\mathrm{PA} \vdash I \leftrightarrow Q(\ulcorner I \urcorner)$, that is,

$\mathrm{PA} \vdash I \leftrightarrow (\mathrm{Bew}(\ulcorner I \urcorner) \rightarrow S)$.

It will enhance readability if we abbreviate "$\mathrm{Bew}(\ulcorner I \urcorner)$, etc., by "$PI$", etc. Thus we have

(1) $\mathrm{PA} \vdash I \leftrightarrow (PI \rightarrow S)$

By (1),

(2) $\mathrm{PA} \vdash I \rightarrow (PI \rightarrow S)$

whence by (i) of Chapter 2,

(3) $\mathrm{PA} \vdash P(I \rightarrow (PI \rightarrow S))$

By (ii) of Chapter 2,

(4) $\mathrm{PA} \vdash P(I \rightarrow (PI \rightarrow S)) \rightarrow (PI \rightarrow P(PI \rightarrow S))$

By (3) and (4),

(5) $\mathrm{PA} \vdash PI \rightarrow P(PI \rightarrow S)$

By (ii) of Chapter 2 again,

(6) $\mathrm{PA} \vdash P(PI \rightarrow S) \rightarrow (PPI \rightarrow PS)$

Thus by (5) and (6),

(7) $\mathrm{PA} \vdash PI \rightarrow (PPI \rightarrow PS)$

By (iii) of Chapter 2,

(8) $\mathrm{PA} \vdash PI \rightarrow PPI$

By (7) and (8),

(9) $\mathrm{PA} \vdash PI \rightarrow PS$

Now suppose that $\mathrm{PA} \vdash \mathrm{Bew}(\ulcorner S \urcorner) \rightarrow S$, i.e., that

(10) $\mathrm{PA} \vdash PS \rightarrow S$

By (9) and (10),

(11) $\mathrm{PA} \vdash PI \rightarrow S$

By (1) and (11),

(12) $\mathrm{PA} \vdash I$

By (i) of Chapter 2,

(13) $\mathrm{PA} \vdash PI$

whence by (11) and (12),

(14) $\mathrm{PA} \vdash S$ $\dashv$

There is a variant proof of Löb's theorem due to Kreisel and Takeuti. Suppose that

(1) $\mathrm{PA} \vdash PS \rightarrow S$

Let $t(x)$ be a Σ pterm for a function whose value for any number that is the Gödel number of a sentence J is the Gödel number of the conditional with antecedent J and consequent S. Setting $P(y) = \mathrm{Bew}(t(y))$ in the diagonal lemma yields a sentence J such that $\mathrm{PA} \vdash J \leftrightarrow \mathrm{Bew}(t(\ulcorner J \urcorner))$. Since $\mathrm{PA} \vdash t(\ulcorner J \urcorner) = \ulcorner (J \rightarrow S) \urcorner$, we have

(2) $\mathrm{PA} \vdash J \leftrightarrow P(J \rightarrow S)$

By (2),

(3) $\mathrm{PA} \vdash P(J \rightarrow S) \rightarrow J$

whence by (i) of Chapter 2,

(4) $\mathrm{PA} \vdash P(P(J \rightarrow S) \rightarrow J)$

By (ii) of Chapter 2,

(5) $\mathrm{PA} \vdash P(P(J \to S) \to J) \to (PP(J \to S) \to PJ)$

whence by (4) and (5),

(6) $\mathrm{PA} \vdash PP(J \to S) \to PJ$

By (iii) of Chapter 2,

(7) $\mathrm{PA} \vdash P(J \to S) \to PP(J \to S)$

By (6) and (7),

(8) $\mathrm{PA} \vdash P(J \to S) \to PJ$

By (ii) of Chapter 2,

(9) $\mathrm{PA} \vdash P(J \to S) \to (PJ \to PS)$

Thus by (8) and (9),

(10) $\mathrm{PA} \vdash P(J \to S) \to PS$

By (1) and (10),

(11) $\mathrm{PA} \vdash P(J \to S) \to S$

whence by (2) and (11),

(12) $\mathrm{PA} \vdash J \to S$

By (i) of Chapter 2,

(13) $\mathrm{PA} \vdash P(J \to S)$

and then by (2) and (13),

(14) $\mathrm{PA} \vdash J$

whence by (12) and (14),

(15) $\mathrm{PA} \vdash S$ $\dashv$

The second incompleteness theorem for PA is an immediate consequence of Löb's theorem:

The second incompleteness theorem for PA. *If* PA *is consistent, then* $\mathrm{PA} \nvdash \neg \mathrm{Bew}(\ulcorner \bot \urcorner)$.

Proof. If $\mathrm{PA} \vdash \neg \mathrm{Bew}(\ulcorner \bot \urcorner)$, then $\mathrm{PA} \vdash \mathrm{Bew}(\ulcorner \bot \urcorner) \to \bot$, whence by Löb's theorem, $\mathrm{PA} \vdash \bot$ and PA is inconsistent. $\dashv$

The *Löb rule* is the modal-logical rule of inference:

$$\text{From} \vdash (\Box A \to A), \quad \text{infer} \vdash A$$

Let K4LR be the system of modal logic whose axioms are those of K4 and whose rules of inference are modus ponens, necessitation and the Löb rule.

According to Theorem 1, if K4$\vdash A$, then for all realizations $*$, PA$\vdash A^*$. We now also know that if K4LR$\vdash$A, then PA$\vdash A^*$. For if PA$\vdash(\Box A \to A)^*$, i.e., if PA$\vdash$Bew($\ulcorner A^* \urcorner$)$\to A^*$, then by Löb's theorem, PA$\vdash A^*$. We now want to see that GL and K4LR have the same theorems.

According to Theorem 18 of Chapter 1, GL$\vdash \Box A \to \Box\Box A$. And GL is closed under the Löb rule, for if
GL$\vdash \Box A \to A$, then by necessitation,
GL$\vdash \Box(\Box A \to A)$. But also
GL$\vdash \Box(\Box A \to A) \to \Box A$, whence by modus ponens
GL$\vdash \Box A$, and by modus ponens again,
GL$\vdash A$.

Thus if K4LR$\vdash A$, GL$\vdash A$. To show the converse, let $B = \Box(\Box A \to A)$, $C = \Box A$, and $D = B \to C$. We are to show that K4LR$\vdash D$. We have that
K$\vdash \Box D \to (\Box B \to \Box C)$ (a distribution axiom) as well as
K$\vdash B \to (\Box C \to C)$ (another distribution axiom). Since B begins with $\Box$,
K4$\vdash B \to \Box B$, whence by the propositional calculus
K4$\vdash \Box D \to (B \to C)$, i.e.,
K4$\vdash \Box D \to D$. By the Löb rule,
K4LR$\vdash D$, Q.E.D. ⊣

Theorem 2. *If* GL$\vdash A$, *then for every realization* $*$, PA$\vdash A^*$.

Proof. K4LR and GL have the same theorems. ⊣

We call a modal sentence A *always provable* if for every realization $*$, PA$\vdash A^*$.

A variant proof of Theorem 2 may be given by appealing to Theorem 1, the diagonal lemma, and Theorem 23 of Chapter 1, according to which, K4$\vdash \Box(q \leftrightarrow (\Box q \to p)) \to (\Box(\Box p \to p) \to \Box p)$. In view of Theorem 1, it suffices to show that for any realization $*$, PA$\vdash(\Box(\Box A \to A) \to \Box A)^*$. Let $P(x)$ be the formula (Bew(x)$\to A^*$).

By the diagonal lemma, there exists a sentence S such that
$\mathrm{PA} \vdash S \leftrightarrow P(\ulcorner S \urcorner)$, i.e.,
$\mathrm{PA} \vdash S \leftrightarrow (\mathrm{Bew}(\ulcorner S \urcorner) \rightarrow A^*)$. By (i) of Chapter 2,
$\mathrm{PA} \vdash \mathrm{Bew}(\ulcorner (S \leftrightarrow (\mathrm{Bew}(\ulcorner S \urcorner) \rightarrow A^*)) \urcorner)$. Let # be a realization such that $^{\#}(p) = A^*$ and $^{\#}(q) = S$. Then
$\mathrm{PA} \vdash \Box(q \leftrightarrow (\Box q \rightarrow p))^{\#}$. By Theorem 23 of Chapter 1 and Theorem 1,
$\mathrm{PA} \vdash (\Box(q \leftrightarrow (\Box q \rightarrow p)) \rightarrow (\Box(\Box p \rightarrow p) \rightarrow \Box p))^{\#}$, and therefore,
$\mathrm{PA} \vdash (\Box(\Box p \rightarrow p) \rightarrow \Box p)^{\#}$, i.e.,
$\mathrm{PA} \vdash \mathrm{Bew}(\ulcorner (\mathrm{Bew}(\ulcorner A^* \urcorner) \rightarrow A^*) \rightarrow A^*) \rightarrow \mathrm{Bew}(\ulcorner A^* \urcorner)$, i.e.,
$\mathrm{PA} \vdash (\Box(\Box A \rightarrow A) \rightarrow \Box A)^*$. $\dashv$

The arithmetical completeness theorem for GL, proved by Robert Solovay, states that the converse of Theorem 2 holds and thus that a modal sentence A is a theorem of GL iff for every realization $*$, $\mathrm{PA} \vdash A^*$, iff A is always provable. Solovay's theorem is proved in Chapter 9.

Let us now look at some elementary examples of the ways in which a study of GL can give us information about provability in arithmetic.

Recall that $\mathrm{Bew}[S]$ is just $\mathrm{Bew}(\ulcorner S \urcorner)$ if S is a sentence.

Terminology. Suppose that S and S' are sentences of the language of arithmetic. Then the arithmetization of the assertion that

...S is provable (in arithmetic) is the sentence $\mathrm{Bew}[S]$;
...S is consistent (with arithmetic) is the sentence $\neg \mathrm{Bew}[\neg S]$;
...S is unprovable is the sentence $\neg \mathrm{Bew}[S]$;
...S is disprovable (refutable) is the sentence $\mathrm{Bew}[\neg S]$;
...S is decidable is the sentence $\mathrm{Bew}[S] \vee \mathrm{Bew}[\neg S]$;
...S is undecidable is the sentence $\neg \mathrm{Bew}[S] \wedge \neg \mathrm{Bew}[\neg S]$;
...S is equivalent to S' is the sentence $\mathrm{Bew}[(S \leftrightarrow S')]$;
...S implies S' (S' is deducible from S, S' follows from S) is the sentence $\mathrm{Bew}[(S \rightarrow S')]$;
...arithmetic is consistent is the sentence $\neg \mathrm{Bew}[\bot]$; and
...arithmetic is inconsistent is the sentence $\mathrm{Bew}[\bot]$.

The arithmetization of the assertion that if...then—is the conditional whose antecedent and consequent are the arithmetizations of the assertion that...and the assertion that—(and similarly for the other propositional connectives). An assertion is said to be provable in PA when its arithmetization is. We shall often say "it is provable that...", meaning "the assertion that...is provable" and shall often allow ourselves a certain amount of stylistic variation in the choice of expressions with which we refer to assertions; for example, we may use "the consistency of arithmetic" to refer to the assertion that arithmetic is consistent or we may anaphorically use "it" in place of "S", etc.

The second incompleteness theorem of Gödel (for PA) is the assertion that if arithmetic is consistent, then the consistency of arithmetic is not provable in arithmetic. An easy argument, which uses the fact that $\Box(\Box\bot \to \bot) \to \Box\bot$ is a theorem of GL, shows that the second incompleteness theorem, which of course is mathematically demonstrable, is in fact *provable in PA*: Since $\mathrm{GL} \vdash \Box(\Box\bot \to \bot) \to \Box\bot$, $\mathrm{GL} \vdash \neg\Box\bot \to \neg\Box\neg\Box\bot$, and then by Theorem 2, $\mathrm{PA} \vdash (\neg\Box\bot \to \neg\Box\neg\Box\bot)^*$, that is, $\mathrm{PA} \vdash \neg\mathrm{Bew}[\bot] \to \neg\mathrm{Bew}[\neg\mathrm{Bew}[\bot]]$. But this theorem of PA is just the arithmetization of the assertion that if arithmetic is consistent, then the consistency of arithmetic is not provable in arithmetic.

Moreover, $\mathrm{GL} \vdash \Box\bot \to \Box\Box\bot$, $\mathrm{GL} \vdash \neg\Box\Box\bot \to \neg\Box\bot$, and so $\mathrm{GL} \vdash \neg\Box\Box\bot \to (\neg\Box\neg\Box\bot \wedge \neg\Box\neg\neg\Box\bot)$. Therefore the following assertion is provable in PA: if the inconsistency of arithmetic is not provable, then the consistency of arithmetic is undecidable.

A theory T whose language is that of PA is said to be ω-consistent if there is no formula $A(x)$ such that both $\mathrm{T} \vdash \exists x A(x)$ and for every number n, $\mathrm{T} \vdash \neg A(\mathbf{n})$. A sentence S in the language of a theory T is said to be *undecidable in* T if neither $\mathrm{T} \vdash S$ nor $\mathrm{T} \vdash \neg S$. And T is *incomplete* if there is at least one sentence[4] that is undecidable in T. The first incompleteness theorem of Gödel is the assertion that if arithmetic is ω-consistent, then arithmetic is incomplete.

A theory T in the language of PA is said to be *1-consistent* if there is no Δ formula $A(x)$ such that both $\mathrm{T} \vdash \exists x A(x)$ and for every number n, $\mathrm{T} \vdash \neg A(\mathbf{n})$.

If PA is ω-consistent, then it is 1-consistent; and if 1-consistent, then consistent (otherwise $\bot$, and hence every sentence, is a theorem).

We recall from Chapter 2 that Proof (y, x) is Δ. Thus if S is not a theorem of PA, then no m is the Gödel number of a proof of S, for every m, $\neg$ Proof $(\mathbf{m}, \ulcorner S \urcorner)$ is a true Σ sentence, and therefore $\mathrm{PA} \vdash \neg \mathrm{Proof}(\mathbf{m}, \ulcorner S \urcorner)$.

If PA is 1-consistent and S is not a theorem of PA, then Bew[S] is not a theorem of PA. For if S is not a theorem, then for every m, PA$\vdash\neg$Proof($\mathbf{m}$,$\ulcorner S\urcorner$); and since Proof(x,$\ulcorner S\urcorner$) is Δ, if PA is 1-consistent, then Bew($\ulcorner S\urcorner$), $=\exists x$ Proof(x,$\ulcorner S\urcorner$) is not a theorem either. Thus if PA is 1-consistent, then $\bot$ is not a theorem, Bew[$\bot$] is not a theorem, Bew[Bew[$\bot$]] is not a theorem,....

The foregoing argument that if PA is 1-consistent, then Bew[$\bot$] is not a theorem can be formalized in PA; it is thus provable in PA that if PA is 1-consistent, then the inconsistency of arithmetic is not provable. As (suitable arithmetizations of) the assertions (a) that if PA is ω-consistent then PA is 1-consistent, (b) that if PA is consistent then the consistency of arithmetic is not provable, and (c) that if the consistency of arithmetic is undecidable then PA is incomplete can all be proved in PA, the first incompleteness theorem of Gödel can also be proved *in PA*.

PA is 1-consistent. (Indeed, PA is ω-consistent. Indeed, every theorem of PA is true.) So none of $\bot$, Bew[$\bot$], Bew[Bew[$\bot$]],... is a theorem of PA; by Theorem 2 it follows that none of $\bot$, $\Box\bot$, $\Box\Box\bot$,... is a theorem of GL.

Löb's theorem states that for every sentence S, if PA$\vdash$Bew[S]$\to S$, then PA$\vdash S$. *Formalized* Löb's theorem states that for every sentence S, PA$\vdash$Bew($\ulcorner$(Bew($\ulcorner S\urcorner$)$\to S$)$\urcorner$)$\to$Bew($\ulcorner S\urcorner$), i.e., for every sentence S, the conditional assertion that S is a theorem of PA if S is deducible from the assertion that S is provable in PA is provable in PA. Since GL$\vdash\Box(\Box p\to p)\to\Box p$, by Theorem 2, for every realization $*$, PA$\vdash(\Box(\Box p\to p)\to\Box p)^*$. Since every sentence S is $^*p$ for some realization $*$, formalized Löb's theorem does indeed hold.

A consequence is a "self–strengthening" of Löb's theorem: If PA$\vdash$Bew($\ulcorner R\urcorner$) $\wedge$ Bew($\ulcorner S\urcorner$)$\to S$, then PA$\vdash$Bew($\ulcorner R\urcorner$)$\to S$. Thus if a statement is deducible from the hypotheses that it and another statement are provable, then the statement is deducible from the sole hypothesis that that other statement is provable: For suppose

PA$\vdash$Bew($\ulcorner R\urcorner$) $\wedge$ Bew($\ulcorner S\urcorner$)$\to S$. By the propositional calculus,
PA$\vdash$Bew($\ulcorner R\urcorner$)$\to$(Bew($\ulcorner S\urcorner$)$\to S$), whence by (i) and (ii) of Chapter 2,
PA$\vdash$Bew($\ulcorner$Bew($\ulcorner R\urcorner$)$\urcorner$)$\to$Bew($\ulcorner$Bew($\ulcorner S\urcorner$)$\to S\urcorner$). By (iii) of Chapter 2,
PA$\vdash$Bew($\ulcorner R\urcorner$)$\to$Bew($\ulcorner$Bew($\ulcorner R\urcorner$)$\urcorner$). By formalized Löb's theorem,
PA$\vdash$Bew($\ulcorner$Bew($\ulcorner S\urcorner$)$\to S\urcorner$)$\to$Bew($\ulcorner S\urcorner$). Thus
PA$\vdash$Bew($\ulcorner R\urcorner$)$\to$Bew($\ulcorner S\urcorner$), and by the supposition,
PA$\vdash$Bew($\ulcorner R\urcorner$)$\to S$.

Can we prove (in PA) that if arithmetic is consistent, then it is

1-consistent? If we let 1Con be a suitable arithmetization of the assertion that arithmetic is 1-consistent, we are asking whether PA$\vdash\neg$Bew[$\bot$]$\to$1Con. Four paragraphs back we saw that PA$\vdash$1Con$\to\neg$Bew[Bew[$\bot$]]. The answer to our question is thus "No, on pain of 1-inconsistency". For if we can prove PA$\vdash\neg$Bew[$\bot$]$\to$1Con, then PA$\vdash\neg$Bew[$\bot$]$\to\neg$Bew[Bew[$\bot$], and so PA$\vdash$Bew[Bew[$\bot$]]$\to$Bew[$\bot$], whence by Löb's theorem, PA$\vdash$Bew[$\bot$], and PA is 1-inconsistent.

A similar argument shows that PA$\nvdash\neg$Bew[Bew[$\bot$]]$\to$1Con. For PA$\vdash$1Con$\to\neg$Bew[Bew[Bew[$\bot$]]], and thus we should otherwise have PA$\vdash\neg$Bew[Bew[$\bot$]]$\to\neg$Bew[Bew[Bew[$\bot$]]], PA$\vdash$Bew[Bew[Bew[$\bot$]]]$\to$Bew[Bew[$\bot$]], and then by Löb's theorem again, PA$\vdash$Bew[Bew[$\bot$]], and PA would again be 1-consistent.[5]

If S is a sentence of the language of PA, then the sentence Bew[S]$\to S$ is called *the reflection principle for S*, or *reflection for S*. Löb's theorem thus asserts that for all sentences S, S is provable if reflection for S is provable. No sentence consistent with PA implies all reflection principles: If PA$\vdash S\to$(Bew[R]$\to R$) for all sentences R, then PA$\vdash S\to$(Bew[$\neg S$]$\to\neg S$), whence by the propositional calculus, PA$\vdash$(Bew[$\neg S$]$\to\neg S$), and by Löb's theorem, PA$\vdash\neg S$, that is, S is not consistent with PA.

$\neg$Bew[$\bot$] is, of course, equivalent to the reflection principle Bew[$\bot$]$\to\bot$. And because PA$\vdash$Bew[$\bot$]$\to$Bew[Bew[$\bot$]], $\neg$Bew[Bew[$\bot$]] is equivalent to the conjunction of the reflection principles Bew[Bew[$\bot$]]$\to$Bew[$\bot$] and Bew[$\bot$]$\to\bot$. But there is no single reflection principle that implies $\neg$Bew[Bew[$\bot$]]. To see this, we appeal to the fact that GL$\vdash\Box((\Box p\to p)\to\neg\Box\Box\bot)\to\Box\Box\bot$. A direct proof of this result is not particularly difficult, and the reader may wish to try to prove it now; however, the semantic techniques to be developed in subsequent chapters yield a proof that is both instructive and satisfying. A proof is given in Chapter 7.

Thus if PA$\vdash$(Bew[S]$\to S$)$\to\neg$Bew[$\neg$Bew[$\bot$]], then where $p^* = S$, $\Box((\Box p\to p)\to\neg\Box\Box\bot)^*$ is true; it follows that $\Box\Box\bot^*$ is true, and thus Bew[$\bot$] is provable, and PA is 1-inconsistent.

According to Theorem 24(a) of Chapter 1, GL$\vdash\Box(p\leftrightarrow\neg\Box p)\to\Box(p\leftrightarrow\neg\Box\bot)$. From Theorem 2 it follows that for every sentence S of the language of arithmetic, it is provable that if S is equivalent to the assertion that S is unprovable, then S is equivalent to the assertion that arithmetic is consistent. Since GL$\vdash\Box(p\leftrightarrow\neg\Box\bot)\to(\Box p\leftrightarrow\Box\neg\Box\bot)$ (normality) and GL$\vdash\Box\neg\Box\bot\leftrightarrow\Box\bot$ by Theorem

21 of Chapter 1, $\mathrm{GL}\vdash\Box(p\leftrightarrow\neg\Box\bot)\rightarrow(\Box p\leftrightarrow\Box\bot)$. Thus, for every S, it is provable that if S is equivalent to the assertion that S is unprovable, then S is provable iff arithmetic is inconsistent.

According to Theorem 24(b) of Chapter 1, $\mathrm{GL}\vdash\Box(p\leftrightarrow\Box p)\rightarrow\Box(p\leftrightarrow\top)$. For every sentence S, therefore, it is provable that if S is equivalent to the assertion that S is provable, then S is equivalent to anything that is provable. And since $\mathrm{GL}\vdash\Box(p\leftrightarrow\Box p)\rightarrow\Box p$, if S is equivalent to the assertion that S is provable, then S is provable. In like manner, Theorem 24(c) shows that it is provable that if S is equivalent to the assertion that S is disprovable, then S is equivalent to the assertion that arithmetic is inconsistent; 24(d) shows that it is provable that if S is equivalent to the assertion that S is consistent with arithmetic, then S is equivalent to anything that is disprovable.

A conjecture arises. Every occurrence of p in each of $\neg\Box p$, $\Box p$, $\Box\neg p$, and $\neg\Box\neg p$ lies in the scope of some occurrence of $\Box$. Let us call a sentence *modalized in p* if every occurrence of p in that sentence lies in the scope of some occurrence of $\Box$.

Is it the case that for every other sentence A modalized in p and containing no sentence letter other than p, there is a letterless sentence H such that $\mathrm{GL}\vdash\Box(p\leftrightarrow A)\rightarrow\Box(p\leftrightarrow H)$? By Theorem 24 of Chapter 1, if $A=\neg\Box p$, $\Box p$, $\Box\neg p$, or $\neg\Box\neg p$, then we may take $H=\neg\Box\bot$, $\top$, $\Box\bot$, or $\bot$, respectively. And for a harder case, if $A=\Box(\neg p\rightarrow\Box\bot)\rightarrow\Box(p\rightarrow\Box\bot)$, then we may take $H=\Box\Box\Box\bot\rightarrow\Box\Box\bot$. (Thus if S is equivalent to the assertion that the inconsistency of arithmetic is deducible from S if deducible from its negation, then S is equivalent to the assertion that if it is provable that the inconsistency of arithmetic is provable, then the inconsistency is provable.) In Chapter 8 we shall show that the answer is *yes* (the Bernardi–Smorynski theorem). Indeed, the theorem holds in general for modal sentences A containing sentence letters other than p: for every sentence A that is modalized in p, there is a sentence H containing only sentence letters found in A other than p, such that $\mathrm{GL}\vdash\Box(p\leftrightarrow A)\rightarrow\Box(p\leftrightarrow H)$ (the fixed point theorem of de Jongh and Sambin). We shall give three different proofs of this beautiful theorem.

One fact about GL and PA might appear to have been overlooked, or at any rate insufficiently attended to, in the foregoing discussion, namely, that every theorem of PA is *true* (in the standard model N). And because every theorem of PA is true, for every sentence S of the language of arithmetic, if $\mathrm{Bew}[S]$ is true, then S is a theorem, and S is thus true. Thus for every realization $*$ and every modal sentence A, $(\Box A \rightarrow A)^*$ is true.

And, of course, if A is a theorem of G, then A^* is a theorem of PA, and therefore A^* is true.

We now introduce a system of propositional modal logic that we shall call GLS ('*S*' for Solovay). The axioms of GLS are all theorems of GL and all sentences $\Box A \rightarrow A$; its sole rule of inference is modus ponens. The following theorem is then evident:

Theorem 3. *If* GLS$\vdash A$, *then for every realization* $*$, A^* *is true.*

We call a modal sentence A *always true* if for every realization $*$, A^* is true.

The second completeness theorem of Solovay, also proved in Chapter 9, is that the converse of Theorem 3 is true. Thus the theorems of GLS are precisely the modal sentences that are always true.

In Chapter 5 and again in Chapter 10 we prove that there is a decision procedure for theoremhood in GL. (We also prove, in Chapter 9, that there is a decision procedure for theoremhood in GLS.) GLS is thus a system of propositional modal logic with a recursive set of axioms.

The axiomatization of GLS given above may be found somewhat opaque, invoking as it does the notion of a *theorem* of GL. There is a more perspicuous axiomatization[6]: Let GLS′ be the system whose sole rule is modus ponens and whose axioms are all necessitations of axioms of GL [i.e., all sentences $\Box B$, where B is either a tautology, a distribution axiom, or a sentence $\Box(\Box A \rightarrow A) \rightarrow \Box A$] and all sentences $\Box A \rightarrow \Box\Box A$ and $\Box A \rightarrow A$.

Theorem 4. *For any modal sentence* B, GLS$\vdash B$ *iff* GLS′$\vdash B$.

Proof. Since all axioms of GLS′ are theorems of GLS, the right–left direction is clear. To show the converse, it suffices to show, by induction on proofs *in GL*, that if B is a theorem of GL, then GLS′$\vdash \Box B$. If B is an axiom of GL, then certainly GLS′$\vdash \Box B$. Suppose that B is inferred from $A \rightarrow B$ and A by modus ponens. By the induction hypothesis, GLS′$\vdash \Box(A \rightarrow B)$ and GLS′$\vdash \Box A$. We now observe that all axioms of GL are theorems of GLS′, for if C is an axiom of GL, then GLS′$\vdash \Box C$ and GLS′$\vdash \Box C \rightarrow C$, whence

GLS′ $\vdash C$. Thus GLS′ $\vdash \Box(A \to B) \to (\Box A \to \Box B)$, and by two applications of modus ponens, GLS′ $\vdash \Box B$. Finally suppose that B is inferred from A by necessitation. Then $B = \Box A$ and by the induction hypothesis, GLS′ $\vdash \Box A$. Then also GLS′ $\vdash \Box B$; i.e., GLS′ $\vdash \Box\Box A$, since GLS′ $\vdash \Box A \to \Box\Box A$. $\dashv$

GLS is not a normal system of modal logic. Although the theorems of GLS are closed under modus ponens and substitution, they are not closed under necessitation. For example, $\neg\Box\bot$, i.e., $\Box\bot \to \bot$, is an axiom and hence a theorem of GLS, but $\Box\neg\Box\bot$ is not a theorem; otherwise by Theorem 3, $\Box\neg\Box\bot^*$ is true, and the consistency of arithmetic is provable, which is not the case. The theorems of GLS are closed under "possibilification," unlike those of GL. (GL $\vdash \top$; GL $\nvdash \Diamond\top$.) For if GLS $\vdash A$, then since GLS $\vdash \Box\neg A \to \neg A$ and GLS $\vdash (\Box\neg A \to \neg A) \to (A \to \neg\Box\neg A)$, GLS $\vdash \neg\Box\neg A$, i.e., GLS $\vdash \Diamond A$. Thus $\top, \Diamond\top, \Diamond\Diamond\top, \ldots$ are all theorems of GLS.

If a correct-modal-principle-when-$\Box$-means-"provable" is an always true modal sentence, then all theorems of GLS are indeed correct-modal-principles-when-$\Box$-means-"provable". Conversely, too, as we shall see.

We conclude with some observations on the way GL and GLS shed light on the first incompleteness theorem.

One quite usual way to prove the first incompleteness theorem for PA involves applying the diagonal lemma to the formula $\neg\mathrm{Bew}(y)$ to obtain a sentence G such that

$$(*) \quad \mathrm{PA} \vdash G \leftrightarrow \neg\mathrm{Bew}[G]$$

One then argues that if PA $\vdash G$, then on the one hand, by condition (i) of Chapter 2, PA $\vdash \mathrm{Bew}[G]$, and on the other, by $(*)$, PA $\vdash \neg\mathrm{Bew}[G]$; therefore if PA $\vdash G$, then PA $\vdash \bot$; and thus if P is consistent, then PA $\nvdash G$. And if PA $\vdash \neg G$, then by condition (i), PA $\vdash \mathrm{Bew}[\neg G]$ and by $(*)$ PA $\vdash \mathrm{Bew}[G]$. But then, since GL $\vdash \Box p \wedge \Box\neg p \to \Box\bot$, PA $\vdash \mathrm{Bew}[\bot]$. Thus if PA $\nvdash \mathrm{Bew}[\bot]$, as is certainly the case, then P is consistent, and G is undecidable: PA $\nvdash G$ and PA $\nvdash \neg G$.

Let us note that $G \leftrightarrow \neg\mathrm{Bew}[G]$ truth-functionally implies $(\mathrm{Bew}[G] \to G) \leftrightarrow G$; therefore, if PA is consistent, then PA does not imply reflection for G. Löb's theorem or no, not every reflection principle is provable.

We have noticed that $\mathrm{GL}\vdash\neg\Box\Box\bot\to(\neg\Box\neg\Box\bot\wedge\neg\Box\neg\neg\Box\bot)$ and $\mathrm{GL}\vdash\Box(p\leftrightarrow\neg\Box p)\to\Box(p\leftrightarrow\neg\Box\bot)$. Thus by normality, $\mathrm{GL}\vdash\Box(p\leftrightarrow\neg\Box p)\wedge\neg\Box\Box\bot\to\neg\Box p\wedge\neg\Box\neg p$. Translating as usual, we see that if, like G, S is equivalent to its own unprovability and inconsistency is unprovable, then S is undecidable. Indeed, S is equivalent to consistency and hence to G. But by Löb's theorem, we cannot hope to prove the undecidability of any such S merely from the assumption that arithmetic is consistent. For then $\mathrm{PA}\vdash S\leftrightarrow\neg\mathrm{Bew}[\bot]$, and thus if $\mathrm{PA}\vdash\neg\mathrm{Bew}[\bot]\to\neg\mathrm{Bew}[S]\wedge\neg\mathrm{Bew}[\neg S]$, then $\mathrm{PA}\vdash\neg\mathrm{Bew}[\bot]\to\neg\mathrm{Bew}[\mathrm{Bew}[\bot]]$, whence by contraposition and Löb, $\mathrm{PA}\vdash\mathrm{Bew}[\bot]$, which is not the case.

We have just seen that there is no sentence equivalent to its own consistency whose undecidability follows (merely) from consistency. We might wonder whether there exists some other sort of sentence whose undecidability does so follow. Now there is a sentence whose undecidability follows from consistency iff $\Box(\Diamond\top\to\neg\Box p\wedge\neg\Box\neg p)$ is "sometimes true", i.e., iff $\neg\Box(\Diamond\top\to\neg\Box p\wedge\neg\Box\neg p)$ is not always true. Once we prove Solovay's result that the theorems of GLS are precisely the always true sentences, it will follow there is a sentence whose undecidability follows from consistency iff $\neg\Box(\Diamond\top\to\neg\Box p\wedge\neg\Box\neg p)$ is not a theorem of GLS. But as we shall then be able to see, it is not a theorem of GLS and there is a sentence of the desired sort (as Rosser was the first to show).

Exercise. Show that for every formula $Q(z)$, there exists a formula $S(z)$ such that for all natural numbers n, $\mathrm{PA}\vdash S(\mathbf{n})\leftrightarrow Q(\ulcorner S(\mathbf{n})\urcorner)$.

Answer. Let $\mathrm{Su}(w,x,y)$ be a Σ pterm for the 2-place function whose value at a,b is the result of substituting the numeral $\mathbf{b}$ for the free variable in the formula with Gödel number a. Let $P(y,z)$ be the formula $Q(\mathrm{su}(y,z))$. By the generalized diagonal lemma, for some formula $S(z)$, $\vdash S(z)\leftrightarrow P(\ulcorner S(z)\urcorner,z)$, $\leftrightarrow Q(\mathrm{su}(\ulcorner S(z)\urcorner,z))$. Then for any natural number n, $\vdash S(\mathbf{n})\leftrightarrow Q(\mathrm{su}(\ulcorner S(z)\urcorner,\mathbf{n}))$. But $\vdash\mathrm{su}(\ulcorner S(z)\urcorner,\mathbf{n})=\ulcorner S(\mathbf{n})\urcorner$. Thus $\vdash S(\mathbf{n})\leftrightarrow Q(\ulcorner S(\mathbf{n})\urcorner)$.

4

Semantics for GL and other modal logics

The semantical treatment of modal logic that we now present is due to Kripke and was inspired by a well-known fantasy often ascribed to Leibniz, according to which we inhabit a place called *the actual world*, which is one of a number of *possible worlds*. (It is a further part of the fantasy, which we can ignore, that because of certain of its excellences God selected the possible world that we inhabit to be the one that he would make actual. Lucky us.) Each of our statements is true or false in – we shall say *at* – various possible worlds. A statement is true at a world if it correctly describes that world and false if it does not. We sometimes call a particular statement true or false, *tout court*, but when we do, we are to be understood as speaking about the actual world and saying that the statement is true or false *at it*. Some of the statements we make are true at all possible worlds, including of course the actual world; these are the so-called *necessary* statements. A statement to the effect that another is necessary will thus be true if the other statement is true at all possible worlds. It follows that if a statement is necessary, then it is true. Some statements are true at at least one possible world; these are the *possible* statements. Since what is true at the actual world is true at at least one possible world, whatever is true is possible. A statement is necessary if and only if its negation is not possible, for the negation of a statement will be true at precisely those worlds at which the statement is false. And if a conditional and its antecedent are both necessary, then the consequent of the conditional is necessary too.

There is a question, raised by Kripke, to which this description of Leibniz's system of possible worlds does not supply the answer. We are said to inhabit the actual world. Are the other possible worlds of whose existence we have been apprised absolutely all of the other worlds that there really are, or are they only those that are possible *relative to* the actual world? The description leaves it open whether or not, if we had inhabited some other world than the actual world, there might have been worlds other than those we now acknowledge that were possible *relative to* that other possible world; in brief, our description does not answer the question whether or not exactly the same worlds are possible relative to each possible world as are possible relative to the actual world.

A possible world is called *accessible from* another if it is possible relative to that other. If we do not assume that the worlds accessible from the actual world are precisely the worlds accessible from each world – even though it may appear self-evident that they are – then questions arise about the nature of the accessibility relation. For example, is the relation transitive? If so, then all worlds accessible from worlds that are accessible from the actual world will themselves be worlds that are accessible from the actual world. It follows that if a statement A is necessary, then A will be true at all worlds x accessible from the actual world; and therefore A will be true at every world y that is accessible from some world x accessible from the actual world (for all such worlds y are accessible from the actual world if accessibility is transitive); and therefore the statement that A is necessary will be true at every world x accessible from the actual world; and therefore the statement that A is necessary will itself be necessary. Thus, on the assumption that the accessibility relation is transitive, if a statement A is necessary, then the statement that A is necessary will also be necessary. In like manner other determinations of the character of the accessibility relation can guarantee the correctness of other modal principles. (The system of semantics for GL that we shall give in this chapter will differ from Leibniz's system in that no world will ever be accessible from itself!)

Set-theoretical analogues of these metaphysical notions were defined by Kripke in providing what has become the standard sort of model-theoretical semantics for the most common systems of propositional modal logic.[1]

Definitions, most of them familiar:

R is a relation *on* W if for all w, x, if wRx, then $w, x \in W$.
A relation R on W is *reflexive on* W if for all w in W, wRw.
R is *irreflexive* if for no w, wRw.
R is *antisymmetric* if for all w, x, if wRx and xRw, then $w = x$.
R is *transitive* if for all w, x, y, if wRx and xRy, then wRy.
R is *symmetric* if for all w, x, if wRx, then xRw.
R is *euclidean* if for all w, x, y, if wRx and wRy, then xRy. (Thus also, if wRx and wRy, then yRx.)

R is an *equivalence relation on* W if R is reflexive on W, symmetric, and transitive.

A symmetric relation is transitive if and only if it is euclidean, and a reflexive relation on W that is euclidean is symmetric. Thus a relation is an equivalence relation on W if and only if it is euclidean and reflexive on W.

A *frame* is an ordered pair $\langle W, R\rangle$ consisting of a nonempty set W and a binary relation R on W. $\langle W, R\rangle$ is finite iff W is. The elements of W are called "possible worlds" or sometimes just "worlds". W is called the *domain* of $\langle W, R\rangle$ and R the *accessibility relation.* (It is occasionally useful to read "R" as "sees". Thus a world *sees* those worlds accessible from it.)

A frame $\langle W, R\rangle$ is said to have some property of binary relations, e.g., transitivity, iff R has that property. ($\langle W, R\rangle$ is called reflexive if R is reflexive on W.)

A *valuation*[2] V on a set W is a relation between members of W and sentence letters, i.e., a set of ordered pairs of members of W and sentence letters. (It is sometimes convenient to read "V" as "verifies".)

A *model* is a triple $\langle W, R, V\rangle$, where $\langle W, R\rangle$ is a frame and V is a valuation on W. A model $\langle W, R, V\rangle$ is said to be *based on* the frame $\langle W, R\rangle$.

A model is finite, reflexive, transitive, etc., iff the frame on which it is based is finite, reflexive, transitive, etc.

For each modal sentence A, each model $M, = \langle W, R, V\rangle$, and each world w in W, we define the relation

$$M, w \vDash A$$

as follows:

if $A = p$ (a sentence letter), then $M, w \vDash A$ iff wVp;
if $A = \bot$, then not: $M, w \vDash A$;
if $A = (B \to C)$, then $M, w \vDash A$ iff either $\neg M, w \vDash B$ or $M, w \vDash C$; and
if $A = \Box B$, then $M, w \vDash A$ iff for all x such that wRx, $M, x \vDash B$.

Some evident consequences of this definition: if $A = \neg B$, then $M, w \vDash A$ iff it is not the case that $M, w \vDash B$; if $A = (B \wedge C)$, then $M, w \vDash$ A iff $M, w \vDash B$ and $M, w \vDash C$; if $A = (B \vee C)$, then $M, w \vDash A$ iff $M, w \vDash B$ or $M, w \vDash C$, etc. Moreover, if $A = \Diamond B$, then $M, w \vDash A$ iff for some x such that wRx, $M, x \vDash B$.

It is worth mentioning that $M, w \models \boxdot A$ iff for all x such that either wRx or $w = x$, $M, x \models A$.

A sentence A is said to be *true* at a world w *in* a model M iff $M, w \models A$. A sentence A is said to be *valid in a model M*, $= \langle W, R, V \rangle$, iff for all w in W, A is true at w in M. And A is said to be *valid in a frame* $\langle W, R \rangle$ iff A is valid in all models based on $\langle W, R \rangle$.

Similarly, a sentence is *satisfiable in a model M*, $= \langle W, R, V \rangle$, iff for some w in W, A is true at w in M. And A is said to be *satisfiable in a frame* $\langle W, R \rangle$ iff A is satisfiable in some model based on $\langle W, R \rangle$.

Important notational conventions. Unless there is some clear indication to the contrary, when 'M' is used to denote a model, it will denote the model also denoted: $\langle W, R, V \rangle$. Moreover, where context makes it clear which model is in question, we shall feel free to write, e.g., '$w \models A$', instead of '$M, w \models A$' or '$\langle W, R, P \rangle, w \models A$'. When we do so, '$w$' is of course understood to denote a member of the set W of worlds of the model M in question.

Suppose that M is a model and $w \in W$. Then every tautology is true at w. And if A and $(A \to B)$ are true at w, so is B. Moreover, every distribution axiom $\Box(A \to B) \to (\Box A \to \Box B)$ is true at w as well: for suppose that $w \models \Box(A \to B)$ and $w \models \Box A$. Then if wRx, both $x \models (A \to B)$ and $x \models A$, whence $x \models B$. Thus if wRx, $x \models B$; $w \models \Box B$. So if $w \models \Box(A \to B)$ and $w \models \Box A$, then $w \models \Box B$; it follows that $w \models \Box(A \to B) \to (\Box A \to \Box B)$.

Thus all tautologies and all distribution axioms are true at every world in every model and the set of sentences true at a world in a model is closed under modus ponens.

Furthermore, if A is valid in M, so is $\Box A$: for assume A valid in M, i.e., true at every world in M. Let w be an arbitrary member of W. Then for all x such that wRx, $x \models A$; therefore, $w \models \Box A$. Since w was arbitrary, $\Box A$ is valid in M.

Thus all tautologies and all distribution axioms are valid in every model and the set of sentences valid in a model is closed under both modus ponens and necessitation.

Thus all theorems of K are valid in all models and hence in all frames.

It is not in general true that if a sentence is valid in a model, then every substitution instance is valid in that model: let $\langle W, R, V \rangle$ be a model in which wVp and not: wVq for every w in W. Then p is valid in $\langle W, R, V \rangle$, but q, which is a substitution instance of p, is not. What *is* true is that if a sentence is valid in a frame, then every substitution instance of it is also true in that frame.

Theorem 1. *Suppose F is valid in the frame $\langle W, R \rangle$. Then every substitution instance $F_p(A)$ of F is also valid in $\langle W, R \rangle$.*

Proof. Let V be an arbitrary valuation on W. Let $M = \langle W, R, V \rangle$. Define the valuation V^* on W by: wV^*p iff $M, w \models A$, and wV^*q iff wVq for every sentence letter q other than p. Let $M^* = \langle W, R, V^* \rangle$. It follows by an easy induction on the complexity of subsentences G of F that $M^*, w \models G$ iff $M, w \models G_p(A)$. So $M^*, w \models F$ iff $M, w \models F_p(A)$. Since F is valid in $\langle W, R \rangle$, $M^*, w \models F$. Thus $M, w \models F_p(A)$. Since w and V were arbitrary, $F_p(A)$ is valid in $\langle W, R \rangle$. $\dashv$

Let R be a binary relation on a set W. For each natural number i, define R^i as follows: R^0 is the identity relation on W; $R^{i+1} = \{\langle w, y \rangle : \exists x(wR^ix \wedge xRy)\}$. Thus $R^1 = R$ and wR^ny iff $\exists x_0 \cdots \exists x_n(w = x_0R \ldots Rx_n = y)$.

Let A be a modal sentence. Define $\Box^i A$ as follows: $\Box^0 A = A$; $\Box^{i+1} A = \Box \Box^i A$. Define $\Diamond^i A$ similarly.

Theorem 2. *$w \models \Box^i A$ iff for all y, if wR^iy, $y \models A$; $w \models \Diamond^i A$ iff for some y, wR^iy and $y \models A$.*

Proof. Induction on i. The basis step is trivial. As for the induction step, $w \models \Diamond^{i+1} A$ iff $w \models \Diamond \Diamond^i A$; iff for some x, wRx and $x \models \Diamond^i A$; iff by the induction hypothesis, for some x, wRx and for some y, xR^iy and $y \models A$; iff for some y, $wR^{i+1}y$ and $y \models A$. The result for $\Box$ holds by de Morgan. $\dashv$

Here is a theorem about what the truth-value of a sentence at a world depends upon. Let A be a modal sentence, M a model, and $w \in W$.

Define $d(A)$ as follows: $d(p) = d(\bot) = 0$; $d(A \to B) = \max(d(A), d(B))$; and $d(\Box A) = d(A) + 1$. Thus $d(A)$ is the maximum number of nested occurrences of $\Box$ in A. $d(A)$ is called the (*modal*) *degree* of A.

Theorem 3 (the "continuity" theorem). *Let M and $N = \langle X, S, U \rangle$ be models, $w \in W$. Let P be a set of sentence letters. Suppose that $d(A) = n$, all sentence letters that occur in A are in P, $X \supseteq \{x : \exists i \leqslant n\ wR^ix\}$, $S = \{\langle x, y \rangle : x, y \in X \wedge xRy\}$,* *and xUp iff xVp for all $x \in X$ and all sentence letters in P. Then $M, w \models A$ iff $N, w \models A$.*

Proof. We show that for all subsentences B of A, if for some i, $wR^i x$ and $d(B) + i \leqslant n$ (so that $i \leqslant n$ and $x \in X$), then $M, x \models B$ iff $N, x \models B$. Since $wR^0 w$ and $d(A) = n$, the theorem follows.

The cases in which $B = \bot$ and B is a sentence letter are trivial. If $B = (C \to D)$, then $d(C)$, $d(D) \leqslant d(B)$, and the result holds for B if it holds for C and D.

Suppose $B = \Box C$, $wR^i x$, and $d(B) + i \leqslant n$. Then $x \in X$ and $d(B) = d(C) + 1$. If xRy, then $wR^{i+1}y$, $d(C) + i + 1 \leqslant n$, $y \in X$, and so xSy, and by the induction hypothesis, $M, y \models C$ iff $N, y \models C$; since $S \subseteq R$, xRy iff xSy. But then $M, x \models B$ iff for all y such that xRy, $M, y \models C$; iff for all y such that xSy, $M, y \models C$; iff, by the i.h., for all y such that xSy, $N, y \models C$; iff $N, x \models B$. $\dashv$

Theorem 4 (the generated submodel theorem). *Let M be a model, $w \in W$, $X = \{x: \exists i\, wR^i x\}$, $S = \{\langle x, y\rangle: x, y \in X \wedge xRy\}$, and xUp iff xVp for all $x \in X$ and all sentence letters p. Let $N = \langle X, S, U\rangle$. Then $M, w \models A$ if $N, w \models A$. (N is called the submodel of M generated from w.)*

Proof. Let P be the set of all sentence letters, and $n = d(A)$. Then $X \supseteq \{x: \exists i \leqslant n\, wR^i x\}$, and the generated submodel theorem follows from the continuity theorem. $\dashv$

The following corollary is a useful immediate consequence of the continuity theorem.

Corollary. *Let A be a sentence. Let M and $N, = \langle W, R, U\rangle$ be models, and wVp iff wUp for all w in W and all p contained in A. Then $M, w \models A$ iff $N, w \models A$.*

We now want to investigate the conditions under which each of the modal sentences $\Box p \to p$, $\Box p \to \Box\Box p$, $p \to \Box\Diamond p$, $\Diamond p \to \Box\Diamond p$, and $\Box(\Box p \to p) \to \Box p$ is valid in a frame $\langle W, R\rangle$.

Theorem 5. *$\Box p \to p$ is valid in $\langle W, R\rangle$ iff R is reflexive on W.*

Proof. Suppose $\Box p \to p$ is valid in $\langle W, R\rangle$. Let w be an arbitrary member of W. We want to show that wRw.

Let V be a valuation on W such that for all x in W, xVp iff wRx.

If wRx, then xVp and $M, x \vDash p$; thus $M, w \vDash \Box p$. Since $M, w \vDash \Box p \to p$, $M, w \vDash p$, wVp, and wRw.

Conversely, suppose R is reflexive on W. Let V be a valuation on W, and suppose $w \in W$. Then if $M, w \vDash \Box p$, for all x such that wRx, $M, x \vDash p$; since wRw by reflexivity, $M, w \vDash p$. Thus if $M, w \vDash \Box p$, then $M, w \vDash p$; so $M, w \vDash \Box p \to p$. ⊣

Theorem 6. *$\Box p \to \Box \Box p$ is valid in $\langle W, R \rangle$ iff R is transitive.*

Proof. Suppose $\Box p \to \Box \Box p$ is valid in $\langle W, R \rangle$, wRx and xRy. Let V be a valuation on W such that for all z in W, zVp iff wRz. Then $w \vDash \Box p$, for if wRz, zVp. So $w \vDash \Box \Box p$, whence $x \vDash \Box p$, $y \vDash p$, and wRy. Conversely, suppose R is transitive. Let V be an arbitrary valuation. Suppose $w \vDash \Box p$ and wRx. If xRy, then by transitivity, wRy and $y \vDash p$. Thus $x \vDash \Box p$. So $w \vDash \Box \Box p$. ⊣

Theorem 7. *$p \to \Box \Diamond p$ is valid in $\langle W, R \rangle$ iff R is symmetric.*

Hint for proof. Suppose wRx. Let V be such that zVp iff $z = w$. ⊣

Theorem 8. *$\Diamond p \to \Box \Diamond p$ is valid in $\langle W, R \rangle$ iff R is euclidean.*

Hint for proof. Suppose wRy, wRx. Let V be such that zVp iff $z = y$. ⊣

Theorem 9 (six soundness theorems)

(a) *if* $\mathrm{K} \vdash A$, *then A is valid in all frames.*
(b) *if* $\mathrm{K4} \vdash A$, *then A is valid in all transitive frames.*
(c) *if* $\mathrm{T} \vdash A$, *then A is valid in all reflexive frames.*
(d) *if* $\mathrm{S4} \vdash A$, *then A is valid in all reflexive and transitive frames.*
(e) *if* $\mathrm{B} \vdash A$, *then A is valid in all reflexive and symmetric frames.*
(f) *if* $\mathrm{S5} \vdash A$, *then A is valid in all reflexive and euclidean frames.*

Proof of (d). Suppose that $\mathrm{S4} \vdash A$ and $\langle W, R \rangle$ is reflexive and transitive. We must show A valid in $\langle W, R \rangle$. But $\Box p \to p$ and $\Box p \to \Box \Box p$ are valid in $\langle W, R \rangle$ by Theorems 5 and 6, and therefore every sentence $\Box A \to A$ and $\Box A \to \Box \Box A$ is valid in $\langle W, R \rangle$, for $\Box A \to A$ is a substitution instance of $\Box p \to p$, as is $\Box A \to \Box \Box A$ of $\Box p \to \Box \Box p$. Since all tautologies and all distribution axioms are valid in all models, all axioms of S4 are valid in $\langle W, R\rangle$. And since the sentences valid in $\langle W, R\rangle$ are closed under modus ponens and necessitation, A is also valid in $\langle W, R\rangle$.

The proofs of (a), (b), (c), (e), and (f) are similar. ⊣

What about GL?

A relation R is called *wellfounded* if for every nonempty set X, there is an R-least element of X, that is to say, an element w of X such that xRw for no x in X.

And a relation R is called *converse wellfounded* if for every nonempty set X, there is an R-greatest element of X, an element w of X such that wRx for no x in X.

If R is converse wellfounded, then R is irreflexive, for if wRw, then $\{w\}$ is a nonempty set with no R-greatest element.

And if R is a converse wellfounded relation on W, then to prove that every member of W has a certain property ψ, it suffices to deduce that an arbitrary object w has ψ from the assumption that all x such that wRx have ψ. (This technique of proof is called *induction on the converse of* R.) To see that the technique works, assume that for all w, w has ψ if all x such that wRx have ψ, and let $X = \{w \in W: w$ does not have $\psi\}$. We show that X has no R-greatest element: suppose $w \in X$. Then w does not have ψ, and by our assumption, for some x, wRx and x does not have ψ. $x \in W$ (since R is a relation on W), and so $x \in X$. Thus X indeed has no R-greatest element. Since R is converse wellfounded, X must be empty, and every w in W has ψ.

Theorem 10. *$\Box(\Box p \to p) \to \Box p$ is valid in $\langle W, R\rangle$ iff R is transitive and converse wellfounded.*

Proof. Suppose that $\Box(\Box p \to p) \to \Box p$ is valid in $\langle W, R\rangle$. Then all sentences $\Box(\Box A \to A) \to \Box A$ are also valid in $\langle W, R\rangle$, and as above, all theorems of GL are valid in $\langle W, R\rangle$. By Theorem 18 of Chapter 1, $\Box p \to \Box\Box p$ is valid in $\langle W, R\rangle$, and so by Theorem 6, $\langle W, R\rangle$ is transitive.

And R is converse wellfounded: for suppose that there is a nonempty set X with no R-greatest element. Let $w \in X$, and let V be a valuation on W such that for every $a \in W$, aVp iff $a \notin X$. We shall show that $w \vDash \Box(\Box p \to p)$ and $w \nvDash \Box p$, contradicting the validity in $\langle W, R\rangle$ of $\Box(\Box p \to p) \to \Box p$.

Suppose wRx, whence $x \in W$. Assume $x \nvDash p$. Then not: xVp, $x \in X$, and therefore for some $y \in X$, xRy, $y \in W$, not: yVp, $y \nvDash p$, and therefore $x \nvDash \Box p$. Thus $x \vDash \Box p \rightarrow p$ and $w \vDash \Box(\Box p \rightarrow p)$.

And since $w \in X$, for some $x \in X$, wRx, and $x \in W$. Thus not: xVp, $x \nvDash p$, and so $w \nvDash \Box p$.

Conversely, suppose that $\langle W, R \rangle$ is transitive and converse wellfounded and that $\langle W, R, V \rangle$, $w \nvDash \Box p$. Let $X = \{x \in W\colon wRx \wedge x \nvDash p\}$. Since $w \nvDash \Box p$, for some z, wRz and $z \nvDash p$. Thus $z \in X$, X is nonempty, and by converse wellfoundedness, for some $x \in X$, xRy for no y in X. Since $x \in X$, wRx, and $x \nvDash p$. Suppose xRy. Then $y \notin X$ and since wRy by transitivity, $y \vDash p$. Thus $x \vDash \Box p$, $x \nvDash \Box p \rightarrow p$, and $w \nvDash \Box(\Box p \rightarrow p)$. So $\Box(\Box p \rightarrow p) \rightarrow \Box p$ is valid in $\langle W, R \rangle$. ⊣

We will need an alternative characterization of the finite transitive and converse wellfounded relations.

Theorem 11. *Suppose that F, $= \langle W, R \rangle$ is finite and transitive. Then F is irreflexive if and only if F is converse wellfounded.*

Proof. We have already observed that if F is converse wellfounded, F is irreflexive. Suppose that F is irreflexive. If $x_1, \ldots, x_n$ is a sequence of elements of W such that $x_i R x_{i+1}$ for all $i < n$, then $x_i \neq x_j$ if $i < j$: otherwise $x_i = x_j$, and by transitivity $x_i R x_j$, contra irreflexivity. Now assume that F is not converse wellfounded. Let X be a nonempty subset of W such that $\forall w \in X \exists x \in X\ wRx$. Then it is clear by induction that for each positive n, there is a sequence $x_1, \ldots, x_n$ of elements of X such that $x_i R x_{i+1}$ for all $i < n$. Therefore for each n, there are at least n elements of $X \subseteq W$. Thus W is infinite, contradiction. ⊣

Thus a frame is finite transitive and converse wellfounded if and only if it is finite transitive and irreflexive.

We thus have established the following soundness theorem for GL.

Theorem 12. *If* GL$\vdash A$, *then A is valid in all transitive and converse wellfounded frames, and A is also valid in all finite transitive and irreflexive frames.*

We conclude with two remarks on the non-characterizability of converse wellfounded frames.

Frames $\langle W, R \rangle$ are naturally thought of as models interpreting formal languages that contain a single two-place predicate letter

ρ. A frame is reflexive, transitive, symmetric, or euclidean if and only if the first-order sentence $\forall w w\rho w$, $\forall w \forall x \forall y(w\rho x \wedge x\rho y \rightarrow w\rho z)$, $\forall w \forall x(w\rho x \rightarrow x\rho w)$, or $\forall w \forall x \forall y(w\rho x \wedge w\rho y \rightarrow x\rho y)$, respectively, is true in the frame. For "converse wellfounded" it is otherwise: there is no first-order sentence that is true in $\langle W, R\rangle$ iff $\langle W, R\rangle$ is converse wellfounded.

Proof. Suppose that σ is a counterexample. Let $\alpha_0, \alpha_1, \ldots$ be an infinite sequence of distinct new constants. Then every finite subset of $\{\sigma\} \cup \{\alpha_i \rho \alpha_j: i < j\}$ has a model, and by the compactness theorem, the entire set has a model $\langle W, R, a_0, a_1, \ldots\rangle$. But the binary relation R that interprets ρ is not converse wellfounded (because $a_0 R a_1 R \ldots$), and thus $\langle W, R\rangle$ is not converse wellfounded either, even though σ is true in $\langle W, R, a_0, a_1, \ldots\rangle$ and hence in $\langle W, R\rangle$. $\dashv$

The same argument also shows that there is no first-order sentence that is true in just those frames that are transitive and converse wellfounded.

We know that $\Box(\Box p \rightarrow p) \rightarrow \Box p$ is a modal sentence that is valid in just the transitive converse wellfounded frames[3]; however, no modal sentence is valid in exactly those frames that are converse wellfounded.

Proof. Suppose that A is a counterexample. Let W be the set of natural numbers and R the successor relation on W, i.e., $\{\langle w, x\rangle: w, x \in W \wedge w + 1 = x\}$. Then $\langle W, R\rangle$ is not converse wellfounded, and so for some valuation V on W, some w in W, $\langle W, R, V\rangle, w \nvDash A$. Let $n = d(A)$, and let $X = \{w, w+1, \ldots, w+n\}$, $S = \{\langle x, y\rangle: x, y \in X$ and $xRy\}$, and xUp iff xVp for every p contained in A. By the continuity theorem, $\langle X, S, U\rangle, w \nvDash A$, But $\langle X, S\rangle$ is converse wellfounded, contradiction. $\dashv$

Exercise. True or false: if A is satisfiable in some finite transitive and irreflexive model and contains at most one sentence letter, then A is satisfiable in some finite transitive and irreflexive model in which for all $w_0, w_1, \ldots, w_{d(A)}$ in W, not: $w_0 R w_1 R \ldots R w_{d(A)}$.

5

Completeness and decidability of GL and K, K4, T, B, S4, and S5

We are now going to establish a completeness theorem for each of the seven modal systems we have considered. We call a frame (or a model) *appropriate to K4, T, B, S4, S5, or GL* if and only if it is transitive, reflexive, symmetric and reflexive, transitive and reflexive, euclidean and reflexive, or transitive and converse well founded, respectively of course. *All* frames are *appropriate* to K. In Chapter 11 we shall give a general definition of a frame's being appropriate to a normal system, but as yet we have only defined the notion with respect to seven particular normal systems.

We are going to show that a modal sentence *A* is a theorem of one of our seven systems L if *A* is valid in all finite frames that are appropriate to L – equivalently, if *A* is valid in all finite models appropriate to L.

Thus, e.g., we shall show that if *A* is valid in all finite transitive and reflexive frames, then *A* is a theorem of S4. When we have done so, we shall have established the coextensiveness of the conditions:

validity in all transitive and reflexive frames;
validity in all finite transitive and reflexive frames;
provability in S4.

For, as we saw in Chapter 4, if *A* is a theorem of S4, *A* is valid in all transitive and reflexive frames, and thus certainly valid in all finite transitive and reflexive frames.

Similar comments apply to the other six systems K, K4, T, B, S5, and GL.

Now let L be one of the seven systems.

Suppose that *D* is a modal sentence that is not a theorem of L.

For want of a better term, we shall call a sentence a *formula* if it is either a subsentence of *D* or the negation of a subsentence of *D*. There are only finitely many subsentences of any sentence, therefore only finitely many formulas, and therefore only finitely many sets of formulas.

We shall call a set X of formulas *L-consistent*, or consistent for short, if $\mathrm{L} \nvdash \neg \bigwedge X$. ($\bigwedge X$ is the conjunction of all members of X.) Thus X is consistent if L does not refute the conjunction of members of X.

A set X of formulas is called *maximal* (*L-*) *consistent*, if X is consistent and for each subsentence A of D, either A or $\neg A$ is a member of X. If A is a subsentence of D and X is a maximal consistent set, then $A \in X$ iff $\neg A \notin X$, for if both A and $\neg A$ belong to X, then since certainly $\mathrm{L} \vdash \neg(A \wedge \neg A)$, $\mathrm{L} \vdash \neg \bigwedge X$.

If X is maximal consistent, $A_1, \ldots, A_n \in X$, $\mathrm{L} \vdash A_1 \wedge \cdots \wedge A_n \rightarrow B$, and B is a subsentence of D, then B is also in X; otherwise $\neg B \in X$, $\mathrm{L} \vdash \neg(A_1 \wedge \cdots \wedge A_n \wedge \neg B)$, and then $\mathrm{L} \vdash \neg \bigwedge X$.

If X is consistent, then X is included in some maximal consistent set: By the propositional calculus $\bigwedge X$ is equivalent to some disjunction $E_1 \vee \cdots \vee E_n$, in each disjunct E_i of which each subsentence of D or its negation occurs,[1] and all members of X occur. At least one disjunct E_i must be L-consistent; otherwise $\mathrm{L} \vdash (\neg E_1 \wedge \cdots \wedge \neg E_n)$, and then $\mathrm{L} \vdash \neg(E_1 \vee \cdots \vee E_n)$, whence $\mathrm{L} \vdash \neg \bigwedge X$. The set of conjuncts of E_i will be a maximal consistent set including X.

Since $\mathrm{L} \nvdash D$, $\{\neg D\}$ is consistent, and therefore included in some maximal consistent set y.

Now let $W =$ the set of maximal consistent sets. Since y is maximal consistent, $y \in W$, and W is nonempty.

For each $w \in W$ and each sentence letter p, let wVp iff p occurs in D and $p \in w$.

We shall define an accessibility relation R, which depends on L, so that the following two conditions are both met:

(1) For every subsentence $\Box B$ of D and every $w \in W$, $\Box B \in w$ iff for all x such that wRx, $B \in x$.
(2) $\langle W, R \rangle$ is appropriate to L.

Assuming that an R has been defined meeting conditions (1) and (2), we complete the proof as follows: Let $M = \langle W, R, V \rangle$ (as ever).

Lemma. *For every subsentence A of D and every $w \in W$, $A \in w$ iff $w \vDash A$.*

Proof. If $A = \bot$, then $A \notin w$, as $\mathrm{L} \vdash \neg \bot$, and w is consistent; but $w \nvDash \bot$. If A is a sentence letter p occurring in D, then $p \in w$ iff wVp, iff $w \vDash p$. Suppose that $A = (B \rightarrow C)$ and the lemma holds for B and

C, which are themselves subsentences of D. Then since $\mathrm{L} \vdash \neg A \to B$, $\mathrm{L} \vdash \neg A \to \neg C$, and $\mathrm{L} \vdash B \to (\neg C \to \neg A)$, $A \notin w$ iff $\neg A \in w$; iff $B \in w$ and $\neg C \in w$; iff by maximal consistency, $B \in w$ and $C \notin w$; iff by the induction hypothesis, $w \vDash B$ and $w \nvDash C$; iff $w \nvDash A$. Thus $A \in w$ iff $w \vDash A$ in this case.

Now suppose that $A = \Box B$ and the lemma holds for the subsentence B of D. Then $A \in w$ iff, by condition (1), for every x such that wRx, $B \in x$. But since B is itself a subsentence of D, $B \in x$ iff $x \vDash B$, by the induction hypothesis. Thus $A \in w$ iff for every x such that wRx, $x \vDash B$; iff $w \vDash \Box B$; iff $w \vDash A$. This proves the lemma. $\dashv$

$y \in W$, y is maximal consistent, and $\neg D \in y$. Thus $D \notin y$ and by the lemma, $y \nvDash D$. D is therefore not valid in the finite frame $\langle W, R \rangle$, which by condition (2) is appropriate to L.

We must now show how to define an accessibility relation R meeting (1) and (2) for each of the seven systems.

K. Define: wRx iff for all $\Box B$ in w, $B \in x$. $\langle W, R \rangle$ is appropriate to K (all frames are), and condition (2) holds. Moreover, it is immediate from the definition of R that one half of condition (1) also holds, for if $\Box B \in w$ and wRx, then certainly $B \in x$. To verify the other half, it has to be shown that if $\Box B \notin w$, then for some x, wRx and $B \notin x$.

Let $X = \{\neg B\} \cup \{C : \Box C \in w\}$. Is X K-consistent? If not, then $\mathrm{K} \vdash \neg \bigwedge X$, i.e., $\mathrm{K} \vdash \neg(\neg B \wedge C_1 \wedge \cdots \wedge C_n)$, where $\Box C_1, \ldots, \Box C_n$ are all the necessitations that belong to w. But then $\mathrm{K} \vdash C_1 \wedge \cdots \wedge C_n \to B$, and by normality $\mathrm{K} \vdash \Box C_1 \wedge \cdots \wedge \Box C_n \to \Box B$. Since $\Box C_1, \ldots, \Box C_n$ are all in w and $\Box B$ is a subsentence of D, $\Box B \in w$. Thus if $\Box B \notin w$, X is consistent, and therefore there is a maximal consistent set $x \supseteq X$. $\neg B \in X \subseteq x$, and therefore $B \notin x$. Moreover, if $\Box C$ is in w, then $C \in X \subseteq x$, and thus by the definition of R, wRx.

K4. Define: wRx iff for all $\Box B$ in w, both $\Box B$ and B are in x. R is evidently transitive and therefore $\langle W, R \rangle$ is appropriate to K4. Moreover, evidently if $\Box B \in w$ and wRx, then $B \in x$.

For the converse of (1), let $X = \{\neg B\} \cup \{C : \Box C \in w\} \cup \{\Box C : \Box C \in w\}$. If X is K4-inconsistent, then, where $\Box C_1, \ldots, \Box C_n$ are all the necessitations in w,

$$\mathrm{K4} \vdash \neg(\neg B \wedge C_1 \wedge \cdots \wedge C_n \wedge \Box C_1 \wedge \cdots \wedge \Box C_n),$$

$\mathrm{K4} \vdash C_1 \wedge \cdots \wedge C_n \wedge \Box C_1 \wedge \cdots \wedge \Box C_n \to B$, whence by normality

$K4 \vdash \Box C_1 \wedge \cdots \wedge \Box C_n \wedge \Box\Box C_1 \wedge \cdots \wedge \Box\Box C_n \rightarrow \Box B$. But since
$K4 \vdash \Box C_i \rightarrow \Box\Box C_i$, we have
$K4 \vdash \Box C_1 \wedge \cdots \wedge \Box C_n \rightarrow \Box B$.

And since $\Box C_1, \ldots, \Box C_n$ are all in w, so is $\Box B$. Thus if $\Box B \notin w$, X is consistent, hence included in some maximal consistent set x. Since $\neg B \in X$, $B \notin x$. And if $\Box C \in w$, then $\Box C$, $C \in x$, and wRx.

T. R is the same as for K. We must see that $\langle W, R \rangle$ is appropriate to T, that is, that R is reflexive on W; i.e., that for all $w \in W$, wRw; i.e., that if $\Box B \in w$, $B \in w$. But since $T \vdash \Box B \rightarrow B$, if $\Box B \in w$, $B \in w$.

S4. R is the same as for K4. Again we must see that R is reflexive on W. But since $T \vdash \Box B \rightarrow B$, the argument given for T works.

B. Define: wRx iff both for all $\Box B \in w$, $B \in x$, and for all $\Box B \in x$, $B \in w$. R is clearly symmetric, and since each sentence $\Box B \rightarrow B$ is a theorem of the system B, R is reflexive on W, and $\langle W, R \rangle$ is appropriate to B. Moreover, it is clear that if $\Box B \in w$ and wRx, then $B \in x$.

Now let $X = \{\neg B\} \cup \{C : \Box C \in w\} \cup \{\neg \Box E : \Box E$ is a subsentence of D and $\neg E \in w\}$. If X is B-inconsistent then $B \vdash C_1 \wedge \cdots \wedge C_n \wedge \neg \Box E_1 \wedge \cdots \neg \Box E_m \rightarrow B$, where $\Box C_1, \ldots, \Box C_n$ are all the necessitations that are in w, and $\neg \Box E_1, \ldots, \neg \Box E_m$ are all the sentences $\neg \Box E$ such that $\Box E$ is a subsentence of D and $\neg E \in w$. But then,

$B \vdash \Box C_1 \wedge \cdots \wedge \Box C_n \wedge \Box \neg \Box E_1 \wedge \cdots \wedge \Box \neg \Box E_m \rightarrow \Box B$. And since
$B \vdash \neg E_i \rightarrow \Box \Diamond \neg E_i$,
$B \vdash \neg E_i \rightarrow \Box \neg \Box E_i$, and
$B \vdash \Box C_1 \wedge \cdots \wedge \Box C_n \wedge \neg E_1 \wedge \cdots \wedge \neg E_m \rightarrow \Box B$.

Since all conjuncts of the antecedent are in w, if $\Box B \notin w$, X is consistent, hence included in some maximal consistent set x. But then $B \notin x$, and if $\Box C \in w$, $C \in x$. Moreover, if $\Box E \in x$ but $E \notin w$, then $\neg E \in w$, and $\neg \Box E \in X \subseteq x$, impossible. Thus wRx.

S5. Define: wRx iff both for all $\Box B$, $\Box B \in w$ iff $\Box B \in x$. R is clearly reflexive on W, transitive, and symmetric, and therefore condition

(2) holds. But both halves of condition (1) now require argument.

Suppose $\Box B \in w$. Then if wRx, $\Box B \in x$, and since $\mathrm{S5} \vdash \Box B \rightarrow B$, $B \in x$.

Conversely, suppose $\Box B \notin w$. Let $X = \{\neg B\} \cup \{\Box C : \Box C \in w\} \cup \{\neg \Box E : \neg \Box E \in w\}$. If X is inconsistent, then $\mathrm{S5} \vdash \Box C_1 \wedge \cdots \wedge \Box C_n \wedge \neg \Box E_1 \wedge \cdots \wedge \neg \Box E_m \rightarrow B$, where $\Box C_1, \ldots, \Box C_n$ are all the sentences $\Box C$ in w, and $\neg \Box E_1, \ldots, \neg \Box E_m$ are all the sentences $\neg \Box E$ in w. By normality.

$\mathrm{S5} \vdash \Box \Box C_1 \wedge \cdots \wedge \Box \Box C_n \wedge \Box \neg \Box E_1 \wedge \cdots \wedge \Box \neg \Box E_m \rightarrow \Box B$. Since
$\mathrm{S5} \vdash \Box C \rightarrow \Box \Box C$ and
$\mathrm{S5} \vdash \neg \Box E \rightarrow \Box \neg \Box E$, we have
$\mathrm{S5} \vdash \Box C_1 \wedge \cdots \wedge \Box C_n \wedge \neg \Box E_1 \wedge \cdots \wedge \neg \Box E_m \rightarrow \Box B$,

and therefore $\Box B \in w$. Thus if $\Box B \notin w$, then X is consistent, and there is a maximal consistent $x \supseteq X$ containing $\Box C_1, .., \Box C_n$ and omitting $\Box E_1, \ldots, \Box E_m$. Thus if $\Box C \in w$, $\Box C \in x$; and if $\Box E \in x$, but $\Box E \notin w$, then $\neg \Box E \in w$, and then by the definition of X, $\neg \Box E \in X \subseteq x$, impossible. So wRx.

GL.[2] Define: wRx iff both for all $\Box B$ in w, $\Box B$ and B are in x and for some $\Box E$ in x, $\neg \Box E$ is in w.

R is transitive. Suppose wRx and xRy. Then if $\Box C \in w$, $\Box C \in x$ and $\Box C, C \in y$. Moreover since wRx, for some $\Box E$, $\neg \Box E \in w$ and $\Box E \in x$, and then $\Box E \in y$. So wRx.

And R is irreflexive. If wRw, then for some $\Box E$, $\neg \Box E \in w$ and $\Box E \in w$, which is impossible as w is consistent.

$\langle W, R \rangle$ is finite transitive and irreflexive, and therefore by Theorem 11 of Chapter 4, $\langle W, R \rangle$ is transitive and converse well-founded, i.e., appropriate to GL. Thus condition (2) holds. We now show that condition (1) holds.

If $\Box B \in w$ and wRx, then clearly $B \in x$.

Let $X = \{\neg B, \Box B\} \cup \{C, \Box C : \Box C \in w\}$.

If X is inconsistent, then

$\mathrm{GL} \vdash \neg(\neg B \wedge \Box B \wedge C_1 \wedge \Box C_1 \wedge \cdots \wedge C_n \wedge \Box C_n)$; by the propositional calculus,
$\mathrm{GL} \vdash C_1 \wedge \Box C_1 \wedge \cdots \wedge C_n \wedge \Box C_n \rightarrow (\Box B \rightarrow B)$, whence by normality,
$\mathrm{GL} \vdash \Box C_1 \wedge \Box \Box C_1 \wedge \cdots \wedge \Box C_n \wedge \Box \Box C_n \rightarrow \Box(\Box B \rightarrow B)$; but since
$\mathrm{GL} \vdash \Box(\Box B \rightarrow B) \rightarrow \Box B$ and

$GL \vdash \Box C \to \Box\Box C$, we have
$GL \vdash \Box C_1 \wedge \cdots \wedge \Box C_n \to \Box B$.

Suppose now that $\Box B \notin w$. Then, since $\Box C_1, \ldots, \Box C_n$ are all in w, X is consistent and for some maximal consistent set x, $X \subseteq x$. Since $\neg B \in X$, $\neg B \in x$ and $B \notin x$. If $\Box C$ is in w, then $\Box C$ and C are in $X \subseteq x$. Moreover, since $\Box B \notin w$, $\neg \Box B \in w$, and $\Box B \in X \subseteq x$. Thus wRx, and condition (1) holds.

A familiar sort of consideration shows that the proof of completeness we have just given for each of the seven systems L shows that L is decidable, i.e., that there is an effective method for deciding whether or not an arbitrary modal sentence D is a theorem of L. For let k be the number of subsentences of D. No consistent set contains any subsentence of D and its negation, and there are therefore at most 2^k consistent sets of formulas. Our proof shows that if D is not a theorem of L, then there is a finite model $\langle W, R, V \rangle$ appropriate to L, in which W contains no more than 2^k members, at one of whose worlds D is false, and such that for any sentence letter p, wVp only if p occurs in D. Thus D is a theorem of L if and only if D is valid in all models $\langle \{1, \ldots, n\}, R, V \rangle$, where $n \leqslant 2^k$, R is appropriate to L, and wVp only if p occurs in D. There are only finitely many such models. Since effective procedures exist for finding all such models from D and for deciding whether or not D is valid in any given finite model, L is decidable.

We close with two disparate remarks.

1. A slight strengthening of the completeness theorem for GL is worth stating: A transitive frame $\langle W, R \rangle$ is called a *tree* if for every $w, x, y \in W$, if wRy and xRy, then either wRx or $w = x$ or xRw.

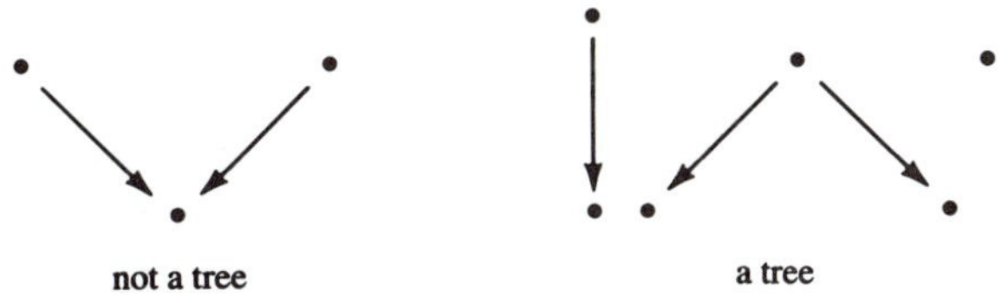

The term "tree" will often be more appropriate to a generated submodel of a tree than to the original model. Finite transitive and irreflexive trees, or generated submodels of them, are in general easier to visualize than arbitrary finite transitive and irreflexive frames. And as the following theorem shows, it turns out that a sentence is a theorem of GL iff it is valid in all finite transitive and irreflexive trees.

Theorem. *A sentence is valid in all finite transitive and irreflexive frames iff it is valid in all finite transitive and irreflexive frames that are trees.*

Proof. Let $\langle W, R, V \rangle$ be a finite transitive and irreflexive model.

Call a function x an R-sequence if for some natural number m, $x: \{0, 1, \ldots, m\} \to W$, and for all $i < m$, $x(i)\ Rx(i+1)$.

Let X be the set of all R-sequences. Say that xSy if x is properly extended by y, i.e., if for some m, n, $x: \{0, 1, \ldots, m\} \to W$, $y: \{0, 1, \ldots, n\} \to W$, and for all $i \leqslant m$, $x(i) = y(i)$.

X is finite if W is.

$\langle X, S \rangle$ is clearly a transitive, irreflexive tree.

For $x \in X$, $x: \{0, 1, \ldots, m\} \to W$, let xUp iff $x(m)Vp$.

Let $N = \langle X, S, U \rangle$.

An obvious induction on the complexity of A shows that if $x \in X$, $x: \{0, 1, \ldots, m\} \to W$, then $N, x \models A$ iff $M, x(m) \models A$. $\dashv$

2. The completeness proof for K4 may be applied to give an alternative proof of Theorem 23 of Chapter 1:

Let M be an arbitrary transitive model, $w \in W$. Then

$$(*)\quad \text{If } w \models \Box q \text{ and } w \models \Box\,(q \leftrightarrow (\Box q \to p)), \quad \text{then } w \models \Box p$$

For if wRx but $x \not\models p$, then $x \models q$, $x \models (q \leftrightarrow (\Box q \to p))$, and thus $x \not\models \Box q$, whence for some y, xRy and $y \not\models q$; but by transitivity wRy, and $y \models q$.

Now if $w \models \Box(q \leftrightarrow (\Box q \to p))$, $w \models \Box(\Box p \to p)$ but $w \not\models \Box p$, then by $(*)$, $w \not\models \Box q$, and for some x, wRx, $x \not\models q$, $x \models (q \leftrightarrow (\Box q \to p))$, $x \models \Box q$, $x \not\models p$, $x \models \Box p \to p$, and $x \not\models \Box p$; but also $x \models \Box(q \leftrightarrow (\Box q \to p))$, contra $(*)$, with x playing the role of w: for if xRy, wRy by transitivity, and $y \models (q \leftrightarrow (\Box q \to p))$.

Thus $\Box(q \leftrightarrow (\Box q \to p)) \to (\Box(\Box p \to p) \to \Box p)$ is valid in M, and by the completeness theorem for K4, it is a theorem of K4.

6

Canonical models

We shall now present a method[1] for constructing modal-logical models. The method enables us to construct from each consistent normal system L of propositional modal logic a model M_L, $= \langle W_L, R_L, V_L \rangle$, called the *canonical model for L*, in which all and only the theorems of L are valid. Although canonical models are of great interest in the study of systems of modal logic other than GL, the canonical model for GL is not particularly useful for the study of GL itself. (Outside this chapter, the notion of a canonical model is used to prove only one theorem in this book, Theorem 3 of Chapter 13.)

We shall begin by defining the canonical model for a consistent normal system L and then prove a completeness theorem for each member of a quite large family of systems that includes K, K4, T, S4, B, and S5 – but not GL, alas.

Let L be a consistent system of normal modal propositional logic. Thus $\mathrm{L} \nvdash \bot$.

A set X of arbitrary modal sentences is called (*L-*) *consistent* iff for no finite subset Y of X, $\mathrm{L} \vdash \neg \bigwedge Y$. If X is consistent, at most one of A and $\neg A$ belongs to X; otherwise, evidently, $\mathrm{L} \vdash \neg(A \wedge \neg A)$, and X is not consistent.

Lemma 1. *If S is consistent, then either $S \cup \{A\}$ is consistent or $S \cup \{\neg A\}$ is consistent.*

Proof. Suppose both inconsistent. Then for some finite sets Y and Z, $Y \subseteq S \cup \{A\}$, $Z \subseteq S \cup \{\neg A\}$, $\mathrm{L} \vdash \neg \bigwedge Y$, and $\mathrm{L} \vdash \neg \bigwedge Z$. Let $U = Y - \{A\}$ and $V = Z - \{\neg A\}$. Then U and V are finite subsets of S, $\mathrm{L} \vdash \neg(\bigwedge U \wedge A)$, and $\mathrm{L} \vdash \neg(\bigwedge V \wedge \neg A)$. Truth-functionally, then $\mathrm{L} \vdash \neg \bigwedge (U \cup V)$. But $U \cup V$ is a finite subset of S, and S is therefore inconsistent. ⊣

A set X is a *maximal* (*L-*) *consistent* set of sentences if it is consistent and for every modal sentence A, either $A \in X$ or $\neg A \in X$. The following lemma is standard.

Lemma 2. *Every consistent set X of sentences is included in some maximal consistent set.*

Proof. Let $A_0, A_1, \ldots$ be an enumeration of all modal sentences. Define a sequence $S_0, S_1, \ldots$ of sets of sentences as follows:

$$S_0 = X$$

$$S_{i+1} = \begin{cases} S_i \cup \{A_i\} \text{ if } S_i \cup \{A_i\} \text{ is consistent} \\ S_i \cup \{\neg A_i\} \text{ otherwise} \end{cases}$$

Then if $i \leqslant j$, $S_i \subseteq S_j$.

Every S_i is consistent: For $X = S_0$ is consistent. And if S_i is consistent, then either $S_i \cup \{A_i\}$ is consistent, in which case $S_{i+1} = S_i \cup \{A_i\}$, or $S_i \cup \{A_i\}$ is inconsistent, in which case $S_{i+1} = S_i \cup \{\neg A_i\}$, which, by Lemma 1, is consistent. Thus in this case too, S_{i+1} is consistent.

Let $S = \bigcup \{S_i : i \in N\}$. Thus each $S_i \subseteq S$; in particular $X = S_0 \subseteq S$.

S is consistent: otherwise for some finite subset Y of S, $\mathrm{L} \vdash \neg \bigwedge Y$. Every A in Y is in some S_j. For each $A \in Y$, let i_A be the least j such that $A \in S_j$, and let $i = \max\{i_A : A \in Y\}$. Then $Y \subseteq S_i$, and S_i is inconsistent, which is not the case.

Moreover, S is maximal consistent: for if $A_i \notin S$, then $A_i \notin S_{i+1}$, $S_i \cup \{A_i\}$ is inconsistent; thus $S_i \cup \{\neg A_i\} = S_{i+1} \subseteq S$, and therefore $\neg A_i \in S$.

Thus $X \subseteq S$, which is maximal consistent. ⊣

Let us note that if S is maximal consistent and $\mathrm{L} \vdash A$, then $A \in S$; otherwise, $\neg A \in S$, and then $\mathrm{L} \vdash \neg \{\neg A\}$, contra the consistency of S.

Moreover if S is maximal consistent, $\mathrm{L} \vdash A_1 \wedge \cdots \wedge A_n \to B$, and $A_1, \ldots, A_n \in S$, then $B \in S$; otherwise $\neg B \in S$, and $\mathrm{L} \vdash \neg (A_1 \wedge \cdots \wedge A_n \wedge \neg B)$, again contra the consistency of S.

We can now define the canonical model M_L for L.

W_L is the set of all maximal (L-) consistent sets.

For every $w, x \in W$, $wR_L x$ iff for every sentence A, if $\Box A \in w$, then $A \in x$. (Equivalently, $wR_L x$ iff for every sentence $B \in x$, $\Diamond B \in w$.)

For every $w \in W$, every sentence letter p, $wV_L p$ iff $p \in w$.

Then $M_L = \langle W_L, R_L, V_L \rangle$.

Lemma 3. *For every sentence A, every w in W_L, $A \in w$ iff $\langle W_L, R_L, V_L \rangle, w \models A$.*

Proof. $\bot \notin w$ and $w \nvDash \bot$. $p \in w$ iff $wV_L p$, iff $w \vDash p$.

Suppose $A = (B \to C)$ and the lemma holds for B and C. Then $\mathrm{L} \vdash \neg(B \to C) \leftrightarrow (B \wedge \neg C)$, and therefore by maximality of w, $\neg(B \to C) \in w$ iff $B \in w$ and $\neg C \in w$. Thus $(B \to C) \in w$ iff $\neg(B \to C) \notin w$ iff either $B \notin w$ or $\neg C \notin w$, iff, by maximality, either $B \notin w$ or $C \in w$, iff, by the i.h., either $w \nvDash B$ or $w \vDash C$, iff $w \vDash B \to C$.

Suppose $A = \Box B$ and the lemma holds for B. If $\Box B \in w$, and wRx, then by the definition of R, $B \in x$, and $x \vDash B$ by the i.h. Thus if $\Box B \in w$, $w \vDash \Box B$. Conversely, if $\Box B \notin w$, then by maximality of w, $\neg \Box B \in w$. Let $X = \{\neg B\} \cup \{D \colon \Box D \in w\}$. X is consistent. Otherwise, for some $\Box D_1, \ldots, \Box D_n$ in w,

$\mathrm{L} \vdash \neg(\neg B \wedge D_1 \wedge \cdots \wedge D_n)$

$\mathrm{L} \vdash D_1 \wedge \cdots \wedge D_r \to B$, whence by normality,

$\mathrm{L} \vdash \Box D_1 \wedge \cdots \wedge \Box D_n \to \Box B$,

and therefore $\Box B \in w, \neg \Box B \in w$, and w is inconsistent, contradiction. Thus for some maximal x, $X \subseteq x$. Since $\{D \colon \Box D \in w\} \subseteq x$, wRx. Since $\neg B \in X \subseteq x$, and x is consistent, $B \notin x$, whence by the induction hypothesis, $x \nvDash B$, and therefore $w \nvDash \Box B$. ⊣

Another fundamental lemma concerning canonical models is the following.

Lemma 4. *If* $\mathrm{L} \vdash A$ *iff* A *is valid in* M_L.

Proof. If $\mathrm{L} \vdash A$, then for every w in $W_L, A \in w$, whence by Lemma 3, $w \vDash A$. If $\mathrm{L} \nvdash A$, then $\{\neg A\}$ is L-consistent (else $\mathrm{L} \vdash \neg \bigwedge \{\neg A\}$, and then $\mathrm{L} \vdash A$), and by Lemma 2, for some maximal consistent w, $\{\neg A\} \subseteq w$. Thus $\neg A \in w$, $A \notin w$, and by Lemma 3, $w \nvDash A$. Thus A is not valid in M_L. ⊣

We have thus re-established the completeness theorem for K: $\mathrm{K} \vdash A$ if A is valid in all models: for if so, then A is valid in M_K, and therefore $\mathrm{K} \vdash A$.

We are now going to use canonical models to prove a general soundness and completeness theorem that has the soundness and completeness theorems for K, K4, T, S4, B, and S5 as special cases.

We recall from Chapter 4 the definition of R^i, R an arbitrary binary relation and i a natural number:

$$mR^i y \text{ iff } \exists z_0 \cdots \exists z_i (x = z_0 R \cdots R z_i = y)$$

Thus $xR^0 y$ iff $x = y$, and $xR^1 y$ iff xRy.

And we recall the definitions of $\Box^i A$ and $\Diamond^i A$:

$$\Box^i A = \Box\Box\cdots\Box A \ (i\Box s) \text{ and } \Diamond^i A = \Diamond\Diamond\cdots\Diamond A \ (i\Diamond s)$$

First, a lemma relating these notions to canonical models.

Lemma 5. *Let* L *be an arbitrary consistent normal modal logic. Then* $wR^i_L x$ *iff for every sentence* A, *if* $\Box^i A \in w$, *then* $A \in x$. *Therefore also,* $wR^i_L x$ *iff for every sentence* B, *if* $B \in x$, *then* $\Diamond^i B \in w$.

Proof. Induction on i. If $i = 0$, the lemma is trivial. Suppose $wR^{i+1}_L x$ and $\Box^{i+1} A = \Box^i \Box A \in w$. Then for some z, $wR^i_L z$ and $zR_L x$. By the induction hypothesis, $\Box A \in z$, and then by the definition of R_L, $A \in x$.

Conversely, suppose that for every A, if $\Box^{i+1} A \in w$, then $A \in x$. Let $Z = \{\Diamond B : B \in x\} \cup \{C : \Box^i C \in w\}$. We wish to show Z consistent. Suppose that it is not and thus that for some $B_1, \ldots, B_q \in x$, some $C_1, \ldots, C_p$, $\Box^i C_1, \ldots, \Box^i C_p \in w$ and $\mathrm{L} \vdash \neg(\Diamond B_1 \wedge \cdots \wedge \Diamond B_q \wedge C_1 \wedge \cdots \wedge C_p)$. Let $C = C_1 \wedge \cdots \wedge C_p$ and $B = B_1 \wedge \cdots \wedge B_q$. $B \in x$ and $\Box^i C \in w$. By normality, $\mathrm{L} \vdash \Diamond B \to \Diamond B_1 \wedge \cdots \wedge \Diamond B_q$, and therefore $\mathrm{L} \vdash \neg(\Diamond B \wedge C)$, and $\mathrm{L} \vdash C \to \Box \neg B$. But then by normality, $\mathrm{L} \vdash \Box^i C \to \Box^{i+1} \neg B$. Thus $\Box^{i+1} \neg B \in w$, and therefore $\neg B \in x$, contradiction.

Thus Z is consistent, and by Lemma 2, for some maximal consistent z, $Z \subseteq z$. For every C, if $\Box^i C \in w$, $C \in z$; and then by the induction hypothesis, $wR^i_L z$. For every B, if $B \in x$, $\Diamond B \in z$; thus $zR_L x$. So $wR^i_L z R_L x$, and so $wR^{i+1}_L x$. ⊣

Now let i, j, m, n be natural numbers. We say that R is i, j, m, n *convergent* iff for all x, y, if for some w, $wR^i x$ and $wR^j y$, then for some z, $xR^m z$ and $yR^n z$:

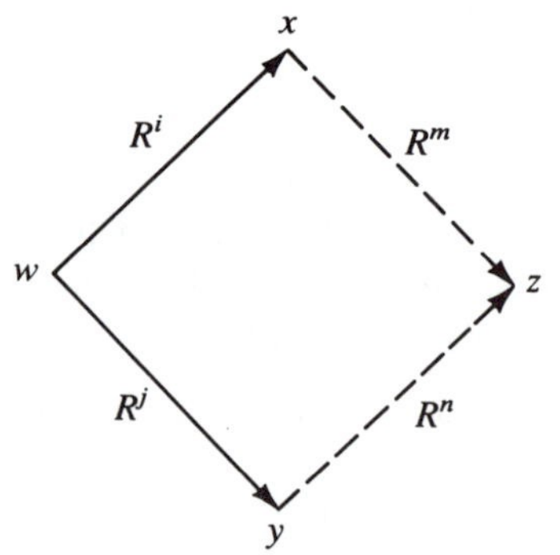

We shall say that L *proves the i, j, m, n scheme* if for all sentences A, $\mathrm{L}\vdash \Diamond^i\Box^m A \to \Box^j\Diamond^n A$.

Theorem 1. *Suppose that R is i, j, m, n convergent. Then every sentence* $\Diamond^i\Box^m A \to \Box^j\Diamond^n A$ *is valid in M.*

Proof. For $a\in W$, $a\vDash \Diamond^k B$ iff for some b such that $aR^k b$, $b\vDash B$, and dually, $a\vDash \Box^k B$ iff for every b such that $aR^k b$, $b\vDash B$.

Suppose now that $w\vDash \Diamond^i\Box^m A$ and $wR^j y$. We must show that for some z, $yR^n z$ and $z\vDash A$. But we have that for some x, $wR^i x$ and $x\vDash \Box^m A$. By i, j, m, n convergence, for some $z, xR^m z$, whence $z\vDash A$, and $yR^n z$, and we are done. ⊣

Theorem 2. *Suppose that* L *proves the i, j, m, n scheme. Then* R_L *is i, j, m, n convergent.*

Proof. Suppose that $wR_L^i x$ and $wR_L^i y$. We must show that there is a z such that $xR_L^m z$ and $yR_L^n z$. Let $Z=\{A\colon \Box^m A\in x\}\cup\{B\colon \Box^n B\in y\}$. If Z is consistent, then by Lemma 2, some maximal consistent z includes Z, and then by Lemma 5, we are done.

So suppose that for some $A_1,\ldots,A_p, B_1,\ldots,B_q$, $\Box^m A_1,\ldots,\Box^m A_p\in x$, $\Box^n B_1,\ldots,\Box^n B_q\in y$, and $\mathrm{L}\vdash\neg(A_1\wedge\cdots\wedge A_p\wedge B_1\wedge\cdots\wedge B_q)$. Let $A=A_1\wedge\cdots\wedge A_p$ and $B=B_1\wedge\cdots\wedge B_q$. Then $\mathrm{L}\vdash A\to\neg B$, whence by normality, $\mathrm{L}\vdash\Diamond^n A\to\Diamond^n\neg B$, and therefore

$$(*)\quad \mathrm{L}\vdash \Diamond^n A\to\neg\Box^n B$$

But also $\Box^m A\in x$ and $\Box^n B\in y$, and then $\Diamond^i\Box^m A\in w$ by Lemma 5. Since $\mathrm{L}\vdash\Diamond^i\Box^m A\to\Box^j\Diamond^n A$, $\Box^j\Diamond^n A\in w$. But $wR_L^j y$, and then again by Lemma 5, $\Diamond^n A\in y$, whence by $(*)$, $\neg\Box^n B\in y$, contradiction. ⊣

Now let α be a set of quadruples (i, j, m, n). Kα will be the system of normal modal logic whose axioms are those of K together with all sentences $\Diamond^i\Box^m A\to\Box^j\Diamond^n A$, $(i, j, m, n)\in\alpha$. We will say that M is α-convergent if for every $(i, j, m, n)\in\alpha$, M is i, j, m, n convergent.

The next theorem is the main result of this chapter.

Thoerem 3. K$\alpha\vdash A$ *iff A is valid in all* α*-convergent models.*

Proof. Suppose K$\alpha\vdash A$ and M is α-convergent. By Theorem 1 every axiom of Kα is valid in M, and therefore A is valid in M. Conversely, by Theorem 2, the canonical model for Kα is α-convergent. Thus if A is valid in every α-convergent model, then A is valid in the canonical model for $K\alpha$, and by Lemma 4, $K\alpha \vdash A$. $\dashv$

Theorem 4 brings Theorem 3 down to earth.

Theorem 4

(a) *R is transitive iff R is* $0, 2, 1, 0$ *convergent.*
(b) *R is reflexive iff R* is $0, 0, 1, 0$ *convergent.*
(c) *R is symmetric iff R* is $0, 1, 0, 1$ *convergent.*
(d) *R is euclidean iff R* is $1, 1, 0, 1$ *convergent.*
(e) K *is* $K\varnothing$.
(f) K4 *is* $K\{(0, 2, 1, 0)\}$.
(g) T *is* $K\{(0, 0, 1, 0)\}$.
(h) S4 *is* $K\{(0, 0, 1, 0), (0, 2, 1, 0)\}$.
(i) B *is* $K\{(0, 0, 1, 0), (0, 1, 0, 1)\}$.
(j) S5 *is* $K\{(0, 0, 1, 0), (1, 1, 0, 1)\}$.

Proof. (e)–(j) are immediate from (a)–(d) and the definitions of the systems. (a)–(d) are exercises in predicate logic with identity. We'll do (a).

By definition, R is $0, 2, 1, 0$ convergent iff $\forall x \forall y(\exists w(w = x \wedge wR^2y) \rightarrow \exists z(xRz \wedge y = z))$, iff $\forall x \forall y(xR^2y \rightarrow xRy)$, iff $\forall x \forall y(\exists v(xRv \wedge vRy) \rightarrow xRy)$, iff $\forall x \forall v \forall y(xRv \wedge vRy \rightarrow xRy)$, iff R is transitive. (b), (c), and (d) fall out in similar fashion. $\dashv$

Theorem 5

(a) $K \vdash A$ *iff A is valid in all models.*
(b) $K4 \vdash A$ *iff A is valid in all transitive models.*
(c) $T \vdash A$ *iff A is valid in all reflexive models.*
(d) $S4 \vdash A$ *iff A is valid in all reflexive and transitive models.*
(e) $B \vdash A$ *iff A is valid in all reflexive and symmetric models.*
(f) $S5 \vdash A$ *iff A is valid in all reflexive and euclidean models.*

Proof. Immediate from Theorems 3 and 4. $\dashv$

GL proves all sentences $\Box A \rightarrow \Box\Box A$; i.e., GL proves the $0, 2, 1, 0$ scheme. By Theorem 2, R_{GL} is $0, 2, 1, 0$ convergent, i.e., transitive. Thus the canonical model for GL is transitive.

Unfortunately, it is not converse wellfounded, as the following argument, due to Giancarlo Meloni, shows: Let $*$ be an arbitrary realization and let $w = \{A : A^* \text{ is true}\}$. w is GL-consistent: otherwise, there are $A_1, \ldots, A_n$ such that $A_1^*, \ldots, A_n^*$ are true and

$\mathrm{GL} \vdash \neg(A_1 \wedge \cdots \wedge A_n)$, and then $\mathrm{PA} \vdash \neg(A_1^* \wedge \cdots \wedge A_n^*)$ and at least one of $A_1^*, \ldots, A_n^*$ is false, contradiction.

Moreover, w is maximal GL-consistent: if $A \notin w$, then A^* is not true, $(\neg A)^*$ is true, and then $\neg A \in w$.

Finally, $w R_{\mathrm{GL}} w$: if $\Box A \in w$, then $(\Box A)^*$ is true, A^* is provable, A^* is true, and $A \in w$. So R_{GL} is not irreflexive, and therefore not converse wellfounded, either.

More work is needed to extract a completeness theorem for GL from results about M_{GL}, about as much, in fact, as it took us to prove the completeness theorem for GL from scratch.

Exercises. 1. A binary relation R is called *serial* if $\forall x \exists y Rxy$, *functional* if $\forall x \forall y \forall z(Rxy \wedge Rxz \to y = z)$, and *dense* if $\forall x \forall y(Rxy \to \exists z(Rxz \wedge Rzy))$. Formulate soundness and completeness theorems concerning these properties of relations.

2. Call R *terminated* if $\forall w(\exists x\, wRx \to \exists x(wRx \wedge \forall y \neg yRx))$. Show that $\mathrm{K} + (\Diamond \top \to \neg \Box \Diamond \top) \vdash A$ iff A is valid in all terminated models. Find a terminated model in which $\Box(\Box p \to p) \to \Box p$ is invalid.

7

On GL

We here present a number of results about the system GL. Some of these will be of direct interest for the study of provability in PA; others are simply independently interesting (we hope), and these occur toward the end of the chapter. The discussion here of letterless sentences and the notions of rank and trace will be particularly important in the next chapter, where we take up the fixed point theorem, certainly one of the most striking applications of modal logic ever made.

We begin with one of the oldest results of the subject of provability logic, the normal form theorem for letterless sentences. Recall that a modal sentence is called *letterless* if it contains no sentence letters, equivalently if it is a member of the smallest class containing $\bot$ and containing $(A \rightarrow B)$ and $\Box A$ whenever it contains A and B.

As ever, $\Box^0 A = A$ and $\Box^{i+1} A = \Box \Box^i A$.

We shall say that a letterless sentence C is in *normal form* if it is a truth-functional combination of sentences of the form $\Box^i \bot$.

The normal form theorem for letterless sentences

If B is a letterless sentence, there is a letterless sentence C in normal form such that $\mathrm{GL} \vdash B \leftrightarrow C$.

Proof. It clearly suffices to show how to construct a letterless sentence in normal form equivalent to $\Box C$ from a letterless sentence C in normal form.

First of all, put C into conjunctive normal form, i.e., rewrite C as a conjunction $D_1 \wedge \cdots \wedge D_k$ of disjunctions of sentences $\Box^i \bot$ and negations of such sentences. Since $\mathrm{GL} \vdash \Box(D_1 \wedge \cdots \wedge D_k) \leftrightarrow (\Box D_1 \wedge \cdots \wedge \Box D_k)$, it suffices to find a suitable equivalent for $\Box D$ from any disjunction D of sentences $\Box^n \bot$ and negations of such sentences.

Let $D = \Box^{n_1} \bot \vee \cdots \vee \Box^{n_p} \bot \vee \neg \Box^{m_1} \bot \vee \cdots \vee \neg \Box^{m_q} \bot$.

If no disjunct of D occurs unnegated, replace D by $\Box^0 \bot \vee D$;

thus we may assume that there is at least one unnegated disjunct $\Box^{n_r}\bot$.

Since $\mathrm{GL}\vdash\Box^i\bot\to\Box^j\bot$ whenever $0\leqslant i\leqslant j$, replace D by $\Box^n\bot\vee\neg\Box^m\bot$, where $n=\max(n_1,\ldots,n_p)$ and $m=\min(m_1,\ldots,m_q)$. Thus replace D by $\Box^n\bot$ if there are no disjuncts $\neg\Box^{m_k}\bot$.

We shall now show that $\Box D$ is equivalent either to $\Box^{n+1}\bot$ or to $\top$, both of which are in normal form. ($\top$ is a 0-place connective, hence a truth-functional compound of letterless sentences.)

If $\neg\Box^m\bot$ is absent, then D is $\Box^n\bot$, and $\mathrm{GL}\vdash\Box D\leftrightarrow\Box^{n+1}\bot$.

Thus we may assume that neither $\Box^n\bot$ nor $\neg\Box^m\bot$ is absent; rewrite D as $\Box^m\bot\to\Box^n\bot$.

If $m\leqslant n$, then $\mathrm{GL}\vdash D$, and therefore $\mathrm{GL}\vdash\Box D\leftrightarrow\top$.

If $m>n$, however, then $n+1\leqslant m$, $\mathrm{GL}\vdash\Box^{n+1}\bot\to\Box^m\bot$, and so $\mathrm{GL}\vdash(\Box^m\bot\to\Box^n\bot)\to(\Box^{n+1}\bot\to\Box^n\bot)$, whence by normality, $\mathrm{GL}\vdash\Box(\Box^m\bot\to\Box^n\bot)\to\Box(\Box^{n+1}\bot\to\Box^n\bot)$; but since $\mathrm{GL}\vdash\Box(\Box^{n+1}\bot\to\Box^n\bot)\to\Box^{n+1}\bot$, $\mathrm{GL}\vdash\Box(\Box^m\bot\to\Box^n\bot)\to\Box^{n+1}\bot$. Conversely, $\mathrm{GL}\vdash\Box^{n+1}\bot\to\Box(\Box^m\bot\to\Box^n\bot)$, and therefore $\mathrm{GL}\vdash\Box D\leftrightarrow\Box^{n+1}\bot$. $\dashv$

If B is a letterless sentence then $B^*=B^\#$ for any realizations $*$ and $\#$. We shall call a sentence of PA a *constant* sentence[1] if it is a member of the smallest class containing $\bot$ and containing $(S\to S')$ and $\mathrm{Bew}(\ulcorner S\urcorner)$ whenever it contains S and S'. For every constant sentence S, there is a letterless sentence B such that for all realizations $*$, $S=B^*$. The class of constant sentences, which contains (arithmetizations of) a large number of assertions that involve the concepts of provability and consistency, is a natural class to investigate. Among the constant sentences are the arithmetizations of the assertion that arithmetic is consistent, that the consistency of arithmetic is not provable, that if arithmetic is consistent, then it is consistent that it is consistent, etc. The arithmetization of the second incompleteness theorem is also a constant sentence, of course. The constant sentences were introduced by Harvey Friedman, who posed the question[2] whether an effective method exists for deciding their truth:

35. Define the set E of expressions by (i) Con is an expression; (ii) if A, B are expressions so are $(\sim A)$, $(A\&B)$, and $\mathrm{Con}(A)$. Each expression ϕ in E determines a sentence ϕ^* in PA by taking Con* to be "PA is consistent," $(\sim A)^*$ to be $\sim(A^*)$, $(A\&B)^*$ to be $A^*\&B^*$, and $\mathrm{Con}(A)^*$ to be "PA + 'A^*' is consistent." The set of expression $\phi\in E$ such that ϕ^* is true is recursive.

The formalized second incompleteness theorem reads $\sim$Con(Con & $\sim$Con(($\sim$Con)))*.[3]

The answer to Friedman's question[4] is yes: From an arbitrary constant sentence S find a letterless B such that $B^* = S$. Put B into normal form. $(\Box^i \bot)^*$ has the same truth-value as $\bot$, for all $i \geqslant 0$. To compute the truth-value of S, then, we may simply delete every occurrence of $\Box$ from the normal form of B and evaluate the result, which will be a truth-functional compound of $\top$ and $\bot$, according to the usual rules of the propositional calculus. We obtain the value $\top$ if and only if S is true.

To decide whether a constant sentence S is provable, find a letterless B such that $B^* = S$ and then decide the truth of $\Box B$.

Rank and trace

In order to study letterless sentences and the constant sentences that are their translations into arithmetic we introduce the notions of the *rank* of a world in a finite transitive and irreflexive frame and the *trace* of a letterless sentence.

Let $\langle W, R \rangle$ be a finite transitive and irreflexive frame. Suppose that for some $w_n, \ldots, w_1, w_0$ in W, $w_n R \ldots R w_1 R w_0$. Then if $j > i$, by transitivity $w_j R w_i$, and by irreflexivity $w_i \neq w_j$. Thus for every w in W, there is a greatest n, which will be less than the number of members of W, such that for some $w_n, \ldots, w_1, w_0$ in W, $w = w_n R \ldots R w_1 R w_0$.

For each $w \in W$, we define the *rank* $\rho_{\langle W,R \rangle}(w)$ of w as the greatest such n. (We omit the subscript "$\langle W, R \rangle$".) Thus if wRx for no x in W, $\rho(w) = 0$.

If wRx, then clearly $\rho(w) \geqslant \rho(x) + 1$ and so $\rho(w) > \rho(x)$.

Moreover, as the following lemma shows, $\rho(w) > i$ iff for some x, wRx and $\rho(x) = i$.

Lemma 1. *If $\rho(w) > i$, then for some x, wRx and $\rho(x) = i$.*

Proof. Suppose $\rho(w) = n > i$ and $w = w_n R \ldots R w_1 R w_0$. Let $x = w_i$. Then wRx by transitivity. We must show that $\rho(x) = i$. Clearly $\rho(x) \geqslant i$. Suppose $\rho(x) = j > i$. Then for some $x_j, \ldots, x_1, x_0$, $x = x_j R \ldots R x_1 R x_0$, $w_i = x_j$, and therefore

$$w = w_n R \ldots R w_{i+1} R w_i = x_j R \ldots R x_1 R x_0$$

Thus $\rho(w) \geqslant n - i + j > n$, contradiction. $\dashv$

If B is a letterless sentence, then we define the *trace*[5] $[\![B]\!]$ of B, which is a set of natural numbers, as follows:

$$[\![\bot]\!] = \varnothing$$
$$[\![B \to C]\!] = (N - [\![B]\!]) \cup [\![C]\!]$$
$$[\![\Box B]\!] = \{n: \forall i < n\; i \in [\![B]\!]\}$$

Thus $[\![\neg B]\!] = N - [\![B]\!]$, $[\![B \wedge C]\!] = [\![B]\!] \cap [\![C]\!]$, $[\![\Diamond B]\!] = \{n: \exists m < n\; m \in [\![B]\!]\}$, and, e.g., $[\![\Box\bot]\!] = \{0\}$, $[\![\Box\Box\bot]\!] = \{0, 1\}$, $[\![\Box\Box\bot \to \Box\bot]\!] = N - \{1\}$.

A set X of natural numbers is said to be *cofinite* if $N - X$ is finite. As any subset of a finite set is finite, any superset of a cofinite set is cofinite.

Lemma 2. *For every letterless B, $[\![B]\!]$ is either finite or cofinite.*

Proof. $[\![\bot]\!]$ is certainly finite. If $[\![B]\!]$ is finite or $[\![C]\!]$ is cofinite, then $N - [\![B]\!]$ is cofinite or $[\![C]\!]$ is cofinite, and then $[\![B \to C]\!]$ is cofinite; but if $[\![B]\!]$ is cofinite and $[\![C]\!]$ is finite, then $N - [\![B]\!]$ is finite and $[\![C]\!]$ is finite, and therefore their union $[\![B \to C]\!]$ is also finite. If $[\![B]\!] = N$, then $[\![\Box B]\!] = N$, which is cofinite; but if $[\![B]\!] \neq N$, then for some least n, $n \notin [\![B]\!]$, and then $[\![\Box B]\!] = \{m: m \leqslant n\}$, which is finite. ⊣

Lemma 3. *Let M be a finite transitive and irreflexive model, $w \in W$, and B letterless. Then $M, w \vDash B$ iff $\rho(w) \in [\![B]\!]$.*

Proof. $w \nvDash \bot$ and $\rho(w) \notin [\![\bot]\!]$.

If the lemma holds for C and D and $B = (C \to D)$, then $w \vDash C \to D$ iff $w \nvDash C$ or $w \nvDash D$, iff $\rho(w) \notin [\![C]\!]$ or $\rho(w) \in [\![D]\!]$, iff $\rho(w) \in [\![C \to D]\!]$.

Suppose $B = \Box C$ and the lemma holds for C. If $w \nvDash \Box C$, then for some x, wRx, $x \nvDash C$, and by the i.h., $\rho(x) \notin [\![C]\!]$. Since wRx, $\rho(x) < \rho(w)$, and therefore $\rho(w) \notin [\![\Box C]\!]$. Conversely, if $\rho(w) \notin [\![\Box C]\!]$, then for some $i < \rho(w)$, $i \notin [\![C]\!]$. By Lemma 1, for some x, $\rho(x) = i$ and wRx. By the i.h., $x \nvDash C$, and therefore $w \nvDash \Box C$. ⊣

It follows that whether or not a letterless sentence holds at a world in a model depends solely on the rank of that world (with respect to the frame on which the model is based).

Lemma 4. *If B is letterless, then* GL $\vdash B$ *iff $[\![B]\!] = N$.*

Proof. Suppose $\mathrm{GL}\vdash B$. For every n, there exists a finite transitive and irreflexive model $M, = \langle W, R, V\rangle$, such that for some $w \in W$, $\rho(w) = n$. But certainly $M, w \vDash B$, and then by Lemma 3, $n = \rho(w) \in [\![B]\!]$. Conversely, if $\mathrm{GL}\nvdash B$, there exist a finite transitive and irreflexive model M and $w \in W$ such that $M, w \nvDash B$. But then by Lemma 3, $\rho(w) \notin [\![B]\!]$. $\dashv$

It follows from Lemma 4 and the definition of $[\![B]\!]$ that if B and C are letterless, then $[\![B]\!] \subseteq [\![C]\!]$ iff $\mathrm{GL}\vdash B \to C$ and $[\![B]\!] = [\![C]\!]$ iff $\mathrm{GL}\vdash B \leftrightarrow C$.

Lemma 5. *For every n, $[\![\Box^n \bot]\!] = \{m: m < n\}$.*

Proof. Induction on n. $[\![\Box^0 \bot]\!] = [\![\bot]\!] = \{m: m < 0\}$. And if $[\![\Box^n \bot]\!] = \{m: m < n\}$, then $[\![\Box^{n+1} \bot]\!] = [\![\Box\Box^n \bot]\!] = \{m: \forall i < m\, i \in [\![\Box^n \bot]\!]\} = \{m: \forall i < m\, i < n\} = \{m: m < n+1\}$. $\dashv$

Lemma 6. *For every n, $[\![\neg(\Box^{n+1}\bot \to \Box^n \bot)]\!] = \{n\}$.*

Proof. By Lemma 5. $\dashv$

Lemma 7. *Suppose $[\![B]\!]$ is finite. Let $C = \bigvee\{\neg(\Box^{n+1}\bot \to \Box^n\bot): n \in [\![B]\!]\}$ (well-defined, since $[\![B]\!]$ is finite.) Then $\mathrm{GL}\vdash B \leftrightarrow C$.*

Proof. Let M be a finite transitive and irreflexive model, $w \in W$. Then by Lemmas 3 and 6, $M, w \vDash B$ iff $\rho(w) \in [\![B]\!]$, iff $\rho(w) = n$ for some $n \in [\![B]\!]$, iff $\rho(w) \in [\![\neg(\Box^{n+1}\bot \to \Box^n\bot)]\!]$ for some $n \in [\![B]\!]$, iff $M, w \vDash \neg(\Box^{n+1}\bot \to \Box^n\bot)$ for some $n \in [\![B]\!]$, iff $M, w \vDash C$. Thus B and C hold at exactly the same worlds in all models, $B \leftrightarrow C$ is valid, and by the completeness theorem for GL, $\mathrm{GL}\vdash B \leftrightarrow C$. $\dashv$

Lemma 8. *Suppose $[\![B]\!]$ is cofinite. Let $C = \bigwedge\{\Box^{n+1}\bot \to \Box^n\bot : n \notin [\![B]\!]\}$. Then $\mathrm{GL}\vdash B \leftrightarrow C$.*

Proof. Like that of Lemma 7. $\dashv$

Lemmas 2, 7, and 8 yield another proof of the normal form theorem: if B is letterless, by Lemma 2, $[\![B]\!]$ is finite or cofinite, and by Lemma 7 or 8 respectively, C is a sentence in normal form such that $\mathrm{GL}\vdash B \leftrightarrow C$. Together with Lemma 4, they also yield proofs of the "letterless" cases of Solovay's completeness for GL and GLS, as the next two theorems show. (The much harder proofs of the full theorems, in which the proviso that B be letterless is absent, are given in Chapter 9.)

Theorem 1. *Let B be letterless, $*$ arbitrary. Then* $\mathrm{GLS} \vdash B$ *iff B^* is true.*

Proof. "Only if" is clear. If $[\![B]\!]$ is finite, then by Lemma 7, $\mathrm{GL} \vdash B \leftrightarrow \bigvee\{\neg(\Box^{n+1}\bot \to \Box^{n}\bot): n \in [\![B]\!]\}$, and, since $(\Box^{n+1}\bot)^*$ is false, B^* is false. (If $[\![B]\!] = \varnothing$, C^* is the empty disjunction, thus equivalent to $\bot$, and B^* is again false.) Thus if B^* is true, $[\![B]\!]$ is cofinite, $\mathrm{GL} \vdash B \leftrightarrow \bigwedge\{\Box^{n+1}\bot \to \Box^{n}\bot : n \notin [\![B]\!]\}$ by Lemma 8, and therefore $\mathrm{GLS} \vdash B$, for then B is equivalent in GL to a conjunction of axioms $\Box D \to D$ of GLS. $\dashv$

Theorem 2. *Let B be letterless, $*$ arbitrary. Then* $\mathrm{GL} \vdash B$ *iff* $\mathrm{PA} \vdash B^*$.

Proof. "Only if" is clear. If $[\![B]\!]$ is finite, B^* is false, as we have just seen, and so unprovable. If $[\![B]\!]$ is cofinite but $i \notin [\![B]\!]$, then $\mathrm{GL} \vdash B \leftrightarrow C$, where $C = \bigwedge\{\Box^{n+1}\bot \to \Box^{n}\bot : n \notin [\![B]\!]\}$ and $\Box^{i+1}\bot \to \Box^{i}\bot$ is a conjunct of C; but $(\Box^{i+1}\bot \to \Box^{i}\bot)^*$ is not provable (Löb), and therefore neither are C^* nor B^*. Therefore if B^* is provable, $[\![B]\!] = N$, and by Lemma 4, $\mathrm{GL} \vdash B$. $\dashv$

Theorem 3 (Goldfarb). *Let B be letterless. Then* $\mathrm{GL} \vdash \neg\Box B \wedge \neg\Box\neg B \to \Diamond\Diamond\top$.

Proof. If $0 \in [\![B]\!]$, $1 \in [\![\Box B]\!]$, and $1 \notin [\![\neg\Box B]\!]$; if $0 \notin [\![B]\!]$, $0 \in [\![\neg B]\!]$, $1 \in [\![\Box\neg B]\!]$, and $1 \notin [\![\neg\Box\neg B]\!]$. In either case, $1 \notin [\![\neg\Box B \wedge \neg\Box\neg B]\!]$. And $0 \in [\![\Box B]\!]$ for all B; thus $0 \notin [\![\neg\Box B \wedge \neg\Box\neg B]\!]$. Since $[\![\Diamond\Diamond\top]\!] = N - \{0, 1\}$, the theorem follows by the remark immediately after Lemma 4. $\dashv$

Theorem 4. *Let B be letterless. Then* $\mathrm{GL} \nvdash \Diamond\top \to \neg\Box B \wedge \neg\Box\neg B$.

Proof. Otherwise, by Theorem 3, $\mathrm{GL} \vdash \Diamond\top \to \Diamond\Diamond\top$, which is not the case. $\dashv$

At the end of Chapter 3 we saw that if S is equivalent to its own unprovability, or, what comes to the same thing, if S is equivalent to the consistency of PA, then the undecidability of S does not follow in PA from the consistency of PA. It follows from Theorems 2 and 4 that the same holds for any letterless sentence S.

Theorem 5. *Let B be letterless. Suppose* $\mathrm{GL} \vdash \Diamond \top \rightarrow B$, *but* $\mathrm{GL} \nvdash B$. *Then* $\mathrm{GL} \vdash B \leftrightarrow \Diamond \top$.

Proof. $[\![\Diamond \top]\!] = N - \{0\}$. By Lemma 4, $[\![\Diamond \top \rightarrow B]\!] = N$, but $[\![B]\!] \neq N$. Then $[\![B]\!] = N - \{0\} = [\![\Diamond \top]\!]$. $\dashv$

Thus no unprovable constant sentence is strictly weaker than consistency. And no consistent constant sentence is stronger than all of consistency, the consistency of consistency, etc.:

Theorem 6. *Let B be letterless. Suppose* $\mathrm{GL} \nvdash \neg B$. *Then for some n,* $\mathrm{GL} \nvdash B \rightarrow \Diamond^n \top$.

Proof. If for all n, $\mathrm{GL} \vdash B \rightarrow \Diamond^n \top$, then by Lemmas 4 and 5, for all n, $[\![B]\!] \subseteq [\![\Diamond^n \top]\!] = N - \{i: i < n\}$, and $[\![B]\!] = \varnothing$, whence $\mathrm{GL} \vdash \neg B$, again by Lemma 4. $\dashv$

Reflection principles and iterated consistency assertions

We now employ GL to examine reflection principles, sentences $(\Box p \rightarrow p)^*$ of arithmetic, and sentences of arithmetic that may be called *iterated consistency assertions*, i.e., sentences $(\Diamond^n \top)^*$. An iterated consistency assertion is a constant sentence of the form $\neg\mathrm{Bew}(\ulcorner \mathrm{Bew}(\ldots \mathrm{Bew}(\ulcorner \bot \urcorner)\ldots)\urcorner)$. The next theorem, for all its simplicity, turns out to be quite useful, and it is applied again in the proof of the main theorem of Chapter 12.

Theorem 7. *Let M be transitive. Suppose that for some natural number n, $w_n R \ldots R w_1 R w_0$, and $X = \{\Box A_i \rightarrow A_i : i < n\}$. Then for some $j \leqslant n$, $w_j \vDash \bigwedge X$.*

Proof. If for every $j \leqslant n$, there is an $i < n$ such that $w_j \nvDash \Box A_i \rightarrow A_i$, then by the pigeonhole principle, for some $i < n$, there are j, k, $0 \leqslant j < k \leqslant n$, such that $w_j \nvDash \Box A_i \rightarrow A_i$ and $w_k \nvDash \Box A_i \rightarrow A_i$. Thus $w_j \nvDash A_i$ and $w_k \vDash \Box A_i$. But by transitivity of R, $w_k R w_j$, contradiction. $\dashv$

In the next two theorems, we assume that $X = \{\Box A_i \rightarrow A_i : i < n\}$.

Theorem 8 (Daniel Leivant). *Suppose* $\mathrm{GL} \vdash \bigwedge X \rightarrow (\Box^k p \rightarrow p)$. *Then $k \leqslant n$.*

Proof. Let $W=\{n,\ldots,1,0,-1\}$, wRx iff $w>x$, and wVp iff $w=-1$. $\langle W,R,V\rangle$ is appropriate to GL. Suppose $k>n$. Then if $0\leqslant j\leqslant n$, $j\nvDash p$ and $j\vDash\Box^{j+1}p$, whence $j\vDash\Box^{k}p$. Thus by the supposition of the theorem and the soundness theorem for GL, for every j, $0\leqslant j\leqslant n$, $j\nvDash\bigwedge X$, contra Theorem 7. $\dashv$

Theorem 9. $\mathrm{GL}\vdash\Box(\bigwedge X\rightarrow\Diamond^{n}\top)\rightarrow(\Diamond^{n}\top\rightarrow\bigwedge X)$.

Proof. Use the completeness theorem. Suppose $w\vDash\Box(\bigwedge X\rightarrow\Diamond^{n}\top)$ and $w\vDash\Diamond^{n}\top$. $\rho(w)\geqslant n$, and then for some $w_n,\ldots,w_1,w_0$, $w=w_nR\ldots Rw_1Rw_0$, and $\rho(w_j)=j$ for $j<n$. By transitivity, if $j<n$, wRw_j and $w_j\vDash(\bigwedge X\rightarrow\Diamond^{n}\top)$. But for $j<n$, $\rho(w_j)<n$, and therefore $w_j\nvDash\Diamond^{n}\top$ and $w_j\nvDash\bigwedge X$. By Theorem 7, $w\vDash\bigwedge X$. $\dashv$

Let $C_n=(\Diamond^{n}\top)^*$; we call C_n the nth *iterated consistency assertion.* C_n asserts the consistency of the consistency of... the consistency of arithmetic (n 'consistency's). It follows from Theorem 9 that *if C_n follows from a conjunction of n reflection principles, then C_n implies that conjunction.* For suppose

$\mathrm{PA}\vdash\bigwedge\{\mathrm{Bew}(\ulcorner S_i\urcorner)\rightarrow S_i: i<n\}\rightarrow C_n$. Then
$\mathrm{PA}\vdash\mathrm{Bew}(\ulcorner\bigwedge\{\mathrm{Bew}(\ulcorner S_i\urcorner)\rightarrow S_i: i<n\}\rightarrow C_n\urcorner)$.

Let $p_0,\ldots,p_{n-1}$ be n distinct sentence letters and let $*$ be such that for each $i<n$, $p_i^*=S_i$. Then

$\mathrm{PA}\vdash\Box(\bigwedge\{\Box p_i\rightarrow p_i): i<n\}\rightarrow\Diamond^{n}\top)^*$. By Theorem 9,
$\mathrm{GL}\vdash\Box(\bigwedge\{\Box p_i\rightarrow p_i): i<n\}\rightarrow\Diamond^{n}\top)\rightarrow(\Diamond^{n}\top\rightarrow\bigwedge\{\Box p_i\rightarrow p_i): i<n\})$,
and therefore
$\mathrm{PA}\vdash(\Diamond^{n}\top\rightarrow\bigwedge\{\Box p_i\rightarrow p_i): i<n\})^*$, i.e.,
$\mathrm{PA}\vdash C_n\rightarrow\bigwedge\{\mathrm{Bew}(\ulcorner S_i\urcorner)\rightarrow S_i: i<n\}$.

The nth iterated consistency assertion $(\Diamond^{n})^*$ is equivalent to $(\Box^{n}\bot\rightarrow\bot)^*$ and (since $\mathrm{GL}\vdash\Box^{i}\bot\rightarrow\Box^{j}\bot$ if $i\leqslant j$) also to $(\Box^{n}\bot\rightarrow\Box^{n-1}\bot)^*\wedge\cdots\wedge(\Box^{2}\bot\rightarrow\Box^{1}\bot)^*\wedge(\Box^{1}\bot\rightarrow\Box^{0}\bot)^*$, a conjunction of n reflection principles.

But no conjunction of fewer than n reflection principles implies C_n: for suppose $m<n$ and a conjunction R of m reflection principles implies C_n. Then since $m<n$, C_n, which is $(\Diamond^{n}\top)^*$, implies C_m, and R implies C_m. Thus C_m implies R back, and therefore C_m implies C_n. But C_m, i.e., $(\Diamond^{m}\top)^*$, certainly does not imply C_n (unless PA is 1-inconsistent).

Thus the nth iterated consistency assertion is equivalent to a conjunction of n fewer reflection principles, but no conjunction of fewer than n reflection principles implies it.

The following result was mentioned in Chapter 3.

Theorem 10. $\mathrm{GL} \vdash \Box((\Box p \to p) \to \neg \Box \Box \bot) \to \Box \Box \bot$.

Proof. Suppose $w \models \Box((\Box p \to p) \to \neg \Box \Box \bot)$, but $w \not\models \Box \Box \bot$. Then $w \models \Diamond \Diamond \top$, and $\rho(w) \geqslant 2$. So for some x, wRx, $\rho(x) = 1$, and $x \models (\Box p \to p) \to \neg \Box \Box \bot$. Since $x \not\models \neg \Box \Box \bot$, $x \not\models (\Box p \to p)$, and $x \models \Box p$. Since $\rho(x) = 1$, for some y, xRy, and $\rho(y) = 0$. But then wRy and $y \models (\Box p \to p) \to \neg \Box \Box \bot$, and since xRy, $y \models p$, $y \models (\Box p \to p)$, and $y \models \neg \Box \Box \bot$, contra $\rho(y) = 0$. $\dashv$

Letterless sentences are unusual in having nice normal forms

According to the normal form theorem for letterless sentences, every letterless sentence is equivalent to a truth-functional combination of sentences $\Box^i \bot$. We now prove a theorem of Solovay's that shows that the letterless sentences are exceptional in possessing such normal forms.

Let H_0 be the set of all sentences containing no sentence letter other than p and equivalent (in GL) to one of p, $\neg p$, $\top$, and $\bot$; let H_{n+1} be the set of all sentences containing no sentence letter other than p and equivalent to some truth-functional combination of sentences $\Diamond^r B$, where $r \geqslant 0$ and $B \in H_n$. Every modal sentence containing no letter but p is in some H_n. By the normal form theorem for letterless sentences, every letterless sentence is in H_1. And since r in the definition of H_{n+1} may equal zero, $H_n \subseteq H_{n+1}$, and thus if $m \leqslant n$, $H_m \subseteq H_n$. Solovay's theorem is that the sequence $\{H_n\}$ is properly increasing.

Theorem 11 (Solovay). *For every* n, $H_n \neq H_{n+1}$.

Proof.[6] Let $A_1 = \Diamond p$; $A_{n+1} = \Diamond(p \wedge A_n)$. Thus, e.g., $A_3 = \Diamond(p \wedge \Diamond(p \wedge \Diamond p))$. $A_1 \in H_1$; if $A_n \in H_n$, then since $p \in H_0 \subseteq H_n$, $p \wedge A_n \in H_n$, and $A_{n+1} \in H_{n+1}$. Thus for every n, $A_n \in H_n$. We shall prove the theorem by showing that $A_{n+1} \notin H_n$.

Consider the model M, where, in the structure depicted below, $W = \{a_{-1}, a_0, b_0, c_0, a_1, b_1, c_1, \ldots\}$, wRx iff there is a nonempty sequence of arrows from w to x, and wVp iff w is one of the as (including a_{-1}) or one of the bs.

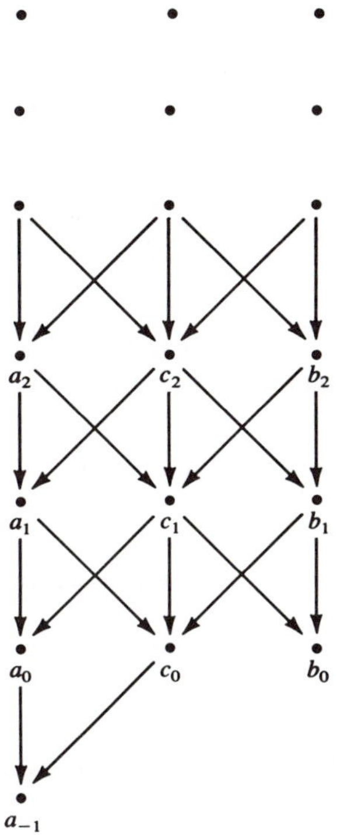

We first show by induction on i that if $A \in H_i$, $i \geqslant 0$, then $a_i \vDash A$ iff $b_i \vDash A$. Since $a_0 \vDash p$ and $b_0 \vDash p$, the basis step is clear. For the induction step, assume $A \in H_{i+1}$ and for all B in H_i, $a_i \vDash B$ iff $b_i \vDash B$. $a_{i+1} \vDash p$ and $b_{i+1} \vDash p$; thus we may assume that $A = \Diamond^r B$, where $r > 0$ and $B \in H_i$.

If $r > 1$, then $a_{i+1} R^r d$ iff $b_{i+1} R^r d$, and therefore $a_{i+1} \vDash \Diamond^r B$ iff for some d, $a_{i+1} R^r d$ and $d \vDash B$; iff for some d, $b_{i+1} R^r d$ and $d \vDash B$; iff $b_{i+1} \vDash \Diamond^r B$. So suppose $r = 1$. If $a_{i+1} Rd$, then either $d = a_i$ or $b_{i+1} Rd$, as a glance at the diagram shows; if $b_{i+1} Rd$, then either $d = b_i$ or $a_{i+1} Rd$; $a_{i+1} Ra_i$; and $b_{i+1} Rb_i$. By the induction hypothesis, $a_i \vDash B$ iff $b_i \vDash B$. Thus $a_{i+1} \vDash \Diamond B$ iff $b_{i+1} \vDash \Diamond B$.

Thus if $A \in H_n$, $a_n \vDash A$ iff $b_n \vDash A$.

Since $a_n R \ldots R a_0 R a_{-1}$, $a_n \vDash A_{n+1}$. But there is no sequence $d_n, \ldots, d_0$ such that $b_n R d_n R \ldots R d_0$ and for all i, $0 \leqslant j \leqslant n$, $d_j V p$. Thus $b_n \nvDash A_{n+1}$. So $A_{n+1} \notin H_n$. $\dashv$

Incompactness

The compactness theorem states that if every finite subset of a set of sentences has a model, so does the entire set. The compactness theorem holds for propositional and first-order logic and fails for (standard) second-order logic. Does it hold for GL? Say that a set of sentences is true at a world w in a model if all its members are true at w. Our question may then be put: Is every set every finite subset of which is true at some world in some model appropriate to GL itself true at some world in some model appropriate to GL?

The answer is *no*, a result due to Kit Fine and Wolfgang Rautenberg. Let $p_0, p_1, p_2, \ldots,$ be an infinite sequence of distinct sentence letters. Let $U = \{\Diamond p_0\} \cup \{\Box(p_i \to \Diamond p_{i+1})\colon i \in N\}$. Then every finite subset of U is a subset of $\{\Diamond p_0\} \cup \{\Box(p_i \to \Diamond p_{i+1})\colon i < n\}$, for some natural number n. And then every sentence in $\{\Diamond p_0\} \cup \{\Box(p_i \to \Diamond p_{i+1})\colon i < n\}$ is true at w in $\langle W, R, V\rangle$, where W is the set of nodes in the diagram:

$$w \to w_0 \to w_1 \to \cdots \to w_n$$

xRy iff there is a nonempty sequence of arrows from x to y, and xVp_j iff $x = w_j$. $\langle W, R, V\rangle$ is finite transitive and irreflexive.

But the whole set U is true at no world in any transitive and converse wellfounded model: for suppose on the contrary that $w \models \Diamond p_0$ and for every i, $w \models \Box(p_i \to \Diamond p_{i+1})$. Let $X = \{x\colon wRx \wedge \text{for some } i,\ x \models p_i\}$. Since $w \models \Diamond p_0$, X is nonempty. Suppose that $x \in X$. Then wRx, and for some i, $x \models p_i$. But $w \models \Box(p_i \to \Diamond p_{i+1})$. Since wRx, $x \models p_i \to \Diamond p_{i+1}$. Thus $x \models \Diamond p_{i+1}$, and for some y, xRy and $y \models p_{i+1}$. By transitivity, wRy, and so $y \in X$. Thus X is nonempty, but every member of X bears R to some member of X. R is therefore not converse wellfounded, contradiction.

There are infinitely many sentence letters in the sentences in U. Is there a set of sentences containing no sentence letter other than p that similarly shows the incompactness of G?

Yes, according to an observation of Goldfarb. For each natural number i, let $C_i = p \wedge \Box^i \bot$, $B_i = \Diamond C_i$, and $A_i = \neg B_i \wedge B_{i+1}$. Then the set $\{\Diamond A_0\} \cup \{\Box(A_i \to \Diamond A_{i+1})\colon i \in N\}$ is true at no world in any model appropriate to GL, as the argument two paragraphs back shows. However, for any n, $\{\Diamond A_0\} \cup \{\Box(A_i \to \Diamond A_{i+1})\colon i < n\}$ has a model $\langle W, R, V\rangle$ appropriate to GL. Consider the transitive frame $\langle W, R\rangle$:

$$
\begin{array}{l}
w \\
\downarrow \\
w_0 \rightarrow x_0 \\
\downarrow \\
w_1 \rightarrow x_1 \rightarrow y_{11} \\
\downarrow \\
w_2 \rightarrow x_2 \rightarrow y_{21} \rightarrow y_{22} \\
\downarrow \\
\vdots \\
\downarrow \\
w_i \rightarrow x_i \rightarrow y_{i1} \rightarrow \cdots \rightarrow y_{ii} \\
\downarrow \\
\vdots \\
\downarrow \\
w_n \rightarrow x_n \rightarrow y_{n1} \rightarrow \cdots \rightarrow y_{nn}.
\end{array}
$$

Let zVp iff $z = x_j$, some j. $\langle W, R, V \rangle$ is clearly appropriate to GL.

$z \vDash C_i$ iff $z = x_j$ for some $j < i$. Then if $z \neq w$, $z \vDash B_i$ iff $z = w_j$ for some $j < i$. And then if $z \neq w$, $z \vDash A_i$ iff $z = w_i$. Thus $w \vDash \Diamond A_0$ and if $i < n$, $w \vDash \Box(A_i \rightarrow \Diamond A_{i+1})$.

8

The fixed point theorem

The beautiful fixed point theorem for GL, due independently to Dick de Jongh and Giovanni Sambin, is the most striking application of modal logic to the study of the concept of provability in formal systems.

We recall the two definitions necessary for the statement of the theorem.

$\boxdot A$ is the sentence $(\Box A \wedge A)$.

A sentence A is said to be *modalized in p* if every occurrence of the sentence letter p in A is in the scope of an occurrence of $\Box$; equivalently, A is modalized in p if and only if A is a truth-functional compound of sentences of the form $\Box D$ and sentence letters other than p.

The fixed point theorem then reads: For every sentence A modalized in p, there is a sentence H containing only sentence letters contained in A, not containing the sentence letter p, and such that $\mathrm{GL} \vdash \boxdot(p \leftrightarrow A) \leftrightarrow \boxdot(p \leftrightarrow H)$.

Any such sentence H is called a *fixed point* of A.

If $\mathrm{GL} \vdash H \leftrightarrow I$, then $\mathrm{GL} \vdash \boxdot(H \leftrightarrow I)$, and therefore $\mathrm{GL} \vdash \boxdot(p \leftrightarrow H) \leftrightarrow \boxdot(p \leftrightarrow I)$. And if $\mathrm{GL} \vdash \boxdot(p \leftrightarrow H) \leftrightarrow \boxdot(p \leftrightarrow I)$ and neither H nor I contains p, then substituting H for p yields $\mathrm{GL} \vdash \boxdot(H \leftrightarrow H) \leftrightarrow \boxdot(H \leftrightarrow I)$, whence $\mathrm{GL} \vdash H \leftrightarrow I$. It follows that any sentence equivalent in GL to a fixed point of A and containing only sentence letters in A other than p is itself a fixed point of A, and that all fixed points of A are equivalent in GL.

A fixed point H does not contain p. Thus writing: $A(p)$ instead of: A, we have that $\mathrm{GL} \vdash \boxdot(H \leftrightarrow A(H)) \leftrightarrow \boxdot(H \leftrightarrow H)$, by substitution in the theorem, and therefore $\mathrm{GL} \vdash H \leftrightarrow A(H)$.

By Theorem 9 of Chapter 1, $\mathrm{GL} \vdash \Box B \leftrightarrow \Box \boxdot B$; by normality it also follows from the theorem that if A is modalized in p, then for some sentence H containing only letters in A but not p, $\mathrm{GL} \vdash \Box(p \leftrightarrow A(p)) \leftrightarrow \Box(p \leftrightarrow H)$.

Notational convention: Until the section of this chapter on the Craig interpolation lemma, A will be a sentence that is modalized in p, n will be the number of boxed subsentences of A, i.e., subsentences of A of the form $\Box D$, and these will be $\Box D_1, \ldots, \Box D_n$. The number n turns out to be a significant constant in the study of fixed points.

The table below provides a number of instances of the theorem. If A is the sentence on the left, H may be taken to be the corresponding sentence on the right:

1. $\neg\Box p$	$\neg\Box\bot$
2. $\Box p$	$\top$
3. $\Box\neg p$	$\Box\bot$
4. $\neg\Box\neg p$	$\neg\Box\bot$
5. $\neg\Box\Box p$	$\neg\Box\Box\bot$
6. $\Box p\to\Box\neg p$	$\Box\Box\bot\to\Box\bot$
7. $\Box(\neg p\to\Box\bot)\to\Box(p\to\Box\bot)$	$\Box\Box\Box\bot\to\Box\Box\bot$
8. $\Box p\to q$	$\Box q\to q$
9. $\Box(p\to q)$	$\Box q$
10. $\Box p\wedge q$	$\Box q\wedge q$
11. $\Box(p\wedge q)$	$\Box q$
12. $q\vee\Box p$	$\top$
13. $\neg\Box(q\to p)$	$\Diamond q$
14. $\Box(p\to q)\to\Box\neg p$	$\Box(\Box\bot\to q)\to\Box\bot$
15. $q\wedge(\Box(p\to q)\to\Box\neg p)$	$q\wedge\Box\neg q$
16. $\Diamond p\to(q\wedge\neg\Box(p\to q))$	$\Diamond\top\to(q\wedge\neg\Box(\Box\bot\to q))$
17. $\Box(\Box(p\wedge q)\wedge\Box(p\wedge r))$	$\Box(\Box q\wedge\Box r)$

According to line 3, GL$\vdash \boxdot(p\leftrightarrow\Box\neg p)\leftrightarrow\boxdot(p\leftrightarrow\Box\bot)$. It follows that S is a sentence that is equivalent (in arithmetic) to its own disprovability if and only if S is equivalent to the assertion that arithmetic is inconsistent. For let $*$ be such that $S = {}^*p$. Then if S is equivalent to its own disprovability, that is, PA$\vdash S\leftrightarrow\mathrm{Bew}(\ulcorner\neg S\urcorner)$, i.e., PA$\vdash(p\leftrightarrow\Box\neg p)^*$, therefore also PA$\vdash\Box(p\leftrightarrow\Box\neg p)^*$, and PA$\vdash\boxdot(p\leftrightarrow\Box\neg p)^*$. But by Theorem 2 of Chapter 3, PA$\vdash(\boxdot(p\leftrightarrow\Box\neg p)\leftrightarrow\boxdot(p\leftrightarrow\Box\bot))^*$, and therefore PA$\vdash\boxdot(p\leftrightarrow\Box\bot)^*$, whence PA$\vdash(p\leftrightarrow\Box\bot)^*$, i.e., PA$\vdash S\leftrightarrow\mathrm{Bew}(\ulcorner\bot\urcorner)$; that is, S is equivalent to the inconsistency of arithmetic. The proof of the converse proceeds in like manner.

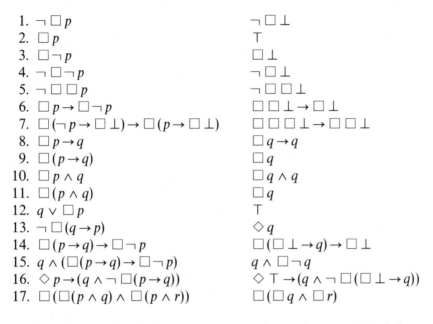

We can similarly infer from lines 1 and 6 of the table that a sentence of arithmetic is equivalent to its own unprovability if and only if it is equivalent to the assertion that arithmetic is consistent and that a sentence is equivalent to the assertion that it is disprovable-if-provable if and only if it is equivalent to the assertion that arithmetic is inconsistent if the inconsistency of arithmetic is provable.

From line 10 we can infer that for arbitrary sentences S and U of arithmetic, S is equivalent to the conjunction of assertions that S is provable and that U is true if and only if S is equivalent to the conjunction of assertion that U is provable and true: let $*$ be such that $*p = S$ and $*q = U$, and argue as above. And so on.

You may have noticed that, roughly speaking, the sentence H in the table has the overall shape of the sentence A of which it is a fixed point. In certain cases, the similarity could have been brought out more sharply by replacing entries by equivalent sentences; e.g., in line 2 we could have replaced $\top$ by $\Box\top$, or $\top$ by $q \vee \Box\top$ in line 12.

From line 6 we see that a fixed point may have a greater modal degree than a sentence of which it is a fixed point. $\Box\Box\bot \rightarrow \Box\bot$, which has degree 2, is a fixed point of the sentence $\Box p \rightarrow \Box\neg p$ of degree 1. Every letterless sentence of degree 1 is equivalent to $\bot$, $\Box\bot$, $\neg\Box\bot$, or $\top$; none of these is equivalent to $\Box\Box\bot \rightarrow \Box\bot$. Thus every fixed point of $\Box p \rightarrow \Box\neg p$ is of higher modal degree than it. Similarly for the sentence A of line 7.

However, as inspection of the table may also suggest, A always has a fixed point whose degree is at most n.

We are going to give three quite different proofs of the fixed point theorem. The first proof will make plain why a sentence modalized in p has a fixed point roughly similar to it in shape. The second will prove that every sentence A modalized in p has a fixed point of modal degree $\leqslant n$. The third proof will obtain the existence of a fixed point as a corollary of a lemma on the uniqueness of fixed points and the Beth definability theorem for GL, which in turn may be derived in the usual manner from the Craig interpolation lemma for GL.

The special case of the fixed point theorem, in which the sentence A modalized in p contains no sentence letter other than p itself, is of great independent interest. The special case was proved before the general case by Claudio Bernardi and Craig Smorynski (independently).

The special case is illustrated in lines 1–6 of the table. The original sentence constructed by Gödel in "On formally undecidable propositions..." can be seen as expressing its own unprovability; line 1 gives us a significant piece of information about such sentences: they are the sentences equivalent to the assertion that arithmetic is consistent. Line 2 encapsulates Löb's answer to Henkin's question. Line 4 tells us that the refutable sentences are those equivalent to their own consistency. Many, perhaps most, questions about the status of arithmetical sentences described "self-referentially" as equivalent to their own satisfaction of some predicate constructed from truth-functional operators and Bew(x) can be answered with the aid of a proof of the special case of the fixed point theorem. Before giving our three proofs of the full fixed point theorem, we shall give a separate proof of the special case, which brings out the close connection between that case and the normal form theorem for letterless sentences. The proof yields a particularly simple procedure for calculating, and determining the truth- and provability-values of, such self-referential sentences of arithmetic.

By Theorem 10 of Chapter 1, if $\mathrm{GL}\vdash \boxdot B\rightarrow C$, then $\mathrm{GL}\vdash \boxdot B\rightarrow \boxdot C$. Then to prove the theorem, it suffices to find a suitable H such that $\mathrm{GL}\vdash \boxdot(p\leftrightarrow A)\rightarrow(p\leftrightarrow H)$ and $\mathrm{GL}\vdash \boxdot(p\leftrightarrow H)\rightarrow(p\leftrightarrow A)$.

We first show that it is enough to find a suitable H such that $\mathrm{GL}\vdash \boxdot(p\leftrightarrow A)\rightarrow(p\leftrightarrow H)$.

Theorem. *Suppose that H does not contain the sentence letter p and $\mathrm{GL}\vdash \boxdot(p\leftrightarrow A)\rightarrow(p\leftrightarrow H)$. Then $\mathrm{GL}\vdash \boxdot(p\leftrightarrow H)\rightarrow(p\leftrightarrow A)$.*

Proof (*Goldfarb*). Suppose that M is a finite transitive and irreflexive model in which $\boxdot(p\leftrightarrow H)\rightarrow(p\leftrightarrow A)$ is invalid. Then for some w, and hence for some w of least rank, $M,w\vDash \boxdot(p\leftrightarrow H)$, whence $M,w\vDash p\leftrightarrow H$, and $M,w\nvDash p\leftrightarrow A$. If wRx, then $M,x\vDash \boxdot(p\leftrightarrow H)$, but since x is of lower rank than w, $M,x\vDash p\leftrightarrow A$. Let V' be just like V, except that $wV'p$ niff[1] wVp. (Thus $xV'q$ iff xVq, provided that either $x\neq w$ or $q\neq p$.) Let $N=\langle W,R,V'\rangle$. N is certainly a finite transitive and irreflexive model.

We now repeatedly appeal to the corollary to the continuity theorem of Chapter 4.

A is a truth-functional compound of sentences $\Box D$ and sentence letters q other than p. $M,w\vDash \Box D$ iff $M,x\vDash D$ for all x such that wRx, iff $N,x\vDash D$ for all x such that wRx (continuity), iff $N,w\vDash \Box D$. Also $M,w\vDash q$ iff $N,w\vDash q$. Thus $M,w\vDash A$ iff $N,w\vDash A$. $M,w\vDash p$ niff $N,w\vDash p$, by the definition of N. Therefore $N,w\vDash p\leftrightarrow A$, and by continuity again, $N,x\vDash p\leftrightarrow A$ for all x such that wRx. Thus $N,w\vDash \boxdot(p\leftrightarrow A)$.

H does not contain p. By continuity, $M,w\vDash H$ iff $N,w\vDash H$. Since

$M, w \vDash p$ niff $N, w \vDash p$, $N, w \nvDash p \leftrightarrow H$ and therefore $\boxdot(p \leftrightarrow A) \rightarrow (p \leftrightarrow H)$ is invalid.

Thus, by soundness and completeness, if $\mathrm{GL} \vdash \boxdot(p \leftrightarrow A) \rightarrow (p \leftrightarrow H)$, then $\mathrm{GL} \vdash \boxdot(p \leftrightarrow H) \rightarrow (p \leftrightarrow A)$. ⊣

To prove the fixed point theorem, it now suffices to prove that $\mathrm{GL} \vdash \boxdot(p \leftrightarrow A) \rightarrow (p \leftrightarrow H)$. We first discuss the special case, where A contains no sentence letters but p.

The special case of the fixed point theorem

Our proof of the special case of the fixed point theorem makes use of the notion of rank ρ and a generalization of the notion of trace; these notions were introduced in Chapter 7.

We shall call a sentence a p *sentence* if it contains no sentence letter other than p. Every p sentence is a truth-functional compound of p and necessitations of p sentences.

Generalizing the notion of trace, we now define the A-trace $[\![B]\!]_A$ of B for each p sentence B.

There is an enumeration $B_0, B_1, \ldots,$ of all p sentences in which p comes after A and in which truth-functional compounds always come after their components. (Thus B_0 is either $\bot$ or a sentence $\Box D$.) We pick one such and call it the standard enumeration. We define whether $m \in [\![B]\!]_A$ or not by a double induction, the outer induction on m, and the inner induction on the standard enumeration:

$$\begin{aligned}
[\![\bot]\!]_A &= \varnothing \\
[\![B \rightarrow C]\!]_A &= (N - [\![B]\!]_A) \cup [\![C]\!]_A \\
[\![\Box D]\!]_A &= \{m : \forall i < m\ i \in [\![D]\!]_A\} \\
[\![p]\!]_A &= [\![A]\!]_A
\end{aligned}$$

$m \notin [\![\bot]\!]_A$; the question whether $m \in [\![B \rightarrow C]\!]_A$ is reduced to the questions whether $m \in [\![B]\!]_A$ and $m \in [\![C]\!]_A$ (the inner induction: $B \rightarrow C$ comes after B and C); the question whether $m \in [\![p]\!]_A$ is reduced to the question whether $m \in [\![A]\!]_A$ (the inner induction: p comes after A); and the question whether $m \in [\![\Box D]\!]_A$ is reduced to questions whether $i \in [\![D]\!]_A$ for $i < m$, (the outer induction).

Thus $[\![B]\!]_A$ is well defined for each p sentence B.

As before, $[\![\neg B]\!]_A = N - [\![B]\!]_A$, $[\![B \wedge C]\!]_A = [\![B]\!]_A \cap [\![C]\!]_A$, etc., and $[\![\Diamond B]\!]_A = \{i : \exists m < i\ m \in [\![B]\!]_A\}$. Moreover, $[\![\Box^i \bot]\!]_A = \{j : j < i\}$ (as one may prove by affixing "$_A$" to "$]\!]$" in the proof of Lemma 5 of Chapter 7). We therefore have the following:

Lemma 1. $[\![\neg(\Box^{i+1}\bot \to \Box^{i}\bot)]\!]_A = \{i\}$.

Henceforth, we shall almost always omit "$_A$" after "$]\!]$".

Lemma 2. *Let M be a finite transitive and irreflexive model in which* $(p \leftrightarrow A)$ *is valid. Let B be a p sentence. Then* $M, w \vDash B$ *iff* $\rho(w) \in [\![B]\!]$.

Proof. We prove the theorem by an outer induction on $\rho(w)$ and an inner induction on the standard enumeration. Since A is a truth-functional compound of p sentences $\Box D$, and $w \vDash p$ iff $w \vDash A$, whence $[\![p]\!] = [\![A]\!]$, we may suppose that $B = \Box D$ and the theorem holds for all $\rho(x) < \rho(w)$. But then the argument of Lemma 3 of Chapter 7 works: If $w \nvDash \Box D$, then for some x, $x \nvDash D$, wRx, and so $\rho(x) < \rho(w)$; by the i.h., $\rho(x) \notin [\![D]\!]$, whence $\rho(w) \notin [\![\Box D]\!]$. Conversely, if $\rho(w) \notin [\![\Box D]\!]$, then for some $i < \rho(w)$, $i \notin [\![D]\!]$; by Lemma 1 of Chapter 7, for some x wRx and $\rho(x) = i$, and then by the i.h., $x \nvDash D$, whence $w \nvDash \Box D$. ⊣

Every subsentence of A is a truth-functional combination of p and $\Box D_1, \ldots, \Box D_n$.

Lemma 3. *Let B be a subsentence of A. Then either* $[\![B]\!] \subseteq \{0, 1, \ldots, n\}$ *or* $N - \{0, 1, \ldots, n\} \subseteq [\![B]\!]$.

Proof. (a) It is evident from the definition of $[\![\Box D]\!]$ that if $k \leqslant j$ and $j \in [\![\Box D]\!]$, then $k \in [\![\Box D]\!]$.

(b) Thus there exists an i, $0 \leqslant i \leqslant n$, such that for every subsentence $\Box D$ of A, $i \in [\![\Box D]\!]$ iff $i+1 \in [\![\Box D]\!]$. Otherwise by (a), for every i, $0 \leqslant i \leqslant n$, there is a subsentence $\Box D$ of A such that $i \in [\![\Box D]\!]$ and $i+1 \notin [\![\Box D]\!]$. But there are only n subsentences $\Box D$ of A, and therefore by the pigeonhole principle, there is a subsentence $\Box D$ of A such that for some i, j, $0 \leqslant i < j \leqslant n$, $i \in [\![\Box D]\!]$, $i+1 \notin [\![\Box D]\!]$, $j \in [\![\Box D]\!]$, and $j+1 \notin [\![\Box D]\!]$, which is absurd, again by (a).

(c) If for every subsentence $\Box D$ of A, $j \in [\![\Box D]\!]$ iff $j+1 \in [\![\Box D]\!]$, then (since A is a truth-functional compound of $\Box D_1, \ldots, \Box D_n$, $j \in [\![A]\!]$ iff $j+1 \in [\![A]\!]$, whence $j \in [\![p]\!]$ iff $j+1 \in [\![p]\!]$ and therefore) for every subsentence B of A, $j \in [\![B]\!]$ iff $j+1 \in [\![B]\!]$.

(d) If for every subsentence B of A, $j \in [\![B]\!]$ iff $j+1 \in [\![B]\!]$, then (where D is a subsentence of A, for all $k < j+1$, $k \in [\![D]\!]$ iff for all $k < j+2$, $k \in [\![D]\!]$ and therefore) for every subsentence $\Box D$ of A, $j+1 \in [\![\Box D]\!]$ iff $j+2 \in [\![\Box D]\!]$.

By (b), (c), and (d), there exists an $i \leqslant n$ such that for every subsentence B of A and every $j \geqslant i$, $i \in [\![B]\!]$ iff $j \in [\![B]\!]$. The lemma now follows at once. ⊣

By Lemma 3, either $[\![A]\!] \subseteq \{0,1,\ldots,n\}$ or $N - \{0,1,\ldots,n\} \subseteq [\![A]\!]$. If the former, let $H = \bigvee\{\neg(\Box^{i+1}\bot \rightarrow \Box^{i}\bot): i \in [\![A]\!]\}$; if the latter, let $H = \bigwedge\{(\Box^{i+1}\bot \rightarrow \Box^{i}\bot): i \notin [\![A]\!]\}$. By Lemma 1, $[\![H]\!] = [\![A]\!] = [\![p]\!]$, and so $[\![p \leftrightarrow H]\!] = N$. We now show that $\mathrm{GL} \vdash \boxdot(p \leftrightarrow A) \rightarrow (p \leftrightarrow H)$.

> ***The special case of the fixed point theorem.*** *Suppose that A contains no sentence letter other than p. Then* $\mathrm{GL} \vdash \boxdot(p \leftrightarrow A) \rightarrow (p \leftrightarrow H)$.

Proof. Suppose that M' is an arbitrary finite transitive and irreflexive model and $M', w \models \boxdot(p \leftrightarrow A)$. Let M be the submodel of M' generated from w. (Cf. Chapter 4.) M is finite transitive and irreflexive since M' is. By the generated submodel theorem, $M, w \models \boxdot(p \leftrightarrow A)$. By the definition of M, $W = \{w\} \cup \{x: wRx\}$. Thus for all $x \in W$, $M, x \models p \leftrightarrow A$, and $p \leftrightarrow A$ is valid in M.

By Lemma 2, $M, w \models p \leftrightarrow H$ iff $\rho(w) \in [\![p \leftrightarrow H]\!]$. But, as we saw, $[\![p \leftrightarrow H]\!] = N$. Thus $M, w \models p \leftrightarrow H$, and by the generated submodel theorem again, $M', w \models p \leftrightarrow H$.

Thus $M', w \models \boxdot(p \leftrightarrow A) \rightarrow (p \leftrightarrow H)$; by the completeness theorem for GL, $\mathrm{GL} \vdash \boxdot(p \leftrightarrow A) \rightarrow (p \leftrightarrow H)$. ⊣

Thus a fixed point of A is true iff $[\![A]\!]_A$ is cofinite; a fixed point of A is provable iff $[\![A]\!]_A$ is the entire set N of natural numbers.

The proof of the special case of the fixed point theorem yields a proof of the normal form theorem for letterless sentences: Suppose A letterless. Then $\mathrm{GL} \vdash \boxdot(p \leftrightarrow A) \rightarrow (p \leftrightarrow H)$. By substitution, $\mathrm{GL} \vdash \boxdot(A \leftrightarrow A) \rightarrow (A \leftrightarrow H)$. Since $\mathrm{GL} \vdash \boxdot(A \leftrightarrow A)$, $\mathrm{GL} \vdash A \leftrightarrow H$. And H is in normal form.

There is a simple truth-table-like procedure for calculating fixed points; we shall not describe the method in full but will give a completely typical illustration of it, in which the sentence A, whose fixed point is to be found, is $\Box p \rightarrow \Box\neg p$:

	$\Box p$	$\Box\neg p$	$\Box p \rightarrow \Box\neg p$	p	$\neg p$	$\bot$	$\Box\bot$	$\Box\Box\bot$
0	⊤	⊤	⊤	⊤	⊥	⊥	⊤	⊤
1	⊤	⊥	⊥	⊥	⊤	⊥	⊥	⊤
2	⊥	⊥	⊤	⊤	⊥	⊥	⊥	⊥
3	⊥	⊥	⊤	⊤	⊥	⊥	⊥	⊥

The lines of the table correspond to ranks of worlds. On the top line, line 0, all sentences $\Box D$ get $\top$; truth-functional compounds inherit their truth-values on a line from those of their components as usual (thus $\bot$ gets $\bot$ on every line), on any line $\Box A$ gets $\top$ iff A gets $\top$ on all lines with lower numbers, and p gets $\top$ on a line iff A does. (Since A is a truth-functional combination of sentences $\Box D$, its truth-value on any line can be calculated before the truth-value of p on that line.) Line 3 repeats line 2, and therefore any later line would also repeat line 2 (cf. Lemma 3); thus we need not write any line >3. A is false at line 1 and nowhere else; thus $[\![A]\!]_A = N - \{1\}$, and $H = \Box\Box\bot \rightarrow \Box\bot$. Note that, had it been in the table, $\Box\Box\bot \rightarrow \Box\bot$ would also have gotten $\bot$ on line 1 and nowhere else.

We turn now to the general case, whose proof seems to require far more than the mere insertion of a sequence of parameters into a proof of the special case. It is noteworthy that none of the three proofs we shall give can be considered a generalization of the proof we have given for the special case. Whether there is such a generalization would appear to be an open question. In view of the existence of simple normal forms for letterless sentences, the non-equivalence of $\Diamond(p \wedge \Diamond p)$ to any truth-functional compound of sentences $\Box^i\bot$, $\Box^i p$ and $\Box^i\neg p$ (cf. Theorem 11 of Chapter 7), and the facts that $\mathrm{GL}\vdash \bot \rightarrow \Box\bot$ but $\mathrm{GL}\nvdash p \rightarrow \Box p$, it would not be surprising if no such proof existed.

First proof of the (general) fixed point theorem

The first proof we shall give is due to Giovanni Sambin and Lisa Reidhaar-Olson.[2]

Call F *k-decomposable* if for some (possibly empty) sequence $q_1, \ldots, q_k$ of distinct sentence letters, some sentence $B(q_1, \ldots, q_k)$ not containing p but containing all of $q_1, \ldots, q_k$, and some sequence of distinct sentences $D_1(p), \ldots, D_k(p)$, each containing p,

$$F = B(\Box D_1(p), \ldots, \Box D_k(p))$$

Since A is modalized in p, for some k, A is k-decomposable.

If A is 0-decomposable, then by the definition, for some sentence B not containing p, $A = B$; more simply, A does not contain p, and A is a fixed point of A. To prove the theorem, it thus suffices to suppose that every k-decomposable sentence that is modalized in p

has a fixed point, assume that A is $(k+1)$-decomposable and modalized in p, and show that A has a fixed point.

By our assumption, $A = B(\Box D_1(p), \ldots, \Box D_{k+1}(p))$ for suitable B, $q_1, \ldots, q_{k+1}$, and $D_1(p), \ldots, D_{k+1}(p)$.

For each i, $1 \leqslant i \leqslant k+1$, let A_i be the sentence

$$B(\Box D_1(p), \ldots, \Box D_{i-1}(p), \top, \Box D_{i+1}(p), \ldots, \Box D_{k+1}(p))$$

Each A_i is k-decomposable and modalized in p and thus has a fixed point H_i. Let H be the sentence

$$B(\Box D_1(H_1), \ldots, \Box D_{k+1}(H_{k+1}))$$

We shall show that H is a fixed point of A.

This construction of the fixed point H is due to Sambin, who gave a syntactic proof of its correctness; Reidhaar-Olson showed that the usual semantics could be used to give an exceedingly perspicuous version of his proof.

Recall the substitution theorem: $\mathrm{GL} \vdash \boxdot(B \leftrightarrow B') \rightarrow (F(B) \leftrightarrow F(B'))$ and its consequence: $\mathrm{GL} \vdash \boxdot(B \leftrightarrow B') \rightarrow \boxdot(F(B) \leftrightarrow F(B'))$. In the next four lemmas, M is a finite transitive and irreflexive model, $w, x, y \in W$, and $1 \leqslant i \leqslant k+1$.

Lemma 4. *Suppose that* $y \vDash \boxdot(p \leftrightarrow A)$ *and* $y \vDash \Box D_i(p)$. *Then* $y \vDash D_i(p) \leftrightarrow D_i(H_i)$ *and* $y \vDash \Box D_i(p) \leftrightarrow \Box D_i(H_i)$.

Proof. Since $y \vDash \Box D_i(p)$, for all z such that yRz, $z \vDash \Box D_i(p)$, $y \vDash \Box D_i(p) \leftrightarrow \top$, and for all z such that yRz, $z \vDash \Box D_i(p) \leftrightarrow \top$. Thus $y \vDash \boxdot(\Box D_i(p) \leftrightarrow \top)$. By substitution, $y \vDash \boxdot(A \leftrightarrow A_i)$. Since $y \vDash \boxdot(p \leftrightarrow A)$, $y \vDash \boxdot(p \leftrightarrow A_i)$, and since H_i is a fixed point of A_i, $y \vDash \boxdot(p \leftrightarrow H_i)$. By substitution, $y \vDash D_i(p) \leftrightarrow D_i(H_i)$ and $y \vDash \Box D_i(p) \leftrightarrow \Box D_i(H_i)$. ⊣

Lemma 5. $x \vDash \boxdot(p \leftrightarrow A) \rightarrow \boxdot(\Box D_i(p) \rightarrow \Box D_i(H_i))$.

Proof. Suppose that $x \vDash \boxdot(p \leftrightarrow A)$, xRy or $x = y$, and $y \vDash \Box D_i(p)$. Then $y \vDash \boxdot(p \leftrightarrow A)$ and by Lemma 4, $y \vDash \Box D_i(H_i)$. ⊣

Lemma 6. $w \vDash \boxdot(p \leftrightarrow A) \rightarrow \boxdot(\Box D_i(H_i) \rightarrow \Box D_i(p))$.

Proof. Suppose that $w \vDash \boxdot(p \leftrightarrow A)$, wRx or $w = x$, and $x \vDash \neg \Box D_i(p)$. Then for some y of least rank, xRy and $y \vDash \neg D_i(p)$. Then for all z such that yRz, we have xRz, $\rho(z) < \rho(y)$, and so $z \vDash D_i(p)$, whence $y \vDash \Box D_i(p)$. Since $w \vDash \boxdot(p \leftrightarrow A)$ and wRy, $y \vDash \boxdot(p \leftrightarrow A)$. By Lemma 4, $y \vDash D_i(p) \leftrightarrow D_i(H_i)$. Thus $y \vDash \neg D_i(H_i)$, and therefore $x \vDash \neg \Box D_i(H_i)$. ⊣

Lemma 7. $w \vDash \boxdot(p \leftrightarrow A) \rightarrow \boxdot(\Box D_i(p) \leftrightarrow \Box D_i(H_i))$.

Proof. By Lemmas 5 and 6. ⊣

The fixed point theorem is now immediate. Using Lemma 7 and repeatedly substituting, we have that

$$\begin{aligned} w \vDash \boxdot(p \leftrightarrow A) \rightarrow & B(\Box D_1(p), \Box D_2(p), \ldots, \Box D_{k+1}(p)) \\ & \leftrightarrow B(\Box D_1(H_1), \Box D_2(p), \ldots, \Box D_{k+1}(p)) \\ & \leftrightarrow B(\Box D_1(H_1), \Box D_2(H_2), \ldots, \Box D_{k+1}(p)) \leftrightarrow \cdots \\ & \leftrightarrow B(\Box D_1(H_1), \Box D_2(H_2), \ldots, \Box D_{k+1}(H_{k+1})), \end{aligned}$$

i.e., $w \vDash \boxdot(p \leftrightarrow A) \rightarrow (A \leftrightarrow H)$. Thus $\boxdot(p \leftrightarrow A) \rightarrow (A \leftrightarrow H)$ is valid in all finite transitive and irreflexive models and by the completeness theorem is a theorem of GL.

Note that in this proof H comes from A by substituting various fixed points for various occurrences of p in A; the results of these substitutions can often be simplified internally. It is therefore unsurprising that a fixed point of A has an overall aspect similar to that of A.

The analysis of A as obtained from B by substitution of sentences $\Box D(p)$ into B need not be unique. E.g., if $A = \Box\Box p$, then we may take $B(q_1) = q$ and $D_1(p) = \Box p$, or we may take $B(q_1) = \Box q_1$ and $D_1(p) = p$. When applied to different analyses of A, the algorithm may yield fixed points that differ considerably in complexity (though of course they are equivalent in GL).

For example, let $A = \Box(\Box(p \wedge q) \wedge \Box(p \wedge r))$; then $n = 3$. If we take $B = q_1$, so that $D_1(p) = \Box(p \wedge q) \wedge \Box(p \wedge r)$, then we obtain $H = \Box(\Box(\top \wedge q) \wedge \Box(\top \wedge r))$, of degree 2, the degree of A. But if we take $B = \Box(q_1 \wedge q_2)$, so that $D_1(p) = p \wedge q$ and $D_2(p) = p \wedge r$, we obtain $H = \Box(\Box(\Box(\top \wedge \Box(\Box(\top \wedge \top) \wedge r)) \wedge q) \wedge$ $\Box(\Box(\Box(\Box(\top \wedge \top) \wedge q) \wedge \top) \wedge r))$, whose degree is 5. (Both fixed points are equivalent to $\Box\Box q \wedge \Box\Box r$.) Thus an injudicious analysis of A may produce a fixed point of needlessly high modal degree.

But simplification of H to a sentence of the degree of A is not always possible: as we have seen, $\Box\Box\bot \rightarrow \Box\bot$ is a fixed point of $\Box p \rightarrow \Box\neg p$, but it is equivalent to no sentence of degree 1. In the next proof, we obtain a fixed point whose degree is guaranteed to be no greater than n, but at a cost: the fixed point will be a disjunction of sentences of low degree but one that is very long.

Second proof of the fixed point theorem

The second proof of the full fixed point theorem is a semantical version, discovered by Zachary Gleit, of a proof given by the author. The fixed point of A will be seen to be of modal degree $\leqslant n$.

Let s be the number of sentences other than p that occur in A. ($s = 0$ iff there are no letters other than p in A.) Let these be $q_1, \ldots, q_s$.

We now define the notion of an m-character, $m \geqslant 0$.[3]

The 0-characters are the 2^s sentences $\pm q_1 \wedge \cdots \wedge \pm q_s$. (Of course, $\pm B$ is either B or $\neg B$. If $s = 0$, $\top$ is the sole 0-character.)

Suppose that the m-characters are the t sentences $V_1, \ldots, V_t$. Then the $(m+1)$-characters are the 2^{s+t} sentences

$$\pm q_1 \wedge \pm \cdots \wedge \pm q_s \wedge \pm \Diamond V_1 \wedge \pm \cdots \wedge \pm \Diamond V_t$$

For any fixed m, the disjunction of all m-characters is a tautology and any two m-characters are truth-functionally inconsistent. Thus for any model, M and any w in W, there is exactly one m-character U – call it $U(m, w, M)$, or $U(m, w)$ for short – such that $M, w \vDash U$.

Conventions: $w, w', w_0 \in W$, $N = \langle X, S, Q \rangle$, and $x, x', x_0 \in X$. We will often omit "M" and "N".

Lemma 8. *Suppose that M and N are finite transitive and irreflexive models, $M, w_0 \vDash \boxdot(p \leftrightarrow A)$, $N, x_0 \vDash \boxdot(p \leftrightarrow A)$, and $U(n, w_0, M) = U(n, x_0, N)$. Then $M, w_0 \vDash p$ iff $N, x_0 \vDash p$.*

Proof. Suppose $w_0 \vDash p$ niff $x_0 \vDash p$.

Let $P(i, Z, w, x, D)$ if and only if the following eight conditions hold:

(1) Z is a set of subsentences of A of the form $\Box B$;
(2) Z contains i members;
(3) $w_0 R w$ or $w_0 = w$;
(4) $x_0 S x$ or $x_0 = x$;
(5) for every sentence $\Box B$ in Z, $w \vDash \Box B$ and $x \vDash \Box B$;
(6) $U(n-i,\ w, M) = U(n-i,\ x, N)$;
(7) $\Box D$ is a subsentence of A; and
(8) $w \vDash \Box D$ niff $x \vDash \Box D$ (whence $\Box D \notin Z$).

Then

(*) if $i < n$ and for some Z, w, x, D, $P(i, Z, w, x, D)$, then for some Z', w', x', D', $P(i+1, Z', w', x', D')$.

For suppose that $i < n$ and $P(i, Z, w, x, D)$. Without loss of generality we may assume that $w \nvDash \Box D$ and $x \vDash \Box D$. Then for some w',

wRw', whence w_0Rw' (3′), $w' \vDash \Box D$ and $w' \nvDash D$. Since $i < n$, $n-(i+1)$ and $U(n-(i+1), w')$ are defined. Let $V = U(n-(i+1), w')$. Then $w' \vDash V$, and $w \vDash \Diamond V$. Thus $\Diamond V$ is a conjunct of $U(n-i, w) = U(n-i, x)$. So $x \vDash \Diamond V$, and thus for some x', xSx', whence x_0Sx' (4′), and $x' \vDash V$. Thus $U(n-(i+1), x') = V = U(n-(i+1), w')$ (6′). Since xSx', $x' \vDash \Box D$ and $x' \vDash D$. Let $Z' = Z \cup \{\Box D\}$ (1′). Then Z' contains $i+1$ members (2′). Since wRw' and xSx', for every sentence $\Box B$ in Z', $w' \vDash \Box B$ and $x' \vDash \Box B$ (5′). It remains to find a suitable D'.

D is a subsentence of A, $w' \nvDash D$, and $x' \vDash D$. Thus either

(a) $w' \vDash p$ niff $x' \vDash p$ or
(b) $w' \vDash q_k$ niff $x' \vDash q_k$ for some k, $1 \leqslant k \leqslant s$, or
(c) $w' \vDash \Box D'$ niff $x' \vDash \Box D'$ for some subsentence $\Box D'$ of A.

But since w_0Rw' and x_0Sx', $w' \vDash p \leftrightarrow A$ and $x' \vDash p \leftrightarrow A$. Thus if (a) holds, $w' \vDash A$ niff $x' \vDash A$, and thus either (b) or (c) holds, since A is a truth-functional compound of the sentence letters $q_1, \ldots, q_s$ and boxed sentences. But (b) does not hold, for $U(n-(i+1), w') = U(n-(i+1), x')$. Thus (c) holds (7′, 8′), and (∗) is established.

Since $w_0 \vDash p \leftrightarrow A$, $x_0 \vDash p \leftrightarrow A$, and $U(n, w_0) = U(n, x_0)$, it follows in exactly the same way that for some subsentence $\Box D$ of A, $w_0 \vDash \Box D$ niff $x_0 \vDash \Box D$; thus $P(0, \varnothing, w_0, x_0, D)$. By induction, for some Z', w', x', D', $P(n, Z', w', x', D')$. But it is absurd that Z' is a set of boxed subsentences of A, Z' contains n members, $\Box D'$ is a subsentence of A, and $\Box D' \notin Z'$: n *is* the number of boxed subsentences of A. ⊣

We now complete the second proof of the fixed point theorem. Let $H = \bigvee \{U : U$ is an n-character and $\mathrm{GL} \vdash \boxdot(p \leftrightarrow A) \wedge U \to p\}$. We shall show that $\mathrm{GL} \vdash \boxdot(p \leftrightarrow A) \to (p \leftrightarrow H)$.

Let M be a finite transitive and irreflexive model. Suppose $w \vDash \boxdot(p \leftrightarrow A)$. Let $U = U(n, w)$. U is the only n-character that holds at w, and thus if $w \vDash H$, then U is a disjunct of H, and $\mathrm{GL} \vdash \boxdot(p \leftrightarrow A) \wedge U \to p$; since $w \vDash U$, $w \vDash p$. Therefore $w \vDash H \to p$.

Now assume $w \vDash p$. If U is not a disjunct of H, $\mathrm{GL} \nvdash \boxdot(p \leftrightarrow A) \wedge U \to p$, and for some finite transitive and irreflexive model N, some world x of N, $x \vDash \boxdot(p \leftrightarrow A)$, $x \vDash U$, and $x \nvDash p$. But the only n-character that holds at x is $U(n, x)$. Thus $U(n, w) = U = U(n, x)$, contra Lemma 8. So U is a disjunct of H, and since $w \vDash U$, $w \vDash H$. Thus $w \vDash p \to H$, and so $w \vDash p \leftrightarrow H$.

By the completeness theorem for GL, $\mathrm{GL} \vdash \boxdot(p \leftrightarrow A) \to (p \leftrightarrow H)$, and the fixed point theorem is proved.

It is immediate by induction on m that the degree of each m-character is m; therefore the degree of H, which is a disjunction of n-characters is n, and we have proved that a fixed point of A always exists whose modal degree is no greater than the number of boxed subsentences of A. Thus although fixed points of A may have to be more complex than A, on the most natural measure of complexity, they need not be much more complex.

It is instructive to examine the m-characters when there are no sentence letters $q_1, \ldots, q_s$, i.e., when $s = 0$. Then the sole 0-character is $\top$, which is the same sentence as $\Diamond^0\top$, and it is consistent.

Suppose that the consistent m-characters are equivalent to $\Diamond^m\top$, $\neg\Diamond^m\top \wedge \Diamond^{m-1}\top, \ldots, \neg\Diamond^2\top \wedge \Diamond^1\top, \neg\Diamond^1\top \wedge \Diamond^0\top$. From $\mathrm{GL} \vdash \Box(\Box^{i+1}\bot \rightarrow \Box^i\bot) \leftrightarrow \Box^{i+1}\bot$, we have $\mathrm{GL} \vdash \Diamond(\neg\Diamond^{i+1}\top \wedge \Diamond^i\top) \leftrightarrow \Diamond^{i+1}\top$. Then the consistent $(m+1)$-characters are equivalent to those of $\pm\Diamond^{m+1}\top \wedge \pm\Diamond^m\top \wedge \cdots \wedge \pm\Diamond^1\top$ that are consistent. But $\mathrm{GL} \vdash \Diamond^{k+i}\top \rightarrow \Diamond^i\top$; thus the consistent $(m+1)$-characters are equivalent to $\Diamond^{m+1}\top$, $\neg\Diamond^{m+1}\top \wedge \Diamond^m\top, \ldots$, $\neg\Diamond^2\top \wedge \Diamond^1\top$, and $\neg\Diamond\top$. So for all m, the consistent m-characters are equivalent to $\Diamond^m\top$, $\neg\Diamond^m\top \wedge \Diamond^{m-1}\top, \ldots, \neg\Diamond^2\top \wedge \Diamond^1\top$, $\neg\Diamond\top$, in other words, to the letterless sentences with traces $\{i: i \geqslant m\}$, $\{m-1\}, \ldots, \{1\}$, and $\{0\}$.

The role of modalization

The somewhat mysterious presence of the rather technical condition on A, that it be modalized in p, may require explanation.

It is certainly not the case that arbitrary sentences B have fixed points. For example, if B is p itself, then a fixed point of B would be a letterless sentence H such that $\mathrm{GL} \vdash (p \leftrightarrow H)$; there is no such H. If B is $\neg p$, a fixed point of B would be a sentence H such that $\mathrm{GL} \vdash (H \leftrightarrow \neg H)$; again, there is no such H.

Moreover, as we shall shortly show, p is not equivalent to any sentence modalized in p, and therefore neither is $\neg p$.

There are, however, sentences equivalent to no sentence modalized in p for which fixed points exist. $\Box p \vee p$ is one example.

Proposition 1. *Suppose that B is modalized in p. If* $\mathrm{GL} \vdash p \rightarrow B$, *then* $\mathrm{GL} \vdash B$.

Proof. Suppose $\mathrm{GL} \nvdash B$. Then for some finite transitive and irreflexive M and some $w, M, w \nvDash B$. Let V' be such that $wV'p$ and otherwise just like V, and let $M' = \langle W, R, V' \rangle$. B is a truth-functional compound of sentences $\Box D$ and sentence letters other than p. By continuity, $M', w \nvDash B$. But $M', w \vDash p$. Thus $M', w \nvDash p \to B$, and $\mathrm{GL} \nvdash p \to B$. ⊣

Thus p is equivalent to no sentence modalized in p.

Proposition 2. *For no B modalized in p,* $\mathrm{GL} \vdash B \leftrightarrow (\Box p \vee p)$.

Proof. Otherwise, $\mathrm{GL} \vdash p \to B$, whence by Lemma 1, $\mathrm{GL} \vdash B$, $\mathrm{GL} \vdash \Box p \vee p$, whence $\mathrm{GL} \vdash \Box \bot \vee \bot$ by substitution, which is certainly not the case. ⊣

Proposition 3. $\mathrm{GL} \vdash \boxdot(p \leftrightarrow \Box p \vee p) \leftrightarrow \boxdot(p \leftrightarrow \top)$.

Proof. The right–left direction is clear. For the left–right direction:

$$\begin{aligned}\mathrm{GL} \vdash \boxdot(p \leftrightarrow \Box p \vee p) &\to \boxdot(\Box p \to p)\\ &\to \boxdot\boxdot(\Box p \to p) \quad \text{(Theorem 9 of Chapter 1)}\\ &\to \boxdot(\Box(\Box p \to p) \wedge (\Box p \to p))\\ &\to \boxdot(\Box p \wedge (\Box p \to p))\\ &\to \boxdot p\\ &\to \boxdot(p \leftrightarrow \top) \quad ⊣\end{aligned}$$

Thus although B's being modalized in p is, as the fixed point theorem tells us, a sufficient condition for a fixed point of B to exist, it is by no means a necessary one. Is there an interesting necessary and sufficient condition on B for there to be a fixed point of B? (Not a rhetorical question.)

The interest of the condition *being modalized in p* is that, as it happens, a great many assertions about which we are curious because they can be characterized as equivalent to their own satisfaction of some formula can also be described as sentences S such that for some $*$ such that $S = p^*$ and some sentence B *that is modalized in p*, $\mathrm{PA} \vdash (p \leftrightarrow B)^*$. For example, the sentences equivalent to their own unprovability are the sentences S such that $\mathrm{PA} \vdash (p \leftrightarrow \neg \Box p)^*$, if $S = p^*$. The fixed point theorem can then be invoked to give us further information about those assertions.

There is a natural correspondence between sentences B modalized in p and the formulas $[B](x)$ of arithmetic containing just x free defined below; under the correspondence, $\mathrm{PA} \vdash B^* \leftrightarrow [B](\ulcorner S \urcorner)$, and therefore $\mathrm{PA} \vdash (p \leftrightarrow B)^*$ iff $\mathrm{PA} \vdash S \leftrightarrow [B](\ulcorner S \urcorner)$, provided that $p^* = S$.

(Under the correspondence the sentence letter p turns into the free variable x of the formula $[B](x)$.) The formulas $[B](x)$ are frequently the formulas involved in the characterization of the assertions that interest us.

Let $\mathrm{cond}(x, y)$ be a Σ pterm for a function whose value for any i, j is the Gödel number of $(F \rightarrow G)$ whenever i is the Gödel number of a formula F and j that of a formula G, and let $\mathrm{bew}(x)$ be a Σ pterm for a function whose value for any i is the Gödel number of $\mathrm{Bew}(\ulcorner F \urcorner)$ whenever i is the Gödel number of a formula F.

For every modal sentence B containing no letter other than p we define the pterm $\{B\}(x)$:

$\{p\}(x)$ is x;
$\{\bot\}(x\}$ is $\ulcorner \bot \urcorner$;
$\{(B \rightarrow C)\}(x)$ is $\mathrm{cond}(\{B\}(x), \{C\}(x))$; and
$\{\Box B\}(x)$ is $\mathrm{bew}(\{B\}(x))$.

It is entirely routine to prove that if $p^* = S$, then for every modal sentence B, $\mathrm{PA} \vdash \{B\}(\ulcorner S \urcorner) = \ulcorner B^* \urcorner$.

For every truth-functional combination B of sentences $\Box D$, we define the formula $[B](x)$:

$[\bot](x)$ is $\bot$;
$[(B \rightarrow C)](x)$ is $([B](x) \rightarrow [C](x))$; and
$[\Box B](x)$ is $\mathrm{Bew}(\{B\} - (x))$.

It is also routine to prove that if $p^* = S$, then for every such B, $\mathrm{PA} \vdash B^* \leftrightarrow [B](\ulcorner S \urcorner)$. Since the sentences modalized in p are the truth-functional combinations of sentence letters other than p and sentences $\Box D$, $[B](x)$ has been defined for every sentence B modalized in p.

Thus if $p^* = S$ and B is modalized in P, $\mathrm{PA} \vdash B^* \leftrightarrow [B](\ulcorner S \urcorner)$.

The correspondence can be generalized to one taking pairs $(B, \#)$ of sentences modalized in p and realizations # to formulas $[B, \#](x)$ of arithmetic such that $\mathrm{PA} \vdash B^* \leftrightarrow [B, \#](\ulcorner S \urcorner)$ whenever $p^* = S$ and $q^* = q^{\#}$ for sentence letters q other than p occurring in B, but we shall omit the definition of $[B, \#](x)$.

The Craig interpolation lemma for GL

The Craig interpolation lemma[4] for GL, from which we shall derive our third proof of the fixed point theorem, reads: If $\mathrm{GL} \vdash A \rightarrow C$, then there is some sentence B such that GL$\vdash A \to B$, GL$\vdash B \to C$, and every sentence letter that occurs in B occurs in both A and C.

Proof (Smorynski[5]*).* Let A and C be modal sentences. Let $\mathscr{L}_0$ be the set of sentences all of whose sentence letters occur in A. Let $\mathscr{L}_1$ be the set of sentences all of whose sentence letters occur in C. Let $\mathscr{L} = \mathscr{L}_0 \cap \mathscr{L}_1$. Let $X = \{D: D$ is a subsentence of A or of $\neg C\}$. Let $Y = \{\neg D: D \in X\}$. For $S \subseteq X \cup Y$, $i = 0, 1$, let $S_i = S \cap \mathscr{L}_i$. Then $S = S_0 \cup S_1$. A sentence B is said to *separate* a set $S, \subseteq X \cup Y$, iff $B \in \mathscr{L}$, GL$\vdash \bigwedge S_0 \to B$, and GL$\vdash \bigwedge S_1 \to \neg B$.

S is *inseparable* iff no sentence B separates S.

If S is consistent, S is inseparable; and if S is inseparable, each S_i is consistent (otherwise one of $\bot$ or $\top$ could be used as a B separating S). ⊣

Lemma 9. *Suppose S is inseparable and $D \in X$. Then either $S \cup \{D\}$ or $S \cup \{\neg D\}$ is inseparable.*

Proof. Suppose not. Either $D \in \mathscr{L}$, $D \in \mathscr{L}_0 - \mathscr{L}_1$, or $D \in \mathscr{L}_1 - \mathscr{L}_0$.

If $D \in \mathscr{L}$, then for some $B, B' \in \mathscr{L}$,

GL$\vdash \bigwedge S_0 \wedge D \to B$,

GL$\vdash \bigwedge S_1 \wedge D \to \neg B$,

GL$\vdash \bigwedge S_0 \wedge \neg D \to B'$, and

GL$\vdash \bigwedge S_1 \wedge \neg D \to \neg B'$.

Let $B^* = (D \to B) \wedge (\neg D \to B')$. $B^* \in \mathscr{L}$. Then

GL$\vdash \bigwedge S_0 \to B^*$, and

GL$\vdash \bigwedge S_1 \to (D \to \neg B) \wedge (\neg D \to \neg B')$, whence

GL$\vdash \bigwedge S_1 \to \neg B^*$.

Thus B^* separates S, which is not the case.

If $D \in \mathscr{L}_0 - \mathscr{L}_1$, then for some $B, B' \in \mathscr{L}$,

GL$\vdash \bigwedge S_0 \wedge D \to B$,

GL$\vdash \bigwedge S_1 \to \neg B$,

GL$\vdash \bigwedge S_0 \wedge \neg D \to B'$, and

GL$\vdash \bigwedge S_1 \to \neg B'$. Let $B^* = B \vee B'$. $B^* \in \mathscr{L}$. Then

GL$\vdash \bigwedge S_0 \to B^*$ and

GL$\vdash \bigwedge S_1 \to \neg B^*$.

Again B^* separates S, which is not the case.

And similarly, not: $D \in \mathscr{L}_1 - \mathscr{L}_0$. ⊣

Call w *maximal* if w is inseparable and for every $D \in X$, either $D \in w$ or $\neg D \in w$. By Lemma 9, every inseparable set is included in some maximal set.

As in the completeness proof for GL, let W be the set of maximal sets; let wRx iff for all $\Box E \in w$, $\Box E, E \in x$ and for some $\Box E \in x$, $\Box E \notin w$; and let wVp iff $p \in w$. Then W is finite, and R is transitive and irreflexive.

Lemma 10. *Let $w \in W$, $D \in X$. Then $M, w \vDash D$ iff $D \in w$.*

Proof. The lemma is trivial if $D = p$.

Since $D \in X$, either $D \in \mathscr{L}_0$ or $D \in \mathscr{L}_1$. Let i $(=0,1)$ be such that $D \in \mathscr{L}_i$ and let $w_i = w \cap \mathscr{L}_i$. Then $D \in w$ iff $D \in w_i$, and if E is a subsentence of D or the negation of one, then $E \in w$ iff $E \in w_i$.

If $D = \bot$ and $D \in w$, then $\bot \in w_i$ and w_i is inconsistent, contra inseparability of w; but also $w \nvDash \bot$. Thus the lemma holds if $D = \bot$.

Suppose $D = (E \to E')$. $E \in w_i$ iff $E \in w$, iff $\neg E \notin w$, iff $\neg E \notin w_i$, and similarly $E' \in w_i$ iff $\neg E' \notin w_i$. If $D \in w_i$, then by consistency of w_i either $E \notin w_i$ or $\neg E' \notin w_i$, whence $E \notin w_i$ or $E' \in w_i$; conversely, if $E \notin w_i$ or $E' \in w_i$, then $\neg E \in w_i$ or $E' \in w_i$, and therefore $D \in w_i$ (otherwise $\neg D \in w_i$, contra consistency). Thus $D \in w$ iff $D \in w_i$, iff either $E \notin w_i$ or $\neg E' \notin w_i$, iff either $E \notin w$ or $E' \in w$, iff (i.h.) $w \nvDash E$ or $w \vDash E'$, iff $w \vDash D$.

Suppose $D = \Box E$. Assume $\Box E \in w$. If wRx, then $E \in x$, and by the i.h., $x \vDash E$; thus $w \vDash \Box E$.

So assume $\Box E \notin w$. Then $\neg \Box E \in w$. Let $S = \{\Box H_1, H_1, \ldots, \Box H_m, H_m, \Box I_1, I_1, \ldots, \Box I_n, I_n, \Box E, \neg E\}$, where $\Box H_1, \ldots, \Box H_m$ are all the sentences of the form $\Box G$ in w_i and $\Box I_1, \ldots, \Box I_n$ are all the sentences of the form $\Box G$ in w_{1-i}. Suppose S is not inseparable.

Case 1. $D \notin \mathscr{L}_{1-i}$. Then for some $B \in \mathscr{L}$,

$\mathrm{GL} \vdash \Box H_1 \wedge H_1 \wedge \cdots \wedge \Box H_m \wedge H_m \wedge \Box E \wedge \neg E \to B$ and

$\mathrm{GL} \vdash \Box I_1 \wedge I_1 \wedge \cdots \wedge \Box I_n \wedge I_n \to \neg B$. Then

$\mathrm{GL} \vdash \Box H_1 \wedge H_1 \wedge \cdots \wedge \Box H_m \wedge H_m \wedge \neg B \to (\Box E \to E)$,

$\mathrm{GL} \vdash \Box \Box H_1 \wedge \Box H_1 \wedge \cdots \wedge \Box \Box H_m \wedge \Box H_m \wedge \Box \neg B \to \Box(\Box E \to E)$,

$\mathrm{GL} \vdash \Box H_1 \wedge \cdots \wedge \Box H_m \wedge \Box \neg B \to \Box E$, and

$\mathrm{GL} \vdash \Box H_1 \wedge \cdots \wedge \Box H_m \wedge \neg \Box E \to \neg \Box \neg B$; also

$\mathrm{GL} \vdash \Box \Box I_1 \wedge \Box I_1 \wedge \cdots \wedge \Box \Box I_n \wedge \Box I_n \to \Box \neg B$, and

$\mathrm{GL} \vdash \Box I_1 \wedge \cdots \wedge \Box I_n \to (\neg\neg) \Box \neg B$.

If $i = 0$, $\neg \Box \neg B$ separates w; if $i = 1$, $\Box \neg B$ does; but w is inseparable, contradiction.

Case 2. $D \in \mathscr{L}_{1-i}$, as well as $\mathscr{L}_i$. Then for some $B \in \mathscr{L}$,

$\mathrm{GL} \vdash \Box H_1 \wedge H_1 \wedge \cdots \wedge \Box H_m \wedge H_m \wedge \Box E \wedge \neg E \to B$ and

$\mathrm{GL} \vdash \Box I_1 \wedge I_1 \wedge \cdots \wedge \Box I_n \wedge I_n \wedge \Box E \wedge \neg E \to \neg B$. We have

$\mathrm{GL} \vdash \Box I_1 \wedge I_1 \wedge \cdots \wedge \Box I_n \wedge I_n \to (B \to (\Box E \to E))$, whence, as usual,

$\mathrm{GL}\vdash \Box I_1 \wedge \cdots \wedge \Box I_n \to \Box(B\to(\Box E\to E))$. Also
$\mathrm{GL}\vdash \Box H_1 \wedge H_1 \wedge \cdots \wedge \Box H_m \wedge H_m \to (\neg B\to(\Box E\to E))$, whence
$\mathrm{GL}\vdash \Box H_1 \wedge \cdots \wedge \Box H_m \to \Box(\neg B\to(\Box E\to E))$, and therefore
$\mathrm{GL}\vdash \Box H_1 \wedge \cdots \wedge \Box H_m \to (\Box(B\to(\Box E\to E))\to \Box(\Box E\to E))$,
$\mathrm{GL}\vdash \Box H_1 \wedge \cdots \wedge \Box H_m \to (\Box(B\to(\Box E\to E))\to \Box E)$, and
$\mathrm{GL}\vdash \Box H_1 \wedge \cdots \wedge \Box H_m \wedge \neg\Box E \to \neg\Box(B\to(\Box E\to E))$.

All of $\Box H_1,\ldots,\Box H_m$, $\Box I_1,\ldots,\Box I_n$, and $\neg\Box E$ are in w, and $\Box(B\to(\Box E\to E))\in\mathscr{L}$. Thus either $\neg\Box(B\to(\Box E\to E))$ or $\Box(B\to(\Box E\to E))$ separates w, which is not the case.

Thus S is inseparable and included in some maximal x. Since $S\subseteq x$, wRx ($\Box E\notin w$, but $\Box E\in x$), $\neg E\in x$, and so $E\notin x$, whence by the i.h. $x\nvDash E$, and $w\nvDash \Box E$. $\dashv$

Now suppose that there is no sentence B whose sentence letters all occur in both A and C such that $\mathrm{GL}\vdash A\to B$ and $\mathrm{GL}\vdash B\to C$. Then $\{A,\neg C\}$ is inseparable and by Lemma 9 is included in some maximal inseparable set w. By Lemma 10, $w\vDash A$, $w\vDash\neg C$, $w\nvDash C$, $w\nvDash A\to C$, and thus $\mathrm{GL}\nvdash A\to C$.

Thus if $\mathrm{GL}\vdash A\to C$, then there is some sentence B whose sentence letters all occur in both A and C and such that $\mathrm{GL}\vdash A\to B$ and $\mathrm{GL}\vdash B\to C$: the Craig interpolation lemma for GL is proved.

Third proof of the fixed point theorem

Our third proof of the fixed point theorem begins with a proof of the analogue for GL of Beth's well-known theorem on definability in the predicate calculus; the standard derivation of the Beth definability theorem from the Craig interpolation lemma for the predicate calculus carries over to GL.

The Beth definability theorem for GL. *Suppose that $q\neq p$, D' is exactly like D except for containing an occurrence of q at all and only those places where D contains an occurrence of p, and* $\mathrm{GL}\vdash D\wedge D'\to(p\leftrightarrow q)$. *Then for some sentence H containing only sentence letters both contained in D and other than p,* $\mathrm{GL}\vdash D\to(p\leftrightarrow H)$.

Proof. By the supposition, $\mathrm{GL}\vdash D\wedge p\to(D'\to q)$. $D'\to q$ does not contain p nor does $D\wedge p$ contain q; any letter contained in both $D\wedge p$ and $D'\to q$ is thus contained in D and other than p. By the Craig interpolation lemma for GL, there is a sentence H, containing only sentence letters contained in D and other than p, such that

$\mathrm{GL} \vdash D \wedge p \to H$ and $\mathrm{GL} \vdash H \to (D' \to q)$. Then $\mathrm{GL} \vdash D \to (p \to H)$, $\mathrm{GL} \vdash D' \to (H \to q)$, and therefore by the substitution of p for q ir the latter, $\mathrm{GL} \vdash D \to (H \to p)$. Thus $\mathrm{GL} \vdash D \to (p \leftrightarrow H)$. ⊣

We now prove a lemma on the uniqueness of fixed points.

Lemma 11 (Bernardi). *Suppose that q does not occur in A, A is modalized in p, and A' is exactly like A except for containing an occurrence of q at all and only those places where A contains an occurrence of p. Then* $\mathrm{GL} \vdash \boxdot(p \leftrightarrow A) \wedge \boxdot(q \leftrightarrow A') \to (p \leftrightarrow q)$.

Proof. For every subsentence B of $A \wedge p$, let B' be the result of replacing every occurrence of p in B by an occurrence of q. Thus p' is q. We shall prove that for every subsentence B of $A \wedge p$, $\mathrm{GL} \vdash \boxdot(p \leftrightarrow A) \wedge \boxdot(q \leftrightarrow A') \to (B \leftrightarrow B')$; the lemma follows.

So suppose that for some finite transitive and irreflexive model M and some w of least rank, $M, w \vDash \boxdot(p \leftrightarrow A) \wedge \boxdot(q \leftrightarrow A')$ but $M, w \nvDash B \leftrightarrow B'$ for some subsentence B of $A \wedge p$. Since $w \vDash p \leftrightarrow q$ if $w \vDash A \leftrightarrow A'$, it is clear that we may suppose $B = \Box D$ and $B' = \Box D'$ for some D. But then, if wRx, $x \vDash \boxdot(p \leftrightarrow A) \wedge \boxdot(q \leftrightarrow A')$, and by leastness of the rank of w, $x \vDash D$ iff $x \vDash D'$, but then $w \vDash B$ iff $x \vDash D$ for all x such that wRx, iff $x \vDash D'$ for all x such that wRx, iff $w \vDash B$, contradiction. ⊣

The fixed point theorem is an immediate consequence of Lemma 11 and the Beth definability theorem for GL:

Let A be modalized in p. Let $q, \neq p$, be a sentence letter not in A, and let A' be the result of replacing each occurrence of p in A by one of q. By Lemma 11, $\mathrm{GL} \vdash \boxdot(p \leftrightarrow A) \wedge \boxdot(q \leftrightarrow A') \to (p \leftrightarrow q)$. The hypothesis of the Beth definability theorem for GL is now satisfied, with $D = \boxdot(p \leftrightarrow A)$ and $D' = \boxdot(q \leftrightarrow A')$. By the theorem, for some sentence H containing only sentence letters both contained in $\boxdot(p \leftrightarrow A)$ and other than p, i.e., both contained in A and other than p, $\mathrm{GL} \vdash \boxdot(p \leftrightarrow A) \to (p \leftrightarrow H)$.

Exercises. 1. (de Jongh) Suppose that A is modalized in p and that B does not contain p. Show, without using the fixed point theorem, that if $\mathrm{GL} \vdash \boxdot(p \leftrightarrow A) \to B$, then $\mathrm{GL} \vdash B$. (Hint: by induction on rank, adjust the truth-value of p at each world of some M in which B is invalid to make $p \leftrightarrow A$ true at each world.)

2. (Osamu Sonobe) Suppose that A is modalized in all sentence letters. Show that either $\mathrm{GL} \vdash \Diamond \top \to \Diamond A$ or $\mathrm{GL} \vdash \Diamond \top \to \Diamond \neg A$. (*Hint*: A is either true at all worlds of rank 0 or false at all worlds of rank 0.)

3. (Smullyan) Formulate and prove a double analogue of the fixed point theorem beginning, "Suppose that A and B are modalized in both p and q. Then there exists a sentence $H \ldots$".

4. Let S be an arbitrary sentence of arithmetic. Show that there is a sentence G^+ such that $\mathrm{PA} \vdash G^+ \leftrightarrow \neg \mathrm{Bew}(\ulcorner S \to G^+ \urcorner)$. Show that for any such G^+, $\mathrm{PA} \vdash G^+ \leftrightarrow \neg \mathrm{Bew}(\ulcorner \neg S \urcorner)$. (*Hint*: line 13.)

5. "If this statement is consistent, then you will have a test tomorrow but you cannot deduce from this statement that you will have a test tomorrow." Discuss.

9

The arithmetical completeness theorems for GL and GLS

GL, we know, is sound and complete with respect to transitive converse wellfounded models. That is, the modal sentences that are theorems of GL are precisely the sentences that are valid in all and only the models of that sort. We also know that all translations of all theorems of GL are theorems of PA. We are now going to prove the converse, the arithmetical completeness theorem for GL, due to Robert Solovay, which asserts that a modal sentence is a theorem of GL if it is always provable, that is, if all of its translations are theorems of PA. The arithmetical completeness theorem for GL thus tells us that if a modal sentence A is not a theorem of GL, then there is a realization $*$, possibly depending on A, such that A^* is not a theorem of PA.

It would be a mistake to suppose the arithmetical completeness theorem for GL to be of interest merely because it informs us about the power of the modal calculus GL; the theorem tells us much that is of interest about PA (and other systems too). For example, consider the sentence $\Box(\Box p \vee \Box\neg p)\rightarrow(\Box p \vee \Box\neg p)$, which, though evidently a theorem of GLS, fails at 1 in the converse wellfounded model

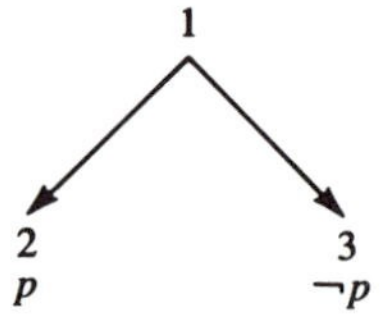

and therefore is not a theorem of GL. By the theorem, for some sentence S,

$$\mathrm{Bew}(\ulcorner(\mathrm{Bew}(\ulcorner S\urcorner) \vee \mathrm{Bew}(\ulcorner\neg S\urcorner))\urcorner)\rightarrow(\mathrm{Bew}(\ulcorner S\urcorner) \vee \mathrm{Bew}(\ulcorner\neg S\urcorner))$$

is not a theorem of PA, and thus, perhaps surprisingly, there is a sentence S such that it is consistent with PA that both S is undecidable and it is provable that S is decidable.

If a modal sentence A is a theorem of GLS, then it is always true: all translations of A are true. Solovay's arithmetical completeness theorem for GLS asserts that the converse also holds. We shall prove the arithmetical completeness theorem for GLS after proving the arithmetical completeness theorem for GL. The proof of the theorem for GLS will show the decidability of GLS, for it will show how to effectively associate with each modal sentence A a sentence A^s such that $\mathrm{GLS} \vdash A$ iff $\mathrm{GL} \vdash A^s$. Since, as we have seen, GL is decidable, it follows that GLS is decidable as well.

Towards the end of the chapter, we shall prove a strengthened theorem, the *uniform* arithmetical completeness theorem for GL, due to Sergei Artemov, Franco Montagna, Arnon Avron, Albert Visser, and the author, according to which there exists a single realization $*$ such that for every modal sentence A, if A is not a theorem of GL, then A^* is not a theorem of PA. Thus for any such $*$, for all A, $\mathrm{GL} \vdash A$ iff $\mathrm{PA} \vdash A^*$. We end with a theorem of Visser's that describes the provability logic of Σ sentences. Our primary goal, though, is to prove the arithmetical completeness theorems for GL and GLS.

The arithmetical completeness theorem for GL

We begin the proof by appealing to the semantical completeness theorem for GL that was established in Chapter 5.

Suppose that $\mathrm{GL} \nvdash A$. Then there is a finite transitive and converse wellfounded model $M, = \langle W, R, V \rangle$, such that for some $w \in W$, $w \nvDash A$.

We shall construct an interpretation $*$ from M and w such that $\mathrm{PA} \nvdash A^*$. We are now dealing with PA, and it will help if our "possible worlds" are natural numbers.

So since W is finite, we assume without loss of generality that $W = \{1, \ldots, n\}$, $w = 1$, and $1Ri$ iff $1 < i \leqslant n$. Thus $M, 1 \nvDash A$.

We are going to find sentences $S_0, S_1, \ldots, S_n$ of PA for which we can prove a certain lemma, Lemma 1 below: taking p^* (for any sentence letter p) as the disjunction of all S_i such that iVp, we will prove there that for $i \in W$ and B a subsentence of A, if $M, i \vDash B$, then $\mathrm{PA} \vdash S_i \to B^*$; but if $M, i \nvDash B$, then $\mathrm{PA} \vdash S_i \to \neg B^*$. Once we do so, we shall have shown that $\mathrm{PA} \vdash S_1 \to \neg A^*$ (since $1 \in W$ and A is a subsentence of itself).

What about S_0? We will also show that $\mathrm{PA} \vdash S_0 \to \neg \mathrm{Bew}(\ulcorner \neg S_1 \urcorner)$ and that S_0 is true. And once we have shown all this, we shall argue: since $\mathrm{PA} \vdash S_1 \to \neg A^*$,

$PA \vdash A^* \to \neg S_1$,
$PA \vdash \text{Bew}(\ulcorner A^* \urcorner) \to \text{Bew}(\ulcorner \neg S_1 \urcorner)$,
$PA \vdash \neg \text{Bew}(\ulcorner \neg S_1 \urcorner) \to \neg \text{Bew}(\ulcorner A^* \urcorner)$, and therefore
$PA \vdash S_0 \to \neg \text{Bew}(\ulcorner A^* \urcorner)$.

Therefore, since whatever PA proves is true, $S_0 \to \neg \text{Bew}(\ulcorner A^* \urcorner)$ is true. But S_0 is true, and consequently so is $\neg \text{Bew}(\ulcorner A^* \urcorner)$; that is to say, A^* is not provable in PA.

But how shall we find the "Solovay sentences" $S_0, S_1, \ldots, S_n$?

We begin by expanding M to a new model M'. Let $W' = W \cup \{0\}$; $R' = R \cup \{\langle 0, i \rangle : 1 \leqslant i \leqslant n\}$. Like R, R' is transitive and converse wellfounded. For all sentence letters p and all i, $1 \leqslant i \leqslant n$, let $iV'p$ iff iVp and $0V'p$ iff $1Vp$. Let $M' = \langle W', R', V' \rangle$. So our new model has a new world 0 from which the other worlds are accessible and which treats sentence letters as 1 does. It is M' that we shall actually embed into PA.

Each sentence S_j will be a sentence asserting that the values of a certain function h of natural numbers has the *limit* j.

Suppose that h is some function whose domain is N. We shall say that the *limit* of h is j if $h(m) = j$ for all sufficiently large m, that is, if for some m, $h(m) = j$ and also for all $m' > m$, $h(m') = j$.

Suppose further that the values of h all lie in W' and that if $h(m) = i$, then either $h(m+1) = i$ or $h(m+1) = j$ for some j such that $iR'j$. Since W' is finite, and R is transitive and irreflexive, it is clear that (a) the limit of h exists.

Moreover, it is clear from the transitivity of R' that (b) if $h(m) = i$ for some m, then either the limit of $h = i$ or the limit of $h = j$ for some j such that $iR'j$.

The h that we are going to define in PA will have the further properties that (c) $h(0) = 0$ and (d) if $h(m) = i$, then $h(m+1) = i$ *unless* m is the Gödel number of a proof in PA of the sentence $\neg S_j$ stating that it is *not* the case that the limit of $h = j$, for some j such that $iR'j$, in which case $h(m+1) = j$.[1]

We appear to be in a circle: Our function h is defined in terms of proofs of negations of sentences S_j; but each S_j asserts that the limit of h is a certain number. Of course we shall use the diagonal lemma to break out.

We begin the escape by noting that if $H(a, b)$ is a formula of PA defining the binary relation $\{\langle a, b \rangle : h(a) = b\}$, then the sentence S_j may (and will) be taken to be $\exists c \forall a (a \geqslant c \to \exists b (b = \mathbf{j} \wedge H(a, b)))$. [Informally, S_j says that for all sufficiently large a, $h(a) = j$.]

But how to define $H(a,b)$? Informally, $h(a)=b$ if and only if there is a finite sequence s of length $a+1$ such whose first value is 0 [since $h(0)=0$], whose last value is b, and such that for each $x<a$, if $s_x=i$, then $s_{x+1}=j$ if x is the Gödel number of a proof of

$$\neg\exists c\forall a(a\geqslant c\rightarrow\exists b(b=\mathbf{j}\wedge H(a,b)))$$

for some j such that $iR'j$; but $s_{x+1}=s_x$ provided that x is not the Gödel number of a proof of $\neg\exists c\forall a(a\geqslant c\rightarrow\exists b(b=\mathbf{j}\wedge H(a,b)))$ for any j such that $iR'j$.

We now use the diagonal lemma to convert this heuristic account of h into proper definitions of $H(a,b)$ and the S_j in six stages.

First of all, let F_m be the formula with Gödel number m.

Secondly, let $\mathrm{notlim}(x_1,x_2)$ be a Σ pterm for a function whose value for each m, j is the Gödel number of the formula

$$\neg\exists c\forall a(a\geqslant c\rightarrow\exists b(b=\mathbf{j}\wedge F_m))$$

(m goes with x_1, j with x_2.)

Thus if some formula $F(a,b)$ with Gödel number m defines a function, then $\mathrm{notlim}(\mathbf{m},\mathbf{j})$ denotes the Gödel number of the negation of the sentence saying that j is the limit of the function defined by $F(a,b)$.

Thirdly, let $B(y,a,b)$ be the formula

$$\begin{aligned}&\exists s(\mathrm{FinSeq}(s)\wedge \mathrm{lh}(s)=a+\mathbf{1}\wedge s_0=\mathbf{0}\wedge s_a=b\wedge\\ &\forall x<a\textstyle\bigwedge_{i:0\leqslant i\leqslant n}[s_x=\mathbf{i}\rightarrow\{\bigwedge_{j:iR'j}[\mathrm{Pf}(x,\mathrm{notlim}(y,\mathbf{j}))\rightarrow s_{x+1}=\mathbf{j}]\\ &\wedge[\{\textstyle\bigwedge_{j:iR'j}\neg\mathrm{Pf}(x,\mathrm{notlim}(y,\mathbf{j}))\}\rightarrow s_{x+1}=s_x]\}])\end{aligned}$$

If (the value of) y is the Gödel number of some formula F defining a function f, then $B(y,a,b)$ says there is a finite sequence of length $a+1$ with first value 0, last value b, and such that for each $x<a$, if $s_x=i$, then $s_{x+1}=j$ provided that $iR'j$ and x is the Gödel number of a proof of the negation of the sentence $\exists c\forall a(a\geqslant c\rightarrow\exists b(b=\mathbf{j}\wedge F))$ to the effect that j is the limit of f; and $=s_x$ if x is not the Gödel number of any such proof.

Fourthly, by the generalized diagonal lemma (Chapter 3), there is a formula $H(a,b)$ with just the variables a and b free such that

$$\mathrm{PA}\vdash H(a,b)\leftrightarrow B(\ulcorner H(a,b)\urcorner,a,b)$$

Fifthly, let m be the Gödel number of $H(a,b)$. So $H(a,b)$ is F_m.

And sixthly, for each j, $0\leqslant j\leqslant n$, let S_j be

$$\exists c\forall a(a\geqslant c\rightarrow\exists b(b=\mathbf{j}\wedge H(a,b)))$$

Then

$$\mathrm{PA} \vdash \mathrm{notlim}(\ulcorner H(a,b)\urcorner, \mathbf{j}) = \mathrm{notlim}(\mathbf{m}, \mathbf{j}) = \ulcorner \neg \exists c \forall a(a \geqslant c \rightarrow \exists b(b = \mathbf{j} \wedge H(a,b))\urcorner = \ulcorner \neg S_j \urcorner$$

and so

(1) $\mathrm{PA} \vdash H(a,b) \leftrightarrow \exists s(\mathrm{FinSeq}(s) \wedge \mathrm{lh}(s) = a + \mathbf{1} \wedge s_0 = \mathbf{0} \wedge s_a = b \wedge \forall x < a \bigwedge_{i:0 \leqslant i \leqslant n} [s_x = \mathbf{i} \rightarrow \{\bigwedge_{j:iR'j}[\mathrm{Pf}(x, \ulcorner \neg S_j \urcorner) \rightarrow s_{x+1} = \mathbf{j}] \wedge [\{\bigwedge_{j:iR'j} \neg \mathrm{Pf}(x, \ulcorner \neg S_j \urcorner)\} \rightarrow s_{x+1} = s_x]\}])$

Note that since $\mathrm{Pr}(x, y)$ is a Δ formula, $H(a,b)$ is a Σ formula. $H(a,b)$ defines the function h described above, and for each $j \leqslant n$, S_j is the sentence of PA that states that the limit of $h = j$.

Having found $H(a,b)$, we are now going to show that PA proves various facts about the Solovay sentences S_j constructed from it. We shall see that PA proves that h has a unique limit $\leqslant n$ (2,4); that if $iR'j$, PA proves ($S_i \rightarrow$ "S_j is consistent") (5); that if $i \geqslant 1$, then PA proves ($S_i \rightarrow$ "S_i is refutable") (6); and that if $i \geqslant 1$, then PA also proves ($S_i \rightarrow$ "the limit of h is some j such that $iR'j$") (7).

Since $\mathrm{PA} \vdash \exists! b H(a,b)$, as may be readily seen by an induction on the variable a, we clearly have

(2) $\mathrm{PA} \vdash \neg(S_i \wedge S_j)$ if $0 \leqslant i < j \leqslant n$

$\langle W', R' \rangle$ is a finite frame that is transitive and converse well-founded. We now show by induction on the converse of R' (otherwise put, by induction on rank) that

(3) $\mathrm{PA} \vdash H(a, \mathbf{i}) \rightarrow (S_i \vee \bigvee_{j:iR'j} S_j)$

So we may assume that for all j such that $iR'j$,

$\mathrm{PA} \vdash H(a, \mathbf{j}) \rightarrow (S_j \vee \bigvee_{k:jR'k} S_k)$. From (1), we have that
$\mathrm{PA} \vdash H(a, \mathbf{i}) \rightarrow \forall c(c \geqslant a \rightarrow [H(c, \mathbf{i}) \vee \bigvee_{j:iR'j} H(c, \mathbf{j})])$,

which, together with the inductive assumption, yields

$\mathrm{PA} \vdash H(a, \mathbf{i}) \rightarrow \forall c(c \geqslant a \rightarrow [H(c, \mathbf{i}) \vee \bigvee_{j:iR'j}(S_j \vee \bigvee_{k:jR'k} S_k)])$, whence
$\mathrm{PA} \vdash H(a, \mathbf{i}) \rightarrow (\forall c(c \geqslant a \rightarrow H(c, \mathbf{i})) \vee \bigvee_{j:iR'j}(S_j \vee \bigvee_{k:jR'k} S_k))$, i.e.,
$\mathrm{PA} \vdash H(a, \mathbf{i}) \rightarrow (S_i \vee \bigvee_{j:iR'j}(S_j \vee \bigvee_{k:jR'k} S_k))$.

Since R' is transitive, (3) holds.

It follows from (3) that $\mathrm{PA} \vdash H(a, \mathbf{0}) \to (S_0 \vee S_1 \vee \cdots \vee S_n)$. Since $\mathrm{PA} \vdash H(\mathbf{0}, \mathbf{0})$, we have

(4) $\mathrm{PA} \vdash (S_0 \vee S_1 \vee \cdots \vee S_n)$

Now suppose that $iR'j$. Note that PA proves that every theorem of PA has infinitely many proofs (any proof can be lengthened by repeating its last formula). Thus for every S,

$$\mathrm{PA} \vdash \mathrm{Bew}(\ulcorner S \urcorner) \to \forall x \exists y (y > x \wedge \mathrm{Pf}(y, \ulcorner S \urcorner))$$

The following argument can then be formalized in PA: Suppose that the limit of $h = i$. Let m be the least number such that for all $r \geqslant m$, $h(r) = h(m) = i$. Since each theorem of PA has infinitely many proofs, if $\neg S_j$ is a theorem of PA, for some least $k > m$, k is the Gödel number of a proof of $\neg S_j$, and then $h(k+1) = j \neq i$, contradiction. Thus $\neg S_j$ is not a theorem of PA. Formalizing this argument shows that

(5) If $iR'j$, then $\mathrm{PA} \vdash S_i \to \neg \mathrm{Bew}(\ulcorner \neg S_j \urcorner)$

(6) If $i \geqslant 1$, then $\mathrm{PA} \vdash S_i \to \mathrm{Bew}(\ulcorner \neg S_i \urcorner)$

Proof. Suppose that $i \geqslant 1$. By (1),
$\mathrm{PA} \vdash H(a, \mathbf{i}) \to \exists x \, \mathrm{Pf}(x, \ulcorner \neg S_i \urcorner)$. Since
$\mathrm{PA} \vdash S_i \to \exists a H(a, \mathbf{i})$, we have
$\mathrm{PA} \vdash S_i \to \mathrm{Bew}(\ulcorner \neg S_i \urcorner)$. ⊣

(7) If $i \geqslant 1$, then $\mathrm{PA} \vdash S_i \to \mathrm{Bew}(\ulcorner \bigvee_{j:iR'j} S_j \urcorner)$

Proof. By (3), $\mathrm{PA} \vdash \exists a H(a, \mathbf{i}) \to (S_i \vee \bigvee_{j:iR'j} S_j)$. Thus
$\mathrm{PA} \vdash \mathrm{Bew}(\ulcorner \exists a H(a, \mathbf{i}) \urcorner) \to \mathrm{Bew}(\ulcorner S_i \vee \bigvee_{j:iR'j} S_j \urcorner)$. But
$\mathrm{PA} \vdash \mathrm{Bew}(\ulcorner \neg S_i \urcorner) \wedge \mathrm{Bew}(\ulcorner (S_i \vee \bigvee_{j:iR'j} S_j) \urcorner) \to \mathrm{Bew}(\ulcorner \bigvee_{j:iR'j} S_j \urcorner)$.
$\mathrm{PA} \vdash \exists a H(a, \mathbf{i}) \to \mathrm{Bew}(\ulcorner \exists a H(a, \mathbf{i}) \urcorner)$ since $H(a, b)$ is Σ, and
$\mathrm{PA} \vdash S_i \to \exists a H(a, \mathbf{i})$. By (6), if $\mathbf{i} \geqslant 1$,
$\mathrm{PA} \vdash S_i \to \mathrm{Bew}(\ulcorner \neg S_i \urcorner)$. These last five theorems yield (7). ⊣

For each sentence letter p, let $p^* = \bigvee_{i:iV'p} S_i$.

Lemma 1. *For all i, $1 \leqslant i \leqslant n$ [n.b.], and all subsentences B of A, if $M, i \vDash B$, then $\mathrm{PA} \vdash S_i \to B^*$; and if $M, i \nvDash B$, then $\mathrm{PA} \vdash S_i \to \neg B^*$.*

Proof. Induction on the complexity of B. Suppose that $B = p$. Then $B^* = \bigvee_{i:iV'p} S_i$.

If $i \vDash p$, then iVp, whence $iV'p$, and so $\mathrm{PA} \vdash S_i \to p^*$, i.e., $\mathrm{PA} \vdash S_i \to B^*$.

If $i \nvDash p$, then not: iVp, whence not $iV'p$, as $i \neq 0$. Then for every disjunct S_j of p^*, S_i is different from S_j, and then by (2), $\mathrm{PA} \vdash S_i \to \neg S_j$; therefore $\mathrm{PA} \vdash S_i \to \neg p^*$, i.e., $\mathrm{PA} \vdash S_i \to \neg B^*$.

The truth-functional cases are completely straightforward.

Now suppose that $B = \Box C$. Then $B^* = \mathrm{Bew}(\ulcorner C^* \urcorner)$.

If $i \vDash B$, then for all j such that iRj, $j \vDash C$, and then by the induction hypothesis, for all j such that iRj,
$\mathrm{PA} \vdash S_j \to C^*$. Since $i \geqslant 1$, iRj iff $iR'j$, and so
$\mathrm{PA} \vdash \bigvee_{j:iR'j} S_j \to C^*$.
$\mathrm{PA} \vdash \mathrm{Bew}(\ulcorner \bigvee_{j:iR'j} S_j \urcorner) \to B^*$, whence by (7),
$\mathrm{PA} \vdash S_i \to B^*$.

Finally if $i \nvDash B$, then for some j, $j \geqslant 1$, iRj, whence $iR'j$, and $j \nvDash C$; thus by the induction hypothesis,
$\mathrm{PA} \vdash S_j \to \neg C^*$, and so
$\mathrm{PA} \vdash \neg \mathrm{Bew}(\ulcorner \neg S_j \urcorner) \to \neg \mathrm{Bew}(\ulcorner C^* \urcorner)$. By (5),
$\mathrm{PA} \vdash S_i \to \neg \mathrm{Bew}(\ulcorner \neg S_j \urcorner)$, and therefore
$\mathrm{PA} \vdash S_i \to \neg B^*$. $\dashv$

It follows from Lemma 1 that

$\mathrm{PA} \vdash S_1 \to \neg A^*$, and therefore
$\mathrm{PA} \vdash A^* \to \neg S_1$,
$\mathrm{PA} \vdash \mathrm{Bew}(\ulcorner A^* \urcorner) \to \mathrm{Bew}(\ulcorner \neg S_1 \urcorner)$, and
$\mathrm{PA} \vdash \neg \mathrm{Bew}(\ulcorner \neg S_1 \urcorner) \to \neg \mathrm{Bew}(\ulcorner A^* \urcorner)$. By (5),
$\mathrm{PA} \vdash S_0 \to \neg \mathrm{Bew}(\ulcorner \neg S_1 \urcorner)$, and therefore

(8) $\mathrm{PA} \vdash S_0 \to \neg \mathrm{Bew}(\ulcorner A^* \urcorner)$

We now conclude the proof of Solovay's completeness theorem for GL; this part of the argument *cannot* be formalized in PA: Every theorem of PA is true. If $i \geqslant 1$, then according to (6), if S_i is true, so is $\mathrm{Bew}(\ulcorner \neg S_i \urcorner)$, and then $\neg S_i$ is a theorem of PA, and so $\neg S_i$ is true. Thus if $i \geqslant 1$, S_i is *not* true. But according to (4), at least one of $S_0, S_1, \ldots, S_n$ is true. So S_0 is true. According to (8), $S_0 \to \neg \mathrm{Bew}(\ulcorner A^* \urcorner)$ is also true, and therefore so is $\neg \mathrm{Bew}(\ulcorner A^* \urcorner)$. But then A^* is not a theorem of PA, Q.E.D.

(What *can* be proved in PA is the sentence
$\bigwedge_{i:1 \leqslant i \leqslant n} [\mathrm{Bew}(\ulcorner \neg S_i \urcorner) \to \neg S_i] \to \neg \mathrm{Bew}(\ulcorner A^* \urcorner)$, which follows from

(4), (6), and (8). However, the antecedent of this conditional, true though it is, cannot be proved in PA.)

The arithmetical completeness theorem for GLS

We now prove Solovay's theorem on the arithmetical completeness of GLS, that a modal sentence A is always true, i.e., true under all translations, if and only if it is a theorem of GLS.

For each modal sentence A, let A^s be $(\bigwedge\{(\Box C \to C): \Box C \text{ is a subsentence of } A\} \to A)$.

Theorem (the arithmetical completeness theorem for GLS). *For every modal sentence A, the following three conditions are equivalent:* (*a*) $\mathrm{GL} \vdash A^s$; (*b*) $\mathrm{GLS} \vdash A$; (*c*) *A is always true.*

Proof. (a) implies (b): if $\mathrm{GL} \vdash A^s$, then $\mathrm{GLS} \vdash A^s$; since GLS is closed under truth-functional consequence and $\mathrm{GLS} \vdash (\Box C \to C)$, it follows that $\mathrm{GLS} \vdash A$.

(b) implies (c): this is the arithmetical soundness of GLS and was proved in Chapter 3.

(c) implies (a): suppose that $\mathrm{GL} \nvdash A^s$. We must show that A^* is false for some realization $*$. By the semantical completeness theorem for GL, we have that for some $M, = \langle\{1, \ldots, n\}, R, V\rangle$, with R transitive and irreflexive, $M, 1 \nvDash A^s$, and $1Ri$ iff $1 < i \leqslant n$. Let W', R', V', $S_0, S_1, \ldots, S_n$, and $*$ be defined from M as above. We shall show that A^* is false. Let us observe that we are entitled to use Lemma 1 for all subsentences of A^s, and hence certainly for all subsentences of A (a subsentence of A^s).

Since $1 \nvDash A^s$, for all subsentences $\Box C$ of A, $1 \vDash \Box C \to C$, and $1 \nvDash A$. We shall now show that for all subsentences B of A, if $1 \vDash B$, then $\mathrm{PA} \vdash S_0 \to B^*$, and if $1 \nvDash B$, then $\mathrm{PA} \vdash S_0 \to \neg B^*$.

Suppose that $B = p$. If $1 \vDash p$, then $1Vp$, $0V'p$ by the definition of V', and S_0 is one of the disjuncts of p^*. Thus $\vdash S_0 \to p^*$. But if $1 \nvDash p$, then S_0 is not one of the disjuncts of p^*, and so by (2), $\vdash S_0 \to \neg p^*$.

The truth-functional cases are straightforward.

Suppose that $B = \Box C$.

If $1 \vDash \Box C$, then for all i, $1 < i \leqslant n$, $i \vDash C$, and so by Lemma 1, $\mathrm{PA} \vdash S_i \to C^*$. Since $1 \vDash \Box C \to C$, $1 \vDash C$, whence by Lemma 1, $\mathrm{PA} \vdash S_1 \to C^*$, and by the hypothesis of the induction (C being simpler than B), $\mathrm{PA} \vdash S_0 \to C^*$. But by (4), $\mathrm{PA} \vdash S_0 \vee S_1 \vee \cdots \vee S_n$. Thus $\mathrm{PA} \vdash C^*$, and so $\mathrm{PA} \vdash \mathrm{Bew}(\ulcorner C^* \urcorner)$, i.e., $\mathrm{PA} \vdash (\Box C)^*$, and therefore $\mathrm{PA} \vdash S_0 \to (\Box C)^*$.

And if $1 \nVdash \Box C$, then for some i, $1 < i \leqslant n$, $i \nVdash C$, and by lemma 1, $\mathrm{PA} \vdash S_i \to \neg C^*$, whence $\mathrm{PA} \vdash \neg \mathrm{Bew}(\ulcorner \neg S_i \urcorner) \to \neg(\Box C)^*$. Since $0R'i$, by (5) we have $\mathrm{PA} \vdash S_0 \to \neg \mathrm{Bew}(\ulcorner \neg S_i \urcorner)$, and therefore $\mathrm{PA} \vdash S_0 \to \neg(\Box C)^*$.

$1 \nVdash A$, so $\mathrm{PA} \vdash S_0 \to \neg A^*$, and therefore $S_0 \to \neg A^*$ is true. But since S_0 is also true, A^* is false, which establishes Solovay's theorem on the arithmetical completeness of GLS. ⊣

The uniform arithmetical completeness theorem for GL

Neither p nor $\neg p$ is a theorem of GLS, but for any realization $*$, either p^* or $\neg p^*$ is true. Thus there is no one realization $*$ such that for all modal sentences A, if A^* is true, then $\mathrm{GLS} \vdash A$. Moreover, there is no realization $*$ such that for all A and $\#$, $\mathrm{PA} \vdash (A^* \to A^\#)$; otherwise let $A_1 = p$, $p^{\#_1} = \bot$, $A_2 = \neg p$, and $p^{\#_2} = \top$; then $\mathrm{PA} \vdash p^* \to \bot$ and $\mathrm{PA} \vdash \neg p^* \to \neg \top$, whence $\mathrm{PA} \vdash \bot$, which is not the case.

But there is a single realization $*$ such that for all A and $\#$, if $\mathrm{PA} \vdash A^*$, then $\mathrm{PA} \vdash A^\#$, and by the arithmetical completeness theorem for GL, such that if $\mathrm{PA} \vdash A^*$, then $\mathrm{GL} \vdash A$.

The uniform arithmetical completeness theorem for GL (Artemov, Avron, Montagna, Visser, Boolos). *There exists a realization $*$ such that for all modal sentences A, if $\mathrm{PA} \vdash A^*$, then $\mathrm{GL} \vdash A$.*

The idea of the proof is simple. For each modal sentence that is not a theorem of GL, pick a finite transitive and irreflexive countermodel, taking the domains of the countermodels to contain only positive integers and to be disjoint from one another, paste the models together with 0 at the top to obtain an infinite but transitive converse wellfounded model, and carry through the construction of h as before. The only change needed is that since h can now take infinitely many values, we must define a predicate $S(x)$ for which $S(\mathbf{i})$ can play the role of S_i in the proof of the arithmetical completeness theorem for GL. Details follow.

Let $Q(x, y)$ be a Σ pterm for a function f such that for every natural number k, $f(k)$ is a code for a quintuple $\langle W_k, R_k, V_k, w_k, A_k \rangle$, where W_k is a finite set of positive integers, R_k is a transitive and irreflexive relation on W_k, $W_k = \{w_k\} \cup \{i\colon w_k R_k i\}$, if $i \in W_k$ and p_n is a sentence letter not in A_k, not: $i V_k p_n$, and $\langle W_k, R_k, V_k \rangle, w_k \nVdash A_k$; for every j, k, if $j \neq k$, W_j and W_k are disjoint; for every $i \geqslant 1$, $i \in \bigcup W_k$; and every modal sentence that is not a theorem of GL is A_k for some k.

The existence of such a Σ pterm is evident in view of the fact that if A is a sentence containing k symbols that is not a theorem of GL, then there is a countermodel $\langle W, R, V \rangle$ to A such that for some $n \leqslant 2^k$, $W = \{1, \ldots, n\}$; if wRx, then $1 \leqslant w, x \leqslant n$; and V contains at most nk pairs $\langle w, p \rangle$. There are at most $2^k \times 2^{(2^k)^2} \times 2^{(2^k k)}$ such $\langle W, R, V \rangle$.

Let $R' = \bigcup R_k \cup \{\langle 0, i \rangle$: for some $k, i \in W_k\}$. R' is thus transitive and converse wellfounded. Each $i \geqslant 1$ bears R' to finitely many numbers.

Let $V' = \bigcup V_k$.

Now let $R(x, y)$ be a Δ formula constructed from $Q(x, y)$ such that

(i) $\mathrm{PA} \vdash R(\mathbf{0}, y) \leftrightarrow y \neq \mathbf{0}$,

(ii) $\mathrm{PA} \vdash R(\mathbf{i}, y) \leftrightarrow \bigvee_{j:iR'j} y = \mathbf{j}$, if $i \geqslant 1$,

(iii) $\mathrm{PA} \vdash \forall x \forall y \forall z (R(x, y) \wedge R(y, z) \rightarrow R(x, z))$, and

(iv) $\mathrm{PA} \vdash \forall x (\forall y (R(x, y) \rightarrow F(y)) \rightarrow F(x)) \rightarrow \forall x F(x)$ for all formulas $F(x)$ of PA.

By (i) and (ii) $R(x, y)$ defines R' in PA: if $iR'j$, $\mathrm{PA} \vdash R(\mathbf{i}, \mathbf{j})$, and if not: $iR'j$, $\mathrm{PA} \vdash \neg R(\mathbf{i}, \mathbf{j})$. (iii) and (iv) formalize the transitivity and converse wellfoundedness of R'.

Let $\mathrm{ex}(x_1, x_2)$ be a Σ pterm for a function whose value at m, r is j if r is the Gödel number of a proof of $\neg \exists c \forall a (a \geqslant c \rightarrow \exists b (b = \mathbf{j} \wedge F_m))$ and is 0 otherwise. (ex *ex*tracts j from the last line of suitable proofs; m goes with x_1, r with x_2.) Note that $iR'0$ for no i.

We may suppose nonlim and ex have been so chosen that

(v) $\mathrm{PA} \vdash \mathrm{ex}(x_1, x_2) \neq 0 \rightarrow \mathrm{Pf}(x_2, \mathrm{nonlim}(x_1, \mathrm{ex}(x_1, x_2)))$.

By the generalized diagonal lemma there is a formula $G(a, b)$ with Gödel number g such that

$$(1') \quad \mathrm{PA} \vdash G(a, b) \leftrightarrow \exists s (\mathrm{FinSeq}(s) \wedge \mathrm{lh}(s) = a + \mathbf{1} \wedge s_0 = \mathbf{0} \wedge s_a = b \wedge \forall x < a \{ [R(s_x, \mathrm{ex}(\mathbf{g}, x)) \rightarrow s_{x+\mathbf{1}} = \mathrm{ex}(\mathbf{g}, x)] \wedge [\neg R(s_x, \mathrm{ex}(\mathbf{g}, x)) \rightarrow s_{x+\mathbf{1}} = s_x] \})$$

Since $R(x, y)$ is a Δ formula and $\mathrm{ex}(x_1, x_2)$ a Σ pterm, $G(a, b)$ is Σ.

We let $S(x)$ be the formula $\exists c \forall a (a \geqslant c \rightarrow \exists b (b = x \wedge G(a, b)))$.

Like H, G defines a function h such that $h(0) = 0$ and $h(r + 1) = h(r)$ unless r is the Gödel number of a proof that it is not the case that the limit of h is j for some j such that $h(r)R'j$, in which case $h(r + 1) = j$. For each j, $S(\mathbf{j})$ says that the limit of h is j.

We now prove analogues (2′)–(7′) of (2)–(7).

(2′) $\mathrm{PA} \vdash S(x) \wedge S(y) \rightarrow x = y$

Proof. As before, $\mathrm{PA} \vdash \exists! b G(a, b)$. ⊣

(3′) $\mathrm{PA} \vdash G(a, x) \rightarrow S(x) \vee \exists y(R(x, y) \wedge S(y))$

Proof. Induction, this time in PA, on the converse wellfounded relation R' defined by $R(x, y)$. Let $F(x)$ be $G(a, x) \rightarrow S(x) \vee \exists y(R(x, y) \wedge S(y))$. Now work in PA. Suppose $\forall y(R(x, y) \rightarrow F(y))$ and $G(a, x)$. By (1′), $G(a, x)$, provable transitivity, and induction on d, we have $\forall d(d \geqslant a \rightarrow G(d, x) \vee \exists y(R(x, y) \wedge G(d, y))$. By $\forall y(R(x, y) \rightarrow F(y))$, we have $\forall d(d \geqslant a \rightarrow G(d, x) \vee \exists y(R(x, y) \wedge (S(y) \vee \exists z(R(y, z) \wedge S(z)))))$, and so $S(x) \vee \exists y(R(x, y) \wedge (S(y) \vee \exists z(R(y, z) \wedge S(z))))$, whence $S(x) \vee \exists y(R(x, y) \wedge S(y))$.

As before, $\mathrm{PA} \vdash G(a, \mathbf{0}) \rightarrow S(\mathbf{0}) \vee \exists y(R(\mathbf{0}, y) \wedge S(y))$, and $\mathrm{PA} \vdash G(\mathbf{0}, \mathbf{0})$. Thus,

(4′) $\mathrm{PA} \vdash \exists x S(x)$ ⊣

(5′) If $iR'j$, then $\mathrm{PA} \vdash S(\mathbf{i}) \rightarrow \neg \mathrm{Bew}(\ulcorner \neg S(\mathbf{j}) \urcorner)$

Proof. Like that of (5). ⊣

(6′) If $i \geqslant 1$, then $\mathrm{PA} \vdash S(\mathbf{i}) \rightarrow \mathrm{Bew}(\ulcorner \neg S(\mathbf{i}) \urcorner)$

Proof. Assume $G(a, \mathbf{i})$. Since $i \geqslant 1$ and $G(\mathbf{0}, \mathbf{0})$ holds, $a > 0$. Thus for some s, c, $\mathrm{lh}(s) = a + 1$, $c < a$, $s_c \neq s_{c+1} = s_a = \mathbf{i} = \mathrm{ex}(\mathbf{g}, c)$ and $R(s_c, \mathrm{ex}(\mathbf{g}, c))$ hold. Since $\mathbf{i} \neq \mathbf{0}$ holds, so does $\mathrm{Pf}(c, \mathrm{nonlim}(\mathbf{g}, \mathrm{ex}(\mathbf{g}, c)))$ by (v), and therefore so does $\mathrm{Bew}(\ulcorner \neg S(\mathbf{i}) \urcorner)$. Formalizing, we obtain $\mathrm{PA} \vdash G(a, \mathbf{i}) \rightarrow \mathrm{Bew}(\ulcorner \neg S(\mathbf{i}) \urcorner)$, and then (6′) follows as did (6). ⊣

(7′) If $i \geqslant 1$, then $\mathrm{PA} \vdash S(\mathbf{i}) \rightarrow \mathrm{Bew}(\ulcorner \bigvee_{j: iR'j} S(\mathbf{j}) \urcorner)$

Proof. By (3′),
$\mathrm{PA} \vdash \exists a G(a, \mathbf{i}) \rightarrow S(\mathbf{i}) \vee \exists y(R(\mathbf{i}, y) \wedge S(y))$. By (ii),
$\mathrm{PA} \vdash \exists a G(a, \mathbf{i}) \rightarrow S(\mathbf{i}) \vee \bigvee_{j: iR'j} S(\mathbf{j})$.
The rest of the proof is like that of (7), with an appeal to (6′) instead of (6). ⊣

Now let $V(x, y)$ be a Δ formula [obtained from $Q(x, y)$] defining the relation $\{\langle i, n\rangle : iV'p_n\}$.

For each n, let $p_n^* = \exists x(S(x) \wedge V(x, \mathbf{n}))$.

Lemma. *For all k, all subsentences B of A_k, and all $i \in W_k$, if $\langle W_k, R_k, V_k\rangle, i \vDash B$, then $\mathrm{PA} \vdash S(\mathbf{i}) \to B^*$, and if $\langle W_k, R_k, V_k\rangle, i \nvDash B$, then $\mathrm{PA} \vdash S(i) \to \neg B^*$.*

Proof. Induction on the complexity of B. (We drop '$\langle W_k, R_k, V_k\rangle$'.)

Suppose $B = p_n$. If $i \vDash B$, then $iV_k p_n$, $iV'p_n$, $\mathrm{PA} \vdash V(\mathbf{i}, \mathbf{n})$, and $\mathrm{PA} \vdash S(\mathbf{i}) \to \exists x(S(x) \wedge V(x, \mathbf{n}))$, i.e., $\mathrm{PA} \vdash S(\mathbf{i}) \to B^*$. If $i \nvDash B$, then not $iV_k p_n$, not $iV'p_n$, $\mathrm{PA} \vdash \neg V(\mathbf{i}, \mathbf{n})$, whence by (2′), $\mathrm{PA} \vdash S(\mathbf{i}) \to \neg \exists x(S(x) \wedge V(x, \mathbf{n}))$, i.e., $\mathrm{PA} \vdash S(\mathbf{i}) \to \neg B^*$.

The truth-functional cases are unproblematic. The argument for the case in which $B = \Box C$ proceeds as in the earlier proof, with appeals to (7′) and (5′) in place of those to (7) and (5), except that we must now observe that since $i \in W_k$, $iR_k j$ iff $iR'j$, and if $iR_k j$, $j \in W_k$. $\dashv$

To complete the proof of the theorem, suppose that $\mathrm{GL} \nvdash A$. Then for some k, $A = A_k$, and therefore $\langle W_k, R_k, V_k\rangle, w_k \nvDash A_k$. Let $i = w_k$. By the lemma, $\mathrm{PA} \vdash S(\mathbf{i}) \to \neg A^*$, and therefore $\mathrm{PA} \vdash \neg \mathrm{Bew}(\ulcorner \neg S(\mathbf{i}) \urcorner) \to \neg \mathrm{Bew}(\ulcorner A^* \urcorner)$. $0R'i$, and thus by (5′), $\mathrm{PA} \vdash S(\mathbf{0}) \to \neg \mathrm{Bew}(\ulcorner A^* \urcorner)$.

By (2′) and (4′), $S(\mathbf{i})$ is true for exactly one i. By (7′), $S(\mathbf{i})$ is true for no i other than 0. Thus $S(\mathbf{0})$ is true, and A^* not provable.

The provability logic of Σ sentences

Σ sentences, which figure prominently in our subject, enjoy an extra modal property not in general possessed by arbitrary sentences of arithmet‑ .. S is Σ and $p^* = S$, then $\mathrm{PA} \vdash (p \to \Box p)^*$. We end with a characterization, due to Albert Visser, of their provability logic.

We shall call a realization $*$ a Σ realization iff p^* is a Σ sentence for every sentence letter p. We wish to characterize the modal sentences A such that for every Σ realization $*$, $\mathrm{PA} \vdash A^*$, and those such that for every Σ realization $*$, A^* is true. To this end, we introduce two systems, GLV and GLSV.

The axioms of GLV are those of GL together with all sentences $p \to \Box p$ (p a *sentence letter*); the rules of inference of GLV are modus ponens and necessitation. GLV is not a normal system, for it is not closed under substitution.

The axioms of GLSV are the theorems of GLV and all sentences $\Box A \to A$; its sole rule of inference is modus ponens.

A model M is *appropriate to GLV* if W is finite, R is irreflexive and transitive, and V meets a special condition: For all $w, x \in W$ and all sentence letters p, if wRx and wVp, then xVp.

Theorem (Visser)

(a) GLV$\vdash A$ *iff* A *is valid in all appropriate models; iff for all* Σ *realizations* $*$, PA$\vdash A^*$.

(b) GLSV$\vdash A$ *iff for all* Σ *realizations* $*$, A^* *is true.*

Proof. (a) It is clear that if GLV$\vdash A$, then for all Σ realizations $*$, PA$\vdash A^*$.

We now want to show that if A is valid in all appropriate models, then GLV$\vdash A$. So suppose GLV$\nvdash A$.

Let $\mathscr{A} = \{B: B$ is a subsentence of $A\}$, $\mathscr{B} = \mathscr{A} \cup \{\Box p: p \in \mathscr{A}\}$, and $\mathscr{C} = \mathscr{B} \cup \{\neg B: B \in \mathscr{B}\}$. Let W be the set of maximal GLV-consistent subsets of $\mathscr{C}$. Define R, V, and M as in the completeness proof for GL. We can then prove as before that for any subsentence B of A and any $w \in W$, $B \in w$ iff $w \vDash B$, and that therefore A is invalid in M (since for some maximal consistent w, $A \notin w$). To prove that M is appropriate, we must also show that V meets the special condition. So suppose wRx and wVp. We are to show xVp.

But since wVp and p is a sentence letter, $w \vDash p$ and $p \in \mathscr{A}$, whence $p \in w$ and $\Box p \in \mathscr{B}$. Since GLV$\vdash p \to \Box p$, $\Box p \in w$, and since wRx, $p \in x$, $x \vDash p$, and so xVp.

So if A is valid in all appropriate models, GLV$\vdash A$.

The Solovay construction is as before, but we must now show that p^*, $= \bigvee \{S_i: iV'p \wedge 0 \leqslant i \leqslant n\}$, is Σ. Let $S = \bigvee \{\exists a H(a, \mathbf{i}): iV'p \wedge 0 \leqslant i \leqslant n\}$. It is enough to show that $\vdash p^* \leftrightarrow S$, for since $H(a, b)$ is Σ, S is Σ. And since PA$\vdash S_i \to \exists a H(a, \mathbf{i})$, it is enough to show that PA$\vdash S \to p^*$. There are two cases:

(1) $1Vp$. Then by the special condition, for all i, $1 \leqslant i \leqslant n$, iVp, and also $0V'p$. Thus for all i, $0 \leqslant i \leqslant n$, $iV'p$. By (4), PA$\vdash S_0 \vee S_1 \vee \cdots \vee S_n$, i.e., PA$\vdash p^*$, and so certainly PA$\vdash S \to p^*$.

(2) Not: $1Vp$. Then neither $0V'p$ nor $1V'p$, and $S = \bigvee \{\exists a H(a, \mathbf{i}): iVp \wedge 1 < i \leqslant n\}$ and $p^* = \bigvee \{S_i: iVp \wedge 1 < i \leqslant n\}$. If iVp and $1 < i \leqslant n$, then by (3), PA$\vdash H(a, \mathbf{i}) \to (S_i \vee \bigvee_{j:iR'j} S_j)$, and there-

fore $\mathrm{PA} \vdash H(a, \mathbf{i}) \rightarrow p^*$, for S_i is a disjunct of p^*, and if $iR'j$, then iRj, $1 < j$, and by the special condition, jVp, and so S_j is also a disjunct of p^*. Thus again $\mathrm{PA} \vdash S \rightarrow p^*$.

As for (b), the left–right direction is clear, and if $\mathrm{GLV} \nvdash A^s$, then for some M appropriate to GLV and $*$ constructed from M as in the proof of the arithmetical completeness theorem for GLS, A^* is false. Since M is appropriate to GLV, $*$ is Σ. ⊣

10

Trees for GL

The method of truth-trees, due to Smullyan, is a proof procedure for propositional and predicate logic that is an attractive simplification of the proof procedure due to Beth called the method of semantic tableaux, which is in turn an adaptation of proof procedures due to Gentzen and Herbrand. Kripke showed how the method of semantic tableaux for the propositional calculus could be extended to provide completeness proofs for several systems of propositional modal logic. In the present chapter we shall adapt Kripke's methods to show how the method of trees may be extended to prove the completeness of GL with respect to finite transitive and irreflexive models. The extension to GL of the method of trees also supplies us with a quite practical decision procedure for GL. We shall assume that the reader is already familiar with some presentation of the method of truth-trees for the propositional calculus, such as the one in Smullyan's *First-Order Logic*, Jeffrey's *Formal Logic: Its Scope and Limits*, or Hodges's *Logic*.

Let us first take a look at a few examples before formally describing our extension of the method of trees.

To test a sentence for theoremhood (or validity) in the method of trees, one tests its negation for consistency (satisfiability). Let us test $\Box(\Box p \to p) \to \Box p$ for theoremhood in GL (Example 1).

Example 1

$$\text{GL} \vdash \Box(\Box p \to p) \to \Box p \ ?$$

$(1) \ \checkmark \ \neg(\Box(\Box p \to p) \to \Box p)$

$(2) \quad \begin{array}{c} \Box(\Box p \to p) \\ \checkmark \ \neg\Box p \end{array}$

$(3) \quad \begin{array}{c} \neg p \\ \Box p \\ \checkmark \ \Box p \to p \\ \Box(\Box p \to p) \end{array}$

$\begin{array}{ccc} \neg\Box p & & p \\ \times & (4) & \times \end{array}$

$\times$

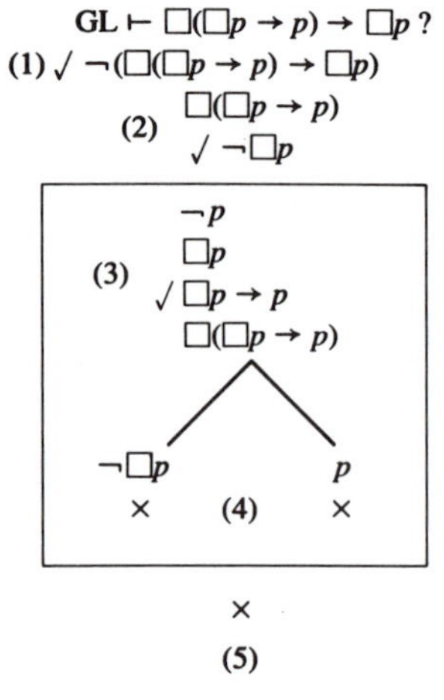

In step (1) we write down its negation $\neg(\Box(\Box p \to p) \to \Box p)$. In step (2) we apply the propositional calculus rules as many times as we can, inferring $\Box(\Box p \to p)$ and $\neg\Box p$ from $\neg(\Box(\Box p \to p) \to \Box p)$ and checking it to indicate that we have finished with it. (Recall that we apply propositional calculus rules only to unchecked occurrences of sentences; that when we apply a propositional calculus rule to an occurrence of a sentence, we check that occurrence; and that we write: $\times$ at the bottom of a branch to indicate that it is closed.) In step (3) we "open a window onto a possible world." We (guess how much space we will later need and) write:

$$\neg p$$
$$\Box p$$
$$\Box p \to p$$
$$\Box(\Box p \to p)$$

meaning: $\Diamond(\neg p \wedge \Box p \wedge (\Box p \to p) \wedge \Box(\Box p \to p))$. The justification for doing so is that

$$\mathrm{GL} \vdash \neg\Box p \wedge \Box(\Box p \to p) \to \Diamond(\neg p \wedge \Box p \wedge (\Box p \to p) \wedge \Box(\Box p \to p))$$

We then check $\neg\Box p$. Since there are no further sentences $\neg\Box A$ in our tree, in step (4) we apply the propositional calculus rules inside the window as many times as possible, obtaining a closed tree in the window. In step (5) we close the branch on which the window lies because there is a closed tree in the window. Our justification here is that if $\mathrm{GL} \vdash \neg F$ and $\mathrm{GL} \vdash E \to \Diamond F$, then $\mathrm{GL} \vdash \Box\neg F$, and so $\mathrm{GL} \vdash \neg E$. Since all branches of the outermost tree are closed, the tree is closed, and $\neg(\Box(\Box p \to p) \to \Box p)$ is not consistent with GL, that is, $\Box(\Box p \to p) \to \Box p$ is a theorem of GL (as of course we knew).

In Example 2, we negate the sentence that we are testing for theoremhood and apply the propositional calculus rules as many times as we can. We obtain a tree with a single branch; there are two sentences $\neg\Box C$: $\neg\Box p$ and $\neg\Box\Box p$ and one sentence $\Box D$: $\Box(p \vee \Box p)$ on the branch. We then open two windows, one for each of the sentences $\neg\Box C$, on the branch. At the top of one of them we write $\neg p$, $\Box p$, $p \vee \Box p$, and $\Box(p \vee \Box p)$; at the top of the other, we put $\neg\Box p$, $\Box\Box p$, $p \vee \Box p$, and $\Box(p \vee \Box p)$. We then apply the propositional calculus rules as many times as possible. We have then

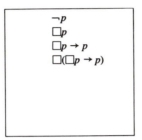

Example 2   GL ⊢ □(p ∨ □p) → (□p ∨ □□p) ?

$\checkmark\ \neg(\Box(p \vee \Box p) \to (\Box p \vee \Box\Box p))$

$\Box(p \vee \Box p)$

$\checkmark\ \neg(\Box p \vee \Box\Box p)$

$\checkmark\ \neg\Box p$

$\checkmark\ \neg\Box\Box p$

$\neg p$
$\Box p$
$\checkmark\ p \vee \Box p$
$\Box(p \vee \Box p)$

$p \qquad \Box p$
$\times$

$\checkmark\ \neg\Box p$
$\Box\Box p$
$\checkmark\ p \vee \Box p$
$\Box(p \vee \Box p)$

$p \qquad \Box p$
$\qquad\ \times$

$\neg p$
$\Box p$
$\Box p$
$\Box\Box p$
$\checkmark\ p \vee \Box p$
$\Box(p \vee \Box p)$

$p \qquad \Box p$
$\times$

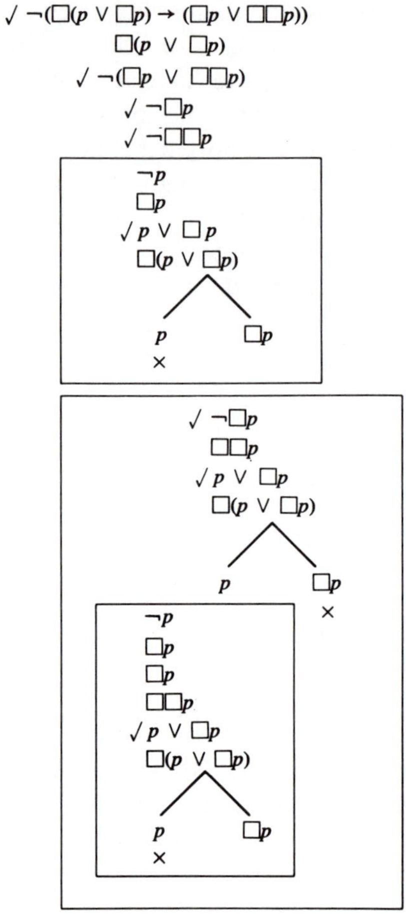

finished with the top window: one branch is closed, but the other is open. In the bottom window, one branch is closed, the other is open, but we have not finished, since there is a sentence ¬ □C, namely ¬□p, on this open branch. We therefore open a window on this open branch: since two sentences □D, namely □□p and □(p ∨ □p), lie on the branch, we write ¬ p, □p, □ p, □□p, p ∨ □p, and □(p ∨ □p) on the top. (We can omit the repetition of □p if we like.) We then again apply the propositional calculus rules as many times as possible. One branch is closed, but the other remains open. There is then nothing more to do, and we have in fact constructed a model in which the sentence that we were testing is invalid. The model looks like this:

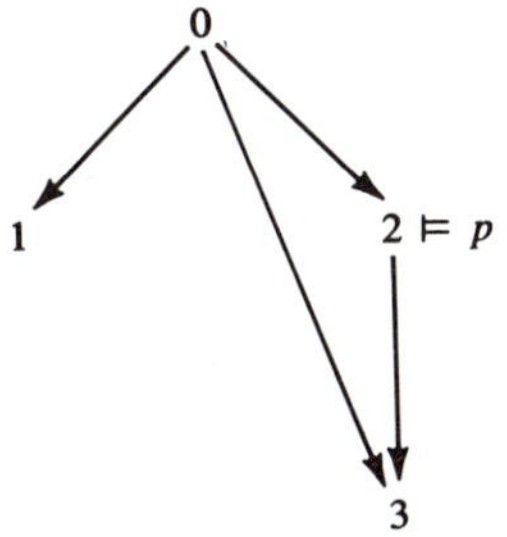

At world 2, p is true; but p is false at worlds 0, 1 and 3. Worlds 1 and 2 correspond to the open branches of the trees in the top and bottom windows, and world 3 corresponds to the open branch of the tree in the window within the bottom window. World 0 is the world at which the negation of the original sentence is true.

So if we take $W = \{0, 1, 2, 3\}$ and $R = \{\langle 0, 1\rangle, \langle 0, 2\rangle, \langle 2, 3\rangle, \langle 0, 3\rangle\}$, and let wVp iff $w = 2$, then $0 \models \neg(\Box(p \vee \Box p) \rightarrow (\Box p \vee \Box\Box p))$, as an easy calculation shows. W is finite and R is transitive and irreflexive. Thus $\mathrm{GL} \nvdash \Box(p \vee \Box p) \rightarrow (\Box p \vee \Box\Box p)$.

We now describe the extension to GL of the method of trees for the propositional calculus. We must first define the degree of a tree, define "closed", and then state *the modal rule*.

The degree of a tree is the least number greater than the degrees of all trees in windows on branches of the tree. Thus a tree with no windows on any of its branches has degree 0, and a tree has degree $n + 1$ if and only if some tree of degree n is in a window on one of its branches, but no tree of degree $> n$ is.

All trees in windows of a tree of degree n are of degree $< n$. So, inductively, we call a tree (of degree n) closed if all its branches are closed, and call a branch (of a tree of degree n) closed if it either contains $\bot$ or contains some sentence and its negation or contains a window in which there is a closed tree (which will be of degree $< n$). "Open" means "not closed".

The modal rule. If there is an unchecked occurrence of $\neg\Box C$ on a branch b, write down on b a window containing the (one-branch) tree

$$\begin{array}{c} \neg C \\ \Box C \\ D_1 \\ \Box D_1 \\ \vdots \\ D_n \\ \Box D_n \end{array}$$

where $\Box D_1, \ldots, \Box D_n$ are all the sentences $\Box B$ on b, and then check the occurrence of $\neg\Box C$.

Our procedure for developing trees to test a sentence for theoremhood in GL is this: Write down the negation of the sentence, then apply the propositional calculus rules as many times as possible, then apply the modal rule as many times as possible, then apply the propositional calculus rules as many times as possible, then apply the modal rule as many times as possible,.... We come to a stop if we cannot make any changes to the tree. (Thus if after completing a cycle of applications of propositional calculus rules, no changes to the tree can be made, we stop and do not go through another cycle of applications of the modal rule.)

We thus develop a tree as far as we can using the propositional calculus rules, then use the modal rule as many times as we can to open windows (perhaps within windows, etc.) containing one-branch trees, then develop the trees in those windows as far as we can using the propositional calculus rules, etc.

A point of terminology: an occurrence of a sentence A on a branch c of a tree in a window on a branch b is not on b. (Some other occurrence of A may be on b, of course.)

We shall show that no matter which sentence we apply it to, the procedure eventually comes to a stop, that if we stop with a closed tree, the sentence under test is a theorem of GL, and that if we stop with an open tree, the sentence is invalid in some finite transitive and irreflexive model. We will have thus reproved the completeness theorem for GL, if A is valid in all finite transitive and irreflexive models, then (when the procedure is applied to A, we come to a stop with a closed tree and) $\mathrm{GL} \vdash A$. We will also, of course, have reproved the decidability of GL.

Now let A be the sentence to which the procedure is applied.

We first show that the procedure always comes to a stop.

Let n be the number of subsentences of A of the form $\Box B$. We want to see that in applying the procedure for developing trees, we go through the modal cycle at most n times and therefore go through the propositional calculus cycle at most $n+1$ times.

Note that before we go through the modal cycle for the kth time, there is no sequence $b_0, b_1, \ldots, b_k$ of open branches, each, except the first, a branch of a tree in a window on its predecessor; after we have gone through the modal cycle for the kth time, there is at least one such sequence, obtained from some sequence $b_0, b_1, \ldots, b_{k-1}$ by opening a window on b_{k-1}.

To see that we cannot go through the modal cycle more than n times, let us observe that if c is an open branch of a tree in a window on an open branch b, then every sentence $\Box D$ on b is also on c, and there is a sentence $\neg\Box C$ on b such that $\Box C$ is also on c. Thus c will contain at least one more *un*negated subsentence $\Box D$ of A than does b. If $k > n$, then, there can then be no sequence $b_0, b_1, \ldots, b_k$ of open branches, each, except the first, a branch of a tree in a window on its predecessor. Thus we do not go through the modal cycle more than n times and our procedure eventually comes to a stop.

We now show that if the procedure comes to a stop with a closed tree, then A is a theorem of GL. To this end, we (simultaneously) define the notions of the *characteristic sentence* (T) *of a tree* T and the *characteristic sentence* (b) *of a branch* b, as follows:

$$(T) = \bigvee\{(b)\text{: } b \text{ is a branch of } T\};\ (b) = \bigwedge\{E\text{: } E \text{ is a sentence on } b\} \wedge \bigwedge\{\Diamond(T)\text{: } T \text{ is a tree in a window on } b\}.$$

(The definition is not circular; trees in windows on branches of T have degrees lower than that of T.)

Suppose that U is the tree that results from a tree T when one of the rules is applied to an occurrence of a sentence E on a branch b of T. We want to see that $\mathrm{GL} \vdash (T) \leftrightarrow (U)$. Note that E is a conjunct of (b).

Case 1. The rule is the modal rule. Then E is a sentence $\neg\Box C$. Let $\Box D_1, \ldots, \Box D_n$ be all the sentences $\Box B$ that occur on b. Let c be the branch of U obtained from b by this application. Then $(c) = (b) \wedge \Diamond(\neg C \wedge \Box C \wedge D_1 \wedge \Box D_1 \wedge \cdots \wedge D_n \wedge \Box D_n)$. Since $\neg\Box C$ and $\Box D_1, \ldots, \Box D_n$ are all conjuncts of b and

$$\mathrm{GL} \vdash (\neg\Box C \wedge \Box D_1 \wedge \cdots \wedge \Box D_n) \to \Diamond(\neg C \wedge \Box C \wedge D_1 \wedge \Box D_1 \wedge \cdots \wedge D_n \wedge \Box D_n),$$

$\mathrm{GL} \vdash (b) \leftrightarrow (c)$, and so $\mathrm{GL} \vdash (T) \leftrightarrow (U)$.

Case 2. The rule is the positive rule for $\to$. Then E is a sentence $(F \to G)$. After the rule is applied, b will have split into two branches of U, c and d, with $(c) = (b) \wedge \neg F$ and $(d) = (b) \wedge G$. Since $(F \to G)$ is a conjunct of (b), (b) is truth-functionally equivalent to $(c) \vee (d)$, and so $\mathrm{GL} \vdash (T) \leftrightarrow (U)$.

Case 3. The rule is the negative rule for $\rightarrow$. Then E is a sentence $\neg(F \rightarrow G)$. Let c be the branch of U obtained from b by this application. Then $(c) = (b) \wedge F \wedge \neg G$, (b) is truth-functionally equivalent to (c), and again $\mathrm{GL} \vdash (T) \leftrightarrow (U)$.

The case for any other propositional calculus rule is perfectly analogous to Case 2 or Case 3.

In all cases, then, $\mathrm{GL} \vdash (T) \leftrightarrow (U)$. If T is in a window on a branch d of a tree X, and U, e, and Y are the tree, branch, and tree that result from d when a rule is applied to an occurrence of a sentence in T, then since $\mathrm{GL} \vdash (T) \leftrightarrow (U)$, $\mathrm{GL} \vdash \Diamond(T) \leftrightarrow \Diamond(U)$, $\mathrm{GL} \vdash (d) \leftrightarrow (e)$, and $\mathrm{GL} \vdash (X) \leftrightarrow (Y)$.

By induction on degree, we infer that if U is the tree that results when a rule is applied *anywhere* in T, then $\mathrm{GL} \vdash (T) \leftrightarrow (U)$. Furthermore, if V is a tree that contains just one branch and that one branch contains just the one sentence $\neg A$, then $(V) = \neg A$. It follows that if T is the tree produced when we stop, then $\mathrm{GL} \vdash \neg A \leftrightarrow (T)$. And since $\mathrm{GL} \vdash \neg \Diamond E$ if $\mathrm{GL} \vdash \neg E$, it follows by induction on degree that if T is a closed tree, then $\mathrm{GL} \vdash \neg (T)$: for if b is a branch of T, then either $\bot$ is on b, or some sentence and its negation are, or some window on b contains a closed tree of lower degree, and in each of these cases, $\mathrm{GL} \vdash \neg (b)$.

Thus if T is the tree generated by our procedure when it stops and T is closed, then $\mathrm{GL} \vdash \neg (T)$, $\mathrm{GL} \vdash \neg A \leftrightarrow \neg (T)$, and therefore $\mathrm{GL} \vdash A$.

It remains to show that if our procedure stops with an open tree T, there is a finite transitive irreflexive model $\langle W, R, V \rangle$ in which A is invalid. W will turn out to be a certain set of open branches obtained from T.

If U is an open tree, then U contains at least one open branch.

Define S, a relation on branches: xSy iff x is open and y is the leftmost open branch of a tree in a window on b.

Let w be the leftmost open branch of the open tree T.

Recall that xS^0y iff $x = y$ and $xS^{i+1}y$ iff $\exists x(xS^iz \wedge zSy)$.

Let $W = \{x \colon \exists i \geqslant 0\ wS^ix\}$, $w \in W$. The degree of T is finite, and therefore W is finite. Every member of W is open.

Let xRy iff $\{\langle x, y \rangle \colon x, y \in W \wedge \exists i \geqslant 1\ xS^iy\}$.

Thus the worlds of our model are the leftmost open branch of T, the leftmost open branches of any trees in windows on that branch of T, the leftmost branches of any trees in windows on those branches of those trees, etc. And if x and y are worlds in our model, then xRy iff y is an open branch of a tree in a window on x or an open branch of a tree in a window on an open branch of a tree in a window on x or....

R is transitive and irreflexive.

Let xVp iff the sentence letter p is one of the sentences lying on branch x.

Our desired model is $\langle W, R, V \rangle$.

Lemma. *For every sentence E and every x in W, if E lies on x, then* $x \vDash E$, *and if* $\neg E$ *lies on x, then* $\nvDash E$.

Proof. Induction on E. There are four cases.

(i) E is $\bot$. Since x is open, $\bot$ does not lie on x. And whether or not $\neg\bot$ lies on x, $x \nvDash \bot$.

(ii) E is a sentence letter p. If p lies on x, then xVp and $x \vDash p$. If $\neg p$ lies on x, then since x is open, p does not lie on x, not: xVp, and $x \nvDash p$.

(iii) E is $(F \to G)$. If $(F \to G)$ lies on x, then the positive rule for $\to$ has been applied to all occurrences of $(F \to G)$ on x, and therefore either $\neg F$ lies on x or G lies on x. By the i.h., either $x \nvDash F$ or $x \vDash G$. In either case, $x \vDash (F \to G)$. If $\neg(F \to G)$ lies on x, then the negative rule has been applied to all occurrences of $\neg(F \to G)$ on x, and therefore F and $\neg G$ both lie on x. By the i.h., $x \vDash F$ and $x \nvDash G$, and therefore $x \nvDash (F \to G)$.

(iv) E is $\Box B$. if $\neg\Box B$ lies on x, then there is a window on x in which there is a tree U at whose very top the sentence $\neg B$ occurs. Since x is open, there is at least one branch of U. Let y be the leftmost open branch of U. xSy, and since $x \in W$, $y \in W$. $\neg B$ lies on every branch of U, and hence on y. By the i.h., $y \nvDash B$. But since xSy, xRy, and $x \nvDash \Box B$. Finally, suppose that $\Box B$ lies on x. If we can show that B lies on y whenever xRy, we shall be done, for then by the i.h., $y \vDash B$ whenever xRy, and $x \vDash \Box B$. But observe that if z, a are both in W, zSa, and $\Box B$ lies on z, then both $\Box B$ and B lie on a: for since zSa, a is a branch of a tree U in a window on z; at the top of U, and hence on every branch of U including a, are $\neg C$, $\Box C$, D_1, $\Box D_1, \ldots, D_n$, $\Box D_n$, where $\neg\Box C$ is some sentence on z and $\Box D_1, \ldots, \Box D_n$ are all the sentences $\Box D$ on z, one of which is $\Box B$. Thus if for some $i \geqslant 1$, xS^iy, both $\Box B$ and B lie on y, and therefore if xRy, B lies on y. ⊣

We are thus done. $\neg A$ lies on every branch of T, and hence on w. By the lemma, $w \nvDash A$. Therefore A is invalid in the finite transitive and irreflexive model $\langle W, R, V \rangle$. In fact, $\langle W, R \rangle$ is a *tree* in the different sense of Chapter 5: for every $x, y, z \in W$, if xRz and yRz, then either xRy or $x = y$ or yRx. Thus the theorems of GL are precisely the sentences valid in all finite transitive and irreflexive trees. Furthermore, if A is not a theorem of GL and there are n subsentences of A of the form $\Box D$, then A is invalid in some finite irreflexive transitive tree $\langle W, R \rangle$ such that $w_0 R w_1 R \ldots R w_n R w_{n+1}$, for no $w_0, w_1, \ldots, w_n, w_{n+1}$ in W.

Like GL, K is closed under the Löb rule

An easy modification of the argument just given shows that if $\mathrm{K} \vdash A$, then A is invalid in some finite frame $\langle W, R \rangle$ in which for all $w_0, w_1, \ldots, w_n$ in W, not $w_0 R w_1 R \ldots R w_n R w_0$. Thus R "contains no loops" and is therefore converse wellfounded.

First of all, change the modal rule to: If $\neg \Box C$ occurs on a branch b, write down on b a window containing the (one-branch) tree

$$\begin{array}{c} \neg C \\ D_1 \\ \vdots \\ D_n, \end{array}$$

where $\Box D_1, \ldots, \Box D_n$ are all the sentences $\Box B$ on b, and then check the occurrence of $\neg \Box C$.

Then observe that the procedure always terminates, in this case because the maximum of the modal degrees of sentences on b is strictly greater than that of the degrees of sentences on c. As for showing that $\mathrm{K} \vdash A$ if we stop with a closed tree, the key observation is that $\mathrm{K} \vdash (\neg \Box C \wedge \Box D_1 \wedge \cdots \wedge \Box D_n) \rightarrow \Diamond(\neg C \wedge D_1 \wedge \cdots \wedge D_n)$. To show that if we stop with an open tree, then A is invalid in a model of the desired sort, we define w, W, and V as before, but now let R simply equal S and note that if $z, a \in W$, zSa, and $\Box B$ lies on z, then B lies on A.

(We thus have another way to see that there is no sentence valid in all and only those frames that are converse wellfounded. Suppose A is a counterexample. Since there are some frames that are not converse wellfounded, A is not valid in *all* frames. Therefore $\mathrm{K} \nvdash A$. Therefore, as we have just seen, A is not valid in some frame that is converse wellfounded, contradiction.)

It follows that for any sentence A, if $\mathrm{K} \vdash \Box A \to A$, then $\mathrm{K} \vdash A$, i.e., that K is closed under the Löb rule. For if $\mathrm{K} \nvdash A$, then A is invalid in some finite frame $\langle W, R \rangle$ in which for all $w_0, w_1, \ldots, w_n$ in W, not: $w_0 R w_1 R \ldots R w_n R w_0$. Then for some w in W, $w \nvDash A$, but for all x, $x \vDash A$ if wRx. (Otherwise, there would be an R-loop.) Thus $w \vDash \Box A$, and $w \nvDash \Box A \to A$, $\Box A \to A$ is invalid in $\langle W, R \rangle$, and $\mathrm{K} \nvdash \Box A \to A$.

Exercise 1. Use the procedure to determine which of these are theorems of GL:

a. $\Box(\Box p \vee \Box \neg p) \to (\Box p \vee \Box \neg p)$.
b. $\Box(\Box(p \wedge q) \to p) \to \Box(\Box q \to p)$.
c. $\Box(p \leftrightarrow (\Box p \to q)) \to \Box(p \leftrightarrow (\Box q \to q))$.
d. $\Box(p \leftrightarrow (\Box(p \vee \Box \bot) \to \Box(p \to \Box \bot))) \to$
$\Box(p \leftrightarrow (\Box \Box \Box \bot \to \Box \bot))$.
e. $\Box p \wedge \Diamond q \to \Diamond(p \wedge \Box \bot)$
f. $\Box(p \to \Box(p \to q)) \to \Box(p \to \Box q)$
g. $\neg \Box \bot \wedge \Box(p \leftrightarrow \neg \Box p) \to (\neg \Box p \wedge \neg \Box \neg p)$.

Exercise 2. Modify our completeness proof to prove the completeness of other modal systems with respect to appropriate sorts of models.

11

An incomplete system of modal logic

Löb's theorem states that a sentence S is a theorem of PA if the apparently weaker sentence $\text{Bew}(\ulcorner S \urcorner) \to S$ is a theorem. As PA is closed under tautological consequence, it follows from Löb's theorem that for any sentence S, if $S \leftrightarrow \text{Bew}(\ulcorner S \urcorner)$ is provable in PA, then so is S. Henkin's question (for PA), whether or not the sentence expressing its own provability is provable,[1] thus receives an affirmative answer.

Let us use "YES" to refer to the statement that for all sentences S, if $S \leftrightarrow \text{Bew}(\ulcorner S \urcorner)$ is a theorem of PA, then so is S. (YES for: the answer to Henkin's question is *yes*, for all such S.) Thus YES follows from Löb's theorem. Conversely, with the aid of the Hilbert–Bernays–Löb derivability conditions (i), (ii), and (iii), which are used to prove Löb's theorem, YES easily implies Löb's theorem: for if

$\vdash \text{Bew}(\ulcorner S \urcorner) \to S$, then by (i) and (ii),
$\vdash \text{Bew}(\ulcorner \text{Bew}(\ulcorner S \urcorner) \to \text{Bew}(\ulcorner S \urcorner)$. But by (iii),
$\vdash \text{Bew}(\ulcorner S \urcorner) \to \text{Bew}(\ulcorner \text{Bew}(\ulcorner S \urcorner) \urcorner)$, whence
$\vdash \text{Bew}(\ulcorner S \urcorner) \leftrightarrow \text{Bew}(\ulcorner \text{Bew}(\ulcorner S \urcorner) \urcorner)$. By YES,
$\vdash \text{Bew}(\ulcorner S \urcorner)$, and therefore by modus ponens,
$\vdash S$.

The use of (i), (ii), and (iii) in this derivation of Löb's theorem from YES and their absence from the converse derivation might suggest that in some sense Löb's theorem is a better result than YES. By considering the question from the point of view of modal logic, we can in fact define a sense in which this is so.

YES and Löb's theorem may be formalized as rules:

$$\text{If } \vdash A \leftrightarrow \Box A, \text{ then } \vdash A \quad \text{(YR)}$$
$$\text{If } \vdash \Box A \to A, \text{ then } \vdash A \quad \text{(LR)}$$

or as schemata:

$$\Box(A \leftrightarrow \Box A) \to \Box A \quad \text{(YS)}$$
$$\Box(\Box A \to A) \to \Box A \quad \text{(LS)}$$

To raise questions about the strength of these four modal principles, we need to choose a background system. Two obvious candidates are K and K4.

Adding any one of (YR), (LR), (YS), or (LS) to K4 yields a system whose theorems are the same as those of GL, for by Theorem 18 of Chapter 1, all sentences $\Box A \rightarrow \Box\Box A$ are theorems of GL; as was shown in Chapter 3, GL is the result of adding (LR) to K4; and by an argument that parallels the foregoing deduction of Löb's theorem from YES, GL is also the result of adding (YR) to K4. Finally, adding (YS) to any normal system such as K4 gives closure under (YR): If $\vdash A \leftrightarrow \Box A$, then $\vdash \Box(A \leftrightarrow \Box A)$, whence $\vdash \Box A$ and $\vdash A$. Thus K4 is too strong a system to enable us to distinguish the four principles.

With K taken as the background system, however, interesting differences among them appear. Unlike K4, K is closed under (LR), as we saw at the end of the previous chapter, and hence under (YR).

Let us use H (for Henkin) to refer to the system that results when (YS) is added to K, i.e., H is the normal system whose new axioms are all sentences $\Box(A \leftrightarrow \Box A) \rightarrow \Box A$. H is clearly a proper extension of K, since $\Box(p \leftrightarrow \Box p) \rightarrow \Box p$ is not a theorem of K. For let $M = \langle N, <, V \rangle$, where for all n in N, not: nVp. Then p is false, $\Box p$ is false, $p \leftrightarrow \Box p$ is true, $\Box(p \leftrightarrow \Box p)$ is true, and therefore $\Box(p \leftrightarrow \Box p) \rightarrow \Box p$ is false, at all n in M.

It is evident that GL is an extension of H. We shall show that it is in fact a proper extension, that neither $\Box p \rightarrow \Box\Box p$ nor $\Box(\Box p \rightarrow p) \rightarrow \Box p$ is a theorem of H, and that although H, as we saw three paragraphs back, is closed under (YR), it is not closed under (LR).

As we shall see, H turns out to be an example of an *incomplete* system of modal logic.

A frame is said to be *appropriate to* a normal modal logic L if and only if all theorems of L are valid in the frame. The definition agrees with the particular definitions of "appropriate to" that we gave in Chapter 5 for the particular logics K, K4, T, S4, B, S5, and GL. E.g., we there called a frame appropriate to K4 iff it is transitive, and indeed all theorems of K4 are valid in very transitive frame.

A system L of propositional modal logic is called *complete* if every sentence that is valid in every frame appropriate to L is a theorem of L.

So to continue the example, K4 is complete: for if A is valid in every frame appropriate to K4, A is valid in every transitive frame, and therefore, as we saw in Chapter 5, A is a theorem of K4.

We have also seen that GL, K, T, S4, B, and S5 are complete, and in Chapter 12 we shall see that the system Grz defined there is complete as well.

Let us forestall a possible confusion. The theorems of any normal logic L are precisely the sentences valid in all *models* in which all theorems of L are valid, for if a sentence is not a theorem of L, then it is not valid in the canonical model for L. The definition of "complete" mentions *frames*, however, and not models.

All tautologies and all distribution axioms are valid in all frames, and the rules of modus ponens, necessitation, and substitution preserve validity in a frame. Thus all theorems of H are valid in a frame if and only if $\Box(p\leftrightarrow\Box p)\rightarrow\Box p$ is valid in that frame.

We are going to show that the frames in which $\Box(p\leftrightarrow\Box p)\rightarrow\Box p$ is valid are exactly the same frames as those in which $\Box(\Box p\rightarrow p)\rightarrow \Box p$ are valid, i.e., the transitive and converse wellfounded frames. Thus a frame is appropriate to H if and only if it is appropriate to GL. We shall then show that the sentence $\Box p\rightarrow\Box\Box p$ is not a theorem of H. It follows that H is incomplete, since $\Box p\rightarrow\Box\Box p$ is a theorem of GL, and therefore valid in every frame appropriate to GL, that is to say, valid in every frame appropriate to H.

Recall from Chapter 4 that the degree of a modal sentence A is the maximum number of nested occurrences of $\Box$ in A. The sentence $\Box(p\leftrightarrow\Box p)\rightarrow\Box p$ is of degree 2 and contains one sentence letter, p. After proving the incompleteness of H, we shall also prove that if X is a set of sentences of degree 1 and L is the normal logic obtained from K whose new axioms are all substitution instances of all members of X, then L is complete. Thus, on one natural measure of simplicity, H is an incomplete modal logic that is as simple as possible.

We begin by proving a theorem due to Lon Berk.

Theorem 1. $\Box(p\leftrightarrow\Box p)\rightarrow\Box p$ *and* $\Box(\Box p\rightarrow p)\rightarrow\Box p$ *are valid in the same frames.*

Proof. It is clear that $\Box(p\leftrightarrow\Box p)\rightarrow\Box p$ is valid in every frame in which $\Box(\Box p\rightarrow p)\rightarrow\Box p$ is valid. For the converse, suppose $\Box(p\leftrightarrow\Box p)\rightarrow\Box p$ valid in $\langle W,R\rangle$, $M=\langle W,R,V\rangle$, $M,w\models\Box(\Box p\rightarrow p)$, and wRx. We must show that $M,x\models p$.

For y in W, let yUp iff for all $n\geqslant 0$, $M,y\models\Box^n p$. Let $N=\langle W,R,U\rangle$. Suppose wRy. Then

$$(*)\quad M,y\models\Box p\rightarrow p$$

and the following are equivalent:
$N, y \vDash p$;
yUp;
for all $n \geqslant 0$, $M, y \vDash \Box^n p$;
for all $n \geqslant 1$, $M, y \vDash \Box^n p$ [by (*)];
for all $n \geqslant 0$, for all z such that yRz, $M, z \vDash \Box^n p$;
for all z such that yRz, for all $n \geqslant 0$, $M, z \vDash \Box^n p$;
for all z such that yRz, zUp;
for all z such that yRz, $N, z \vDash p$;
$N, y \vDash \Box p$.

Thus if wRy, then $N, y \vDash p \leftrightarrow \Box p$. Therefore $N, w \vDash \Box(p \leftrightarrow \Box p)$. By the validity in $\langle W, R \rangle$ of $\Box(p \leftrightarrow \Box p) \rightarrow \Box p$, $N, w \vDash \Box p$; and then since $wRx, N, x \vDash p$; xUp; for all $n \geqslant 0$, $M, x \vDash \Box^n p$; and $M, x \vDash \Box^0 p$, i.e., $M, x \vDash p$. $\dashv$

It follows from Theorem 1 that all theorems of GL, including $\Box p \rightarrow \Box\Box p$, are valid in all frames in which $\Box(p \leftrightarrow \Box p) \rightarrow \Box p$ is valid. As we shall now show, $\Box p \rightarrow \Box\Box p$ is not a theorem of H, and therefore neither is $\Box(\Box p \rightarrow p) \rightarrow \Box p$. So H is incomplete. The incompleteness of H was conjectured by the author and proved by Roberto Magari, who in 1980 constructed a model in which all axioms of H are valid, but in one of whose worlds $\Box p \rightarrow \Box\Box p$ is false, proving thereby that $\Box p \rightarrow \Box\Box p$ is not a theorem of H. A number of years later, Max Cresswell considerably simplified Magari's original construction.

Following Cresswell's argument, we let $N^*, = \{0^*, 1^*, 2^*, \ldots\}$ be a disjoint copy of $N, = \{0, 1, 2, \ldots\}$. Define $m^* < n^*$ iff $m < n$.

Let $W = N \cup N^*$. Let wRx iff either for some $m, n \in N$, $w = m^*$, $x = n^*$ and $m \leqslant n + 1$, or w is in N^* and x is in N, or w, x are in N and $w > x$. Note that for all n, n^*Rn^* and $(n+1)^*Rn^*$, and also $n^*R(n+1)^*$, $n^*R(n+2)^*, \ldots$.

Let wVp iff $w \neq 0^*$. Cresswell's model is $\langle W, R, V \rangle$, depicted here:

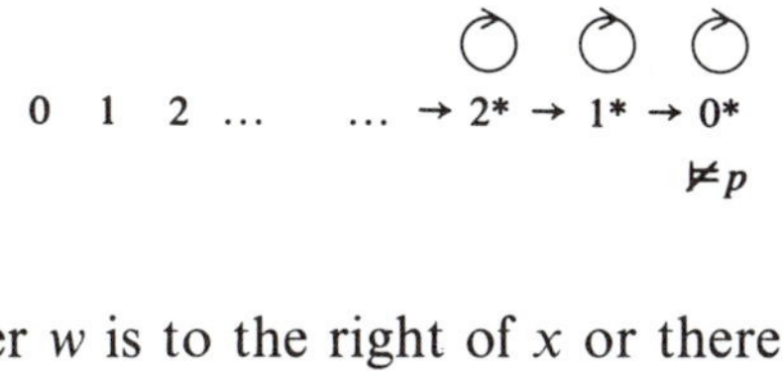

wRx iff either *w* is to the right of *x* or there is a (single) arrow from *w* to *x*. *p* is false at 0* and nowhere else.

(The right-hand piece of the frame on which Cresswell's model is based is known as *the recession frame*.)

For any modal sentence A, let $[A] = \{w\colon w \vDash A\}$. A subset X of W is *cofinite* if $W - X$ is finite.

Lemma. *For every sentence A, $[A]$ is either finite or cofinite.*

Proof. Induction on A. For every sentence letter p, $[p] = W - \{0^*\}$, which is cofinite. $[\bot] = \varnothing$, which is certainly finite. And $[A \to B] = (W - [A]) \cup [B]$. Thus if $[A]$ is cofinite and $[B]$ is finite, then $[A \to B]$ is finite. But if $[A]$ is finite or $[B]$ is cofinite, $[A \to B]$ is cofinite.

For the step from A to $\Box A$, we distinguish two cases.

Case 1. For some n in N, $n \notin [A]$. Then $[\Box A]$ is finite, for if either $w \in N^*$ or $w \in N$ and $w > n$, then wRn and $w \notin [\Box A]$.

Case 2. $N \subseteq [A]$. By the induction hypothesis, $[A]$ is either finite or cofinite and is therefore cofinite. Thus there is some k such that for all $x \notin [A]$, $x \in N^*$ and $x \leqslant k^*$. It follows that $[\Box A]$ is cofinite, for if $w \notin [\Box A]$, then for some x, wRx and $x \notin [A]$, and thus $x \in N^*$ and $x \leqslant k^*$; but then $w \in N^*$ and $w \leqslant (k+1)^*$, and there are only finitely many such w. ⊣

Theorem 2. *$\Box p \to \Box\Box p$ is not a theorem of* H.

Proof. We first show that every sentence $\Box(A \leftrightarrow \Box A) \to \Box A$ is valid in M. Assume that for some w in W, $w \vDash \Box(A \leftrightarrow \Box A)$ and $w \nvDash \Box A$.

We distinguish the same cases.

Case 1. For some n in N, $n \nvDash A$; we may assume n the least such. Then $n \vDash \Box A$, $n \nvDash (A \leftrightarrow \Box A)$, not: wRn, and $w \neq n$. Since R is connected (for all $y, z \in W$, yRz or $y = z$ or zRy), nRw. Thus $w \in N$ and $n > w$. Since $w \nvDash \Box A$, for some x, $x \nvDash A$, wRx, $x \in N$, $n > w > x$, contra leastness of n.

Case 2. $N \subseteq [A]$. By the lemma, $W - [A]$ is finite. Since $w \nvDash \Box A$, $W - [A]$ is nonempty. Let k^* be its greatest member. Then $k^* \nvDash A$, $(k+1)^* \vDash A$, and $(k+1)^* \nvDash \Box A$ since $(k+1)^* R k^*$. For some x, wRx and $x \nvDash A$, and since $N \subseteq [A]$, $x \in N^*$ and for some n, $x = n^*$ and $n \leqslant k$. Since wRx, $w \in N^*$ and for some m, $w = m^*$ and $m \leqslant n + 1$. Then $m \leqslant (k+1) + 1$ and $wR(k+1)^*$, whence $(k+1)^* \vDash (A \leftrightarrow \Box A)$, contradiction.

Thus all the axioms of H are valid in the model M, for all tautologies and distribution axioms are valid in M. Consequently, all theorems of H are valid in M, since modus ponens and necessitation preserve validity in M.

But 2^*Rx iff $x = 1^*, 2^*, 3^*, \ldots$, or x is in N; thus 2^*Rx iff $x \neq 0^*$. Hence $2^* \vDash \Box p$. But $0^* \nvDash p$, $1^* \nvDash \Box p$, $2^* \nvDash \Box\Box p$, whence $2^* \nvDash \Box p \to \Box\Box p$.

Thus $\Box p \to \Box\Box p$ is not valid in M and is therefore not a theorem of H. ⊣

It follows from Theorem 2 and the next result that H is not closed under (LR).

Theorem 3. $\mathrm{H} \vdash \Box(\Box p \to \Box\Box p) \to \Box p \to \Box\Box p$.

Proof. Let $A = \Box(\Box p \to \Box\Box p)$. Then
$\mathrm{K} \vdash A \to \Box(p \wedge \Box p \to \Box p \wedge \Box\Box p)$ and
$\mathrm{K} \vdash \Box p \to \Box(\Box p \wedge \Box\Box p \to p \wedge \Box p)$. Thus
$\mathrm{K} \vdash A \to (\Box p \to \Box(p \wedge \Box p \leftrightarrow \Box p \wedge \Box\Box p))$ and
$\mathrm{K} \vdash A \to (\Box p \to \Box(p \wedge \Box p \leftrightarrow \Box(p \wedge \Box p)))$, whence
$\mathrm{H} \vdash A \to (\Box p \to \Box(p \wedge \Box p))$, and finally,
$\mathrm{H} \vdash A \to (\Box p \to \Box\Box p)$. ⊣

Before the discovery of Magari's theorem it was known that there is a sentence of degree 2 containing two sentence letters of which the result to adding all substitution instances as new axioms to K is incomplete; and similarly for a sentence of degree 3 containing one sentence letter. The following theorem, due to David Lewis, shows that Magari's theorem is best possible.

Theorem 4. *Let X be a set of sentences and suppose that the degree of every sentence in X is $\leqslant 1$. Let* L *be the system obtained from* K *by taking as new axioms all substitution instances of members of X. Then* $\mathrm{L} \vdash A$ *iff A is valid in every frame in which all theorems of* L *are valid, and* L *is complete.*

Proof. The left–right direction is obvious. Suppose then that $\mathrm{L} \nvdash A$. Fix an enumeration $A_0, A_1, \ldots$ of all modal sentences. Let $\mathscr{A}$ be the set of all subsentences of A, $\mathscr{B}$ be the set of truth-functional combinations of members of $\mathscr{A}$, and $\mathscr{C}$ be the set of maximal L-consistent conjunctions of subsentences of A and negations of subsentences of A that occur earlier in the enumeration than any other conjunction with exactly the same conjuncts.

For each C in $\mathscr{C}$ let w_C be a maximal L-consistent set containing C. (Cf. Lemma 2 of Chapter 6.) Let $W = \{w_c\colon C \in \mathscr{C}\}$. Let wRx iff for all B in $\mathscr{B}$, if $\Box B \in w$, then $B \in x$. We shall show A invalid, but all members of X valid, in the frame $\langle W, R\rangle$. The theorem follows since validity in a frame is preserved under substitution.

Let wVp iff $p \in w$. Let $[B] = \{w \in W\colon M, w \vDash B\}$, and $|B| = \{w \in W\colon B \in w\}$.

Lemma. *(1)* $[p] = |p|$; *(2)* $[\bot] = |\bot| = \varnothing$; *(3) if* $[B] = |B|$ *and* $[C] = |C|$, *then* $[B \to C] = |B \to C|$; *(4) if* $B \in \mathscr{B}$ *and* $[B] = |B|$, *then* $[\Box B] = |\Box B|$.

Proof. (1) and (2) are clear and (3) follows in the usual way from the fact that members of W are maximal L-consistent sets. As for (4), assume that $B \in \mathscr{B}$ and $[B] = |B|$. Let $w \in W$. If $w \in |\Box B|$, then $\Box B \in w$, and thus if wRx, $B \in x$, $x \in |B| = [B]$ and so $x \vDash B$; thus $w \vDash \Box B$ and $w \in [\Box B]$. Therefore $|\Box B| \subseteq [\Box B]$. Conversely, suppose that $w \notin |\Box B|$. Then $\neg \Box B \in w$. Let $Y = \{\neg B\} \cup \{C \in \mathscr{B}\colon \Box C \in w\}$. $Y \subseteq \mathscr{B}$. If Y is not L-consistent, then for some $C_1, \ldots, C_k$ in $\mathscr{B}$, $\Box C_1, \ldots, \Box C_k \in w$, and $\mathrm{L} \vdash C_1 \wedge \cdots \wedge C_k \to B$, whence by the normality of L, $\mathrm{L} \vdash \Box C_1 \wedge \cdots \wedge \Box C_k \to \Box B$, and w is inconsistent, contradiction. Thus Y is L-consistent. For some C in $\mathscr{C}$, then, $\mathrm{L} \vdash C \to E$ for all E in Y and $Y \subseteq w_C$, whence wRw_C. Thus $\neg B \in Y \subseteq w_C$, $B \notin w_C$, $w_C \notin |B| = [B]$, $w_C \nvDash B$, $w \nvDash \Box B$, and $w \notin [\Box B]$. The lemma is proved.

It follows from the lemma that for every B in $\mathscr{B}$, $[B] = |B|$.

Since $\mathrm{L} \nvdash A$, for some w in W, $\neg A \in w$, $A \notin w$, and $w \notin |A|$. Thus $w \notin [A]$, $w \nvDash A$, and A is invalid in $\langle W, R\rangle$.

We now show all members of X valid in $\langle W, R\rangle$. Let V' be a valuation on W, and $M' = \langle W, R, V'\rangle$. For any sentence D, let $[D]' = \{w \in W\colon M', w \vDash D\}$. Now suppose $D \in X$. We must show that $[D]' = W$.

For each sentence letter p, let $E_p = \bigvee \{C \in \mathscr{C}\colon w_C V'p\}$. C is the unique member of $\mathscr{C}$ in w_C, and therefore $E_p \in w_C$ iff C is a disjunct of E_p, iff $w_C V'p$. Thus $|E_p| = [p]'$. Since $E_p \in \mathscr{B}$, $[E_p] = |E_p|$. For any sentence D, let D' be the result of substituting E_p for each p in D. Then $p' = E_p$, and therefore $[p'] = [p]'$. By a straightforward induction on subsentences of D, $[D'] = [D]'$. As the degree of $D \leqslant 1$ and each $E_p \in \mathscr{B}$, D' is a truth-functional combination of necessitations of members of $\mathscr{B}$, and by the lemma, $[D'] = |D'|$. Since $D \in X$, $\mathrm{L} \vdash D'$, and $|D'| = W$. Thus $[D]' = W$. $\dashv$

12

An S4-preserving proof-theoretical treatment of modality

The unprovability of consistency, and hence of reflection, is a striking feature of the concept of formal provability. $\mathrm{Bew}(\ulcorner S \urcorner) \rightarrow S$ is not, in general, a provable sentence of PA, and $(\Box p \rightarrow p)$ is therefore not an always provable sentence of modal logic.

However, there is an interpretation of the language of propositional modal logic that makes use of the notion of formal provability and preserves not only $(\Box p \rightarrow p)$ but all other theorems of S4 as well: interpret $\Box$ to mean: $\boxdot$.

We have defined the notation: $\boxdot A$ to mean: $(\Box A \wedge A)$. It is obvious that $(\boxdot A \rightarrow A)$ is a tautology, and it is also evident that $\mathrm{K} \vdash \boxdot(A \rightarrow B) \rightarrow (\boxdot A \rightarrow \boxdot B)$; Theorem 9 of Chapter 1 asserts that $\mathrm{K4} \vdash \boxdot A \rightarrow \boxdot \boxdot A$. Moreover if $\mathrm{K4} \vdash A$, then also $\mathrm{K4} \vdash \Box A$, whence $\mathrm{K4} \vdash \boxdot A$. Thus the result of "dotting" all boxes in any theorem of S4 is a theorem of K4.

More precisely, we define the modal sentence ${}^{t}A$ for all modal sentences A:

${}^{t}p = p$ (p a sentence letter);
${}^{t}\bot = \bot$;
${}^{t}(A \rightarrow B) = ({}^{t}A \rightarrow {}^{t}B)$; and
${}^{t}\Box A = (\Box\, {}^{t}A \wedge {}^{t}A)$.

${}^{t}A$ is then the result of dotting all boxes in A. Then if $\mathrm{S4} \vdash A$, $\mathrm{K4} \vdash {}^{t}A$. (The proof of the converse will be left as an exercise.)

For any realization $*$ and any modal sentence A, we define the sentence ${}^{*}A$ of arithmetic as follows:

${}^{*}p = p^{*} = {}^{*}(p)$;
${}^{*}\bot = \bot$;
${}^{*}(A \rightarrow B) = ({}^{*}A \rightarrow {}^{*}B)$; and
${}^{*}\Box A = (\mathrm{Bew}(\ulcorner {}^{*}A \urcorner) \wedge {}^{*}A)$.

We may call ${}^{*}A$ the *truth-translation* of A under the realization $*$.

We cannot define the notion *true sentence* by a formula of arithmetic – that is, no formula $T(x)$ of arithmetic defines the set of Gödel numbers of true sentences of arithmetic – but for each particular sentence S of arithmetic, we may take the arithmetization of the assertion that S is true to be S itself. If $p^* = S$, then $*\Box p$ will assert that S is provable and true.

If $*A = ({}^tA)^*$, then $*\Box A = (\mathrm{Bew}(\ulcorner *A \urcorner) \wedge *A) = (\mathrm{Bew}(\ulcorner ({}^tA)^* \urcorner) \wedge ({}^tA)^*) = (\Box {}^tA \wedge {}^tA)^* = ({}^t\Box A)^*$. Thus for every modal sentence A, $*A = ({}^tA)^*$.

We are thus led to ask the questions: Which modal sentences are provable under all truth-translations? and: Which modal sentences are true under all truth-translations? It turns out, perhaps surprisingly, that these questions have the same answer, and that the answer is *not*: exactly the theorems of S4.

We shall give the name Grz, after Andrzej Grzegorczyk, to the modal system whose rules of inference are those of K and whose axioms are those of K and all sentences

$$\Box(\Box(A \to \Box A) \to A) \to A$$

S4Grz is the system that similarly results from adjoining to S4 all those sentences as new axioms.

S4Grz properly extends S4, for $\Box(\Box(p \to \Box p) \to p) \to p$ is not a theorem even of S5: Let $W = \{0, 1\}$, R is the universal relation $\{\langle 0,0\rangle, \langle 0,1\rangle, \langle 1,0\rangle, \langle 1,1\rangle\}$ on W, which is an equivalence relation, not: $0 V p$ and $1 V p$ (any sentence letter p). Then $0 \nvDash p$, $1 \nvDash \Box p$, $1 \vDash p$, $1 \nvDash p \to \Box p$, $0 \nvDash \Box(p \to \Box p)$, $0 \vDash \Box(p \to \Box p) \to p$, $1 \vDash \Box(p \to \Box p) \to p$, $0 \vDash \Box(\Box(p \to \Box p) \to p)$, and $0 \nvDash \Box(\Box(p \to \Box p) \to p) \to p$.

A relation R is *antisymmetric* if for all w, x, if wRx and xRw, then $w = x$.

A relation R is called *converse weakly wellfounded* if for every nonempty set X, there is an *R-maximal* element of X, that is, an element w of X such that wRx for no x in X *other than* w.

We use "reflexive" to mean: reflexive on W, when the context makes it clear which set W is meant.

The main result of this chapter is the equivalence of the following ten conditions:

(1) S4Grz $\vdash A$;
(2) Grz $\vdash A$;
(3) GL $\vdash {}^tA$;
(4) for all realizations $*$, PA $\vdash *A$;
(5) GLS $\vdash {}^tA$;

(6) for all realizations $*$, $^*A$ is true;
(7) for any such realization $*$ as in the uniform arithmetical completeness theorem for GL, $\mathrm{PA} \vdash {}^*A$;
(8) for any such realization $*$ as in the uniform arithmetical completeness theorem for GL, $\mathrm{PA} \vdash ({}^tA)^*$;
(9) A is valid in all finite transitive, reflexive, and antisymmetric frames;
(10) A is valid in all transitive, reflexive, and converse weakly well-founded frames.

$^*A$, we have observed, is identical with $({}^tA)^*$. Thus (7) is equivalent to (8), and by the arithmetical completeness theorem for GL, (3) is equivalent to (4). (5) is equivalent to (6) by the arithmetical completeness theorem for GLS, and (3) to (8) by the uniform arithmetical completeness theorem for GL. Moreover, (1) evidently implies (2), and (3) evidently implies (5).

(2) implies (1).[1]

Proof. We must show that $\mathrm{Grz} \vdash \Box A \to A$ and $\mathrm{Grz} \vdash \Box A \to \Box\Box A$.
$\Box A \to A$ is easy: we have that
$\mathrm{K} \vdash A \to (\Box(A \to \Box A) \to A)$,
$\mathrm{K} \vdash \Box A \to \Box(\Box(A \to \Box A) \to A)$; but
$\mathrm{Grz} \vdash \Box(\Box(A \to \Box A) \to A) \to A$, whence
$\mathrm{Grz} \vdash \Box A \to A$.

As for $\Box A \to \Box\Box A$, let $B = \Box A \to \Box\Box A$ and let $C = B \wedge A$. Then by the propositional calculus, we have
$\mathrm{K} \vdash (((\Box A \to \Box\Box A) \wedge A) \to \Box A) \to (A \to \Box A)$, i.e.,
$\mathrm{K} \vdash (C \to \Box A) \to (A \to \Box A)$. Since
$\mathrm{K} \vdash C \to A$,
$\mathrm{K} \vdash \Box C \to \Box A$, and thus
$\mathrm{K} \vdash (C \to \Box C) \to (A \to \Box A)$; therefore, by the normality of K,
$\mathrm{K} \vdash \Box(C \to \Box C) \to (\Box A \to \Box\Box A)$, i.e.,
$\mathrm{K} \vdash \Box(C \to \Box C) \to B$, and then by necessitation,

$$(*) \quad \mathrm{K} \vdash \Box[\Box(C \to \Box C) \to B]$$

Now
$\mathrm{K} \vdash \Box A \to \Box[\Box(C \to \Box C) \to A]$, which with $(*)$ yields
$\mathrm{K} \vdash \Box A \to \Box[\Box(C \to \Box C) \to (B \wedge A)]$, i.e.,
$\mathrm{K} \vdash \Box A \to \Box[\Box(C \to \Box C) \to C]$. But since
$\mathrm{Grz} \vdash \Box[\Box(C \to \Box C) \to C] \to C$,
$\mathrm{Grz} \vdash \Box A \to C$, whence since
$\mathrm{Grz} \vdash C \to (\Box A \to \Box\Box A)$,

$\mathrm{Grz} \vdash \Box A \rightarrow (\Box A \rightarrow \Box\Box A)$, and therefore
$\mathrm{Grz} \vdash \Box A \rightarrow \Box\Box A$. ⊣

(1) implies (10).

Proof. Suppose that $\langle W, R\rangle$ is transitive, reflexive, and converse weakly wellfounded. $\Box p \rightarrow p$ and $\Box p \rightarrow \Box\Box p$ are valid in $\langle W, R\rangle$. It suffices to show $\Box(\Box(p \rightarrow \Box p) \rightarrow p) \rightarrow p$ valid in $\langle W, R\rangle$. Let V be a valuation on $\langle W, R\rangle$.

Let $X_0 = \{w \in W: w \vDash \Box(\Box(p \rightarrow \Box p) \rightarrow p)$ and $w \nvDash p\}$, and $X_1 = \{w \in W: w \vDash \Box(\Box(p \rightarrow \Box p) \rightarrow p)$, $w \nvDash \Box p$, and $w \vDash p\}$. $X_0 \cap X_1 = \varnothing$.

If $w \in X_0$, by reflexivity, $w \vDash \Box(p \rightarrow \Box p) \rightarrow p$, and then $w \nvDash \Box(p \rightarrow \Box p)$. Therefore, for some x, wRx, $x \vDash p$, and $x \nvDash \Box p$. Since wRx, by transitivity, $x \vDash \Box(\Box(p \rightarrow \Box p) \rightarrow p)$. Thus $x \in X_1$.

If $w \in X_1$, then for some x, wRx, and $x \nvDash p$. By transitivity again, $x \vDash \Box(\Box(p \rightarrow \Box p) \rightarrow p)$. Thus $x \in X_0$.

Thus for every w in X_i $(i = 0, 1)$, there is an x in X_{1-i} such that wRx. Let $X = X_0 \cup X_1$. Since $X_0 \cap X_1 = \varnothing$, for every w in X, there is an x in X such that wRx and $w \neq x$. By converse weak wellfoundedness, $X = \varnothing$, and therefore $X_0 = \varnothing$. Thus for every $w \in W$, $w \vDash \Box(\Box(p \rightarrow \Box p) \rightarrow p) \rightarrow p$. ⊣

(10) implies (9).

Proof. It suffices to show that if $\langle W, R\rangle$ is finite, transitive, reflexive, and antisymmetric, then R is converse weakly wellfounded. But if W is finite and $\langle W, R\rangle$ is (merely) transitive and antisymmetric, then $\langle W, R\rangle$ is converse weakly wellfounded: For if X is a nonempty set, of which each member bears R to some other member, then for every n, there is a sequence $x_1, \ldots, x_n$ of n distinct members of X, each of which bears R to all later members, contra the supposition that W is finite. (If $x_1, \ldots, x_n$ is such a sequence, then for some y in X, $x_n R y$ and $x_n \neq y$. By transitivity $x_i R y$ for all $i \leqslant n$; if $y = x_i$ for some $i < n$, then by transitivity, $y R x_n$, and by antisymmetry, $x_n = y$, contradiction. Then $x_1, \ldots, x_n, y$ is such a sequence of $n+1$ distinct members of x.) ⊣

(9) implies (1) (the completeness theorem for S4Grz).[2]

Proof. Let A be an arbitrary sentence. Let $\mathscr{A} = \{B: B$ is a subsentence of $A\}$, let $\mathscr{B} = \mathscr{A} \cup \{\Box(C \rightarrow \Box C): \Box C \in \mathscr{A}\}$, and let $\mathscr{C} = \mathscr{B} \cup \{\neg B: B \in \mathscr{B}\}$.

Let $W = \{w\colon w$ is a maximal Grz-consistent subset of $\mathscr{C}\}$. As usual, every Grz-consistent subset of $\mathscr{C}$ is included in some w in W.

Let wQx iff for every $\Box C$ in $\mathscr{C}$, if $\Box C \in w$, then $\Box C \in x$.

Let wRx iff both wQx and if xQw, then $w = x$.

Q is transitive. R is clearly reflexive and antisymmetric. And R is transitive: Suppose $wRxRy$. Then $wQxQy$, whence wQy. Suppose yQw. Then $yQwQx$, whence yQx. Since xRy, $y = x$, and so wRy.

W is finite and so $\langle W, R\rangle$ is a finite transitive, reflexive, and antisymmetric frame.

For p a sentence letter, $w \in W$, let wVp iff $p \in w$. ⊣

Lemma. *For all B in $\mathscr{A}$, w in W, $B \in w$ iff $M, w \vDash B$.*

Proof. The atomic case is immediate from the definition of V. $\bot \notin w$ and $w \nvDash \bot$. If $B = C \rightarrow D$, then $C, D \in \mathscr{A}$, and therefore $C \rightarrow D \in w$ iff either $C \notin w$ or $D \in w$ (maximal consistency), iff either $w \nvDash C$ or $w \vDash D$ (induction hypothesis), iff $w \vDash C \rightarrow D$.

Assume $B = \Box C$. Suppose $\Box C \in w$. If wRx, then wQx, $\Box C \in x$, and since $\mathrm{Grz} \vdash \Box C \rightarrow C$ and x is maximal consistent, $C \in x$, and by the i.h., $x \vDash C$. Thus $w \vDash \Box C$.

Now suppose $\Box C \notin w$. Then $\neg \Box C \in w$. If $C \notin w$, then by the i.h., $w \nvDash C$ and since wRw, $w \nvDash \Box C$. So we may assume $C \in w$. Then, since $\Box(C \rightarrow \Box C) \in \mathscr{B}$, $\Box(C \rightarrow \Box C) \notin w$; otherwise since $C \in w$ and $\mathrm{Grz} \vdash \Box(C \rightarrow \Box C) \wedge C \rightarrow \Box C$, $\Box C \in w$. Let $\Box D_1, \ldots, \Box D_k$ be all the sentences $\Box D$ in w. Let $X = \{\Box D_1, \ldots, \Box D_k, \Box(C \rightarrow \Box C), \neg C\}$. If X is inconsistent, then

$\mathrm{Grz} \vdash \Box D_1 \wedge \cdots \wedge \Box D_k \rightarrow (\Box(C \rightarrow \Box C) \rightarrow C)$,

$\mathrm{Grz} \vdash \Box\Box D_1 \wedge \cdots \wedge \Box\Box D_k \rightarrow \Box(\Box(C \rightarrow \Box C) \rightarrow C)$,

$\mathrm{Grz} \vdash \Box\Box D_1 \wedge \cdots \wedge \Box\Box D_k \rightarrow C$,

$\mathrm{Grz} \vdash \Box\Box\Box D_1 \wedge \cdots \wedge \Box\Box\Box D_k \rightarrow \Box C$, and since

$\mathrm{Grz} \vdash \Box D_i \rightarrow \Box\Box\Box D_i$,

$\mathrm{Grz} \vdash \Box D_1 \wedge \cdots \wedge \Box D_k \rightarrow \Box C$, which is impossible, for $\Box D_1, \ldots, \Box D_k, \neg \Box C \in w$ and w is Grz-consistent. So X is also Grz-consistent and is thus included in some x in W. Since $\Box D_1, \ldots, \Box D_k \in x$, wQx. Since $\Box(C \rightarrow \Box C) \in x$, but $\notin w$, not xQw. Thus wRx. But $\neg C \in x$, $C \notin x$, by the i.h. $x \nvDash C$, and so $w \nvDash \Box C$. ⊣

Then if $\mathrm{Grz} \nvdash A$, $\{\neg A\}$ is a consistent subset of $\mathscr{C}$, $\neg A$ is in some w in W, $A \notin w$, and by the lemma $w \nvDash A$, and therefore A is invalid in the finite transitive, reflexive, and antisymmetric frame $\langle W, R\rangle$. Thus (9) implies (1).

(9) is equivalent to (3).[3]

Proof. Suppose that R is a relation on W. Let $R^+ = R \cup \{\langle x,x\rangle: x \in W\}$ and $R^- = R - \{\langle x,x\rangle: x \in W\}$. R^+ is reflexive and R^- is irreflexive. If R is irreflexive, then $R^{+-} = R$; if R is reflexive, then $R^{-+} = R$. Moreover, as is easily verified, if R is transitive, reflexive, and antisymmetric, then R^- is transitive and irreflexive; if R is transitive and irreflexive, then R^+ is transitive, reflexive, and antisymmetric.

If R is a transitive and irreflexive relation on W, then $\langle W, R, V\rangle$, $w \vDash {}^tB$ iff $\langle W, R^+, V\rangle$, $w \vDash B$, as we may see by induction on the complexity of B; the only case that requires attention is the one in which $B = \Box C$. But then $\langle W, R, V\rangle, w \vDash {}^t\Box C$, iff $\langle W, R, V\rangle, w \vDash (\Box {}^tC \wedge {}^tC)$, iff $\langle W, R, V\rangle$, $w \vDash \Box {}^tC$ and $\langle W, R, V\rangle$, $w \vDash {}^tC$, iff for all x such that wRx, $\langle W, R, V\rangle$, $x \vDash {}^tC$ and $\langle W, R, V\rangle$, $w \vDash {}^tC$, iff for all x such that wR^+x, $\langle W, R, V\rangle$, $x \vDash {}^tC$, iff by the i.h., for all x such that wR^+x, $\langle W, R^+, V\rangle$, $x \vDash C$, iff $\langle W, R^+, V\rangle$, $w \vDash \Box C$.

Thus if $\mathrm{GL} \nvdash {}^tA$, then for some finite transitive and irreflexive model $\langle W, R, V\rangle$, some $w \in W$, $\langle W, R, V\rangle$, $w \nvDash {}^tA$, whence $\langle W, R^+, V\rangle$, $w \nvDash A$, and A is invalid in the finite transitive, reflexive, and antisymmetric frame $\langle W, R^+\rangle$. Conversely, if $\langle W, R\rangle$ is a finite transitive, reflexive, and antisymmetric frame and $\langle W, R, V\rangle$, $w \nvDash A$, then $R = R^{-+}$ and $\langle W, R^{-+}, V\rangle$, $w \nvDash A$, $\langle W, R^-, V\rangle$, $w \nvDash {}^tA$, ${}^tA$ is invalid in the transitive and irreflexive frame $\langle W, R^-\rangle$, and therefore $\mathrm{GL} \nvdash {}^tA$. ⊣

(5) implies (3).[4] Suppose $\mathrm{GL} \nvdash {}^tA$. Then there is a finite transitive and irreflexive model M such that W contains 0, W contains no positive integers, $W = \{0\} \cup \{x: 0Rx\}$, and $M, 0 \nvDash {}^tA$.

Let n be the number of subsentences of ${}^tA$ of the form $\Box C$.

Let $X = W \cup \{i: 1 \leqslant i \leqslant n\}$. Let $Q = \{\langle j, i\rangle: 1 \leqslant i < j \leqslant n\} \cup \{\langle i, x\rangle: 1 \leqslant i \wedge x \in W\} \cup R$. $\langle X, Q\rangle$ is a finite transitive and irreflexive frame. Let $U = V \cup \{\langle i, p\rangle: 1 \leqslant i \leqslant n \wedge 0Vp\}$. Let $N = \langle X, Q, U\rangle$.

Lemma. *For any sentence B, any i, $0 \leqslant i < n$, $N, i+1 \vDash {}^tB$ iff $N, i \vDash {}^tB$.*

Proof. (We drop "N".) If B is a sentence letter p, ${}^tB = p$, and $i+1 \vDash p$ iff $i+1Up$, iff $0Vp$, iff iUp, iff $i \vDash p$. The truth-functional cases are straightforward.

Note that $i+1Sx$ iff $x = i$ or iSx; thus for any sentence D, $i+1 \vDash \Box D$ iff $i \vDash \Box D$ and $i \vDash D$. Now suppose $B = \Box C$. Then $i+1 \vDash {}^t\Box C$ iff $i+1 \vDash \Box {}^tC \wedge {}^tC$, iff $i+1 \vDash \Box {}^tC$ and $i+1 \vDash {}^tC$, iff $i \vDash \Box {}^tC$ and $i \vDash {}^tC$ and $i+1 \vDash {}^tC$, iff (by the i.h.) $i \vDash \Box {}^tC$ and $i \vDash {}^tC$, iff $i \vDash \Box {}^tC \wedge {}^tC$, iff $i \vDash {}^t\Box C$. ⊣

By continuity, $N, 0 \nVdash {}^tA$, and by the lemma, for all $i, 0 \leqslant i \leqslant n, N, i \nVdash {}^tA$.

Let $X = \{\Box C \rightarrow C: \Box C$ is a subsentence of ${}^tA\}$. X contains n members. By Theorem 7 of Chapter 7,[5] for some i, $0 \leqslant i \leqslant n$, N, $i \vDash \Box C \rightarrow C$ for all subsentences $\Box C$ of ${}^tA$. $({}^tA)^s = (\bigwedge \{\Box C \rightarrow C: \Box C$ is a subsentence of ${}^tA\} \rightarrow {}^tA)$. Thus $N, i \nvDash ({}^tA)^s$, $({}^tA)^s$ is invalid in the finite transitive irreflexive frame $\langle X, Q \rangle$, and $\mathrm{GL} \nvdash ({}^tA)^s$. By the arithmetical completeness theorem for GLS, $\mathrm{GLS} \nvdash {}^tA$.

Thus the ten conditions are indeed equivalent. The equivalence of (2) and (9) shows the decidability of Grz in the usual manner.

The schema: $\Box(\Box(A \rightarrow \Box A) \rightarrow A) \rightarrow A$ came to light in the investigation of the connections between intuitionistic and modal logic. (For an account of intuitionistic logic, the reader may be referred to Heyting's *Intuitionism: an Introduction* and Dummett's *Elements of Intuitionism.*) In his 1933 paper "An interpretation of the intuitionistic propositional calculus," Gödel asserted that the intuitionistic propositional calculus I could be interpreted in the modal system S4 if the following translation scheme were used:

$\neg A$	is to be translated as	$\neg \Box A$
$A \rightarrow B$		$\Box A \rightarrow \Box B$
$A \vee B$		$\Box A \vee \Box B$
$A \wedge B$		$A \wedge B$

Gödel's claim was that for any sentence A built up from sentence letters by $\neg, \rightarrow, \vee$, and $\wedge$, if $\mathrm{I} \vdash A$, then $\mathrm{S4} \vdash A'$, where A' is the translation of A under this scheme. Gödel conjectured that the converse holds; McKinsey and Tarski proved the conjecture.[6] Grzegorczyk showed that the Gödel–McKinsey–Tarski result also holds if one replaces S4 by a system deductively equivalent to S4Grz.[7] Thus for all sentences A as above, $\mathrm{I} \vdash A$ iff $\mathrm{S4Grz} \vdash A'$.[8]

Stringing together the equivalences of the main theorem yields a translation of the intuitionistic propositional calculus into (classical) arithmetic: $\mathrm{I} \vdash A$ iff $\mathrm{S4Grz} \vdash A'$, iff $\mathrm{GL} \vdash {}^t(A')$, iff ${}^t(A')$ is always provable, iff ${}^t(A')$ is always true. (Shades of the intuitionists' doctrine that mathematical truth is to be identified with provability!) By the uniform arithmetical completeness theorem for GL, there is a realization $*$ under which all and only the theorems of GL are provable in PA. Thus also $\mathrm{I} \vdash A$ iff $\mathrm{PA} \vdash ({}^t(A'))^*$. This result is an analogue, for classical arithmetic, of an earlier theorem of de Jongh[9] that states that there is a translation scheme $\circ$ under which for all sentences A of the intuitionistic propositional calculus, $\mathrm{I} \vdash A$ iff

$\mathrm{HA}\vdash A^\circ$, i.e., iff A° is provable in Heyting (intuitionistic) Arithmetic.

We close with five disjointed remarks on Grz.

1. Let $B(p) = \Box p \wedge p$. By the equivalence of (3) and (1), ^{t} is a function from and to modal sentences that commutes with truth-functional operators and is such that for all sentences A, $^t(\Box A) = B(^tA)$ and $\mathrm{Grz}\vdash A$ iff $\mathrm{GL}\vdash {^tA}$. But there can be no analogous converse reduction of GL to Grz given by a sentence like $B(p)$:

For $\mathrm{K}\vdash \Box\top \leftrightarrow \top$ and $\mathrm{T}\vdash \Box\bot \leftrightarrow \bot$. Therefore any letterless sentence is equivalent in T either to $\top$ or to $\bot$, and the same holds for Grz, which extends T. Thus if $B'(p)$ is a sentence containing a single sentence letter p and f is a function from and to modal sentences that commutes with truth-functional operators and is such that for all sentences A, $f(\Box A) = B'(f(A))$, then either $f(\neg\Box\bot)$ or $f(\Box\bot)$ is equivalent in Grz to $\top$, and therefore either $\mathrm{Grz}\vdash f(\neg\Box\bot)$ or $\mathrm{Grz}\vdash f(\Box\bot)$. But $\mathrm{GL}\nvdash \neg\Box\bot$ and $\mathrm{GL}\nvdash \Box\bot$.

2. A system L of propositional modal logic is *complete* if every sentence valid in all frames appropriate to L, i.e., all frames in which all theorems of L are valid, is itself a theorem of L. Like GL, K, K4, T, S4, B, and S5, Grz is complete: (2) implies (10), and therefore if A is valid in all frames in which all theorems of Grz are valid, then A is valid in all transitive, reflexive and converse weakly wellfounded frames, and then $\mathrm{Grz}\vdash A$, since (10) also implies (2).

3. In which frames are $\Box(\Box(p\to\Box p)\to p)\to p$ valid?

(1) implies (10), and therefore if $\langle W, R\rangle$ is a transitive, reflexive, and converse weakly wellfounded frame, then $\Box(\Box(p\to\Box p)\to p)\to p$ is valid in $\langle W, R\rangle$. And conversely, as the following theorem states:

Theorem. *Suppose that* $\Box(\Box(p\to\Box p)\to p)\to p$ *is valid in* $\langle W, R\rangle$. *Then* $\langle W, R\rangle$ *is transitive, reflexive, and converse weakly wellfounded.*

Proof. By the equivalence of (2) and (1), $\Box p\to p$ and $\Box p\to\Box\Box p$ are also valid in $\langle W, R\rangle$, and thus $\langle W, R\rangle$ is reflexive and transitive. Suppose that $\langle W, R\rangle$ is not converse weakly wellfounded. Then there is a nonempty set X and such that $\forall w\in X\,\exists x\in x(wRx \wedge w\neq x)$.

According to the axiom of dependent choice, a consequence of the axiom of choice, if X is a nonempty set and S a relation on X such that $\forall w\in X\,\exists x\in X\; wSx$, then there exists a function f such that for every natural number i, $f(i)Sf(i+1)$. Thus there exists a sequence $w_0, w_1, w_2, \ldots$ of elements of W such that for all i, w_iRw_{i+1} and $w_i\neq w_{i+1}$.

Let $I = \{i : \forall j < i \, w_i \neq w_j\}$. $0, 1 \in I$. If $2n \in I$, then for some m, $2m+1 \in I$ and $w_{2n} R w_{2m+1}$: for either $2n+1 \in I$, in which case we may take $m = n$, or for some $j \in I$, $j < 2n+1$, and $w_{2n+1} = w_j$. But in this case we may take $m = n-1$. For since $w_{2n+1} \neq w_{2n}$, $j \leqslant 2n-1 = 2m+1$. Then $w_{2n} R w_{2n+1} = w_j$. By transitivity $w_j R w_{2m+1}$ and therefore $w_{2n} R w_{2m+1}$.

Similarly, if $2m+1 \in I$, then for some n, $2n \in I$ and $w_{2m+1} R w_{2n}$.

Now for all w in W, let wVp iff for no n, $2n \in I$ and $w = w_{2n}$.

Suppose now that $2n$, $2m+1 \in I$; then $w_{2n} \nvDash p$ and $w_{2m+1} \vDash p$, $w_{2n} \nvDash \Box p$ and $w_{2m+1} \nvDash \Box p$, $w_{2n} \vDash p \rightarrow \Box p$ and $w_{2m+1} \nvDash p \rightarrow \Box p$, $w_{2n} \nvDash \Box(p \rightarrow \Box p)$ and $w_{2m+1} \nvDash \Box(p \rightarrow \Box p)$, $w_{2n} \vDash \Box(p \rightarrow \Box p) \rightarrow p$ and $w_{2m+1} \vDash \Box(p \rightarrow \Box p) \rightarrow p$, $w_{2n} \vDash \Box(\Box(p \rightarrow \Box p) \rightarrow p)$ (because if $w_{2n} R x$ but $x = w_i$ for no $i \in I$, then $x \vDash p$, and therefore $x \vDash \Box(p \rightarrow \Box p) \rightarrow p$), and thus $w_{2n} \nvDash \Box(\Box(p \rightarrow \Box p) \rightarrow p) \rightarrow p$, contradiction: $0 \in I$. $\dashv$

4. Open (?) problem. If $\langle W, R \rangle$ is transitive, reflexive, and converse weakly wellfounded, then $\Box(\Box(p \rightarrow \Box p) \rightarrow p) \rightarrow p$ is valid in $\langle W, R \rangle$; if $\Box(\Box(p \rightarrow \Box p) \rightarrow p) \rightarrow p$ is valid in $\langle W, R \rangle$, then $\langle W, R \rangle$ is transitive and reflexive and there is no sequence $w_0, w_1, w_2, \ldots$ of elements of W such that for all i, $w_i R w_{i+1}$ and $w_i \neq w_{i+1}$. Can either "if" be strengthened to "iff" in ZF set theory alone, and hence without appeal to the axiom of dependent choice?

5. From the equivalence of (2) and (3) it of course follows that $\mathrm{GL} \vdash \boxdot(\boxdot(p \rightarrow \boxdot p) \rightarrow p) \rightarrow p$. It is a good puzzle to see what an actual derivation might look like, and in order not to spoil the pleasure of the reader who might like to solve it, we have printed the solution overleaf:

By Theorem 9 of Chapter 1,

$\mathrm{GL} \vdash \Box(p \to \boxdot p) \to \Box \boxdot(p \to \boxdot p)$, and so by normality,
$\mathrm{GL} \vdash \Box(\boxdot(p \to \boxdot p) \to p) \to (\Box(p \to \boxdot p) \to \Box p)$, whence
$\mathrm{GL} \vdash \Box(\boxdot(p \to \boxdot p) \to p) \to (\Box(p \to \boxdot p) \to (p \to \boxdot p))$. And since
$\mathrm{GL} \vdash \Box(\boxdot(p \to \boxdot p) \to p) \to \Box\Box(\boxdot(p \to \boxdot p) \to p)$, by normality we have
$\mathrm{GL} \vdash \Box(\boxdot(p \to \boxdot p) \to p) \to \Box(\Box\boxdot(p \to \boxdot p) \to \Box p)$, whence by Theorem 9 of Chapter 1 again,
$\mathrm{GL} \vdash \Box(\boxdot(p \to \boxdot p) \to p) \to \Box(\Box(p \to \boxdot p) \to (p \to \boxdot p))$, and thus
$\mathrm{GL} \vdash \Box(\boxdot(p \to \boxdot p) \to p) \to \Box(p \to \boxdot p)$, whence

$$\text{(A)} \quad \mathrm{GL} \vdash \boxdot(\boxdot(p \to \boxdot p) \to p) \to \Box(p \to \boxdot p)$$

By the propositional calculus,

$\mathrm{GL} \vdash (\boxdot(p \to \boxdot p) \to p) \to (\Box(p \to \boxdot p) \to p)$. So
$\mathrm{GL} \vdash \boxdot(\boxdot(p \to \boxdot p) \to p) \to (\Box(p \to \boxdot p) \to p)$, and by (A),
$\mathrm{GL} \vdash \boxdot(\boxdot(p \to \boxdot p) \to p) \to p$, as desired.

13

Modal logic within set theory

In the present chapter we are going to investigate the connections between modal logic and set theory, i.e., Zermelo–Fraenkel set theory, "ZF", for short.

This chapter and the next, which deals with second-order arithmetic, or *analysis* as it is sometimes called, are, unfortunately, not self-contained. In order even to explain, let alone prove, their most interesting results we are forced to assume a level of knowledgeability about logical matters quite a bit higher than was necessary for the understanding of previous chapters. (Including the necessary background material would entail a lengthy exposition of matters largely irrelevant to the aims of this work.) The present chapter consists mainly of the proofs of two striking completeness theorems that concern interesting weakenings of the notion of provability: truth in all transitive models of set theory and truth in all models V_κ (alias R_κ), κ inaccesssible. The theorems were discovered by Robert Solovay in the fall of 1975; their proofs have not hitherto appeared in print.

To understand the proofs of these results, one has to have a reasonable acquaintance with basic set theory, as well as some basic notions involved in proofs of independence à la Gödel and Cohen. An excellent source for this material is Kunen's *Set Theory.*[1] The relevant system of modal logic for the notion: truth in all V_κ, κ inaccessible, is stronger than that for: truth in all transitive models, which is itself stronger than GL. (When treating inaccessibles, we assume that ZF includes the axiom of choice; otherwise not.)

GL, not at all surprisingly, turns out to be the modal logic of (ordinary) provability in ZF. The proofs of the arithmetical completeness theorems for GL and GLS carry over without essential change from PA to ZF. To prove that the theorems of GL are *all* the sentences all of whose translations into the language of ZF are provable, we must of course appeal to certain facts that cannot be proved in set theory, as we appealed to certain facts that could not be proved in PA in order to establish the arithmetical completeness theorem for GL.

We have seen that if A is not a theorem of GL, there are sentences $S_0, S_1, \ldots, S_n$ and a realization $*$ such that

$\mathrm{PA} \vdash S_0 \vee S_1 \vee \cdots \vee S_n$,
$\mathrm{PA} \vdash S_i \to \mathrm{Bew}(\ulcorner \neg S_i \urcorner)$ if $i \geqslant 1$, and
$\mathrm{PA} \vdash S_0 \to \neg \mathrm{Bew}(\ulcorner A^* \urcorner)$.

[These are (4), (6), and (8) of Chapter 9.] It follows that

$$\mathrm{PA} \vdash \bigwedge_{i:1 \leqslant i \leqslant n} [\mathrm{Bew}(\ulcorner \neg S_i \urcorner) \to \neg S_i] \to \neg \mathrm{Bew}(\ulcorner A^* \urcorner)$$

and therefore the unprovability of A^* in PA is implied in PA by a conjunction of reflection principles. Under appropriate translation of the language of arithmetic into that of ZF, the antecedent conjunction of reflection principles can be proved in ZF, and therefore so can the consequent statement that A^* is not provable in PA.

Similarly the unprovability of A^* in ZF for a suitably defined $*$ is implied in ZF by a conjunction of set-theoretical reflection principles, which of course cannot now be proved *in ZF* (provided that ZF is consistent, of course), but only with the aid of principles not themselves provable in ZF. In order to obtain completeness theorems for the notions of truth in all transitive models and truth in all models V_κ, κ inaccessible, we shall again, predictably enough, have to appeal to principles not themselves provable in set theory.

Truth in all transitive models of set theory

Let $*$ be a function that assigns to each sentence letter a sentence of the language of set theory, and for each modal sentence A, now define A^* as follows

$p^* = {*}(p)$,
$\bot^* = \bot$,
$(A \to B)^* = (A^* \to B^*)$, and
$(\Box A)^* =$ the sentence of the language of set theory that translates "A^* holds in all transitive models of ZF".

A *finite prewellordering* is a frame $\langle W, R \rangle$, where W is finite and R is a transitive and irreflexive relation such that for every w, x, y in W, if wRx, then either wRy or yRx.

Lemma 1. *Let* $\langle W, R\rangle$ *be a finite transitive and irreflexive frame. Then* $\langle W, R\rangle$ *is a finite prewellordering iff for some* $f: W \to N$, *for all* $w, x \in W, f(w) > f(x)$ *iff* wRx.

Proof. Suppose $\langle W, R\rangle$ is a finite prewellordering. $\langle W, R\rangle$ is appropriate to GL. Let f be ρ. [For the notion of rank $\rho = \rho_{\langle W,R\rangle}$, see Chapter 7.] Then if wRx, $\rho(w) > \rho(x)$. And if $i = \rho(w) > \rho(x) = j$, then for some $w_i, \ldots, w_0, x_j, \ldots, x_0$, $w = w_i R \ldots R w_0$ and $x = x_j R \ldots R x_0$. By the transitivity of R, wRw_j, and thus either wRx or xRw_j. But if xRw_j, then $xRw_j R \ldots R w_0$, and $\rho(x) \geqslant j+1$, impossible. Thus wRx.

Conversely, if for all $w, x \in W$, $f(w) > f(x)$ iff wRx, then $\langle W, R\rangle$ is a finite prewellordering. For suppose wRx and $y \in W$; then since $f(w) > f(x)$, either $f(w) > f(y)$, whence wRy, or $f(y) > f(x)$, whence yRx. ⊣

Let I be the system of modal logic that results when all sentences

$$\Box(\Box A \to \Box B) \vee \Box(\Box B \to \boxdot A)$$

are added to GL as new axioms.

Theorem 1 (Solovay). *Let* A *be a modal sentence. Then* (A), (B), *and* (C) *are equivalent*:
(A) *For all* $*$, $\mathrm{ZF} \vdash A^*$.
(B) A *is valid in all finite prewellorderings.*
(C) $\mathrm{I} \vdash A$.

In order to prove the theorem, we shall assume that there are infinitely many α such that L_α is a model of $\mathrm{ZF} + V = L$. We shall prove that (A) implies (B), (B) implies (C), and (C) implies (A).

(A) implies (B): Suppose that $\langle W, R\rangle$ is a finite prewellordering, V is a valuation on W, and $\langle W, R, V\rangle, w \nvDash A$. In view of Lemma 1, we may suppose without loss of generality that for some natural numbers $n, r_0, \ldots, r_n$, $W = \{(i, j): i \leqslant n \text{ and } j \leqslant r_i\}$ and $(i, j)R(k, m)$ iff $i > k$.

Let $W' = W \cup \{0\}$ and $R' = R \cup \{\langle 0, z\rangle : z \in W\}$.

It suffices to find sentences S_x for x in W' such that

(a) if $x \neq y$, then $\mathrm{ZF} \vdash \neg(S_x \wedge S_y)$;
(b) $\mathrm{ZF} \vdash \bigvee\{S_x : x \in W'\}$;
(c) if $xR'y$, then $\mathrm{ZF} \vdash S_x \to$ "S_y holds in some transitive model";

(d) if $x \neq 0$, then $\mathrm{PA} \vdash S_x \to$ "$\bigvee_{y:xR'y} S_y$ holds in every transitive model"; and
(e) S_0 is true.

[(a), (b), (c), and (d) correspond to (2), (4), (5), and (7) of the proof of the arithmetical completeness theorem.]

For if we define $p^* = \bigvee \{S_x : xVp\}$, then the argument at the end of the proof of the arithmetical completeness theorem shows that $\mathrm{ZF} \vdash S_w \to \neg A^*$ and $\mathrm{ZF} \vdash S_0 \to$ "S_w holds in some transitive model". Since S_0 is true, so is "$\neg A^*$ holds in some transitive model". By the soundness of logic, it follows that $\mathrm{ZF} \nvdash A^*$.

We let S_0 be the sentence "there are at least $n+1$ transitive models of $\mathrm{ZF} + V = L$". By our assumption, (e) holds.

If $i \leqslant n$ and $j < r_i$, we let $S_{(i,j)}$ be "$2^{\aleph_0} = \aleph_{j+1}$ and there are exactly i transitive models of $\mathrm{ZF} + V = L$". And if $i \leqslant n$ and $j = r_i$, we let $S_{(i,j)}$ be "$2^{\aleph_0} \geqslant \aleph_{r_i+1}$ and there are exactly i transitive models of $\mathrm{ZF} + V = L$".

(a) and (b) are clearly satisfied. As for (c), suppose $xR'y$, $y = (k, m)$. Now working in ZF, we have that if S_x holds, there are at least $k+1$ transitive models of $\mathrm{ZF} + V = L$. Take the $(k+1)^{\mathrm{st}}$ model of $\mathrm{ZF} + V = L$, counting the minimal model as the first, and expand if necessary à la Cohen to a transitive model $\mathscr{M}$ of $2^{\aleph_0} = \aleph_{m+1}$ *with the same ordinals*. By the absoluteness of "transitive model of $\mathrm{ZF} + V = L$", S_y holds in $\mathscr{M}$. Thus (c) holds.

And as for (d), suppose that $x \neq 0$. Let $x = (i, j)$. then $\bigvee_{y:xR'y} S_y$ is equivalent to the statement "there are $< i$ transitive models of $\mathrm{ZF} + V = L$". Now working in ZF, we have that if S_x holds, then for some $i \leqslant n$, there are exactly i transitive models of $\mathrm{ZF} + V = L$. Let $\mathscr{M}$ be a transitive model of ZF. We must show that $\bigvee_{y:xR'y} S_y$ holds in $\mathscr{M}$. But $\mathscr{M} \cap L$ is a transitive model of $\mathrm{ZF} + V = L$ with the same ordinals as $\mathscr{M}$, $\mathscr{M} \cap L$ is thus not in $\mathscr{M}$, and so there are $< i$ transitive models of $\mathrm{ZF} + V = L$ in $\mathscr{M}$. By absoluteness, $\bigvee_{y:xR'y} S_y$ holds in $\mathscr{M}$. So (d) holds.

The proof that (B) implies (C) is a standard sort of maximal set construction of a model $\langle W, R, V \rangle$ in which a given non-theorem A of I is invalid, but the members of W will be maximal sets consistent with a certain conjunction Δ of sentences of the form $\boxdot(E \to F)$ that is consistent with $\neg A$. R and V are then defined as in the completeness proof for GL. Lemma 1 is used to show $\langle W, R \rangle$ a finite prewellordering. The proof that for subsentences of A, "true at" = "in" is as usual.

Here are the details. For all sentences C, D,

$$\mathrm{K4} \vdash \Box(\Box C \to \Box D) \to [\boxdot(\Box C \to \Box D) \vee (\boxdot(\Box D \to \Box C) \wedge \boxdot(\Box D \to C))],$$
$$\mathrm{K4} \vdash \Box(\Box D \to \boxdot C) \to [\boxdot(\Box C \to \Box D) \vee \boxdot(\Box D \to \Box C)], \text{ and}$$
$$\mathrm{K4} \vdash \Box(\Box D \to \boxdot C) \to [\boxdot(\Box C \to \Box D) \vee \boxdot(\Box D \to C)].$$

Since $\mathrm{I} \vdash \Box(\Box C \to \Box D) \vee \Box(\Box D \to \boxdot C)$ and I extends K4, $\mathrm{I} \vdash \boxdot(\Box C \to \Box D) \vee (\boxdot(\Box D \to \Box C) \wedge \boxdot(\Box D \to C))$.

Suppose now that $\mathrm{I} \nvdash A$. Then $\{\neg A\}$ is I-consistent. Let $\mathscr{A} = \{B: B$ is a subsentence of A or the negation of a subsentence of $A\}$. Let $\mathscr{B} = \{\boxdot(E \to F): E, F \in \mathscr{A}\}$. Let $B_1, \ldots, B_r$ be an enumeration of $\mathscr{B}$. Let $\mathscr{C}_1 = \{B_1\}$ if $\{\neg A\} \cup \{B_1\}$ is I-consistent; otherwise let $\mathscr{C}_1 = \{\neg B_1\}$, and for $i < r$ let $\mathscr{C}_{i+1} = \mathscr{C}_i \cup \{B_{i+1}\}$ if $\{\neg A\} \cup \mathscr{C}_i \cup \{B_{i+1}\}$ is I-consistent; otherwise let $\mathscr{C}_{i+1} = \mathscr{C}_i \cup \{\neg B_{i+1}\}$. For each $i \leqslant r$, $\{\neg A\} \cup \mathscr{C}_i$ is I-consistent. Let $\Delta = \bigwedge(\mathscr{C}_r \cap \mathscr{B})$. Then $\mathrm{I} \nvdash \Delta \to A$, and $\mathrm{I} \vdash \Delta \to \Box\Delta$, since Δ is a conjunction of sentences $\boxdot M$.

Let $W =$ the set of maximal subsets w of $\mathscr{A}$ such that $\mathrm{I} \nvdash \Delta \to \neg \bigwedge w$. If $X \subseteq \mathscr{A}$ and $\mathrm{I} \nvdash \Delta \to \neg \bigwedge X$, then for some w in W, $X \subseteq w$, and therefore for some w_0 in W, $\neg A \in w_0$. If $w \in W$ and $B \to C \in \mathscr{A}$, then $B \to C \in w$ iff either $B \notin w$ or $C \in w$. And W is finite.

Let wRx iff $w, x \in W$, for every $\Box C \in w$, $\Box C \in x$ and $C \in x$; and for some $\Box D \in x$, $\neg \Box D \in w$. R is irreflexive. And R is transitive, for if $wRxRy$, then for some $\Box D \in y$, $\neg \Box D \in x$, whence $\neg \Box D \in w$. We shall use Lemma 1 to show $\langle W, R\rangle$ a finite prewellordering. Let $f(w)$ be the number of sentences $\neg \Box C$ in w. If wRx, then $f(w) > f(x)$. Suppose $f(w) > f(x)$. Then for some $\Box D$ in $\mathscr{A}$, $\neg \Box D \in w$ and $\Box D \in x$. To show that wRx it thus suffices to show that if $\Box C \in w$, then $\Box C \in x$ and $C \in x$.

So suppose $\Box C \in w$. Since $\mathrm{I} \vdash \boxdot(\Box C \to \Box D) \vee (\boxdot(\Box D \to \Box C) \wedge \boxdot(\Box D \to C))$, either $\boxdot(\Box C \to \Box D)$ is a conjunct of Δ or $\boxdot(\Box D \to \Box C)$ and $\boxdot(\Box D \to C)$ are both conjuncts of Δ. If $\boxdot(\Box C \to \Box D)$ is a conjunct, then $\mathrm{I} \vdash \Delta \to \neg(\Box C \wedge \neg \Box D)$, and so $\mathrm{I} \vdash \Delta \to \neg \bigwedge w$, contra $w \in W$. Thus both $\boxdot(\Box D \to \Box C)$ and $\boxdot(\Box D \to C)$ are conjuncts. So $\mathrm{I} \vdash \Delta \to \neg(\Box D \wedge \neg \Box C)$ and $\mathrm{I} \vdash \Delta \to \neg(\Box D \wedge \neg C)$. If either $\Box C \notin x$ or $C \notin x$, then $\neg \Box C \in x$ or $\neg C \in x$, and then $\mathrm{I} \vdash \Delta \to \neg \bigwedge x$, contra $x \in W$. Thus $\Box C \in x$ and $C \in x$, and $\langle W, R\rangle$ is a finite prewellordering.

As usual, let wVp if $p \in W$.

Lemma 2. *If $w \in W$ and $B \in \mathscr{A}$, then $M, w \vDash B$ iff $B \in w$.*

Proof. Induction on B. The only non-trivial case is the one in which $B = \Box C$. If $\Box C \in w$, then as usual, $w \models \Box C$. Suppose then that $\Box C \notin w$. Then $\neg \Box C \in w$. Let $\Box D_1, \ldots, \Box D_n$ be all the sentences $\Box D$ in w. Let $X = \{\Box D_1, D_1, \ldots, \Box D_n, D_n, \Box C, \neg C\}$. If
$\mathrm{I} \vdash \Delta \to \neg \bigwedge X$, then
$\mathrm{I} \vdash \Delta \to (\Box D_1 \wedge D_1 \wedge \cdots \wedge \Box D_n \wedge D_n \to (\Box C \to C))$, and so
$\mathrm{I} \vdash \Box \Delta \to (\Box D_1 \wedge \cdots \wedge \Box D_n \to \Box C)$ (since I extends GL),
$\mathrm{I} \vdash \Delta \to \neg(\Box D_1 \wedge \cdots \wedge \Box D_n \wedge \neg \Box C)$ (since $\mathrm{I} \vdash \Delta \to \Box \Delta$), and
$\mathrm{I} \vdash \Delta \to \neg \bigwedge w$, contra $w \in W$.
Thus $\mathrm{I} \nvdash \Delta \to \neg \bigwedge X$, and so for some $x \in W$, $X \subseteq x$, whence wRx. And as usual, since $\neg C \in X \subseteq x$, $C \notin x$, and $x \nvDash C$ by the induction hypothesis. Thus $w \nvDash \Box C$. ⊣

$A \notin w_0$ and $w_0 \in W$; by Lemma 2, $w_0 \nvDash A$, and A is invalid in the finite prewellordering $\langle W, R \rangle$.

(C) implies (A): It is a routine matter to verify that if $\mathrm{GL} \vdash A$, then $\mathrm{ZF} \vdash A^*$. In the case of $\Box(\Box A \to A) \to \Box A$, we argue: If $\neg S$ holds in some transitive model (of ZF), then for some least α, $\neg S$ holds in some transitive model $\mathcal{M}$ such that $|\mathcal{M}| = \alpha$. (Here and below $|\ \ |$ is ordinal rank.) There is no transitive model of $\neg S$ in $\mathcal{M}$, and so by the absoluteness of "... is a transitive model of ——", $\mathcal{M}$ is also a transitive model of "S holds in all transitive models". In the case of $\Box(\Box A \to \Box B) \vee \Box(\Box B \to \boxdot A)$, we appeal to the following theorem.[2]

> **Theorem (Jensen–Karp).** *If $\mathcal{C}$ and $\mathcal{D}$ are transitive models, $|\mathcal{C}| < |\mathcal{D}|$, and $\mathcal{C} \models \chi$, then $\mathcal{D} \models$ "χ holds in some transitive model". (The theorem is not obvious, as $\mathcal{C}$ need not be in $\mathcal{D}$.)*

Using the theorem, we may argue in ZF: Suppose that for some transitive models $\mathcal{M}$, $\mathcal{N}$ and some sentences σ, τ,

$\mathcal{M} \models$ "σ holds in all transitive models",
$\mathcal{M} \models$ "$\neg \tau$ holds in some transitive model",
$\mathcal{N} \models$ "τ holds in all transitive models", and either
$\mathcal{N} \models \neg \sigma$ or $\mathcal{N} \models$ "$\neg \sigma$ holds in some transitive model".

Let $\mathcal{A}$ be a transitive model of $\neg \tau$ that belongs to $\mathcal{M}$. Then $|\mathcal{A}| < |\mathcal{M}|$ and by the theorem, $|\mathcal{N}| < |\mathcal{M}|$. If $\mathcal{N} \models \neg \sigma$, the theorem yields a contradiction. Thus for some transitive model $\mathcal{B}$ in $\mathcal{N}$,

$\mathscr{B} \models \neg\sigma$ and $|\mathscr{B}| < |\mathscr{N}|$. But then $|\mathscr{B}| < |\mathscr{M}|$ and the theorem again gives a contradiction.

We now prove the theorem[3]

We begin with a theorem of Skolem: for any sentence σ there is an $\forall\exists$ sentence τ, i.e., a prenex sentence τ in whose prefix all universal quantifiers precede all existential quantifiers, such that any model of σ has an expansion that is a model of τ and the reduct of any model of τ to the language of σ is a model of σ. (τ may contain new predicate letters.) One example will prove the theorem: if $\sigma = \exists x \forall y \exists z \exists a \forall b \exists c Wxyzabc$, W a quantifier-free formula, then we may take τ to be the result of suitably prenexing the sentence:

$$\begin{aligned}
&\exists x Rx \wedge \\
&\forall x(Rx \leftrightarrow \forall y Sxy) \wedge \\
&\forall x \forall y(Sxy \leftrightarrow \exists z Txyz) \wedge \\
&\forall x \forall y \forall z(Txyz \leftrightarrow \exists a Uxyza) \wedge \\
&\forall x \forall y \forall z \forall a(Uxyza \leftrightarrow \forall b Vxyzab) \wedge \\
&\forall x \forall y \forall z \forall a \forall b(Vwyzab \leftrightarrow \exists c Wxyzabc).
\end{aligned}$$

Now let $\sigma_1, \sigma_2, \ldots$ be a recursive enumeration of χ and the axioms of ZF. Let $\tau_1, \tau_2, \ldots$ be a recursive enumeration of $\forall\exists$ sentences constructed from $\sigma_1, \sigma_2, \ldots$ as in our example, such that no predicate letter other than '$\in$' occurs in both τ_i and τ_j if $i \neq j$, and $\tau_i = \forall x_1 \cdots \forall x_{n_i} \psi_i(x_1, \ldots, x_{n_i})$, where $\psi_i = \exists y_1 \cdots \exists y_{m_i} \theta_i(x_1, \ldots, x_{n_i}, y_1, \ldots, y_{m_i})$ and θ_i is quantifier-free. Thus any model of σ_i has an expansion that is a model of τ_i and the reduct to the language of ZF of any model of τ_i is a model of σ_i.

Let $\mathscr{A} = \langle A, \in|A, R_1, R_2, \ldots\rangle$ be an expansion of $\mathscr{C}$ that is a model of all τ_i. (Since the τ_i have been suitably constructed from the σ_i, the axiom of choice is not needed to guarantee the existence of $\mathscr{A}$.) We may assume that the sequence $\rho_1, \rho_2, \ldots$ of predicate letters interpreted in $\mathscr{A}$ by $R_1, R_2, \ldots$ can be recursively encoded. Let no(j) be the least integer k such that all predicate letters in $\tau_1, \ldots, \tau_j$ are among $\rho_1, \ldots, \rho_k$.

If $\mathscr{P} = \langle P_0, E_0, S_1, \ldots, S_k\rangle$ and $\mathscr{P}_1 = \langle P_1, E_1. T_1, \ldots, T_k, \ldots\rangle$ where the final "..." may represent a finite or infinite sequence of relations and $\mathscr{P}_0$ is a substructure of $\langle P_1, E_1, T_1, \ldots, T_k\rangle$, then we shall call $\mathscr{P}_0$ an almost-substructure of $\mathscr{P}_1$ and write $\mathscr{P}_0 \sqsubseteq \mathscr{P}_1$.

Let X be the set of all $\langle j, \mathscr{P}, f\rangle$, where $j \geqslant 1$, $\mathscr{P}, = \langle P, E, S_1, \ldots, S_{no(j)}\rangle$, is a structure with P a finite subset of ω, $f: P \to |A|$, and for all p, q in P, if pEq, then $f(p) < f(q)$.

Let $x_1 \prec x_0$ if $x_0, x_1 \in X$, $j_0 < j_1$, $\mathscr{P}_0 \subseteq \mathscr{P}_1, f_0 \subseteq f_1$, and for all $i \leqslant j_0$ and all $p_1, \ldots, p_{n_i}$ in P_0, $\mathscr{P}_1 \vDash \psi_i[p_1, \ldots, p_{n_i}]$.

Lemma 3. $\langle X, \prec \rangle$ is not wellfounded.

Proof. Let $Y \subseteq X$ be the set of those $\langle j, \mathscr{P}, f \rangle$ in X such that for some isomorphism e of $\mathscr{P}$ onto an almost-substructure of $\mathscr{A}$, $f(p) = |e(p)|$ for all p in P. Y is not empty. Let $\mathscr{A}' = \langle \{0\}, \in|\{0\}, R_1|\{0\}, \ldots, R_{no(1)}|\{0\} \rangle$. Then $\langle 1, \mathscr{A}', \{\langle 0,0 \rangle\} \rangle \in Y$. Moreover, for every x_0 in Y, there is some x_1 in Y such that $x_1 \prec x_0$: Suppose that $\mathscr{P}_0 = \langle P_0, E_0, S_1, \ldots, S_{no(j_0)} \rangle$, $x_0 = \langle j_0, \mathscr{P}_0, f_0 \rangle$ is in X, there is an isomorphism e_0 of $\mathscr{P}_0$ onto an almost-substructure $\mathscr{A}_0 = \langle A_0, \in|A_0, R_1|A_0, \ldots, R_{no(j_0)}|A_0 \rangle$ of $\mathscr{A}$, and for every p in $P_0, f_0(p) = |e_0(p)|$. Then $A_0 = e_0[P_0]$. A_0 is a finite subset of A. Moreover, for all $i \leqslant j_0$, $\mathscr{A} \vDash \tau_i$. Thus if $i \leqslant j_0$ and $a_1, \ldots, a_{n_i}$ are in A_0, $\mathscr{A} \vDash \psi_i[a_1, \ldots, a_{n_i}]$ and thus for some $b_1, \ldots, b_{m_i}$ in A, $\mathscr{A} \vDash \theta_i[a_1, \ldots, a_{n_i}, b_1, \ldots, b_{m_i}]$. Thus there are a finite set A_1, $A_0 \subseteq A_1 \subseteq A$, and a structure $\mathscr{A}_1 = \langle A_1, \in|A_1, R_1|A_1, \ldots, R_{no(j_0+1)}|A_1 \rangle$ such that $\mathscr{A}_0 \subseteq \mathscr{A}_1 \subseteq \mathscr{A}$ and for every $i \leqslant j_0$, every $a_1, \ldots, a_{n_i}$ in A_0, there are $b_1, \ldots, b_{m_i}$ in A_1 for which $\mathscr{A}_1 \vDash \theta_1[a_1, \ldots, a_{n_i}, b_1, \ldots, b_{m_i}]$, and therefore $\mathscr{A}_1 \vDash \psi_i[a_1, \ldots, a_{n_i}]$. Consequently we may extend $P_0, \mathscr{P}_0$, and e_0 to $P_1, \mathscr{P}_1$, and e_1 so that $P_0 \subseteq P_1 \subseteq \omega$, P_1 is finite, $\mathscr{P}_0 \subseteq \mathscr{P}_1$ is of the form $\langle P_1, E_1, T_1, \ldots, T_{no(j_0+1)} \rangle$, $e_0 \subseteq e_1$ is an isomorphism of $\mathscr{P}_1$ with $\mathscr{A}_1$, and for all $i \leqslant j_0$, all $p_1, \ldots, p_{n_i}$ in P_0, $\mathscr{P}_1 \vDash \psi_i[p_1, \ldots, p_{n_i}]$. If we let $j_1 = j_0 + 1$, $f_1(p) = |e_1(p)|$ for all p in P_1, and $x_1 = \langle j_1, \mathscr{P}_1, f_1 \rangle$, then $x_1 \prec x_0$. ⊣

Observe now that since $|A|$, the least ordinal not in $\mathscr{C}$, is in $\mathscr{D}$, $\langle X, \prec \rangle$ is itself in $\mathscr{D}$. And $\langle X, \prec \rangle$ is not wellfounded *in* $\mathscr{D}$: otherwise there are an ordinal ξ in $\mathscr{D}$ and in function $h: X \to \xi$ in $\mathscr{D}$ such that if $x_0, x_1 \in X$ and $x_0 \prec x_1$, $h(x_0) < h(x_1)$. But then $\langle X, \prec \rangle$ *is* wellfounded, contra Lemma 3.

Replacing $\mathscr{D}$ by $\mathscr{D} \cap L$ if necessary, we may assume that the axiom of choice holds in $\mathscr{D}$. Then $\mathscr{D}$ contains a sequence $x_0, x_1, x_2, \ldots$ of members of X such that $\cdots \prec x_2 \prec x_1 \prec x_0$, where $x_k = \langle j_k, \mathscr{P}_k, f_k \rangle$ and $\mathscr{P}_k = \langle P_k, E_k, S_{1,k}, \ldots, S_{no(j_k),k} \rangle$. Let $\mathscr{P}$ be the union, or more properly, the direct limit of the $\mathscr{P}_k$, thus is, $\mathscr{P} = \langle \bigcup P_k, \bigcup E_k, \bigcup S_{1,k}, \ldots, \bigcup S_{i;k}, \ldots \rangle$, where $S_{i;k} = S_{i,k}$ if $S_{i,k}$ is defined and $S_{i,k} = \varnothing$ otherwise, $\mathscr{P} \in \mathscr{D}$. Let $P = \bigcup P_k$; $E = \bigcup E_k$.

All τ_i hold in $\mathscr{P}$: Suppose $p_1, \ldots, p_{n_i} \in P$. Then for some k, $p_1, \ldots, p_{n_i} \in P_k$ and $i \leqslant j_k$. Then $\mathscr{P}_{k+1} \vDash \psi_i[p_1, \ldots, p_{n_i}]$, and for some $q_1, \ldots, q_{m_i}$, $\mathscr{P}_{k+1} \vDash \theta_i[p_1, \ldots, p_{n_i}, q_1, \ldots, q_{m_i}]$. Since $P_{k+1} \subseteq P$ and θ_i is quantifier free, $\mathscr{P} \models \theta_i[p_1, \ldots, p_{n_i}, q_1, \ldots, q_{m_i}]$ and $\mathscr{P} \models \psi_i[p_1, \ldots, p_{n_i}]$. Thus $\mathscr{P} \models \tau_i$.

Let $\mathscr{B} = \langle P, E \rangle$. All σ_i hold in $\mathscr{B}$, whence $\mathscr{B}$ is a model of ZF and of χ. In particular, $\mathscr{B}$ is a model of the axiom of extensionality.

$\mathscr{B}$ is wellfounded: Let $f = \bigcup f_k$. If $i \leqslant j$, $f_i \subseteq f_j$; thus f is a function mapping P into $|A|$. If $p, q \in P$ and pEq, then for some $k, p, q \in P_k$, pE_kq and $f(p) = f_k(p) < f_k(q) = f(q)$.

Thus $\mathscr{B}$ is a wellfounded model of extensionality, ZF, and χ that belongs to $\mathscr{D}$. Since $\mathscr{D}$ is a model of ZF, by the Gödel–Mostowski isomorphism theorem, there is a transitive model of ZF and of χ that belongs to $\mathscr{D}$. Thus $\mathscr{D} \models$ "χ holds in some transitive model".

Truth in all universes

A universe is a set V_κ, where κ is inaccessible. The sets V_κ are sometimes denoted: R_κ. If κ is inaccessible, then V_κ is a model of ZF.

Now define A^* as before, except that we now redefine $(\Box A)^*$ as the sentence of the language of set theory that translates "A^* holds in all universes".

A finite strict linear ordering is a frame $\langle W, R \rangle$, where W is finite and R is a transitive and irreflexive relation that is connected on W, i.e., for all w, x in W, either wRx or $w = x$ or xRw.

Let J be the system that results when all sentences

$$\Box(\Box A \to B) \vee \Box(\boxdot B \to A)$$

are added to GL as new axioms.

The final result of this chapter is another completeness theorem of Solovay's.

Theorem 2 (Solovay). *Let A be a modal sentence. Then* (A), (B), *and* (C) *are equivalent*:
(A) *For all* $*$, ZF $\vdash A^*$.
(B) *A is valid in all finite strict linear orderings.*
(C) J $\vdash A$.

In order to prove the theorem, we shall assume that there are infinitely many inaccessibles.

(A) implies (B): Let M be a finite strict linear ordering. We may suppose $W = \{1, \ldots, n\}$ and $R = <|W$, and $M, 1 \nvDash A$. Let $W' = \{0\} \cup W$ and $R' = <|W'$. Then let

S_0 = "there are at least n universes",
S_1 = "there are exactly $n-1$ universes",
S_2 = "there are exactly $n-2$ universes",...,
S_{n-1} = "there is exactly 1 universe", and
S_n = "there are no universes".

Thus by our assumption, S_0 is true. The analogues of (2) and (4) are clear. Note that "universe" is absolute between universes and V. As for the analogue of (5), if $i<j$ and S_i holds, then there is a universe in which S_j holds. And as for that of (7), if $i \geqslant 1$ and S_i holds, then in every universe, the disjunction of the S_j, $j \geqslant i$, holds. The proof then goes through as before.

(C) implies (A): The axioms of GL are treated as in the proof of Theorem 1. As for the new axiom $\Box(\Box A \to B) \vee \Box(\boxdot B \to A)$ of J, we argue in ZF: if $\mathcal{M}$ and $\mathcal{N}$ are universes,

$\mathcal{M} \models$ "σ holds in all universes",
$\mathcal{M} \models \neg\tau$,
$\mathcal{N} \models$ "τ holds in all universes",
$\mathcal{N} \models \tau$, and
$\mathcal{N} \models \neg\sigma$,

then $\mathcal{M} \neq \mathcal{N}$. Then either $\mathcal{N} \in \mathcal{M}$ or $\mathcal{M} \in \mathcal{N}$, and by the absoluteness in universes of "... is a universe that is a model of ——", we have a contradiction.

(B) implies (C): For once, canonical models (cf. Chapter 6) come in handy. $\langle W_J, R_J, V_J \rangle$ is the canonical model for J.

R_J is transitive: suppose wR_JxR_Jy, and $\Box A \in w$. We must show $A \in y$. But since J extends GL and GL$\vdash \Box A \to \Box\Box A$, $\Box\Box A \in w$. And then by the definition of R_J, $\Box A \in x$ and so $A \in y$.

R_J is also "piecewise connected": If wR_Jx and wR_Jy, then either xR_Jy or $x=y$ or yR_Jx. For if wR_Jx, wR_Jy, not: xR_Jy, $x \neq y$, and not: yR_Jx, then for some B, C, D, $B \in x$, $B \notin y$, $\Box C \in x$, $C \notin y$, $\Box D \in y$, and $D \notin x$. Let $E = \neg B \vee D$. Then $\Box C \to E \notin x$, $\boxdot E \in y$, $\boxdot E \to C \notin y$, $\Box(\Box C \to E) \notin w$, $\Box(\boxdot E \to C) \notin w$. Since J $\vdash \Box(\Box C \to E) \vee \Box(\boxdot E \to C)$, $\Box(\Box C \to E) \vee \Box(\boxdot E \to C) \in w$, contradiction.

Assume now that J$\nvdash A$. Then for some u in W_J, $A \notin u$. If $\Box A \in u$, let $v=u$. But if $\neg\Box A \in u$, then since J extends G, J$\vdash \neg\Box A \to$

$\Diamond(\Box A \wedge \neg A)$, and for some w in W_J, $uR_J w$, $\Box A \in w$ and $\neg A \in w$; in this case let $v = w$. In either case, $\Box A, \neg A \in v$. Similarly, if $\Box C$ is a subsentence of A and $\neg \Box C \in v$, then for some x in W_J, $vR_J x$, $\Box C \in x$, and $\neg C \in x$; moreover, any such x is unique: if $y \in W_J$, $vR_J y$, $\Box C \in y$, and $\neg C \in y$, then by piecewise connectedness, either $xR_J y$ (but then $C \in y$ since $\Box C \in x$) or $yR_J x$ (but then $C \in x$) or $x = y$ (the only possible case).

Let $W = \{v\} \cup \{x : vR_J x$ and for some subsentence $\Box C$ of A, $\neg \Box C \in v$, $\Box C \in x$ and $\neg C \in x\}$. W is finite. Let $R = R_J | W$. R is transitive, for R_J is. R is irreflexive: if $w \in W$, then for some sentence $\Box B$, $\Box B \in w$, and $\neg B \in w$; thus not $wR_J w$. And R is connected: suppose $x, y \in W$, $x \neq y$. If either is v, it bears R_J to the other; and if $x \neq v \neq y$, then $vR_J x$ and $vR_J y$, whence by piecewise connectedness $xR_J y$ or $yR_J x$. Thus $\langle W, R \rangle$ is a finite strict linear ordering.

Let wVp iff $p \in w$.

Lemma 4. *If $w \in W$ and B is a subsentence of A, then $B \in w$ iff $w \models B$.*

Proof. Induction on B. As usual the only non-trivial case is: $B = \Box C$. If $w \not\models \Box C$, then for some x, wRx and $x \not\models C$; but then $wR_J x$ and, by the i.h., $C \notin x$, whence $\Box C \notin w$. Conversely, suppose $\Box C \notin w$. Then $\neg \Box C \in w$, and so $\neg \Box C \in v$ (otherwise $\Box C \in w$, as either $v = w$ or $vR_J w$). So for some x in W, $vR_J x$, $\Box C \in x$, and $\neg C \in x$. Thus $x \neq w$, and therefore either xRw or wRx. But if xRw, $xR_J w$, and $\Box C \in w$, which is impossible. So wRx, $C \notin x$, $x \not\models C$ (i.h.), and thus $w \not\models \Box C$. ⊣

Since $\neg A \in v$, $A \notin v$, and by Lemma 4, $M, v \not\models A$. Thus A is invalid in the finite strict linear ordering $\langle W, R \rangle$.

Always truth[4]

We extended GL to GLS and can likewise extend I to a system IS, with axioms all theorems of I and all sentences $\Box A \to A$ and sole rule of inference modus ponens. The system JS is similarly obtained from J. Can we prove the adequacy of these systems?

As in Chapter 9, let $A^s = \bigwedge \{\Box D \to D : \Box D$ is a subsentence of $A\} \to A$. Then it is immediate that if $I \vdash A^s$, then $\mathrm{IS} \vdash A$. And with $(\Box A)^*$ defined to mean "A^* is true in all transitive models of ZF", the argument given in the proof of the arithmetical completeness theorem for GLS shows that if $I \nvdash A^s$, then for some $*$, A^* is false.

Analogously for J and JS, when $(\Box A)^*$ is defined to mean "A^* is true in all universes". Thus each of the systems IS and JS is complete (for an appropriate interpretation of $\Box$).

It is the soundness of these systems that is problematic. We can close the circle and prove that if IS$\vdash A$, then for all $*$, A^* is true, and similarly for JS, but only by assuming one or more principles of set theory not provable in ZF.

Consider IS first. To show its soundness, we need to show that for all $A, *$, $(\Box A \to A)^*$ is true, or, equivalently, that for all $A, *$, $(A \to \Diamond A)^*$ is true. Thus we must show that every instance of the schema ($S \to$ "S is true in some transitive model of ZF") holds, S a sentence of the language of set theory.

For JS, we must show that every instance of the stronger schema ($S \to$ "S is true in some v_κ, κ inaccessible") holds.

Lévy has shown that the latter schema, and hence the former, is implied by the following schema: If F is a strictly increasing and continuous definable function on all ordinals, there is at least one inaccessible in the range of F. The plausibility of this schema is briefly discussed in Drake's *Set Theory*.[5] Whether the deduction of the soundness of IS and JS from this schema should count as an outright proof that these systems are sound is a question we must leave unanswered.

14

Modal logic within analysis

We are going to examine some of the connections between modal logic and analysis (second-order arithmetic).

The main theorem of the present chapter, announced in Solovay's 1976 paper, but not proved there, is that the modal logic of provability in analysis under the ω-rule is GL. To understand the proof, one needs some familiarity with notations for constructive ordinals. Most of this material is contained in Rogers's *Theory of Recursive Functions and Effective Computability* or Sacks's *Higher Recursion Theory.*[1]

The modal logic of provability in analysis

Analysis is second-order arithmetic, the theory that results when the recursion axioms

$$\mathbf{0} \neq \mathbf{s}x \quad \text{and} \quad \mathbf{s}x = \mathbf{s}y \rightarrow x = y$$

for successor and the induction axiom

$$X0 \wedge \forall x(Xx \rightarrow X\mathbf{s}x) \rightarrow X\mathbf{x}$$

(which is a single second-order formula) are added to axiomatic second-order logic. Noteworthy among the principles of axiomatic second-order logic is the comprehension scheme: for any formula $A(\mathrm{x})$ of the language of analysis, the formula $\exists X \forall \mathrm{x}(X\mathrm{x} \leftrightarrow A(\mathrm{x}))$, asserting the existence of the class of numbers satisfying $A(\mathrm{x})$ is one of the axioms of analysis. [X is not free in $A(\mathrm{x})$; x is any sequence of first- or second-order variables.] As Dedekind showed, addition and multiplication can be defined from zero and successor in analysis and the recursion axioms for these operations proved in analysis. Each of the induction axioms for PA then follows from the induction axiom for analysis and the comprehension scheme, and therefore analysis is an extension of PA. Robbin's *Mathematical Logic: A First Course*[2] contains a good discussion of second-order logic and analysis (which Robbin calls "second-order Peano arithmetic").

The proofs of the arithmetical completeness theorems for GL and GLS carry over without essential change from PA to analysis, as was the case for ZF.

The modal logic of provability in analysis under the ω-rule

The ω-rule reads: infer $\forall x A(x)$ from all (the infinitely many sentences) $A(\mathbf{n})$, n a natural number. (Thus one might identify the ω-rule for T with the set-theoretical object $\{\langle\{A(\mathbf{n}): n\in N\}, \forall x A(x)\rangle : A(x)$ a formula of the language of $T\}$.) At one time Hilbert entertained the idea that the Gödel incompleteness theorems might be "overcome" through use of the ω-rule; the rule was also studied in the 1930s by Carnap, Tarski, and Rosser.

Anω is analysis plus the ω-rule. The theorems of Anω are the sentences that belong to all classes that contain all axioms of analysis and are closed under the ω-rule as well as the ordinary logical rules of inference.

'$\vdash$' means "provable in analysis"; '$\omega\vdash$', "provable in Anω". F said to be provable (in analysis) under the ω-rule iff $\omega\vdash F$. Note that provability under the ω-rule is *not* the dual of ω-consistency; a formula is ω-inconsistent if and only if it is provable with the aid of *one* application of the ω-rule.[3]

We now prove Solovay's theorem that GL is the modal logic of provability in analysis under the ω-rule. The completeness proof will differ in structure from that of the arithmetical completeness theorem in Chapter 9: instead of using the diagonal lemma to construct a predicate $H(a, b)$ containing a and b free and then forming "Solovay sentences" $S_0, S_1, \ldots, S_n$ from $H(a, b)$, we shall use Corollary 1 of the diagonal lemma to construct the Solovay sentences directly, by a simultaneous diagonalization. The technique is due to Dzhaparidze, and de Jongh, Jumelet, and Montagna. It will be used again in the next chapter to prove the arithmetical completeness of a certain system of bimodal logic with two boxes, one for provability, the other for the dual of ω-consistency.

Let θ be the set of Gödel numbers of theorems of Anω. θ is Π^1_1, as it is the intersection of all sets meeting a certain arithmetical condition. Let $\Theta(x)$ be a Π^1_1 formula of the language of analysis that naturally defines θ.

A realization $*$ is now a function that assigns to each sentence letter a sentence of the language of analysis; for each modal sentence A, we define A^* in the obvious manner:

$$p^* = *(p)$$
$$\bot^* = \bot$$
$$(A \to B)^* = (A^* \to B^*)$$
$$\Box(A)^* = \Theta(\ulcorner A^* \urcorner)$$

Theorem 1 (Solovay). *Let A be a modal sentence. Then* (A), (B), *and* (C) *are equivalent:*
(A) GL$\vdash A$.
(B) *For all* $*$, $\vdash A^*$.
(C) *For all* $*$, $\omega\vdash A^*$.

(B) obviously implies (C).

We first show that $\Theta(x)$ and analysis satisfy the following three analogues of the Hilbert–Bernays–Löb derivability conditions:

(i) if $\vdash S$, then $\vdash \Theta(\ulcorner S \urcorner)$;
(ii) $\vdash \Theta(\ulcorner (S \to S) \urcorner) \to (\Theta(\ulcorner S \urcorner) \to \Theta(\ulcorner S' \urcorner))$; and
(iii) $\vdash \Theta(\ulcorner S \urcorner) \to \Theta(\ulcorner \Theta(\ulcorner S \urcorner) \urcorner)$

(for all sentences S, S').

Showing that (i), (ii), and (iii) hold is sufficient to show that (A) implies (B); we simply repeat the derivation of Löb's theorem, using $\Theta(x)$ instead of Bew(x). (i) and (ii) are sufficiently evident. Since $\Theta(\ulcorner S \urcorner)$ is a Π^1_1 sentence, (iii) follows from (iv):

(iv) If S is a Π^1_1 sentence, then $\vdash S \to \Theta(\ulcorner S \urcorner)$.

And the formalization in analysis of the following argument, which shows that if S is a true Π^1_1 sentence then S is provable in Anω, establishes (iv):

Suppose that $\forall f \exists x R\bar{f}(x)$, R a primitive recursive relation such that if $R\bar{f}(x)$ holds, so does $R\bar{f}(y)$, all $y \geqslant x$. ($\bar{f}(x)$ is the standard code for the finite sequence $[f(0), \ldots, f(x-1)]$ of length x.) We wish to show that $\omega \vdash \forall f \exists x R\bar{f}(x)$.

Let Sec $= \{s$: s codes a finite sequence and $\omega \vdash \forall f \exists x \mathbf{Rs}^* \bar{f}(x)\}$.

Lemma 1. *If Rs, then* $s \in$ Sec.

Proof. Suppose Rs. Then $\vdash \mathbf{Rs}$, $\omega \vdash \mathbf{Rs}$, $\omega \vdash \mathbf{Rs}^*[\,]$, and therefore $\omega \vdash \forall f \exists x \mathbf{Rs}^* \bar{f}(x)$. $\dashv$

Lemma 2. *If for all i*, $s^*i \in$ Sec, *then* $s \in$ Sec.

Proof. Suppose that for all i, $\omega \vdash \forall f \exists x \mathbf{R}\mathbf{s}^* i^* \bar{f}(x)$. Then by the ω-rule, $\omega \vdash \forall y \forall f \exists x \mathbf{R}\mathbf{s}^* y^* \bar{f}(x)$. Thus $\omega \vdash \forall g \forall f \exists x \mathbf{R}\mathbf{s}^* g(\mathbf{0})^* \bar{f}(x)$, and so $\omega \vdash \forall f \exists x \mathbf{R}\mathbf{s}^* \bar{f}(x)$. ⊣

Suppose now that $[\,] \notin \mathrm{Sec}$. Define h by $h(0) = [\,]$ and $h(n+1) = h(n)^* \mu i[h(n)^* i \notin \mathrm{Sec}$ if $h(n)^* i \notin \mathrm{Sec}$ for some i, and $i = 0$ otherwise]. By Lemma 2, for every n, $h(n) \notin \mathrm{Sec}$. By Lemma 1, for every n, not: $Rh(n)$. Let $f(n) = (h(n+1))_n$. Then for every n, not: $R\bar{f}(n)$, which contradicts our supposition that $\forall f \exists n R \bar{f}(n)$. Thus $[\,] \in \mathrm{Sec}$, i.e., $\omega \vdash \forall f \exists x R [\,]^* \bar{f}(x)$, and so $\omega \vdash \forall f \exists x R \bar{f}(x)$.

Hence if S is a Π^1_1 sentence and thus equivalent to a sentence $\forall f \exists x R \bar{f}(x)$ (R primitive recursive), then S is provable in Anω if it is true. Thus (iv) holds.

We now show that (C) implies (A). We shall need certain definitions and lemmas concerning the constructive ordinals. Since we shall want to see that our treatment of these matters can be formalized in analysis, we shall proceed rather carefully. At the outset let us note that since all ordinals under discussion are countable, we may regard quantification over such ordinals as disguised quantification over well-orderings of natural numbers (which, in turn, is to be understood as quantification over whatever objects the second-order variables of analysis range over) and mention of ordinal relations (e.g., $<$ or $=$) and ordinal functions (e.g., $+$) as involving claims about the existence of appropriate wellorderings of natural numbers and order-preserving maps between them (à la Cantor). The existence of the necessary relations and maps will be guaranteed by the (unrestricted) comprehension schema of analysis.

$\langle O, <_O \rangle$ is the standard system of notations for the constructive ordinals. If $a \in O$, $|a|$ is the ordinal denoted by a, and then $2^a \in O$ and denotes $|a| + 1$. The wellfoundedness of $<_O$ and the scheme of transfinite induction on $<_O$ can of course be proved in analysis.

$O_a = \{b \in O : |b| < |a|\}$. The following result is well-known, but it will not be amiss to present a proof of it here. We follow Sacks's *Higher Recursion Theory*, but with a slight emendation.

Lemma 3. *$\{\langle a, b \rangle : a \in O \wedge b \notin O_a\}$ is Π^1_1.*

Proof. The existence of an r.e. relation $<'$ such that for all $a, b \in O$, $a <' b$ iff $a <_O b$ is proved on p. 14 of *Higher Recursion Theory* ($a <' b \equiv a \in W_{p(b)}$). We shall need to observe that

(∗) If $2^d \in O$, $y = 3 \cdot 5^w$, and for all n,
$|\{w\}(n)| < |d|$ and $\{w\}(n) <' \{w\}(n+1)$,
then $y \in O$ and $|y| < |2^d|$

For, if the antecedent holds, then, since $d \in O$ and for every n, $|\{w\}(n)| < |d|$, for every n, $\{w\}(n) \in O$ and therefore $\{w\}(n) <_O \{w\}(n+1)$, whence $y \in O$ and $|y| \leqslant |d| < |2^d|$.
Now let

$$A(R) \equiv \forall x \forall y \forall z(Rx,y,z \rightarrow z = 0 \vee z = 1) \wedge \forall x[\exists y(Rx,y,0 \vee Rx,y,1) \\ \rightarrow \forall y(Rx,y,0 \leftrightarrow \neg Rx,y,1)] \wedge \forall y R1,y,0 \\ \wedge \forall e\{3 \cdot 5^e \in O \rightarrow \forall y(R3 \cdot 5^e, y, 1 \leftrightarrow \exists n R\{e\}(n), y, 1)\} \\ \wedge \forall d\{2^d \in O \rightarrow \forall y(R2^d, y, 1 \leftrightarrow [y = 1 \vee \exists z(y = 2^z \wedge Rd, z, 1) \\ \vee \exists w(y = 3 \cdot 5^w \wedge \forall n(Rd, \{w\}(n), 1 \\ \wedge \{w\}(n) <' \{w\}(n+1)))])\}$$

Let R^*x,y,z iff $x \in O$ and either ($y \in O_x$ and $z = 1$) or ($y \notin O_x$ and $z = 0$).

With the aid of (∗) we have by induction on $<_O$ that $A(R^*)$, and also that if $A(R)$, then for all $x \in O$, $\forall y \forall z(R^*x,y,z \leftrightarrow Rx,y,z)$. Since $x \in O$ if R^*x,y,z, $\forall x \forall y \forall z(R^*x,y,z \rightarrow Rx,y,z)$. Therefore R^*x,y,z iff $\forall R(A(R) \rightarrow Rx,y,z)$. $A(R)$ is a Σ^1_1-condition on R [all occurrences of "$\in O$" are in negative position in $A(R)$, and hence in positive position in "$\forall R(A(R) \rightarrow Rx,y,z)$"]. Thus R^* is Π^1_1, and therefore so is $\{\langle a,b \rangle: a \in O \wedge b \notin O_a\}$, $= \{\langle a,b \rangle: R^*a,b,0\}$. ⊣

Lemma 4. *There is a Π^1_1 relation $\lesssim$ with domain θ such that $\{\langle x,y \rangle: x,y \in \theta \wedge x \lesssim y\}$ reflexively well-orders θ; moreover, if $x \in \theta$ and $y \notin \theta$, then $x \lesssim y$. (Thus $x = y$ if $x \lesssim y$ and $y \lesssim x$.)*

Proof. (Uses no assumption about θ other than that it is Π^1_1.)

Since θ is Π^1_1 and O is Π^1_1-complete, there is a recursive function g such that for all numbers x, $x \in \theta$ iff $g(x) \in O$.

Define $x \lesssim y$ by:

$$(g(x) \in O \wedge g(y) \notin O_{g(x)}) \wedge ((2^{g(x)} \in O \wedge g(y) \notin O_{2^{g(x)}}) \vee x \leqslant y)$$

By Lemma 3, $\lesssim$ is a Π^1_1 relation. We now show that $x \lesssim y$ iff

(∗∗) $g(x) \in O \wedge [g(y) \in O \rightarrow |g(x)| < |g(y)| \vee (|g(x)| = |g(y)| \wedge x \leqslant y)]$

Suppose $x \lesssim y$. Then $g(x) \in O$. Assume $g(y) \in O$. Then $|g(x)|$ and $|g(y)|$ are defined. If $|g(y)| < |g(x)|$, then $g(y) \in O_{g(x)}$, impossible. Thus either $|g(x)| < |g(y)|$ or $|g(x)| = |g(y)|$; but if the latter, then $g(y) \in O_{2^{g(x)}}$, whence $x \leqslant y$, and (**) holds. Conversely, suppose (**) holds. Then $g(x) \in O$, and then also $2^{g(x)} \in O$. If $g(y) \in O_{g(x)}$, then $g(y) \in O$ and $|g(y)| < |g(x)|$, impossible. Thus $g(y) \notin O_{g(x)}$. But if $g(y) \in O_{2^{g(x)}}$, then $g(y) \in O$ and $|g(y)| < |g(x)| + 1$; but since not $|g(y)| < |g(x)|$, $|g(x)| = |g(y)|$, and therefore $x \leqslant y$.

It is clear from the equivalence of $x \lesssim y$ and (**) that x is in the domain of $\lesssim$ iff $g(x) \in O$, i.e., iff $x \in \theta$. Moreover, if $x, y \in \theta$, then $g(x), g(y) \in O$, and then either $|g(x)| < |g(y)|$, $|g(y)| < |g(x)|$, or both $|g(x)| = |g(y)|$ and either $x \leqslant y$ or $y \leqslant x$. Thus $\lesssim$ reflexively well-orders θ. And if $x \in \theta$ and $y \notin \theta$, then (**), and so $x \lesssim y$. ⊣

Let $\rho(x, y)$ be a Π^1_1 formula of analysis naturally defining $\lesssim$. The preceding definitions, claims, lemmas, and proofs can be carried out in analysis, and therefore the sentences (naturally constructed from $\rho(x, y)$ and $\Theta(x)$) stating that $\lesssim$ reflexively linearly orders θ and that $x \lesssim y$ provided that $x \in \theta$ and $y \notin \theta$ can be formulated and proved in analysis.[4]

Suppose now that $\mathrm{GL} \nvdash A$. Then for some n, W, R, V, M, $W = \{1, \ldots, n\}$, $M = \langle W, R, V \rangle$, and $M, 1 \nvDash A$.

We now extend R so that also $0Rx$ for all $x \in W$. (That is, define $R' = R \cup \{\langle 0, x \rangle : x \in W\}$, but drop the prime on R.)

Let $m \leqslant n$. We shall call a function h: $\{0, \ldots, m\} \to W \cup \{0\}$ *w-OK* if $h(0) = 0$, $h(m) = w$, for all $i < m$, $h(i)Rh(i+1)$. Call h *OK* if h is w-OK for some w. W is finite, and thus there are only finitely many w-OK functions h. In what follows we assume that h and h' are OK and that their domains are $\{0, \ldots, m\}$ and $\{0, \ldots, m'\}$.

Let neg be a pterm such that for all sentences S, $\mathrm{An}\omega \vdash \mathrm{neg}(\ulcorner S \urcorner) = \ulcorner \neg S \urcorner$.

For each $w \in W \cup \{0\}$, let $P_w(y_0, \ldots, y_n)$ be the formula

$$\mathbf{w} = \mathbf{w} \wedge \bigvee \{\alpha_h \wedge \beta_h \colon h \text{ is } w\text{-OK}\}$$

where α_h is

$$\bigwedge_{i:i<m} \bigwedge_{x:h(i)Rx} \rho(\mathrm{neg}(y_{h(i+1)}), \mathrm{neg}(y_x))$$

and β_h is

$$\bigwedge_{x:h(m)Rx} \neg\Theta(\mathrm{neg}(y_x))$$

By Corollary 1 to the generalized diagonal lemma, there exist sentences $S_0, S_1, \ldots, S_n$ such that for each $w \in W \cup \{0\}$,

$$\vdash S_w \leftrightarrow \mathbf{w} = \mathbf{w} \wedge \bigvee \{A_h \wedge B_h \colon h \text{ is } w\text{-OK}\}$$

where A_h is

$$\bigwedge_{i:i<m}\bigwedge_{x:h(i)Rx}\rho(\ulcorner\neg S_{h(i+1)}\urcorner,\ulcorner\neg S_x\urcorner)$$

and B_h is

$$\bigwedge_{x:h(m)Rx}\neg\Theta(\ulcorner\neg S_x\urcorner)$$

Because of the conjunct $\mathbf{w}=\mathbf{w}$ in S_w, S_x is not the same sentence as $S_{x'}$ if $x \neq x'$. A_h is a Π^1_1 sentence.

We write: AB_h to abbreviate: $A_h \wedge B_h$.

Say that h' *extends* h if $m < m'$ and for all $i \leqslant m$, $h(i)=h'(i)$.

Lemma 5. *If $h \neq h'$, then* $\vdash\neg(AB_h \wedge AB_{h'})$.

Proof. Case 1. For some j, $h(j)$ and $h'(j)$ are defined and unequal. Let j be the least such. Since $h(0)=0=h'(0)$, $j=i+1$ for some i. Then $h(i)=h'(i)$. Let $x=h(i+1)$, $x'=h'(i+1)$. So $h(i)Rx$, $h'(i)Rx'$, one of the conjuncts of A_h is the sentence $\rho(\ulcorner\neg S_x\urcorner,\ulcorner\neg S_{x'}\urcorner)$, and one of the conjuncts of $A_{h'}$ is the sentence $\rho(\ulcorner\neg S_{x'}\urcorner,\ulcorner\neg S_x\urcorner)$. But $\neg S_x$ is not the same sentence as $\neg S_{x'}$, and therefore these two sentences are incompatible in analysis.

Case 2. h' properly extends h. Then $m<m'$ and $h(m)=h'(m)$. Let $x=h'(m+1)$. Then $h(m)Rx$, and $\neg\Theta(\ulcorner\neg S_x\urcorner)$ is a conjunct of B_h and $\rho(\ulcorner\neg S_x\urcorner)$, $\ulcorner\neg S_x\urcorner)$ is a conjunct of $A_{h'}$. But again, these sentences are incompatible in analysis.

Case 3. h properly extends h'. Like Case 2. $\dashv$

Lemma 6. *If $x,x'\in W\cup\{0\}$, and $x\neq x'$, then* $\vdash\neg(S_x \wedge S_{x'})$.

Proof. Let h be x-OK, h' x'-OK. Since $x\neq x'$, $h\neq h'$. The lemma then follows from Lemma 5. $\dashv$

Let $h{*}x$ be the function g with domain $\{0,\dots,m+1\}$, such that for all $i\leqslant m$, $g(i)=h(i)$ and $g(m+1)=x$.

Lemma 7. $\vdash A_h \to AB_h \vee \bigvee\{A_{h*x}\colon h(m)Rx\}$.

Proof. Formalize in analysis: If A_h holds but B_h does not, then for some x such that $h(m)Rx$, $\neg S_x$ is in θ, and hence for some x, $h(m)Rx$ and for every y such that $h(m)Ry$, $\rho(\ulcorner\neg S_x\urcorner,\ulcorner\neg S_y\urcorner)$ holds. Then $h{*}x$ is OK and A_{h*x} holds. $\dashv$

Lemma 8. $\vdash A_h \to AB_h \vee \bigvee\{AB_{h'}\colon h' \text{ extends } h\}$.

Proof. There is a maximum element, n, that may belong to the domain of any h. But if n is in h's domain, then $h(0)Rh(1)R\dots Rh(n)$, the range of $h = W \cup \{0\}$, $m = n$, $h(m)Rx$ for no x, and B_h is equivalent to $\top$. To prove the lemma, then, it suffices to suppose that it holds for all h' whose domain has maximal element $m+1$ and show that it holds for all h (whose domain has maximal element m). By Lemma 7, $\vdash A_h \rightarrow (B_h \vee \bigvee\{A_{h*x}: h(m)Rx\})$. If $h(m)Rx$, then the domain of $h*x$ has maximal element $m+1$. Thus for each x such that $h(m)Rx$, $\vdash A_{h*x} \rightarrow AB_{h*x} \vee \bigvee\{AB_{h'}: h' \text{ extends } h*x\}$, whence $\vdash A_h \rightarrow (AB_h \vee \bigvee\{(AB_{h*x} \vee \bigvee\{AB_{h'}: h' \text{ extends } h*x\}): h(m)Rx\})$. But then we are done, since h' extends h iff for some x, $h(m)Rx$ and h' is identical with or extends $h*x$. $\dashv$

Lemma 9. $\vdash A_h \rightarrow S_{h(m)} \vee \bigvee\{S_x: h(m)Rx\}$.

Proof. By Lemma 7, $\vdash A_h \rightarrow AB_h \vee \bigvee\{AB_{h*x}: h(m)Rx\}$. h is certainly $h(m)$-OK. Thus $\vdash AB_h \rightarrow S_{h(m)}$. Suppose $h(m)Rx$. $h*x$ is x-OK. By Lemma 8, $\vdash A_{h*x} \rightarrow AB_{h*x} \vee \bigvee\{AB_{h'}: h' \text{ extends } h*x\}$. $\vdash AB_{h*x} \rightarrow S_x$. Suppose h' extends $h*x$. h' is $h'(m')$-OK. Thus $\vdash AB_{h'} \rightarrow S_{h'(m')}$. Since $h(m)RxRh'(m')$, $h(m)Rh'(m')$ – done. $\dashv$

Lemma 10. $\vdash \bigvee\{S_w: w \in W \cup \{0\}\}$.

Proof. Let $h = \{\langle 0, 0\rangle\}$. $m = 0$; $h(m) = 0$. By Lemma 9, $\vdash A_h \rightarrow S_0 \vee \bigvee\{S_x: 0Rx\}$, i.e., $\vdash A_h \rightarrow \bigvee\{S_w: w \in W \cup \{0\}\}$. But since $m = 0$, $\vdash A_h$. $\dashv$

Lemma 11. *Suppose* $w \in W \cup \{0\}$, wRx. *Then* $\vdash S_w \rightarrow \neg\Theta(\ulcorner \neg S_x \urcorner)$.

Proof. Let h be w-OK. Then $h(m) = w$ and $h(m)Rx$. But then we are done: $\vdash B_h \rightarrow \neg\Theta(\ulcorner \neg S_x \urcorner)$. $\dashv$

From this point on, the proof is very much like that of the arithmetical completeness theorem for GL.

Lemma 12. *Let* $w \in W$. *Then* $\vdash S_w \rightarrow \Theta(\ulcorner \neg S_w \urcorner)$.

Proof. Let h be w-OK. $h(m) = w$. Since $w \neq 0$, $h(1)$ is defined, $m = i+1$ for some i, and
$\vdash A_h \rightarrow \rho(\ulcorner \neg S_{h(i+1)} \urcorner, \ulcorner \neg S_{h(i+1)} \urcorner)$, whence
$\vdash A_h \rightarrow \Theta(\ulcorner \neg S_{h(i+1)} \urcorner)$, i.e.,
$\vdash A_h \rightarrow \Theta(\ulcorner \neg S_w \urcorner)$ – done. $\dashv$

Lemma 13. *Let* $w \in W$. *Then* $\vdash S_w \to \Theta(\ulcorner \bigvee \{S_x : wRx\} \urcorner)$.

Proof. Let h be w-OK. $h(m) = w$. By Lemma 9,
$\vdash A_h \to S_w \vee \bigvee \{S_x : wRx\}$, whence
$\vdash \Theta(\ulcorner A_h \urcorner) \to \Theta(\ulcorner S_w \vee \bigvee \{S_x : wRx\} \urcorner)$. Since A_h is Π^1_1,
$\vdash A_h \to \Theta(\ulcorner A_h \urcorner)$. Thus
$\vdash S_w \to \Theta(\ulcorner S_w \vee \bigvee \{S_x : wRx\} \urcorner)$. But by Lemma 12,
$\vdash S_w \to \Theta(\ulcorner \neg S_w \urcorner)$. And so by the derivability conditions for $\Theta(x)$,
$\vdash S_w \to \Theta(\ulcorner \bigvee \{S_x : wRx\} \urcorner)$. $\dashv$

We now define $*$: for any sentence letter p, $*(p) = \bigvee \{S_w : wVp\}$.

Lemma 14. *Let* B *be a subsentence of* A, $w \in W$. *Then if* $M, w \models B$, *then* $\vdash S_w \to B^*$; *and if* $M, w \not\models B$, *then* $\vdash S_w \to \neg B^*$.

Proof. Induction on B. Suppose $B = p$. Then if $w \models p$, S_w is one of the disjuncts of p^*. If $w \not\models p$, then by Lemma 6, S_w is incompatible with each disjunct of p^*.

The propositional calculus cases are routine. Suppose $B = \Box C$.

Assume $M, w \models \Box C$. Then for all x such that wRx, $M, x \models C$. $x \in W$, and so by the i.h., for all x such that wRx, $\vdash S_x \to C^*$, whence
$\vdash \bigvee \{S_x : wRx\} \to C^*$,
$\vdash \Theta(\ulcorner \bigvee \{S_x : wRx\} \vdash) \to \Theta(\ulcorner C^* \urcorner)$, i.e.,
$\vdash \Theta \bigvee \{S_x : wRx\} \urcorner) \to B^*$. But by Lemma 13,
$\vdash S_w \to \Theta(\ulcorner \bigvee \{S_x : wRx\} \urcorner)$.

Assume $M, w \not\models \Box C$. Then for some x such that wRx, $M, x \not\models C$. $x \in W$, and so by the i.h., $\vdash S_x \to \neg C^*$, whence
$\vdash \neg\Theta(\ulcorner \neg S_x \urcorner) \to \neg\Theta(\ulcorner C^* \urcorner)$, i.e.,
$\vdash \neg\Theta(\ulcorner \neg S_x \urcorner) \to \neg B^*$. But by Lemma 11,
$\vdash S_w \to \neg\Theta(\ulcorner \neg S_x \urcorner)$. $\dashv$

Lemmas 6, 9, 10, 11, 12, 13, and 14 are, respectively, the analogues of (2), (3), (4), (5), (6), (7), and Lemma 1 of Chapter 9.

The proof ends the way the proof of the arithmetical completeness theorem ended: Every theorem of Anω is true, If $i \geqslant 1$, then, by Lemma 12, if S_i is true, so is $\Theta(\ulcorner \neg S_i \urcorner)$, and then $\neg S_i$ is a theorem of Anω, and so true. Thus if $i \geqslant 1$, S_i is *not* true. But by Lemma 10, at least one of $S_0, S_1, \ldots, S_n$ is true. So S_0 is true. By Lemma 14,

$\vdash S_1 \to \neg A^*$, and therefore
$\vdash \neg\Theta(\ulcorner \neg S_1 \urcorner) \to \neg\Theta(\ulcorner A^* \urcorner)$. By Lemma 11,
$\vdash S_0 \to \neg\Theta(\ulcorner \neg S_1 \urcorner)$, and therefore
$\vdash S_0 \to \neg\Theta(\ulcorner A^* \urcorner)$.

Since S_0 is true, so is $\neg\Theta(\ulcorner A^* \urcorner)$. But then A^* is not a theorem of Anω, Q.E.D.

The truth case

Theorem 2 (Solovay). *Let A be a modal sentence. Then* (D) *and* (E) *are equivalent:*
(D) GLS$\vdash A$.
(E) *for all* $*$, A^* *is true.*

Since analysis proves only truths, it is clear that (D) implies (E). The proof of the converse is so similar in detail to that of the arithmetical completeness theorem for GL that we place it in a note.[5]

15

The joint provability logic of consistency and ω-consistency

Introduction

We recall from Chapter 3 the definition of the *ω-inconsistency* of a theory T (whose language contains $\mathbf{0}$ and $\mathbf{s}$): T is ω-inconsistent iff for some formula $A(x)$, $\mathrm{T}\vdash \exists x A(x)$, and for every natural number n, $\mathrm{T}\vdash \neg A(\mathbf{n})$. T is *$\omega$-consistent* iff it is not ω-inconsistent. If T is ω-consistent, then $\mathrm{T}\nvdash \exists x\, x \neq x$, and therefore T is consistent.

It is easy to show, however, that the converse does not hold: Let T be the theory that results when $\mathrm{Bew}(\ulcorner\bot\urcorner)$ is added to PA. Since PA does not prove $\neg\mathrm{Bew}(\ulcorner\bot\urcorner)$, T is consistent and for every n, the Δ sentence $\neg\mathrm{Pf}(\mathbf{n}, \ulcorner\bot\urcorner)$ is true. Thus for every n, $\mathrm{PA}\vdash\neg\mathrm{Pf}(\mathbf{n}, \ulcorner\bot\urcorner)$, and so for every n, $\mathrm{T}\vdash\neg\mathrm{Pf}(\mathbf{n}, \ulcorner\bot\urcorner)$ (T extends PA). But $\mathrm{T}\vdash\mathrm{Bew}(\ulcorner\bot\urcorner)$, that is, $\mathrm{T}\vdash\exists y\,\mathrm{Pf}(y, \ulcorner\bot\urcorner)$. So, despite its consistency, T is ω-inconsistent.

As a sentence S is said to be inconsistent with T if the theory whose axioms are those of T together with S itself is inconsistent, so S is *ω-inconsistent* (with T) if the theory whose axioms are those of T together with S is ω-inconsistent. S is ω-consistent iff not ω-inconsistent.

We call a sentence S *ω-provable* in T iff $\neg S$ is ω-inconsistent with T. So if S is provable in T, S is ω-provable in T.

In the present chapter we shall study the joint provability logic of (simple)[1] consistency and ω-consistency with PA, which of course is also the joint provability logic of provability and ω-provability in PA. We shall introduce a modal system GLB ("B" for "bimodal"), which, in addition to the usual modal operators $\Box$ and $\Diamond$ for provability and consistency, contains two new operators $\boxed{1}$ and $\langle 1\rangle$ representing ω-provability and ω-consistency.

The sentences $\Box A \rightarrow \boxed{1} A$ will certainly be among the axioms of GLB.

We are going to prove the arithmetical completeness and decidability of GLB; these theorems are due to Giorgie K. Dzhaparidze. In the next chapter we shall also prove the fixed point theorem for

GLB and give an algorithm for calculating the truth-values of letterless sentences of GLB. These last two results are due to Konstantin N. Ignatiev, who also discovered the simplification that we shall present here of Dzhaparidze's original proof of arithmetical completeness.

We shall also prove the arithmetical completeness and decidability of the system GLSB, related to GLB as GLS is to GL. These theorems are also due to Dzhaparidze.

GLB is a fragment of a system GLP ("P" for "polymodal") introduced by Dzhaparidze; the language of GLP contains a countably infinite sequence of diamonds representing a sequence of ever stronger consistency notions beginning with simple and ω-consistency. We briefly discuss GLP and these notions at the end of the chapter.

Let us straightaway define GLB.

We introduce a new unary operator $\boxed{1}$; the syntax of $\boxed{1}$ is the same as that of $\Box$.

The axioms of GLB are all tautologies and all sentences:

$\Box(A \to B) \to (\Box A \to \Box B)$,
$\boxed{1}(A \to B) \to (\boxed{1} A \to \boxed{1} B)$,
$\Box(\Box A \to A) \to \Box A$,
$\boxed{1}(\boxed{1} A \to A) \to \boxed{1} A$,
$\Box A \to \boxed{1} A$, and
$\neg \Box A \to \boxed{1} \neg \Box A$.

The rules of inference of GLB are modus ponens and $\Box$-necessitation (from A, infer $\Box A$).

If GLB$\vdash A$, then GLB$\vdash \Box A$, whence GLB$\vdash \boxed{1} A$; thus $\boxed{1}$-necessitation is a derived rule of GLB.

As with GL, we have that GLB$\vdash \boxed{1} A \to \boxed{1}\boxed{1} A$ (cf. the proof of Theorem 18, Chapter 1). Moreover, GLB$\vdash \Box A \to \boxed{1}\Box A$, since GLB$\vdash \Box A \to \Box\Box A$ and GLB$\vdash \Box\Box A \to \boxed{1}\Box A$.

Our first main goal is to formulate and prove an arithmetical soundness theorem for GLB.

The *ω-rule*, it may be recalled, runs as follows: infer $\forall x A(x)$ from all (the infinitely many sentences) $A(\mathbf{n})$, n a natural number. A sentence is said to be provable under the ω-rule in T if it belongs to all classes containing the axioms of T and closed under the ordinary rules of inference (modus ponens and generalization) and the ω-rule.

It is clear that the sentences of the language of PA that are true in the standard model N are precisely the sentences provable under the ω-rule in PA (as Hilbert observed). For all sentences so provable are certainly true, and it is evident by induction on complexity that every true sentence of the language of PA is so provable: For all true atomic sentences and negations of atomic sentences are (simply) provable and hence provable under the ω-rule; if $(S \wedge S')$ is true, then S and S' are true, and thus by the i.h. provable under the ω-rule, and hence $(S \wedge S')$ is so provable, for it can be deduced from S and S' (in PA, by the usual rules); similarly for $\vee$; if $\forall x A(x)$ is true, then so are all the sentences $A(\mathbf{n})$, which by the i.h. are all provable under the ω-rule, as therefore is $\forall x A(x)$; if $\exists x A(x)$ is true, then so is some sentence $A(\mathbf{n})$, which by the i.h. is provable under the ω-rule, and from which $\exists x A(x)$ can be deduced. And every sentence is equivalent to one built up from $\wedge$, $\vee$, $\forall$, $\exists$ and in which negation signs occur only in atomic formulas.

Do not confuse the notions "ω-provable" and "provable under the ω-rule". If S is ω-provable in PA, then S is certainly provable in PA under the ω-rule: For if $\neg S$ is ω-inconsistent, then for some formula $A(x)$, $\mathrm{PA} \vdash \neg S \to \exists x \neg A(x)$ and $\mathrm{PA} \vdash \neg S \to A(\mathbf{n})$ (for all n), whence $\forall x(\neg S \to A(x))$ is provable under the ω-rule; but then so is S.

It is evident, however, that since "ω-provable" is definable in arithmetic, it cannot coincide in extension with "provable under the ω-rule", which we have just seen to be coextensive with "true". ["Provable under the ω-rule" was defined with the aid of a quantifier ranging over classes of sentences, as the intersection of all classes of sentences meeting a certain closure condition; such definitions cannot in general be made in the language of (Peano, i.e., first-order) arithmetic, which lacks variables for classes or functions. They can, of course, be made in the language of analysis.] Thus the sentences ω-provable in PA are properly included in those provable in PA under the ω-rule.

We say that a sentence S is provable in PA *by one application of the ω-rule* if for some formula $A(x)$, $\mathrm{PA} \vdash A(\mathbf{n})$ for all n and $\mathrm{PA} \vdash \forall x A(x) \to S$.

If S is ω-provable and so for some formula $B(x)$, $\mathrm{PA} \vdash \neg S \to B(\mathbf{n})$ for all n and $\mathrm{PA} \vdash \neg S \to \exists x \neg B(x)$, then, letting $A(x)$ be $\neg S \to \neg B(x)$, we have that $\mathrm{PA} \vdash A(\mathbf{n})$ for all n, and then by predicate logic, $\mathrm{PA} \vdash \forall x A(x) \to S$ as well. Thus if S is ω-provable it is provable by one application of the ω-rule.

Conversely, if $\mathrm{PA} \vdash A(\mathbf{n})$ for all n and $\mathrm{PA} \vdash \forall x A(x) \rightarrow S$, so that S is provable by one application of the ω-rule, then $\neg S$ is ω-inconsistent.

So S is ω-provable iff provable by one application of the ω-rule.

(We might attempt to define a series of more general notions, calling S provable by $m+1$ applications of the ω-rule if there are formulas $A_1(x), \ldots, A_{m+1}(x)$ such that

$\mathrm{PA} \vdash A_1(\mathbf{n})$ for all n,
$\mathrm{PA} \vdash \forall x A_1(x) \rightarrow A_2(\mathbf{n})$ for all $n, \ldots,$
$\mathrm{PA} \vdash \forall x A_1(x) \wedge \cdots \wedge \forall x A_m(x) \rightarrow A_{m+1}(\mathbf{n})$ for all n, and
$\mathrm{PA} \vdash \forall x A_1(x) \wedge \cdots \wedge \forall x A_{m+1}(x) \rightarrow S$.

But if S is provable by $m+1$ applications, it is provable by one: Let $A(x)$ be

$$[A_1(x) \wedge (\forall x A_1(x) \rightarrow A_2(x)) \wedge \cdots \wedge (\forall x A_1(x) \wedge \cdots \wedge \forall x A_m(x) \rightarrow A_{m+1}(x))]$$

Then $\mathrm{PA} \vdash A(\mathbf{n})$ for all n, and $\mathrm{PA} \vdash \forall x A(x) \rightarrow S$.

We shall call a *sentence* $\forall x A(x) \rightarrow S$ an *ω-proof* of S if $\mathrm{PA} \vdash A(\mathbf{n})$ for all n and $\mathrm{PA} \vdash \forall x A(x) \rightarrow S$. Thus S is ω-provable if it has an ω-proof.

Here is one last definition in the same family. Let PA^+ be the theory whose axioms are those of PA, together with all sentences $\forall x A(x)$ such that for every natural number n, $\mathrm{PA} \vdash A(\mathbf{n})$.

If $\mathrm{PA}^+ \vdash S$, then for some formulas $A_1(x), \ldots, A_m(x)$ of PA, $\mathrm{PA} \vdash \forall x A_1(x) \wedge \cdots \wedge \forall x A_m(x) \rightarrow S$, where for all n, $\mathrm{PA} \vdash A_1(\mathbf{n}), \ldots,$ $\mathrm{PA} \vdash A_m(\mathbf{n})$; but then, where $A(x)$ is $A_1(x) \wedge \cdots \wedge A_m(x)$, $\mathrm{PA} \vdash A(\mathbf{n})$ for all n and $\mathrm{PA} \vdash \forall x A(x) \rightarrow S$, so that S is provable by one application of the ω-rule. Since it is clear that $\mathrm{PA}^+ \vdash S$ if S is provable by one application of the ω-rule, we have established the following theorem:

Theorem 1. *The following are equivalent*:
(a) *S is ω-provable*;
(b) $\mathrm{PA}^+ \vdash S$;
(c) *S is provable by one application of the ω-rule*; *and*
(d) *there is an ω-proof of S.*

It is sufficiently clear that these equivalences are provable in PA. It is also clear that a formalized proof in PA would require about as much work as the proof of the deduction theorem in PA. (The deduction theorem states that $\mathrm{T} \cup \{S\} \vdash A$ iff $\mathrm{T} \vdash S \rightarrow A$.) The reader who has come this far will be willing to suppose the necessary work done.

We now let $\omega\mathrm{Pf}(y,x)$ be a formula of the language of PA that naturally formalizes "is an ω-proof of". We let $\omega\mathrm{Bew}(x)$ be the formula $\exists y\, \omega\mathrm{Pf}(y,x)$. $\omega\mathrm{Bew}(x)$ will then be provably coextensive with each of the formulas naturally formalizing "ω-provable", "provable in PA^+", and "provable by one application of the ω-rule".

So $\mathrm{PA} \vdash \mathrm{Bew}(\ulcorner S \urcorner) \rightarrow \omega\,\mathrm{Bew}(\ulcorner S \urcorner)$ for every sentence S.

The notion of a realization remains defined as in Chapter 3, and we now extend the definition of the translation A^* of a modal sentence A under a realization $*$ by making the obvious stipulation:

(5) $\boxed{1}(A)^* = \omega\,\mathrm{Bew}(\ulcorner A^* \urcorner)$

The arithmetical soundness theorem for GLB will state that if $\mathrm{GLB} \vdash A$, then for every realization $*$, $\mathrm{PA} \vdash A^*$.

To prove the arithmetical soundness theorem, we need to proceed as in Chapter 2, where we introduced the Σ_1 formulas, there called Σ formulas. We will define the notion of a Σ_3 formula, show that $\omega\mathrm{Bew}(x)$ is Σ_3, and show that if S is a Σ_3 sentence, then $\mathrm{PA} \vdash S \rightarrow \omega\mathrm{Bew}(\ulcorner S \urcorner)$. We proceed with greater dispatch than in Chapter 2.

Σ_1 formulas have been defined. Suppose the notion of a Σ_n formula is defined, $n \geqslant 1$. Then $A(\mathsf{x})$ is a Π_n formula if it is equivalent to the negation of a Σ_n formula; $A(\mathsf{x})$ is a Σ_{n+1} formula if for some Π_n formula $B(y, \mathsf{x})$, $A(\mathsf{x})$ is equivalent to $\exists y B(y, \mathsf{x})$.

$\omega\mathrm{Pf}(y,x)$ is Π_2: for let $B(x,y,z)$ be a Σ_1 formula expressing: (the value of) y is the Gödel number of a provable conditional; the consequent of that conditional is the sentence with Gödel number x; and the antecedent is the universal quantification with respect to the sole free variable of a formula E such that the result of substituting in E the numeral for z for that variable is provable in PA. Then $\omega\,\mathrm{Pf}(y,x)$ is equivalent to $\forall z B(x,y,z)$, a Π_2 formula. ($\forall = \neg\exists\neg$.)

It follows that $\omega\mathrm{Bew}(x)$, $= \exists y\, \omega\mathrm{Pf}(y,x)$, is a Σ_3 formula.

We want now to show that every true Σ_3 sentence is ω-provable. So let S be a Σ_3 sentence, provably equivalent to $\exists y \forall z B(y,z)$, with $B(y,z)$ a Σ_1 formula. Then if S is true, for some m, for every n, $B(\mathbf{m},\mathbf{n})$ is true; therefore for some m, for every n, $B(\mathbf{m},\mathbf{n})$ is provable (since every true Σ_1 sentence is provable); thus for some m, $\forall z B(\mathbf{m},z)$ is ω-provable, and therefore so are $\exists y \forall z B(y,z)$ and S.

A formalization of this argument in PA shows that if S is a Σ_3 sentence, then $\mathrm{PA} \vdash S \rightarrow \omega\mathrm{Bew}(\ulcorner S \urcorner)$.

We can now readily prove the arithmetical soundness of GLB:

Theorem 2. *For any modal sentence A and realization* $*$, *if* $\mathrm{GLB} \vdash A$, *then* $\mathrm{PA} \vdash A^*$.

Proof. We need to consider only the "new" axioms $\boxed{1}(A \to B) \to (\boxed{1}A \to \boxed{1}B)$, $\boxed{1}(\boxed{1}A \to A) \to \boxed{1}A$, $\Box A \to \boxed{1}A$, and $\neg \Box A \to \boxed{1}\neg \Box A$; the arguments for the remaining axioms and rules of inference of GLB are as in Chapter 3.

It is evident that if $(S \to S')$ is a theorem of PA^+, then if S is a theorem of PA^+, so is S'. By Theorem 1, if $(S \to S')$ is ω-provable, then if S is ω-provable, so is S'. Formalizing our reasoning in PA, we have that $\mathrm{PA} \vdash \omega\mathrm{Bew}(\ulcorner S \to S' \urcorner) \to (\omega\mathrm{Bew}(\ulcorner S \urcorner) \to \omega\mathrm{Bew}(\ulcorner S' \urcorner))$, and thus that $\mathrm{PA} \vdash (\boxed{1}(A \to B) \to (\boxed{1}A \to \boxed{1}B))^*$.

Since $\omega\mathrm{Bew}(x)$ is Σ_3, and $\mathrm{PA} \vdash S \to \omega\mathrm{Bew}(\ulcorner S \urcorner)$, for any sentence S, $\mathrm{PA} \vdash \omega\mathrm{Bew}(\ulcorner S \urcorner) \to \omega\mathrm{Bew}(\ulcorner \omega\mathrm{Bew}(\ulcorner S \urcorner) \urcorner)$.

In Chapter 3 we proved that $\mathrm{PA} \vdash (\Box(\Box A \to A) \to \Box A)^*$. The only facts about $\mathrm{Bew}(x)$ needed (beyond the provability in PA of all tautologies and the closure of the set of theorems of PA under modus ponens) were that all sentences $\mathrm{Bew}(\ulcorner S \to S' \urcorner) \to (\mathrm{Bew}(\ulcorner S \urcorner) \to \mathrm{Bew}(\ulcorner S' \urcorner))$ and $\mathrm{Bew}(\ulcorner S \urcorner) \to \mathrm{Bew}(\ulcorner \mathrm{Bew}(\ulcorner S \urcorner) \urcorner)$ were theorems and that if S is a theorem so is $\mathrm{Bew}(\ulcorner S \urcorner)$. We now know, though, that all sentences $\omega\mathrm{Bew}(\ulcorner S \to S' \urcorner) \to (\omega\mathrm{Bew}(\ulcorner S \urcorner) \to \omega\mathrm{Bew}(\ulcorner S' \urcorner))$ and $\omega\mathrm{Bew}(\ulcorner S \urcorner) \to \omega\mathrm{Bew}(\ulcorner \omega\mathrm{Bew}(\ulcorner S \urcorner) \urcorner)$ are theorems of PA, and it is evident that $\omega\mathrm{Bew}(\ulcorner S \urcorner)$ is provable if S is, for then $\mathrm{Bew}(\ulcorner S \urcorner)$ is provable. We conclude that the analogue for ω-provability of Löb's theorem holds, that this analogue is also provable in PA, and therefore that $\mathrm{PA} \vdash (\boxed{1}(\boxed{1}A \to A) \to \boxed{1}A)^*$.

We have already observed that $\mathrm{PA} \vdash \mathrm{Bew}(\ulcorner S \urcorner) \to \omega\mathrm{Bew}(\ulcorner S \urcorner)$; so $\mathrm{PA} \vdash (\Box A \to \boxed{1}A)^*$.

For the remaining new axioms, the sentences $\neg \Box A \to \boxed{1}\neg \Box A$, it suffices to observe that the following argument can be formalized in PA, showing that $\mathrm{PA} \vdash (\neg \Box A \to \boxed{1}\neg \Box A)^*$: Suppose S is not provable in PA. Then for all n, n is not the Gödel number of a proof of S in PA. Thus for all n, $\neg \mathrm{Pf}(\mathbf{n}, \ulcorner S \urcorner)$ is true, and therefore for all n, $\mathrm{PA} \vdash \neg \mathrm{Pf}(n, \ulcorner S \urcorner)$. [$\mathrm{Pf}(y, x)$ is Δ.] But then $\forall y \neg \mathrm{Pf}(y, \ulcorner S \urcorner)$ is ω-provable, and therefore so is $\neg \exists y\, \mathrm{Pf}(y, \ulcorner S \urcorner)$, alias $\neg \mathrm{Bew}(\ulcorner S \urcorner)$. ⊣

Thus GLB is arithmetically sound (for provability).

The axioms of GLSB are all theorems of GLS and all sentences $\boxed{1}A \to A$; the sole rule of inference is modus ponens. Thus all sentences $\Box A \to \boxed{1}A$ are axioms of GLSB, and therefore all sentences

$\Box A \to A$ are theorems. Since whatever is ω-provable is true, if GLSB$\vdash A$, then for all $*$, A^* is true: GLSB is arithmetically sound (for truth).

The trouble with GLB

The trouble with GLB is that it has no decent Kripke semantics. The difficulty is not that there are two sorts of boxes, $\Box$ and $\boxed{1}$, for one can easily enough introduce two kinds of accessibility relations, one for each sort of box, and we ourselves shall do so shortly. The problem is that there turns out to be no natural way to do so for GLB.

A frame for a modal logic with two boxes is a triple $\langle W, R, R_1 \rangle$, with R and R_1 both relations on W. A model M is a quadruple $\langle W, R, R_1, V \rangle$, where V is a valuation on W. Truth of a modal sentence at w in M is then defined in the obvious way; the two key clauses of the definition run:

$M, w \models \Box A$ iff (as ever) for all x such that wRx, $M, x \models A$ and
$M, w \models \boxed{1} A$ iff (as expected) for all x such that wR_1x, $M, x \models A$.

The reader may recall from Chapter 4 a theorem stating that $\Diamond p \to \Box \Diamond p$ is valid in a frame $\langle W, R \rangle$ iff R is euclidean, i.e., iff for all w, x, y, if wRx and wRy, then xRy. Equivalently, $\neg \Box p \to \Box \neg \Box p$ is valid in $\langle W, R \rangle$ iff R is euclidean.

It is easy to prove a similar-looking theorem for one of the axioms of GLB: $\neg \Box p \to \boxed{1} \neg \Box p$ is valid in $\langle W, R, R_1 \rangle$ iff for all w, x, y, if wR_1x and wRy, then xRy.

For suppose $\neg \Box p \to \boxed{1} \neg \Box p$ valid in $\langle W, R, R_1 \rangle$, wR_1x and wRy. Let zVp iff $z \neq y$, and let $M = \langle W, R, R_1, V \rangle$. Then $y \nvDash p$, $w \models \neg \Box p$, $w \models \boxed{1} \neg \Box p$, $x \nvDash \Box p$, for some z, xRz and not: zVp, and so xRy. Conversely, suppose that for all w, x, y, if wR_1x and wRy, then xRy, $M = \langle W, R, R_1, V \rangle$, $w \models \neg \Box p$, and wR_1x. Then for some y, wRy and $y \models \neg p$, whence xRy, and $x \models \neg \Box p$.

Moreover, $\Box p \to \boxed{1} p$ is valid in $\langle W, R, R_1 \rangle$ iff for all w, x, if wR_1x, then wRx.

For suppose $\Box p \to \boxed{1} p$ valid in $\langle W, R, R_1 \rangle$ and wR_1x. Let zVp iff $z \neq x$, and let $M = \langle W, R, R_1, V \rangle$. Then $x \nvDash p$, $w \models \neg \boxed{1} p$, $w \models \neg \Box p$, for some y, wRy and $y \nvDash p$ and so wRx. The converse is as easy as can be.

And as usual, if $\Box(\Box p \to p) \to \Box p$ is valid in $\langle W, R, R_1 \rangle$, R is irreflexive. (The behavior of R_1 is irrelevant.)

But now observe (with Dzhaparidze) that if *all* axioms of GLB, including $\neg\Box p \rightarrow \boxed{1}\neg\Box p$, $\Box p \rightarrow \boxed{1} p$, and $\Box(\Box p \rightarrow p) \rightarrow \Box p$, are valid in $\langle W, R, R_1 \rangle$, then for *no* w, x, is it ever the case that wR_1x: For if wR_1x, then wRx, and so xRx, contra irreflexivity of R.

Thus in no frame in which all axioms of GLB are valid is R_1 anything but the empty relation. But if R_1 is empty, $\boxed{1}\bot$ is valid. However, by soundness, $\nvdash \boxed{1}\bot$. Trouble.

Dzhaparidze managed to overcome the difficulty by introducing a *pair* of pairs of accessibility relations, one to take care of some of the axioms, the other to take care of the others, and embedding the resulting models, *unsound* for GLB, into arithmetic.

A more elegant treatment was found by Ignatiev, who isolated a subsystem of GLB that can be given a reasonable Kripke semantics of a quite familiar sort. Ignatiev's central idea was to preserve much of Dzhaparidze's original construction and argumentation, but to demote the axioms $\Box A \rightarrow \boxed{1} A$ of GLB to antecedents of conditionals, in a manner reminiscent of Solovay's treatment of sentences $\Box A \rightarrow A$, while promoting the theorems $\Box A \rightarrow \boxed{1}\Box A$ to axioms. A weaker system, which I shall call *IDzh*,[2] results. Kripke models for IDzh can be embedded into arithmetic à la Solovay. Details begin now.

Semantics for IDzh

The language of IDzh is the same as that of GLB.
The axioms of IDzh are all tautologies and all sentences:

$\Box(A \rightarrow B) \rightarrow (\Box A \rightarrow \Box B)$,
$\boxed{1}(A \rightarrow B) \rightarrow (\boxed{1} A \rightarrow \boxed{1} B)$,
$\Box(\Box A \rightarrow A) \rightarrow \Box A$,
$\boxed{1}(\boxed{1} A \rightarrow A) \rightarrow \boxed{1} A$,
$\Box A \rightarrow \boxed{1}\Box A$, and
$\neg\Box A \rightarrow \boxed{1}\neg\Box A$.

The rules of inference of IDzh are modus ponens, $\Box$-necessitation, and $\boxed{1}$-necessitation.

As in the case of GLB, for any modal sentence A, IDzh$\vdash \Box A \rightarrow \Box\Box A$ and IDzh$\vdash \boxed{1} A \rightarrow \boxed{1}\boxed{1} A$.

A IDzh-model is a quadruple $\langle W, R, R_1, V \rangle$, where W is a finite nonempty set; V is a valuation on W; and R and R_1 are transitive, irreflexive relations on W such that for all w, x, y in W,

$$\text{If } wR_1x, \text{ then } wRy \text{ iff } xRy$$

So not both wRx and wR_1x; for otherwise xRx.

We will use "M" to abbreviate "$\langle W, R, R_1, V\rangle$" and drop "$M$" at every opportunity.

Truth at a world and validity in a model are defined as usual (and as was described above).

Theorem 3 (*the semantical soundness theorem for* IDzh). *If* IDzh $\vdash A$, *then A is valid in all* IDzh-*models.*

Proof. It will suffice to treat only the axioms $\Box A \rightarrow \boxed{1}\Box A$ and $\neg\Box A \rightarrow \boxed{1}\neg\Box A$. Let $M = \langle W, R, R_1, V\rangle$ be a model for IDzh, $w \in W$.

Suppose $w \vDash \Box A$, wR_1x. We must show $x \vDash \Box A$. Suppose xRy. Then wRy, and so $y \vDash A$. Thus $w \vDash \Box A \rightarrow \boxed{1}\Box A$.

Now suppose $w \vDash \neg\Box A$, wR_1x. We must show $x \vDash \neg\Box A$. But for some y, wRy, and $y \vDash \neg A$. But then xRy. Thus $w \vDash \neg\Box A \rightarrow \boxed{1}\neg\Box A$. ⊣

The proof of the semantical completeness theorem for IDzh also offers few difficulties.

Theorem 4 (*the semantical completeness theorem for IDzh*). *If A is valid in all* IDzh-*models, then* IDzh $\vdash A$.

Proof. As usual, suppose IDzh $\nvdash A$. A *formula* is a subsentence of A or the negation of a subsentence of A. A set X of formulas is *consistent* if IDzh $\nvdash \neg \bigwedge X$; X is *maximal consistent* if consistent and for every subsentence B of A, either $B \in X$ or $\neg B \in X$. Every consistent set of formulas is included in some maximal consistent set.

Let W be the set of maximal consistent sets of formulas.

As in the proof for GL, let wRx iff wRx iff (a) for all formulas $\Box B \in w$, $\Box B$ and B are in x; and (b) for some formula $\Box D \in x$, $\Box D \notin w$.

Now, a novelty:

Let wR_1x iff (a) for all formulas $\boxed{1}B \in w$, $\boxed{1}B$ and B are in x; (b) for all formulas $\Box C$, $\Box C \in w$ iff $\Box C \in x$; and (c) for some formula $\boxed{1}D \in x$, $\boxed{1}D \notin w$.

Let wVp iff $p \in w$.

It is *very* easy to verify that M is indeed an IDzh-model. (Pay attention to the condition "$\Box C \in w$ iff $\Box C \in x$".)

We now show by induction on the complexity of subsentences B of A that for any $w \in W$, $B \in w$ iff $w \vDash B$. The argument in the case in which $B = \Box C$ is as in the semantical completeness theorem for GL. The only interesting case is the new one, in which $B = \boxed{1}\, C$.

If $\boxed{1}\, C \in w$, then $w \vDash \boxed{1}\, C$, for if $wR_1 x$, then $C \in x$, whence $x \vDash C$ by the i.h. Thus suppose $\boxed{1}\, C \notin w$. By maximal consistency of w, $\neg \boxed{1}\, C \in w$. Let $X = \{\neg C, \boxed{1}\, C\} \cup \{\boxed{1}\, D, D\colon \boxed{1}\, D \in w\} \cup \{\Box E\colon \Box E \in w\} \cup \{\neg \Box F\colon \neg \Box F \in w\}$.

If $\mathrm{IDzh} \vdash \neg \bigwedge X$, then

$$\begin{aligned}
&\mathrm{IDzh} \vdash \bigwedge \{\boxed{1}\, D, D\colon \boxed{1}\, D \in w\} \wedge \bigwedge \{\Box E\colon \Box E \in w\} \\
&\qquad \wedge \bigwedge \{\neg \Box F\colon \neg \Box F \in w\} \to (\boxed{1}\, C \to C), \\
&\mathrm{IDzh} \vdash \bigwedge \{\boxed{1}\, \boxed{1}\, D, \boxed{1}\, D\colon \boxed{1}\, D \in w\} \wedge \bigwedge \{\boxed{1}\, \Box E\colon \Box E \in w\} \\
&\qquad \wedge \bigwedge \{\boxed{1} \neg \Box F\colon \neg \Box F \in w\} \to \boxed{1}\, (\boxed{1}\, C \to C), \\
&\mathrm{IDzh} \vdash \bigwedge \{\boxed{1}\, D\colon \boxed{1}\, D \in w\} \wedge \bigwedge \{\Box E\colon \Box E \in w\} \\
&\qquad \wedge \bigwedge \{\neg \Box F\colon \neg \Box F \in w\} \to \boxed{1}\, C
\end{aligned}$$

which contradicts the consistency of w. Thus X is consistent, and therefore for some maximal consistent set x, $X \subseteq x$. By the definitions of X and R_1, $wR_1 x$. The rest of the proof is as usual: Since $\neg C \in X$, $\neg C \in x$, $C \notin x$, and by the i.h., $x \nvDash C$. Thus $w \nvDash \boxed{1}\, C$. And since $\mathrm{IDzh} \nvdash A$, $\{\neg A\}$ is consistent, for some maximal consistent set $w \in W$, $\neg A \in w$, $A \notin w$, and by what we have just shown, $w \nvDash A$. It follows that A is not valid in the IDzh-model M. $\dashv$

Before we begin to embed IDzh-models into arithmetic, we need to do some more semantics.

Let $\langle W, R, R_1, V \rangle$ be an IDzh-model.

"$|$" means "relative product"; thus $wR|R_1 x$ iff for some y, $wRyR_1 x$. So $w \vDash \Box\, \boxed{1}\, A$ iff, for all x such that $wR|R_1 x$, $x \vDash A$.

Let wTx iff $w = x \vee wRx \vee wR_1 x \vee wR|R_1 x$. Since R and R_1 are transitive and aRc if $aR_1 bRc$, T is transitive.

Suppose now that M is an IDzh-model and $w \in W$.

Let $T''w = \{x\colon wTx\}$.

Let $M''w = \langle T''w, R \cap (T''w)^2, R_1 \cap (T''w)^2, \{\langle p, x \rangle\colon pVx \wedge x \in T''w\} \rangle$.

Then $M''w$ is an IDzh-model, for $T''w$ is certainly finite and nonempty ($w \in T''w$) and the accessibility relations of $M''w$ are just the restrictions to $T''w$ of those of M.

The generated submodel theorem for IDzh-models states that for all sentences A, if $x \in T''w$, then $M, x \vDash A$ iff $M''w, x \vDash A$. Its proof is perfectly straightforward since $T''w$ is closed under both R and R_1.

Some definitions: For any sentence A, M is *A-complete* if, for all $x \in W$, $M, x \vDash \Box B \to \boxed{1}\, B$ for all subsentences $\Box B$ of A.

For any sentence A, ΔA is the sentence $A \wedge \Box A \wedge \boxed{1} A \wedge \Box \boxed{1} A$. Then $M, w \vDash \Delta A$ iff, for all x such that wTx, $M, x \vDash A$.

UA is $\bigwedge \{\Delta(\Box B \rightarrow \boxed{1} B): \Box B$ is a subsentence of $A\}$. GLB$\vdash UA$, for any sentence A. (But we do not in general have that IDzh$\vdash UA$.)

Lemma 1. *Let $w \in W$. Then $M''w$ is A-complete iff $M, w \vDash UA$.*

Proof. $M''w$ is A-complete iff for all $x \in T''w$, $M''w, x \vDash \Box B \rightarrow \boxed{1} B$ for all subsentences $\Box B$ of A; iff, by the generated submodel theorem, for all subsentences $\Box B$ of A, all x such that wTx, $M, x \vDash \Box B \rightarrow \boxed{1} B$; iff $M, w \vDash UA$. $\dashv$

The proof of the arithmetical completeness of GLB

We are going to prove the equivalence of the three statements: IDzh$\vdash UA \rightarrow A$, GLB$\vdash A$, and PA$\vdash A^*$ for all $*$. Since IDzh $\subseteq$ GLB and GLB$\vdash UA$, the first implies the second; the arithmetical soundness theorem for GLB is the assertion that the second implies the third. So suppose that IDzh$\nvdash UA \rightarrow A$. We must find a realization $*$ such that PA$\nvdash A^*$.

By the completeness theorem for IDzh, there are a model M and a world e such that $M, e \nvDash UA \rightarrow A$, and hence $M, e \vDash UA$ and $M, e \nvDash A$. By the generated submodel theorem, we may suppose that $M = M''e$, and therefore by Lemma 1 that M is A-complete. Without loss of generality, suppose that $W = \{1, \ldots, n\}$ and $e = 1$.

The proof we shall give of the analogue for GLB of Solovay's arithmetical completeness theorem follows a course similar to that of the completeness proof given in Chapter 14, but somewhat different from that of Solovay's original proof of the completeness theorem for GL, found in Chapter 9. Unlike that proof, which invokes the diagonal lemma to produce a formula $H(a, b)$ with two free variables, the proofs in this chapter and the previous one appeal only to Corollary 1 of the diagonal lemma to produce a sequence of closed sentences $S_0, S_1, \ldots, S_n$ with certain desirable and familiar properties. As the present proof presupposes no recursive function theory, we have repeated a number of the details found in the previous chapter in order to keep the treatment self-contained.

Solovay sentences for GLB. We extend R so that also $0Rx$ for all x in W. (I.e., we let $R' = R \cup \{\langle 0, x\rangle : x \in W\}$, but now write R to mean R'.)

Let $m \leqslant n$. We shall call a function $h: \{0, \ldots, m\} \to W \cup \{0\}$ *w-OK* if $h(0) = 0$, $h(m) = w$, for all $i < m$, either $h(i)Rh(i+1)$ or $h(i)R_1 h(i+1)$, and for no i, $h(i)R_1 h(i+1)Rh(i+2)$. Call h *OK* if h is w-OK for some w. W is finite, and thus there are only finitely many w-OK functions h. In what follows we assume that h and h' are OK and that their domains are $\{0, \ldots, m\}$ and $\{0, \ldots, m'\}$. There is a unique least k, $0 \leqslant k \leqslant m$, such that $h(i)R_1 h(i+1)$ for all i, $k \leqslant i < m$. [$k = 0$ iff $m = 0$; for if $m > 0$, then $h(0)Rh(1)$ and $k > 0$.] Thus if $m > 0$, $h(0)Rh(1) \ldots R \ldots Rh(k)R_1 \ldots R_1 \ldots R_1 h(m)$. Let k' be similarly defined from h'.

Until the end of the chapter, '$\vdash$' shall mean 'PA$\vdash$'.

Let neg be a pterm such that for all sentences S, $\vdash \mathrm{neg}(\ulcorner S \urcorner) = \ulcorner \neg S \urcorner$.

For each $w \in W \cup \{0\}$, let $P_w\,(y_0, \ldots, y_n)$ be the formula

$$\mathbf{w} = \mathbf{w} \wedge \bigvee \{\alpha_h \wedge \beta_h \wedge \gamma_h \wedge \delta_h : h \text{ is } w\text{-OK}\}$$

where α_h is

$$\bigwedge_{i:i<k} \bigwedge_{x:h(i)Rx} \exists b(\mathrm{Pf}(b, \mathrm{neg}(y_{h(i+1)})) \wedge \forall a < b \neg \mathrm{Pf}(a, \mathrm{neg}(y_x)))$$

β_h is

$$\bigwedge_{x:h(k)Rx} \neg \mathrm{Bew}(\mathrm{neg}(y_x))$$

γ_h is

$$\bigwedge_{i:k \leqslant i<m} \bigwedge_{x:h(i)R_1x} \exists b(\omega\mathrm{Pf}(b, \mathrm{neg}(y_{h(i+1)})) \wedge \forall a < b \neg \omega\mathrm{Pf}(a, \mathrm{neg}(y_x)))$$

and δ_h is

$$\bigwedge_{x:h(m)R_1x} \neg \omega\,\mathrm{Bew}(\mathrm{neg}(y_x))$$

By Corollary 1 to the generalized diagonal lemma, there exist sentences $S_0, S_1, \ldots, S_n$ such that for each $w \in W \cup \{0\}$,

$$\vdash S_w \leftrightarrow \mathbf{w} = \mathbf{w} \wedge \bigvee \{A_h \wedge B_h \wedge C_h \wedge D_h : h \text{ is } w\text{-OK}\}$$

where A_h is

$$\bigwedge_{i:i<k} \bigwedge_{x:h(i)Rx} \exists b(\mathrm{Pf}(b, \ulcorner \neg S_{h(i+1)} \urcorner) \wedge \forall a < b \neg \mathrm{Pf}(a, \ulcorner \neg S_x \urcorner))$$

B_h is

$$\bigwedge_{x:h(k)Rx} \neg \mathrm{Bew}(\ulcorner \neg S_x \urcorner)$$

C_h is

$$\bigwedge_{i:k \leqslant i<m} \bigwedge_{x:h(i)R_1x} \exists b(\omega\mathrm{Pf}(b, \ulcorner \neg S_{h(i+1)} \urcorner) \wedge \forall a < b \neg \omega\mathrm{Pf}(a, \ulcorner \neg S_x \urcorner))$$

and D_h is

$$\bigwedge_{x:h(m)R_1x} \neg \omega \operatorname{Bew}(\ulcorner \neg S_x \urcorner)$$

Because of the conjunct $\mathbf{w}=\mathbf{w}$ in S_w, if $w \neq w'$, S_w is not the same sentence as $S_{w'}$. Let us observe that A_h is Σ_1, B_h is Π_1, C_h is Σ_3, and D_h is Π_3.

We write: AB_h instead of: $A_h \wedge B_h$, etc.

Lemma 2. *If* $h \neq h'$, *then* $\vdash \neg(ABCD_h \wedge ABCD_{h'})$.

Proof.

Case 1. For some j, $h(j)$ and $h'(j)$ are defined and unequal. Let j be the least such. Since $h(0)=0=h'(0)$, $j=i+1$ for some i. Then $h(i)=h'(i)$. Let $x=h(i+1)$, $x'=h'(i+1)$.

Case a. $i<k$ and $i<k'$. Then $h(i)Rx$, $h'(i)Rx'$, one of the conjuncts of A_h is the sentence $\exists b(\operatorname{Pf}(b,\ulcorner \neg S_x \urcorner) \wedge \forall a<b \neg \operatorname{Pf}(a,\ulcorner \neg S_{x'} \urcorner))$, and one of the conjuncts of $A_{h'}$ is the sentence $\exists b(\operatorname{Pf}(b,\ulcorner \neg S_{x'} \urcorner) \wedge \forall a<b \neg \operatorname{Pf}(a,\ulcorner \neg S_x \urcorner))$. But $\neg S_x$ is not the same sentence as $\neg S_{x'}$, and therefore these two sentences are incompatible in PA.

Case b. $i<k$ and $i \geqslant k'$. Then $i=k'$, $h(i)Rx$, $h'(i)R_1x'$, one of the conjuncts of A_h is the sentence $\exists b(\operatorname{Pf}(b,\ulcorner \neg S_x \urcorner) \wedge \forall a<b \neg \operatorname{Pf}(a,\ulcorner \neg S_{x'} \urcorner))$, and since $h'(k')=h'(i)=h(i)Rx$, one of the conjuncts of $B_{h'}$ is the sentence $\neg \operatorname{Bew}(\ulcorner \neg S_x \urcorner)$. Again, these sentences are incompatible.

Case c. $i \geqslant k$ and $i<k'$. Like case b.

Case d. $i \geqslant k$ and $i \geqslant k'$. Then $h(i)Sx$, $h'(i)Sx'$, one of the conjuncts of C_h is the sentence $\exists b(\omega\operatorname{Pf}(b,\ulcorner \neg S_x \urcorner) \wedge \forall a<b \neg \omega\operatorname{Pf}(a,\ulcorner \neg S_{x'} \urcorner))$, and one of the conjuncts of $C_{h'}$ is the sentence $\exists b(\omega\operatorname{Pf}(b,\ulcorner \neg S_{x'} \urcorner) \wedge \forall a<b \neg \omega\operatorname{Pf}(a,\ulcorner \neg S_x \urcorner))$. Again, these different sentences are incompatible.

Case 2. h' properly extends h. Then $m<m'$ and $h(m)=h'(m)$. Let $x=h'(m+1)$.

Case a. $h(m)Rx$. Then $\neg \operatorname{Bew}(\ulcorner \neg S_x \urcorner)$ is a conjunct of B_h and $\exists b(\operatorname{Pf}(b,\ulcorner \neg S_x \urcorner) \wedge \forall a<b \neg \operatorname{Pf}(a,\ulcorner \neg S_x \urcorner))$ is a conjunct of $A_{h'}$. But these are incompatible.

Case b. $h(m)R_1x$. Then $\neg \omega\operatorname{Bew}(\ulcorner \neg S_x \urcorner)$ is a conjunct of D_h and $\exists b(\omega\operatorname{Pf}(b,\ulcorner \neg S_x \urcorner) \wedge \forall a<b \neg \omega\operatorname{Pf}(a,\ulcorner \neg S_{x'} \urcorner))$ is a conjunct of $C_{h'}$. But these, again, are incompatible.

Case 3. h properly extends h'. Like case 2. ⊣

Call h R_1-*free* if for no $i<m$, $h(i)R_1h(i+1)$. If h is R_1-free, then $k=m$.

Let h^*x be the function g with domain $\{0, \ldots, m+1\}$, such that for all $i \leqslant m$, $g(i) = h(i)$ and $g(m+1) = x$.

Lemma 3. *Let h be R_1-free.* $\vdash A_h \to AB_h \vee \bigvee \{A_{h^*x}: h(m)Rx\}$.

Proof. Since h is R_1-free, $k = m$. Formalize in arithmetic: If A_h holds but B_h does not, then for some x such that $h(m)Rx$, there is a proof of $\neg S_x$, and hence for some x, $h(m)Rx$ and for every $y \neq x$ such that $h(m)Ry$, $\neg S_x$ has a proof with a smaller Gödel number than any proof of $\neg S_y$. Then h^*x is OK and A_{h^*x} holds. $\dashv$

Say that h' *R-extends* h if $m < m'$, for all $i \leqslant m$, $h(i) = h'(i)$, and for all i, $m \leqslant i < m'$, $h'(i)Rh'(i+1)$. R_1*-extends* is defined similarly. If h is R_1-free and h' R-extends h, then h' is also R_1-free.

Lemma 4. *Let h be R_1-free.* $\vdash A_h \to AB_h \vee \bigvee \{AB_{h'}: h'$ *R-extends* $h\}$.

Proof. There is a maximum element n that may belong to the domain of any h. But if n is in h's domain, then $h(0)Rh(1)R\ldots Rh(n)$, the range of $h = W \cup \{0\}$, $m = n$, $h(m)Rx$ for no x, and B_h is equivalent to $\top$. To prove the lemma, then, it suffices to suppose that it holds for all R_1-free h' whose domain has greatest element $m+1$ and show that it holds for all R_1-free h (whose domain has greatest element m). By Lemma 3, $\vdash A_h \to (B_h \vee \bigvee \{A_{h^*x}: h(m)Rx\})$. If $h(m)Rx$, then h^*x is R_1-free and its domain has maximal element $m+1$. Thus for each x such that $h(m)Rx$, $\vdash A_{h^*x} \to AB_{h^*x} \vee \bigvee \{AB_{h'}: h'$ R-extends $h^*x\}$, whence $\vdash A_h \to (AB_h \vee \bigvee \{(AB_{h^*x} \vee R \bigvee \{AB_{h'}: h'$ R-extends $h^*x\}): h(m)Rx\})$. But then we are done, since h' R-extends h iff for some x, $h(m)Rx$ and h' is identical with or R-extends h^*x. $\dashv$

Lemma 5. *Let h be R_1-free.* $\vdash AB_h \to ABCD_h \vee \bigvee \{ABC_{h^*x}: h(m)R_1x\}$.

Proof. Since h is R_1-free, $k = m$. Now formalize in arithmetic: Suppose A_h and B_h hold. Since $k = m$, C_h holds trivially. Then either for no x such that $h(m)R_1x$ is there an ω-proof of $\neg S_x$, in which case D_h also holds, or for some x such that $h(m)R_1x$, there is an ω-proof of $\neg S_x$, and there is then a unique x such that $h(m)R_1x$ and $\exists b(\omega\mathrm{Pf}(b, \ulcorner\neg S_x\urcorner) \wedge \forall a < b \neg\omega\mathrm{Pf}(a, \ulcorner\neg S_y\urcorner))$ holds for all y such that $h(m)R_1y$. And then A_{h^*x}, B_{h^*x}, and C_{h^*x} all hold. $\dashv$

Lemma 6. $\vdash ABC_h \to D_h \vee \bigvee \{ABC_{h*x}: h(m)R_1x\}$.

Proof. Like that of Lemma 3. Formalize in arithmetic: If ABC_h holds but D_h does not, then for some x such that $h(m)R_1x$, there is an ω-proof of $\neg S_x$, and hence for some x, $h(m)R_1x$ and for every y such that $h(m)R_1y$, $\exists b(\omega\,\mathrm{Pf}(b,\ulcorner\neg S_x\urcorner) \wedge \forall a < b \neg\omega\,\mathrm{Pf}(a,\ulcorner\neg S_y\urcorner))$ holds. Then $h{*}x$ is OK and ABC_{h*x} holds. $\dashv$

Lemma 7. $\vdash ABC_h \to ABCD_h \vee \bigvee \{ABCD_{h'}: h'\ R_1\text{-}extends\ h\}$

Proof. Like that of Lemma 4. If n is in h's domain, then the range of $h = W \cup \{0\}$, $m = n$, $h(m)R_1x$ for no x, and D_h is equivalent to $\top$. Thus it suffices to suppose that Lemma 7 holds for all h' whose domain has maximal element $m+1$ and show that it holds for h (whose domain has maximal element m). By Lemma 6, $\vdash ABC_h \to (D_h \vee \bigvee \{ABC_{h*x}: h(m)R_1x\})$. If $h(m)R_1x$, then the domain of $h{*}x$ has maximal element $m+1$. Thus for each x such that $h(m)R_1x$, $\vdash ABC_{h*x} \to ABCD_{h*x} \vee \bigvee \{ABCD_{h'}: h'\ R_1\text{-extends } h{*}x\}$, whence $\vdash ABC_h \to (ABCD_h \vee \bigvee \{(ABCD_{h*x} \vee \bigvee \{ABCD_{h'}: h'\ R_1\text{-extends } h{*}x\}): h(m)R_1x\})$. But then we are done, since $h'\ R_1$-extends h iff for some x, $h(m)R_1x$ and h' is identical with or R_1-extends $h{*}x$. $\dashv$

Lemma 8. *If* $x, x' \in W \cup \{0\}$, *and* $x \neq x'$, *then* $\vdash \neg(S_x \wedge S_{x'})$.

Proof. Let h be x-OK, h' x'-OK. Since $x \neq x'$, $h \neq h'$. Lemma 8 then follows from Lemma 2. $\dashv$

Let wCx iff $wRx \vee wR_1x \vee wR|R_1x$. So wTx iff $w = x \vee wCx$. If wCx, then certainly $x \in W$.

Lemma 9. *Let h be R_1-free.* $\vdash A_h \to S_{h(m)} \vee \bigvee \{S_x: h(m)Cx\}$.

Proof. We first show that

$$(*) \quad \vdash AB_h \to S_{h(m)} \vee \bigvee \{S_x: h(m)Cx\}$$

By Lemma 5, $\vdash AB_h \to ABCD_h \vee \bigvee \{ABC_{h*x}: h(m)R_1x\}$. h is certainly $h(m)$-OK. Thus $\vdash ABCD_h \to S_{h(m)}$. Suppose $h(m)R_1x$. $h{*}x$ is x-OK. By Lemma 7, $\vdash ABC_{h*x} \to ABCD_{h*x} \vee \bigvee \{ABCD_{h'}: h'\ R_1\text{-extends } h{*}x\}$. $\vdash ABCD_{h*x} \to S_x$. And since $h(m)R_1x$, $h(m)Cx$.

Suppose $h'\ R_1$-extends $h{*}x$. h' is $h'(m')$-OK. Thus we have $\vdash ABCD_{h'} \to S_{h'(m')}$. And since $h(m)R_1xR_1h'(m')$, $h(m)Ch'(m')$. Thus $(*)$ is shown.

We now show that

$$(**)\quad \text{If } h' \; R\text{-extends } h, \vdash AB_{h'} \to \bigvee \{S_x : h(m)Cx\}$$

Suppose h' R-extends h. Then h' is R_1-free, By Lemma 5, $\vdash AB_{h'} \to ABCD_{h'} \vee \bigvee \{ABC_{h'*x}: h'(m')R_1x\}$. h' is $h'(m')$-OK. Thus $\vdash ABCD_{h'} \to S_{h'(m')}$. Since $h(m)Rh'(m')$, $h(m)Ch'(m')$.

Suppose $h'(m')R_1x$. $h'*x$ is x-OK. By Lemma 7, $\vdash ABC_{h'*x} \to ABCD_{h'*x} \vee \bigvee\{ABCD_{h''}: h''\ R_1\text{-extends } h'*x\}$. $\vdash ABCD_{h'*x} \to S_x$. Since $h(m)Rh'(m')R_1x$, $h(m)Cx$.

Suppose h'' R_1-extends $h'*x$. Then h'' is $h''(m'')$-OK and so $\vdash ABCD_{h''} \to S_{h''(m'')}$. Since $h(m)Rh'(m')R_1xR_1h''(m'')$, $h(m)Ch''(m'')$.

Thus $(**)$ is shown.

By $(*)$, $(**)$, and Lemma 4, we are done. ⊣

Lemma 10. $\vdash ABC_h \to S_{h(m)} \vee \bigvee \{S_x : h(m)R_1x\}$.

Proof. Since h is $h(m)$-OK, $\vdash ABCD_h \to S_{h(m)}$. And if h' R_1-extends h, then $h(m)R_1h'(m')$, and $\vdash ABCD_{h'} \to S_{h'(m')}$. By Lemma 7 done. ⊣

Lemma 11. $\vdash \bigvee \{S_w : w \in W \cup \{0\}\}$.

Proof. Let $h = \{\langle 0, 0 \rangle\}$. h is R_1-free. By Lemma 9,
$\vdash A_h \to S_{h(m)} \vee \bigvee \{S_x : h(m)Cx\}$, i.e.,
$\vdash A_h \to S_0 \vee \bigvee \{S_x : 0Cx\}$, i.e.,
$\vdash A_h \to \bigvee \{S_w : w \in W \cup \{0\}\}$.
But since $k = m = 0$, $\vdash A_h$. ⊣

Lemma 12. *Suppose* $w \in W \cup \{0\}$, wRx. *Then* $\vdash S_w \to \neg\, \mathrm{Bew}[\neg S_x]$.

Proof. Let h be w-OK. Then $h(m) = w$ and either $h(k) = h(m)$ or $h(k)R_1h(m)$. In either case, $h(k)Rx$. But then we are done: $\vdash B_h \to \neg\, \mathrm{Bew}[\neg S_x]$. ⊣

We write: $\omega\mathrm{Bew}[S]$ to mean: $\omega\mathrm{Bew}(\ulcorner S \urcorner)$.

Lemma 13. *Suppose* wR_1x. *Then* $\vdash S_w \to \neg\, \omega\mathrm{Bew}[\neg S_x]$.

Proof. Let h be w-OK. Then $h(m) = w$ and we are done: $\vdash D_h \to \neg\, \omega\mathrm{Bew}[\neg S_x]$. ⊣

Let wQx iff $wCx \vee \exists z(zR_1w \wedge zCx)$. wQx iff $wCx \vee \exists z(zR_1w \wedge zR_1x)$: for if zR_1w and zRx, then wRx, and so wCx; and if zR_1w and $zRyR_1x$, then $wRyR_1x$, whence again wCx.

Lemma 14. *Suppose* $w \neq 0$. *Then* $\vdash S_w \to \mathrm{Bew}[\bigvee \{S_x : wQx\}]$.

Proof. Let h' be w-OK. Let h be "the initial R-segment" of h', i.e., $h: \{0, \dots, k'\} \to W \cup \{0\}$ and for all $i \leqslant k'$, $h(i) = h'(i)$. Then h is R_1-free, $k = m = k'$, and either $h(m) R_1 w$ or $h(m) = w$. In either case, if $h(m)Cx$, then wQx. By Lemma 9, $\vdash A_h \to S_{h(m)} \vee \bigvee \{S_x : h(m)Cx\}$, and so $\vdash A_h \to S_{h(m)} \vee \bigvee \{S_x : wQx\}$, whence
$\vdash \mathrm{Bew}[A_h] \to \mathrm{Bew}[S_{h(m)} \vee \bigvee \{S_x : wQx\}]$. Since $w \neq 0$, $h(1)$ is defined, $m = k = i + 1$ for some i, and
$\vdash A_h \to \exists b(\mathrm{Pf}(b, \ulcorner \neg S_{h(i+1)} \urcorner) \wedge \forall a < b \neg \mathrm{Pf}(a, \ulcorner \neg S_{h(i+1)} \urcorner))$, whence
$\vdash A_h \to \mathrm{Bew}(\ulcorner \neg S_{h(i+1)} \urcorner)$, i.e.,
$\vdash A_h \to \mathrm{Bew}[\neg S_{h(m)}]$. Since A_h is Σ_1,
$\vdash A_h \to \mathrm{Bew}[A_h]$. So
$\vdash A_h \to \mathrm{Bew}[\bigvee \{S_x : wQx\}]$. $\dashv$

Lemma 15. *Suppose $w \neq 0$. Then $\vdash S_w \to \omega\mathrm{Bew}[\bigvee \{S_x : wR_1 x\}]$.*

Proof. Let h be w-OK. Then $h(m) = w$, and since $w \neq 0$, $m = i + 1$ for some i, and either $k = m$, in which case $\vdash A_h \to \mathrm{Bew}[\neg S_{h(m)}]$, or $k < m$, in which case $\vdash C_h \to \omega\,\mathrm{Bew}[\neg S_{h(m)}]$. Since
$\vdash \mathrm{Bew}(x) \to \omega\mathrm{Bew}(x)$, in either case,
$\vdash ABC_h \to \omega\mathrm{Bew}[\neg S_w]$. By Lemma 10,
$\vdash ABC_h \to S_w \vee \bigvee \{S_x : wR_1 x\}$. Then
$\vdash \omega\mathrm{Bew}[ABC_h] \to \omega\mathrm{Bew}[S_w \vee \bigvee \{S_x : wR_1 x\}]$. Since ABC_h is a Σ_3 sentence,
$\vdash ABC_h \to \omega\mathrm{Bew}[ABC_h]$. Thus
$\vdash ABC_h \to \omega\mathrm{Bew}[S_w \vee \bigvee \{S_x : wR_1 x\}] \wedge \omega\mathrm{Bew}[\neg S_w]$, whence
$\vdash ABC_h \to \omega\mathrm{Bew}[\bigvee \{S_x : wR_1 x\}]$. $\dashv$

Lemma 16. *If $w \in W$, then $\vdash S_w \to \omega\mathrm{Bew}[\neg S_w]$.*

Proof. Let $w \in W$; then $w \neq 0$. By Lemma 15,
$\vdash S_w \to \omega\mathrm{Bew}[\bigvee \{S_x : wR_1 x\}]$. If $wR_1 x$, then $w \neq x$, and by Lemma 8, $\vdash S_x \to \neg S_w$. Thus $\vdash \bigvee \{S_x : wR_1 x\} \to \neg S_w$, and therefore
$\vdash \omega\mathrm{Bew}[\bigvee \{S_x : wR_1 x\}] \to \omega\mathrm{Bew}[\neg S_w]$. $\dashv$

We now define $*$: For any sentence letter p, $*(p) = \bigvee \{S_w : wVp\}$.

Lemma 17. *Let B be a subsentence of A, $w \in W$. Then if $M, w \vDash B$, then $\vdash S_w \to B^*$; and if $M, w \nvDash B$, then $\vdash S_w \to \neg B^*$.*

Proof. Induction on B. Suppose $B = p$. Then if $w \vDash p$, S_w is one of the disjuncts of p^*. If $w \nvDash p$, then by Lemma 8, S_w is incompatible with each disjunct of p^*.

The propositional calculus cases are routine.

Suppose $B = \Box C$. Assume $M, w \vDash \Box C$.

Suppose that for some x, wQx and $M, x \nvDash C$. Clearly not: wRx. If wR_1x, $wRyR_1x$, or both zR_1w and zR_1x, then respectively $M, w \nvDash \boxed{1} C$, $M, y \nvDash \boxed{1} C$, or $M, z \nvDash \boxed{1} C$, and then by A-completeness of M, respectively $M, w \nvDash \Box C$, $M, y \nvDash \Box C$, or $M, z \nvDash \Box C$, whence for some a, $M, a \nvDash C$, and respectively wRa, $wRyRa$, or zR_1w and zRa, and then in each case wRa, whence $M, a \vDash C$, contradiction.

Thus for all x such that wQx, $M, x \vDash C$. Since $x \in W$ whenever wQx, by the i.h., for all x such that wQx, $\vdash S_x \to C^*$. Thus $\vdash \bigvee \{S_x: wQx\} \to C^*$, and so $\vdash \text{Bew}[\bigvee \{S_x: wQx\}] \to B^*$. By Lemma 14, $\vdash S_w \to \text{Bew}[\bigvee \{S_x: wQx\}]$, and so $\vdash S_w \to B^*$.

If $M, w \nvDash \Box C$, then for some x, wRx, $M, x \nvDash C$, and by the i.h., $\vdash S_x \to \neg C^*$, whence $\vdash \neg \text{Bew}[\neg S_x] \to \neg B^*$. By Lemma 12, $\vdash S_w \to \neg \text{Bew}[\neg S_x]$, and so $\vdash S_w \to \neg B^*$.

Suppose $B = \boxed{1} C$.

If $M, w \vDash \boxed{1} C$, then for all x such that wR_1x, $M, x \vDash C$, and by the i.h., for all x such that wR_1x, $\vdash S_x \to C^*$. So $\vdash \bigvee \{S_x: wR_1x\} \to C^*$, and thus $\vdash \omega\text{Bew}[\bigvee \{S_x: wR_1x\}] \to B^*$. By Lemma 15, $\vdash S_w \to \omega\text{Bew}[\bigvee \{S_x: wSx\}]$, whence $\vdash S_w \to B^*$.

If $M, w \nvDash \boxed{1} C$, then for some x, wR_1x, $M, x \nvDash C$, and by the i.h., $\vdash S_x \to \neg C^*$, whence $\vdash \neg \omega\text{Bew}[\neg S_x] \to \neg B^*$. By Lemma 13, $\vdash S_w \to \neg \omega\text{Bew}[\neg S_x]$, $\vdash S_w \to \neg B^*$. $\dashv$

We conclude in the usual manner: By Lemma 17, $\vdash S_1 \to \neg A^*$. Thus $\vdash \neg \text{Bew}[\neg S_1] \to \neg \text{Bew}[A^*]$. By Lemma 12, $\vdash S_0 \to \neg \text{Bew}[\neg S_1]$. So $\vdash S_0 \to \neg \text{Bew}[A^*]$. We now appeal to the soundness of PA^+: By Lemma 16, $\vdash S_w \to \omega\text{Bew}[\neg S_w]$ for all w in W; thus if $w \in W$ and S_w is true, then $\neg S_w$ is ω-provable and therefore S_w is false. By Lemma 12, $\vdash \bigvee \{S_w: w \in W \cup \{0\}\}$, and therefore one of $S_0, S_1, \ldots, S_n$ is true. Thus it is S_0 that is true. And since $\vdash S_0 \to \neg \text{Bew}[A^*]$, $\neg \text{Bew}[A^*]$ is true and A^* is not provable in PA.

The truth case

GLSB is the system whose axioms are all theorems of GLB and all sentences $\boxed{1} A \to A$, and whose sole rule is modus ponens. All sentences $\Box A \to A$ are thus theorems of GLSB.

We want to show that GLSB$\vdash A$ iff A^* is true for all $*$. Let $HA = \bigwedge \{\Box C \to C: \Box C$ is a subsentence of $A\} \wedge \bigwedge \{\boxed{1} C \to C: \boxed{1} C$ is a subsentence of $A\}$. Since soundness is evident, it will suffice to show that if GLB$\nvdash (HA \to A)$, then A^* is false for some $*$.

So suppose that GLB$\nvdash (HA \to A)$. Then for some $W = \{0, \ldots, n\}$, $M = \langle \{0, \ldots, n\}, R, R_1, V \rangle$, M is $(HA \to A)$-complete and hence A-

complete, and $M, 0 \nvDash HA \to A$. (*Note*: Now $0 \in W$, and 0, not 1, is the world at which $HA \to A$ is false.) Thus $M, 0 \vDash HA$ and $M, 0 \nvDash A$.

We now define the Solovay sentences S_w, $0 \leqslant w \leqslant n$, from M as before but without adding a new point or altering R or R_1 in any way. Thus it is now possible that $0R_1w$. We note that none of the proofs of Lemmas 2–13 appealed to the assumption that $0Rh(1)$, i.e., that $m \neq 0$.

Let $wQ'x$ iff $wQx \vee w = x = 0 \vee x = 0R_1w$.

Lemma 14′. *For all* $w \in \{0, \ldots, n\}$, $\vdash S_w \to \mathrm{Bew}[\bigvee \{S_x : wQ'x\}]$.

Proof. Let h' be w-OK. As in the proof of Lemma 14, let h be "the initial R-segment" of h'. Then as before, $\vdash A_h \to S_{h(m)} \vee \bigvee \{S_x : h(m)Cx\}$ and $\vdash \mathrm{Bew}[A_h] \to \mathrm{Bew}[S_{h(m)} \vee \bigvee \{S_x : wQx\}]$.

Case 1. $m = k = i + 1$ for some i. As before, $\vdash A_h \to \mathrm{Bew}[\bigvee \{S_x : wQx\}]$, whence $\vdash A_h \to \mathrm{Bew}[\bigvee \{S_x : wQ'x\}]$.

Case 2. $m = k = 0$. Then $h(m) = 0$ and $\vdash A_h$, and therefore $\vdash S_0 \vee \bigvee \{S_x : 0Cx\}$. Assume $w = 0$. Then if $x = 0$ or $0Cx$, $wQ'x$. Assume $w \neq 0$. Then $0R_1w$, since $k = 0$ and h' is w-OK. Thus if $x = 0$, $wQ'x$, and if $0Cx$, then wQx and thus $wQ'x$. In each case, $\vdash \bigvee \{S_x : wQ'x\}$. Thus $\vdash \mathrm{Bew}[\bigvee \{S_x : wQ'x\}]$, and therefore $\vdash A_h \to \mathrm{Bew}[\bigvee \{S_x : wQ'x\}]$.

In both cases, $\vdash A_h \to \mathrm{Bew}[\bigvee \{S_x : wQ'x\}]$. ⊣

Let wR'_1x iff $wR_1x \vee w = x = 0$.

Lemma 15′. *For all* $w \in \{0, \ldots, n\}$, $\vdash S_w \to \omega\mathrm{Bew}[\bigvee \{S_x : wR'_1x\}]$.

Proof. Let h be w-OK. Then $h(m) = w$.

Case 1. $w \neq 0$. Then, as in the proof of Lemma 15, $\vdash ABC_h \to \omega\mathrm{Bew}[\bigvee \{S_x : wR_1x\}]$, whence $\vdash ABC_h \to \omega\mathrm{Bew}[\bigvee \{S_x : wR'_1x\}]$.

Case 2. $w = 0$. By Lemma 10, $\vdash ABC_h \to S_w \vee \bigvee \{S_x : wR_1x\}$. Then $\vdash \omega\mathrm{Bew}[ABC_h] \to \omega\mathrm{Bew}[S_w \vee \bigvee \{S_x : wR_1x\}]$. Since ABC_h is a Σ_3 sentence, we have $\vdash ABC_h \to \omega\mathrm{Bew}[ABC_h]$. Thus $\vdash ABC_h \to \omega\mathrm{Bew}[S_w \vee \bigvee \{S_x : wR_1x\}]$, i.e., $\vdash ABC_h \to \omega\mathrm{Bew}[\bigvee \{S_x : wR'_1x\}]$. ⊣

Let $*(p) = \bigvee \{S_w : wVp\}$.

Lemma 17′. *Let B be a subsentence of A. Then for all* $w \in \{0, \ldots, n\}$, *if* $M, w \vDash B$, *then* $\vdash S_w \to B^*$; *and if* $M, w \nvDash B$, *then* $\vdash S_w \to \neg B^*$.

Proof. Induction on B. The atomic and propositional calculus cases are as usual. So suppose $B = \Box C$.

Suppose $M, w \vDash \Box C$.

Assume that for some x, $wQ'x$ and $M, x \nvDash C$. Clearly, not: wRx. If wR_1x, $wRyR_1x$, or zR_1w and zR_1x, then we obtain a contradiction as in the proof of Lemma 17. If $w = x = 0$, then since $M, 0 \vDash HA$, $M, 0 \vDash \Box C \to C$, $M, 0 \vDash C$, contradiction. If $x = 0R_1w$, then since $M, x \nvDash C$ and $M, 0 \vDash HA$, $M, 0 \nvDash \Box C$, and then for some a, $0Ra$ and $M, a \nvDash C$; but then since $0R_1w$ and $0Ra$, wRa and so $M, a \vDash C$, contradiction.

Thus for all x such that $wQ'x$, $M, x \vDash C$, whence by the i.h., for all x such that $wQ'x$, $\vdash S_x \to C^*$. Thus $\vdash \bigvee \{S_x : wQ'x\} \to C^*$, and so $\vdash \mathrm{Bew}[\bigvee \{S_x : wQ'x\}] \to B^*$. By Lemma 14′, $\vdash S_w \to \mathrm{Bew}[\bigvee \{S_x : wQ'x\}]$, and so $\vdash S_w \to B^*$.

If $M, w \nvDash \Box C$, then for some x, wRx, $M, x \nvDash C$, and by the i.h., $\vdash S_x \to \neg C^*$, whence $\vdash \neg \mathrm{Bew}[\neg S_x] \to \neg B^*$. By Lemma 12, $\vdash S_w \to \neg \mathrm{Bew}[\neg S_x]$, and so $\vdash S_w \to \neg B^*$.

Suppose $B = \boxed{1}\, C$.

Assume $M, w \vDash \boxed{1}\, C$. Suppose for some x, $wR_1'x$ and $M, x \nvDash C$. Then not: wR_1x, and so $w = x = 0$. But since $M, w \vDash HA$, $M, w \vDash \boxed{1}\, C \to C$, and so $M, w \vDash C$, i.e., $M, x \vDash C$, contradiction.

Thus for all x such that $wR_1'x$, $M, x \vDash C$, and by the i.h., for all x such that $wR_1'x$, $\vdash S_x \to C^*$. So $\vdash \bigvee \{S_x : wR_1'x\} \to C^*$, and thus $\vdash \omega\mathrm{Bew}[\bigvee \{S_x : wR_1'x\}] \to B^*$. By Lemma 15′, $\vdash S_w \to \omega\mathrm{Bew}[\bigvee \{S_x : wR_1'x\}]$, whence $\vdash S_w \to B^*$.

If $M, w \nvDash \boxed{1}\, C$, then for some x, wR_1x, $M, x \nvDash C$, and by the i.h., $\vdash S_x \to \neg C^*$, whence $\vdash \neg \omega\mathrm{Bew}[\neg S_x] \to \neg B^*$. By Lemma 13, $\vdash S_w \to \neg \omega\mathrm{Bew}[\neg S_x]$, and $\vdash S_w \to \neg B^*$. ⊣

Since $M, 0 \nvDash A$, by Lemma 17′, $\vdash S_0 \to \neg A^*$. Since S_0 is true, A^* is false.

Decidability

By the semantical soundness and completeness theorems for IDzh, IDzh $\vdash A$ iff A is valid in all IDzh-models. Since IDzh-models have finite domains, the usual argument shows that IDzh is decidable.

It follows that GLB and GLSB are decidable as well, for GLB $\vdash A$ iff IDzh $\vdash UA \to A$ and GLSB $\vdash A$ iff GLB $\vdash HA \to A$, as we have just seen.

GLP

A sentence S equivalent to its own inconsistency must be both false and consistent. It must also be ω-inconsistent. For if

$\vdash S \leftrightarrow \mathrm{Bew}(\ulcorner \neg S \urcorner)$, then
$\vdash \neg S \leftrightarrow \neg \mathrm{Bew}(\ulcorner \neg S \urcorner)$,
$\vdash \neg S \rightarrow \omega\mathrm{Bew}(\ulcorner \neg \mathrm{Bew}(\ulcorner \neg S \urcorner) \urcorner)$, and
$\vdash \neg S \rightarrow \omega\mathrm{Bew}(\ulcorner \neg S \urcorner)$.

Since $\neg S$ is true, $\neg S$ is ω-provable, i.e., S is ω-inconsistent.

Likewise a sentence equivalent to its own ω-inconsistency must be both false and ω-consistent. Thus any such sentence will suffer from a drawback that is less serious than either simple or ω-inconsistency. Call it ω–ω-inconsistency. Then if PA^{++} is the theory whose axioms are those of PA^{+}, together with all sentences $\forall x A(x)$ such that for every n, $\mathrm{PA}^{+} \vdash A(\mathbf{n})$, ω–ω-inconsistency is simply refutability in PA^{++}.

We might now consider a sentence equivalent to its own ω–ω-inconsistency….

The system GLP contains a countably infinite series of boxes $[0]$ $(=\Box)$, $[1], [2], \ldots$ representing provability in PA, provability in PA^{+}, in $\mathrm{PA}^{++}, \ldots$. (Their duals $\langle 0 \rangle$ $(=\Diamond)$, $\langle 1 \rangle, \langle 2 \rangle, \ldots$ of course then represent consistency, ω-consistency, ω–ω-consistency,…) The axioms of GLP are all tautologies, and all sentences:

$[n](A \rightarrow B) \rightarrow ([n]A \rightarrow [n]B)$,
$[n]([n] \rightarrow A) \rightarrow [n]A$,
$[n]A \rightarrow [n+1]A$, and
$\neg [n]A \rightarrow [n+1]\neg [n]A$;

the rules of inference are modus ponens and [0]-necessitation. The axioms of the associated truth system GLSP are all theorems of GLP and all sentences $[n]A \rightarrow A$; the sole rule of inference is modus ponens. Dzhaparidze actually proved the arithmetical completeness of GLP and GLSP; a simpler and more accessible proof, on which our treatment has been based, was given by Ignatiev. Going from GLB to GLP offers no difficulties remotely comparable to those involved in taking the step needed to extend GL to GLB. (To prove the arithmetical completeness of GLP, though, one must observe that for each modal sentence A there is some n such that A contains $[i]$ only if $i \leqslant n$.)

16

On GLB: The fixed point theorem, letterless sentences, and analysis

Here we prove the fixed point theorem for GLB, prove a normal form theorem for letterless sentences of GLB, and indicate the outlines of a proof of the arithmetical soundness and completeness of GLB and GLSB for the notions "provable" and "provable under the ω-rule" in analysis. The fixed point theorem and normal form theorem are due to Ignatiev.

The fixed point theorem for GLB

Our sentences are now bimodal: they may contain occurrences of the new operator $\boxed{1}$.

A sentence A is *modalized in p* if every occurrence of the sentence letter p in A is in the scope of an occurrence of either $\Box$ or $\boxed{1}$; equivalently, iff A is a truth-functional compound of sentences $\Box B$, sentences $\boxed{1} B$, and sentence letters other than p.

As in Chapter 1, $\boxdot A$ is the sentence $(\Box A \wedge A)$.

The fixed point theorem for GLB reads: For every sentence A modalized in p, there is a sentence H containing only sentence letters contained in A, not containing the sentence letter p, and such that

$$\mathrm{GLB} \vdash \boxdot(p \leftrightarrow A) \leftrightarrow \boxdot(p \leftrightarrow H)$$

H of course might now contain both $\Box$ and $\boxed{1}$. But since GLB extends GL as well as the trivial notational variant of GL obtained by inserting a "1" inside all boxes, and since the fixed point theorem holds for GL and therefore obviously holds for the notational variant as well, H may be chosen not to contain $\boxed{1}$ if A does not contain $\boxed{1}$, not to contain $\Box$ if A does not contain $\Box$, and to contain neither $\Box$ nor $\boxed{1}$ if A contains neither $\Box$ nor $\boxed{1}$.

The proof of the fixed point theorem for GLB closely follows the second proof given in Chapter 8 of the fixed point theorem for GL. We begin by reducing the fixed point theorem for GLB to (a version of) the fixed point theorem for IDzh.

As in the previous chapter, ΔA is the sentence $(A \wedge \Box A \wedge \boxed{1} A \wedge \Box \boxed{1} A)$.

$\mathrm{GLB} \vdash \Box A \rightarrow \Box \Box A$, whence $\mathrm{GLB} \vdash \Box A \rightarrow \Box \boxed{1} A$, and also $\mathrm{GLB} \vdash \Box A \rightarrow \boxed{1} A$; it follows that $\mathrm{GLB} \vdash \boxdot A \leftrightarrow \Delta A$. IDzh is a subsystem of GL; it will therefore suffice to prove that if A is modalized in p, then $\mathrm{IDzh} \vdash \Delta(p \leftrightarrow A) \leftrightarrow \Delta(p \leftrightarrow H)$ for some H containing only sentence letters other than p and contained in A.

Let s be the number of sentences other than p that occur in A. Let these be $q_1, \ldots, q_s$.

We now define the notion of an *m-character*, $m \geqslant 0$.

The 0-characters are the 2^s sentences $\pm q_1 \wedge \pm \cdots \wedge \pm q_s$. (If $s = 0$, $\top$ is the sole 0-character.)

Suppose that the m-characters are the t sentences $V_1, \ldots, V_t$. Then the $(m+1)$-characters are the 2^{s+2t} sentences

$$\pm q_1 \wedge \cdots \wedge \pm q_s \wedge \pm \Diamond V_1 \wedge \cdots \wedge \pm \langle 1 \rangle V_t \pm \langle 1 \rangle V_1 \wedge \cdots \wedge \pm \langle 1 \rangle V_t$$

For any fixed m, the disjunction of all m-characters is a tautology and any two m-characters are truth-functionally inconsistent. Thus for any IDzh-model $M = \langle W, R, R_1, V \rangle$, and any w in W, there is exactly one m-character U – call it $U(m, w, M)$, or $U(m, w)$ for short – such that $M, w \vDash U$.

Conventions: w, w', etc. $\in W$, $N, = \langle X, S, S_1, Q \rangle$, is also a IDzh-model, and x, etc. $\in X$. We will often omit "M" and "N".

Lemma 1. *Suppose that M and N are finite* IDzh-*models, $M, w_0 \vDash \Delta(p \leftrightarrow A)$, $N, x_0 \vDash \Delta(p \leftrightarrow A)$, and $U(n, w_0, M) = U(n, x_0, N)$. Then M, $w_0 \vDash p$ iff N, $x_0 \vDash p$.*

Proof. Suppose $w_0 \vDash p$ niff $x_0 \vDash p$.

Let j be the number of subsentences of A of the form $\Box B$, k the number of subsentences of the form $\boxed{1} B$. If Z is a set containing c subsentences of A of form $\Box B$ and d subsentences of A of form $\boxed{1} B$, then we shall say that the *weight* of Z is $c(k+1) + d$. Let $n = j(k+1) + k$, which is clearly the maximum weight of any set Z.

Let wEw' iff $w = w'$, wRw', wR_1w', or $wR|R_1w'$. Let xFx' if $x = x'$, xSx', xS_1x', or $xS|S_1x'$. E and F are transitive.

Let $P(i, Z, w, x, D)$ iff the following six conditions hold:

(1) the weight of Z is $\geqslant i$;
(2) w_0Ew;
(3) x_0Fx;
(4) if $\Box B \in Z$, $w \vDash \Box B$ and $x \vDash \Box B$, and if $\boxed{1} B \in Z$, $w \vDash \boxed{1} B$ and $x \vDash \boxed{1} B$;

(5) $U(n-i, w, M) = U(n-i, x, N)$;
(6) either $\Box D$ is a subsentence of A, and $w \vDash \Box D$ niff $x \vDash \Box D$ (whence $\Box D \notin Z$) or $\boxed{1} D$ is a subsentence of A, and $w \vDash \boxed{1} D$ niff $x \vDash \boxed{1} D$ (whence $\boxed{1} D \notin Z$).

Then

(*) if $i < n$ and for some Z, w, x, D, $P(i, Z, w, x, D)$, then for some Z', w', x', D', $P(i+1, Z', w', x', D')$.

For suppose that $i < n$ and $P(i, Z, w, x, D)$.

Case 1. $w \nvDash \Box D$ and $x \vDash \Box D$. Then for some w', wRw', whence $w_0 E w'$ (2′), $w \vDash \Box D$ and $w' \nvDash D$. Since $i < n$, $n-(i+1)$ and $U(n-(i+1), w')$ are defined. Let $V = U(n-(i+1), w')$. Then $w' \vDash V$, and $w \vDash \Diamond V$. Thus $\Diamond V$ is a conjunct of $U(n-i, w) = U(n-i, x)$. So $x \vDash \Diamond V$, and thus for some x', xSx', whence $x_0 F x'$ (3′), and $x' \vDash V$. Thus $U(n-(i+1), x') = V = U(n-(i+1), w')$ (5′). Since xSx', $x \vDash \Box D$ and $x' \vDash D$. Let $Z' = \{\Box B: \Box B \in Z\} \cup \{\Box D\}$. Let i' = the weight of Z'. Since $\Box D$ is not in Z but is in Z', along with all sentences $\Box B$ in Z, $i' \geqslant (i-k) + (k+1) = i+1$ (1′). (Although up to k sentences $\boxed{1} B$ in Z may be missing from Z', Z' contains $\Box D$ instead, which adds more to the weight of Z' than all the $\boxed{1}$ Bs combined.) Since wRw' and xSx', for every sentence $\Box B$ in Z, $w' \vDash \Box B$ and $x' \vDash \Box B$, and therefore for every sentence $\Box B$ in Z', $w' \vDash \Box B$ and $x' \vDash \Box B$, and trivially the same holds for every sentence $\boxed{1} B$ in Z' (4′).

Case 2. $x \nvDash \Box D$ and $w \vDash \Box D$. Just like Case 1.

Case 3. $w \nvDash \boxed{1} D$ and $x \vDash \boxed{1} D$. Then for some $w', \ldots$ [as in case 1, but with $R_1, S_1, \boxed{1}$ and $\langle 1 \rangle$ in place or $R, S, \Box$, and $\Diamond$]$\ldots$ and $x' \vDash D$. Let $Z' = Z \cup \{\boxed{1} D\}$. Then the weight of $Z' \geqslant i+1$ (1′) since $\boxed{1} D \notin Z$. Since wR_1w' and xS_1x', $w' \vDash \boxed{1} B$ and $x' \vDash \boxed{1} B$ for every sentence $\boxed{1} B$ in Z'. Suppose $\Box B \in Z'$. Then $\Box B \in Z$, $w \vDash \Box B$, and $x \vDash \Box B$. If $w'Rw''$, then since wR_1w', wRw'', whence $w'' \vDash B$; thus $w' \vDash \Box B$. Similarly, $x' \vDash \Box B$ (4′).

Case 4. $x \nvDash \boxed{1} D$ and $w \vDash \boxed{1} D$. Just like Case 3.

It remains to find a suitable D'.

D is a subsentence of A, and in all four cases, $w' \vDash D$ niff $x' \vDash D$. Thus

(a) $w' \vDash p$ niff $x' \vDash p$,
(b) $w' \vDash q_k$ niff $x' \vDash q_k$ for some k, $1 \leqslant k \leqslant s$,
(c) $w' \vDash \Box D'$ niff $x' \vDash \Box D'$ for some subsentence $\Box D'$ of A, or
(d) $w' \vDash \boxed{1} D'$ niff $x' \vDash \boxed{1} D'$ for some subsentence $\boxed{1} D'$ of A.

But since $w_0 E w'$ and $x_0 F x'$, $w' \vDash p \leftrightarrow A$ and $x' \vDash p \leftrightarrow A$. Thus if (a) holds, $w' \vDash A$ niff $x' \vDash A$, and thus (b), (c), or (d) holds, since A is a truth-functional compound of the sentence letters $q_1, \ldots, q_s$ and sentences $\Box B$ and $\boxed{1} B$. But (b) does not hold, for $U(n-(i+1), w') = U(n-(i+1), x')$. Thus (c) or (d) holds (6′) and (∗) is established.

Since $w_0 \vDash p \leftrightarrow A$, $x_0 \vDash p \leftrightarrow A$, and $U(n, w_0) = U(n, x_0)$, it follows in exactly the same way that either for some subsentence $\Box D$ of A, $w_0 \vDash \Box D$ niff $x_0 \vDash \Box D$, or for some subsentence $\boxed{1} D$, $w_0 \vDash \boxed{1} D$ niff $x_0 \vDash \boxed{1} D$; thus $P(0, \varnothing, w_0, x_0, D)$. By induction, it follows from (∗) that for some Z, w, x, D, $P(n, Z, w, x, D)$. But it is impossible that Z has weight $\geqslant n$, $\Box D$ or $\boxed{1} D$ is a subsentence of A, and either $\Box D$ or $\boxed{1} D \notin Z$; for then $Z \cup \{\Box D\}$ or $Z \cup \{\boxed{1} D\}$ has weight $> n$, which is absurd. ⊣

We now complete the proof of the fixed point theorem. Let $H = \bigvee \{U : U$ is an n-character and $\mathrm{IDzh} \vdash (\Delta(p \leftrightarrow A) \wedge U) \rightarrow p\}$. We shall show that $\mathrm{IDzh} \vdash \Delta(p \leftrightarrow A) \rightarrow (p \leftrightarrow H)$.

Let M be an IDzh-model. Suppose $w \vDash \Delta(p \leftrightarrow A)$. Let $U = U(n, w)$. U is the only n-character that holds at w, and thus if $w \vDash H$, then U is a disjunct of H, and $\mathrm{IDzh} \vdash (\Delta(p \leftrightarrow A) \wedge U) \rightarrow p$; since $w \vDash U$, $w \vDash p$. Therefore $w \vDash H \rightarrow p$.

Now assume $w \vDash p$. If U is not a disjunct of H, $\mathrm{IDzh} \nvdash \Delta(p \leftrightarrow A) \wedge U \rightarrow p$, and for some IDzh-model N, some world x of N, $x \vDash \Delta(p \leftrightarrow A)$, $x \vDash U$, and $x \nvDash p$. But the only character that holds at x is $U(n, x)$. Thus $U(n, w) = U = U(n, x)$, contra the lemma. So U is a disjunct of H, and since $w \vDash U$, $w \vDash H$. Thus $w \vDash p \rightarrow H$, and so $w \vDash p \leftrightarrow H$.

By the completeness theorem for IDzh, $\mathrm{IDzh} \vdash \Delta(p \leftrightarrow A) \rightarrow (p \leftrightarrow H)$.

As in the previous chapter, for arbitrary $w, x \in W$, let wTx iff $w = x \vee wRx \vee wR_1x \vee wR|R_1x$, whence T is transitive. Moreover, $w \vDash \Delta B$ iff for all x such that wTx, $x \vDash B$.

With the aid of the completeness theorem for IDzh, it is easy to see that if $\mathrm{IDzh} \vdash B$, $\mathrm{IDzh} \vdash \Delta B$; $\mathrm{IDzh} \vdash \Delta(B \rightarrow C) \rightarrow (\Delta B \rightarrow \Delta C)$; and $\mathrm{IDzh} \vdash \Delta B \rightarrow \Delta\Delta B$.

So $\mathrm{IDzh} \vdash \Delta\Delta(p \leftrightarrow A) \rightarrow \Delta(p \leftrightarrow H)$, and therefore $\mathrm{IDzh} \vdash \Delta(p \leftrightarrow A) \rightarrow \Delta(p \leftrightarrow H)$: one half of the fixed point theorem for GLB is proved.

To prove the other half, we use a version of the argument due to Goldfarb given in Chapter 8: Let M be an arbitrary IDzh-model. Let wCx iff $wRx \vee wR_1x \vee wR|R_1x$. Thus wTx iff $w = x \vee wCx$. Like R and R_1, C is irreflexive: if $wR|R_1w$, then for some y, $wRyR_1w$, and yR_1wRy, whence wRw, impossible. And C is also transitive.

Suppose now that for some $z \in W$, $M, z \vDash \Delta(p \leftrightarrow H)$, but $M, z \nvDash (p \leftrightarrow A)$. Let m be the cardinality of W. Then since C is transitive and irreflexive, for no $w_0, w_1, \ldots, w_m \in W$, $w_0Cw_1C \ldots Cw_m$. Thus for some

$w \in W$, zTw, $M, w \nvDash (p \leftrightarrow A)$, and for all x such that wCx, $M, x \vDash (p \leftrightarrow A)$. Now let M' be just like M except that wVp niff $wV'p$. Then since A is modalized in p, $M, w \vDash A$ iff $M', w \vDash A$. But since $M, w \vDash p$ niff $M', w \vDash p$, for all x such that wTx, $M', x \vDash (p \leftrightarrow A)$; so $M', w \vDash \Delta(p \leftrightarrow A)$, and therefore by the half of the fixed point theorem just proved, $M', w \vDash p \leftrightarrow H$. H does not contain p, and so $M, w \nvDash p \leftrightarrow H$. But since zTw and $M, z \vDash \Delta(p \leftrightarrow H)$, M, $w \vDash p \leftrightarrow H$, contradiction.

So IDzh$\vdash \Delta(p \leftrightarrow H) \rightarrow (p \leftrightarrow A)$, whence as above, IDzh$\vdash \Delta(p \leftrightarrow H) \rightarrow \Delta(p \leftrightarrow A)$. Thus IDzh$\vdash \Delta(p \leftrightarrow H) \leftrightarrow \Delta(p \leftrightarrow A)$ and we have proved the fixed point theorem for GLB.

A normal form theorem for letterless sentences of GLB

Like ordinary letterless modal sentences, a letterless bimodal sentence is true under all realizations if it is true under any one. We give an algorithm, due to Ignatiev, for telling whether or not any given letterless sentence of GLB is true (under some/every realization).

In what follows, by "ordinal" we shall mean "ordinal $<\omega^\omega$". It is a standard fact from set theory that for any ordinal $\alpha \geqslant 0$, there exist natural numbers $l_1, \ldots, l_n$ such that $l_1 \geqslant \cdots \geqslant l_n$ and $\alpha = \omega^{l_1} + \cdots + \omega^{l_n}$. (If $\alpha = 0$, the sum is empty and $n = 0$.) For the sake of clarity, we shall sometimes write: $\langle l_1, \ldots, l_n \rangle$ instead of: $\omega^{l_1} + \cdots + \omega^{l_n}$. Thus $\langle\ \rangle = 0$. We always assume that $l_1 \geqslant \cdots \geqslant l_n$.

We recall that if $\alpha = \langle l_1, \ldots, l_n \rangle$ and $\beta = \langle k_1, \ldots, k_p \rangle$, then $\alpha > \beta$ iff either for every $i \leqslant p$, $l_i = k_i$ and $n > p$, or for some $i \leqslant p$, $l_i > k_i$ and $l_j = k_j$ for all $j < i$.

We now define some operations on ordinals. Let $\alpha = \langle l_1, \ldots, l_n \rangle$.

If $\alpha > 0$, then $\alpha^- = \langle l_1, \ldots, l_{n-1} \rangle$; $0^- = 0$.
If $\alpha > 0$, then $d\alpha = l_n$. We do not now define $d0$.

Thus certainly if $\alpha > 0$, then $\alpha^- < \alpha$, $d\alpha < \alpha$, and $\alpha = \alpha^- + \omega^{d\alpha}$.

$\alpha^{-j} = \langle l_1, \ldots, l_m \rangle$, where $m \leqslant n$ and $l_1, \ldots, l_m$, are precisely those of $l_1, \ldots, l_n$ that are $\geqslant j$. Thus $\alpha^{-j} \leqslant \alpha$.

$\alpha^{+j} = \langle l_1, \ldots, l_m, j \rangle$, $= \alpha^{-j} + \omega^j$.

We collect in Lemma 2 some technical facts about these operations that we shall need below.

Lemma 2

(a) $\alpha < \alpha^{+j}$.

(b) If $\alpha^{-j} \neq 0$, then $d(\alpha^{-j}) \geqslant j$.

(c) If $\alpha > \beta$, $d\alpha, d\beta \geqslant j$, then $\alpha \geqslant \beta^{+j}$.
(d) $(\alpha^{+j})^{-(j+1)} \leqslant \alpha$.

Proof

(a) With notations as above, either $m = n$, in which case $\alpha < \alpha^{+j}$, or $m < n$, in which case $l_{m+1} < j$, and again $\alpha < \alpha^{+j}$.
(b) If $\alpha^{-j} \neq 0$, then $d(\alpha^{-j}) = l_m \geqslant j$.
(c) $\beta^{+j} = \langle k_1, \ldots, k_p, j \rangle$. Since $\alpha > \beta$, either $n > p$, in which case $l_{p+1} \geqslant l_n \geqslant j$ and $\alpha \geqslant \beta^{+j}$, or for some $i \leqslant p, k_i < l_i$, etc., in which case $\alpha > \beta^{+j}$.
(d) $(\alpha^{+j})^{-(j+1)} = \langle l_1, \ldots, l_m, j \rangle^{-(j+1)} = \langle l_1, \ldots, l_q \rangle$, for some $q \leqslant m$. $\dashv$

We now assign to each ordinal α a formula $D\alpha$: $D0 = \bot$; if $\alpha > 0$, $D\alpha = \Box D\alpha^- \vee \boxed{1}^i \bot$, where $i = d\alpha$. Since $(\alpha+1)^- = \alpha$ and $d(\alpha+1) = 0$, $D(\alpha+1) = \Box D\alpha \vee \bot = \Box D\alpha$. (We often identify obvious equivalents.) If λ is a limit ordinal, then $D(\lambda+\omega) = D(\lambda+\omega^1) = \Box D\lambda \vee \boxed{1}\bot$. And if $j > 0$, $D\omega^j = \Box D0 \vee \boxed{1}^j\bot$, i.e., $\Box\bot \vee \boxed{1}^j\bot$; but since $\vdash \Box\bot \to \boxed{1}^j\bot$, $D\omega^j = \boxed{1}^j\bot$. So, for example,

$$D0 = \bot$$
$$D1 = \Box\bot$$
$$D2 = \Box\Box\bot$$
$$D\omega = \boxed{1}\bot$$
$$D(\omega+1) = \Box\boxed{1}\bot$$
$$D(\omega\cdot 2) = \Box\boxed{1}\bot \vee \boxed{1}\bot$$
$$D(\omega\cdot 3) = \Box(\Box\boxed{1}\bot \vee \boxed{1}\bot) \vee \boxed{1}\bot$$
$$D\omega^2 = \boxed{1}\boxed{1}\bot$$
$$D(\omega^2+\omega) = \Box\boxed{1}\boxed{1}\bot \vee \boxed{1}\bot$$
$$D(\omega^2+\omega\cdot 2) = \Box(\Box\boxed{1}\boxed{1}\bot \vee \boxed{1}\bot) \vee \boxed{1}\bot$$
$$D\omega^3 = \boxed{1}\boxed{1}\boxed{1}\bot$$
$$D(\omega^3+\omega^2) = \Box\boxed{1}^3\bot \vee \boxed{1}^2\bot.$$

We are going to show how to find from any given letterless sentence A of GLB a truth-functional combination of sentences $D\alpha$ that is GLB-equivalent to A. Since nothing false is provable or ω-provable, it is evident from the definition of $D\alpha$ that every $D\alpha$ is false (under every realization). We will therefore have shown how to determine the truth-value of any given letterless sentence.

Let us note that neither of $D\omega = \boxed{1}\bot$ and $D(\omega+1) = \Box\boxed{1}\bot$ implies the other: If $\vdash \Box\boxed{1}\bot \to \boxed{1}\bot$, then, as usual, $\vdash \boxed{1}\bot$, which is impossible. And if $\vdash \boxed{1}\bot \to \Box\boxed{1}\bot$, then

$$(**) \quad \vdash \neg\Box\boxed{1}\bot \to \neg\boxed{1}\bot$$

and so $\vdash \boxed{1}\neg\Box\boxed{1}\bot \to \boxed{1}\neg\boxed{1}\bot$; but $\vdash \neg\Box\boxed{1}\bot \to \boxed{1}\neg\Box\boxed{1}\bot$; thus $\vdash \neg\Box\boxed{1}\bot \to \boxed{1}\neg\boxed{1}\bot$, whence $\vdash \neg\Box\boxed{1}\bot \to \boxed{1}\bot$, and by (**) $\vdash \Box\boxed{1}\bot$, impossible.

Thus although it is in general false that if $\alpha < \beta$, $\vdash D\omega \to D\beta$, we can prove that if $\alpha < \beta$, $\vdash \Box D\alpha \to D\beta$. First, a lemma.

Lemma 3. *Suppose $j < i$. Then*
$\vdash \Box(\Box A \vee \boxed{1}^j\bot) \to \Box A \vee \boxed{1}^i\bot$.

Proof. $\vdash \Box(\Box A \vee \boxed{1}^j\bot) \to \boxed{1}(\Box A \vee \boxed{1}^j\bot)$; $\vdash \neg\Box A \to \boxed{1}\neg\Box A$; $\vdash \boxed{1}(\Box A \vee \boxed{1}^j\bot) \wedge \boxed{1}\neg\Box A \to \boxed{1}^{j+1}\bot$. Since $j < i$, $\vdash \boxed{1}^{j+1}\bot \to \boxed{1}^i\bot$. Then by the propositional calculus, $\vdash \Box(\Box A \vee \boxed{1}^j\bot) \to \Box A \vee \boxed{1}^i\bot$. ⊣

Lemma 4 is fundamental to what follows; on occasion it will be appealed to without explicit mention.

Lemma 4. *Suppose $\alpha < \beta$. Then $\vdash \Box D\alpha \to D\beta$.*

Proof. We may assume that for all γ, $\alpha < \gamma < \beta$, $\vdash \Box D\alpha \to D\gamma$. We may also therefore assume that $\beta^- \leqslant \alpha < \beta$, for if $\alpha < \beta^-$, then since $\beta^- < \beta$, $\vdash \Box D\alpha \to D\beta^-$, whence $\vdash \Box\Box D\alpha \to \Box D\beta^-$; but by the definition of $D\beta$, $\vdash \Box D\beta^- \to D\beta$, and of course $\vdash \Box D\alpha \to \Box\Box D\alpha$, whence $\vdash \Box D\alpha \to D\beta$.

Let us now observe that since $\beta^- \leqslant \alpha < \beta$, there are natural numbers $i_1, \ldots, i_m, j_1, \ldots, j_n$ (where either m or n may be 0), such that $\beta = \langle i_1, \ldots, i_m, i_{m+1}\rangle$, $\alpha = \langle i_1, \ldots, i_m, j_1, \ldots, j_n\rangle$, and $\beta^- = \langle i_1, \ldots, i_m\rangle$, and $i_{m+1} > j_1 \geqslant \cdots \geqslant j_n$.

Let $\Delta_k B = \Box(B \vee \boxed{1}^k\bot)$.

By the definition of $D\beta$, $\vdash \Box D\beta^- \to D\beta$. Since $\alpha = \beta^-$ if $n = 0$, we may assume that $n > 0$. Then $D\alpha = \Box D\alpha^- \vee \boxed{1}^{j_n}\bot$, and $\Box D\alpha = \Delta_{j_n}\Box D\alpha^- = \cdots = \Delta_{j_n}\cdots\Delta_{j_2}\Delta_{j_1}\Box D\beta^-$. By Lemma 3 repeatedly, $\vdash \Delta_{j_1}\Box D\beta^- \to \Box D\beta^- \vee \boxed{1}^{i_{m+1}}\bot$, $\vdash \Delta_{j_2}\Delta_{j_1}\Box D\beta^- \to \Delta_{j_1}\Box D\beta^- \vee \boxed{1}^{i_{m+1}}\bot, \ldots,$ $\vdash \Box D\alpha \to \Box D\beta^- \vee \boxed{1}^{i_{m+1}}\bot$, i.e., $\vdash \Box D\alpha \to D\beta$. ⊣

Lemma 5.

(a) $\vdash \neg\boxed{1}^j\bot \to (\Box D\alpha \leftrightarrow \Box D\alpha^{-j})$.

(b) *If $d\alpha \geqslant j$, then $\vdash D\alpha^{+j} \leftrightarrow \Box D\alpha \vee \boxed{1}^j\bot$.*

Proof

(a) As we have seen, $\alpha^{+j} = \alpha^{-j} + \omega^j$. Thus $D\alpha^{+j} = \Box D\alpha^{-j} \vee \boxed{1}^j\bot$. By Lemma 2(a), $\alpha < \alpha^{+j}$. Thus by Lemma 4, $\vdash \Box D\alpha \rightarrow D\alpha^{+j}$, whence $\vdash \neg \boxed{1}^j\bot \rightarrow (\Box D\alpha \rightarrow \Box D\alpha^{-j})$. But $\alpha^{-j} \leqslant \alpha$ also, and thus $\alpha^{-j} < \alpha + 1$. Since $D(\alpha+1) = \Box D\alpha$, $\vdash \Box D\alpha^{-j} \rightarrow \Box D\alpha$ by Lemma 4, and part (a) follows.

(b) $D\alpha^{+j} = \Box D(\alpha^{+j})^{-} \vee \boxed{1}^j\bot$. But if $d\alpha \geqslant j$, $(\alpha^{+j})^{-} = \langle l_1, \ldots, l_n, j\rangle^{-} = \alpha$. $\dashv$

We now let ∞ be some large number, say ω^ω. Up to now we have taken the variable α to range over the ordinals ($< \omega^\omega$) and the variable i to range over the natural numbers. But henceforth α shall range over ∞ and the ordinals, β over just the ordinals, i over ∞ and the positive integers, and j over just the positive integers.

We now define $H\infty = \top = \boxed{1}^{\infty}\bot$, and if α is an ordinal, we define $H\alpha = \Box D\alpha, = D(\alpha+1)$. We also define $d0 = d\infty = \infty$.

We shall say that a sentence is in normal form if it is a (possibly empty) conjunction of disjunctions, each disjunction having one of the following forms:

(1) $\neg H\alpha \vee \neg \boxed{1}^i\bot$

(2) $\neg H\alpha \vee H\beta \vee \neg \boxed{1}^i\bot, \qquad \alpha > \beta$

(3) $\neg H\alpha \vee H\beta \vee \neg \boxed{1}^i\bot \vee \boxed{1}^j\bot, \qquad \alpha > \beta, \quad i > j > 0, \quad d\alpha, d\beta \geqslant j$

We shall call a sentence *nice* if it is a truth-functional combination of sentences $H\alpha$ and $\boxed{1}^i\bot$. Our main goal is to show how to construct from any given letterless sentence a nice GLB-equivalent. [Since $H\alpha = D(\alpha+1)$ or $\top$ and $\boxed{1}^i\bot = D\omega^i$ or $\top$, any nice sentence is a truth-functional combination of sentences $D\alpha$.] We shall do so in two stages: we first show how to find a sentence in normal form that is equivalent to any nice sentence; we then show how to construct nice sentences equivalent to $\Box A$ and $\boxed{1}A$ from any sentence A in normal form.

Stage 1. We suppose that A is nice. We now show how to find an equivalent of A in normal form.

First rewrite A as a conjunction of disjunctions of sentences $H\alpha$, $\neg H\alpha$, $\boxed{1}^i\bot$, $\neg \boxed{1}^i\bot$. Fix a conjunct B of A. To show how to put A into normal form, it will suffice to determine whether B is equivalent to $\top$, for if so, it may be deleted from A; and if not, to find an equivalent of B in form (1), (2), or (3).

Recalling that $\neg H\infty$ and $\neg \boxed{1}^{\infty}\bot$ are equivalent to $\bot$, we may suppose that for some α, i, $\neg H\alpha$ and $\neg \boxed{1}^i\bot$ are disjuncts of B. And using the equivalence $\vdash \boxed{1}^j\bot \leftrightarrow \boxed{1}^j\bot \vee \Box\bot$, we may suppose that if some sentence $\boxed{1}^j\bot$ is a disjunct of B, so is some sentence $H\beta$. ($\Box\bot = H0$.) Now according to Lemma 4, either $\vdash H\alpha \rightarrow H\beta$ or $\vdash H\beta \rightarrow H\alpha$ [since $H\gamma = \Box D\gamma = D(\gamma+1)$]. Moreover, either $\vdash \boxed{1}^i\bot \rightarrow \boxed{1}^j\bot$ or $\vdash \boxed{1}^j\bot \rightarrow \boxed{1}^i\bot$. Thus by deleting disjuncts $\neg H\alpha$ of B of the form that imply other disjuncts $\neg H\alpha'$, and similarly for disjuncts $H\alpha, \neg\boxed{1}^i\bot, \boxed{1}^i\bot$, we may assume that B has one of the three forms

$\neg H\alpha \vee \neg\boxed{1}^i\bot$,
$\neg H\alpha \vee H\beta \vee \neg\boxed{1}^i\bot$, or
$\neg H\alpha \vee H\beta \vee \neg\boxed{1}^i\bot \vee \boxed{1}^j\bot$.

If B is of the first form, we are done. If B is of the second form but $\alpha \leqslant \beta$, then by Lemma 4, $\vdash H\alpha \rightarrow H\beta$, and therefore B is equivalent to $\top$. But if $\alpha > \beta$, we are also done. Thus we may suppose that B is $\neg H\alpha \vee H\beta \vee \neg\boxed{1}^i\bot \vee \boxed{1}^j\bot$. If $i \leqslant j$, then $\vdash \boxed{1}^i\bot \rightarrow \boxed{1}^j\bot$, and B is equivalent to $\top$. Thus we may suppose $i > j$.

Now if $\alpha \neq \infty$, let $\alpha' = \alpha^{-j}$; otherwise let $\alpha' = \infty$; and let $\beta' = \beta^{-j}$. By Lemma 5(a), $\vdash \neg\boxed{1}^j\bot \rightarrow [H\alpha \leftrightarrow H\alpha'] \wedge [H\beta \leftrightarrow H\beta']$. If $\alpha' = 0, \infty$, then $d\alpha' = \infty \geqslant j$; and otherwise $d\alpha' = d(\alpha^{-j}) \geqslant j$, by Lemma 2(b). Similarly, $d\beta' \geqslant j$. Thus B is equivalent to $\neg H\alpha' \vee H\beta' \vee \neg\boxed{1}^i\bot \vee \boxed{1}^j\bot$, where $i > j$, and $d\alpha', d\beta' \geqslant j$. If $\alpha' \geqslant \beta'$, we are again done, for $\vdash H\alpha' \rightarrow H\beta'$. Thus we may suppose $\alpha' > \beta'$. But now we *are* done.

Stage 2. We now want to show how to find nice equivalents of $\Box A$ and $\boxed{1}A$ from a sentence A in normal form. Since $\Box$ and $\boxed{1}$ distribute over $\wedge$, we may assume that A consists of a single conjunct of one of the forms (1), (2), (3). We first consider $\Box A$: If A is $\neg H\alpha \vee \neg\boxed{1}^i\bot$, then $\Box A$ is equivalent to $\Box\bot$, i.e., to $H0$.

Suppose that A is $\neg H\alpha \vee H\beta \vee \neg\boxed{1}^i\bot$, where $\alpha > \beta$. We shall show that $\Box A$ is equivalent to $H(\beta+1) = \Box H\beta$.

Observe that $\vdash \Box H\beta \rightarrow \Box A$. And since $\beta + 1 \leqslant \alpha$,
$\vdash \neg H\alpha \rightarrow \neg H(\beta+1)$, and therefore
$\vdash \Box A \rightarrow \Box(\neg H(\beta+1) \vee H\beta \vee \neg\boxed{1}^i\bot)$. Recall that $i > 0$; thus $\vdash \neg\boxed{1}^i\bot \rightarrow \neg\boxed{1}\bot$. Moreover, for any sentence C,
$\vdash \neg(\neg\Box\Box C \vee \Box C) \rightarrow (\Box\Box C \wedge \neg\Box C), \rightarrow (\boxed{1}\Box C \wedge \boxed{1}\neg\Box C), \rightarrow \boxed{1}\bot$; thus $\vdash \neg\boxed{1}\bot \rightarrow (\neg\Box\Box C \vee \Box C)$, in particular, since
$H\beta = \Box D\beta, \vdash \neg\boxed{1}\bot \rightarrow (\neg H(\beta+1) \vee H\beta)$, and therefore
$\vdash \Box A \rightarrow \Box(\neg H(\beta+1) \vee H\beta)$, whence
$\vdash \Box A \rightarrow \Box H\beta$ (Löb), and therefore $\vdash \Box A \leftrightarrow H(\beta+1)$.

Finally, suppose that A is $\neg H\alpha \vee H\beta \vee \neg\boxed{1}^i\bot \vee \boxed{1}^j\bot$, where

$\alpha > \beta$, $i > j$, and $d\alpha$, $d\beta \geqslant j$. We shall show that $\Box A$ is equivalent to $H\beta^{+j}$.

By Lemma 2(c), $\alpha \geqslant \beta^{+j}$; thus by Lemma 4, $\vdash A \to H\beta^{+j} \vee H\beta \vee \neg \boxed{1}^i \bot \vee \boxed{1}^j \bot$. By Lemma 5(a), $\vdash \neg \boxed{1}^{j+1} \bot \to (H\beta^{+j} \to H(\beta^{+j})^{-(j+1)})$. By Lemmas 2(d) and 4 and the fact that $i > j$, $\vdash \neg \boxed{1}^i \bot \to (H\beta^{+j} \to H\beta)$. Thus $\vdash A \to \neg H\beta^{+j} \vee H\beta \vee \boxed{1}^j \bot$. But since $d\beta \geqslant j$, by Lemma 5(b), $\vdash D\beta^{+j} \leftrightarrow H\beta \vee \boxed{1}^j \bot$. Thus $\vdash A \to \neg H\beta^{+j} \vee D\beta^{+j}$, i.e., $\vdash A \to \neg \Box D\beta^{+j} \vee D\beta^{+j}$, and so $\vdash \Box A \to \Box D\beta^{+j}$, i.e., $\vdash \Box A \to H\beta^{+j}$. Conversely, again by Lemma 5(b), $\vdash \Box D\beta^{+j} \to \Box(H\beta \vee \boxed{1}^j \bot)$, whence $\vdash H\beta^{+j} \to \Box A$. So $\Box A$ is equivalent to $H\beta^{+j}$.

Now for the easier case of $\boxed{1} A$:

Lemma 6. *Let F be a truth-functional combination of sentences $\Box C$. Then* $\vdash \boxed{1}(F \vee G) \leftrightarrow (F \vee \boxed{1} G)$.

Proof. F is equivalent in the propositional calculus to some conjunction of disjunctions of sentences $\Box C$ and $\neg \Box C$, and so is $\neg F$. But since $\vdash \Box C \to \boxed{1} \Box C$, $\vdash \neg \Box C \to \boxed{1} \neg \Box C$, $\vdash \boxed{1} F_1 \vee \boxed{1} F_2 \to \boxed{1}(F_1 \vee F_2)$, and $\vdash \boxed{1} F_1 \wedge \boxed{1} F_2 \to \boxed{1}(F_1 \wedge F_2)$, it follows that $\vdash F \to \boxed{1} F$, and likewise, $\vdash \neg F \to \boxed{1} \neg F$. Since $\vdash \boxed{1} F \to \boxed{1}(F \vee G)$ and $\vdash \boxed{1} G \to \boxed{1}(F \vee G)$, $\vdash (F \vee \boxed{1} G) \to \boxed{1}(F \vee G)$. Conversely, $\vdash \neg F \to \boxed{1} \neg F$, whence $\vdash \neg F \wedge \boxed{1}(F \vee G) \to \boxed{1} G$, and therefore $\vdash \boxed{1}(F \vee G) \to (F \vee \boxed{1} G)$. $\dashv$

Sentences $H\alpha$ are of course truth-functional combinations of sentences $\Box C$. (If $\alpha = \infty$, $H\alpha$ is $\top$, which certainly is such a combination.) If A is of form (1), then by Lemma 6, $\boxed{1} A$ is equivalent to $\neg H\alpha \vee \boxed{1} \neg \boxed{1}^i \bot$, and hence to $\neg H\alpha \vee \boxed{1} \bot$. If A is of form (2), $\boxed{1} A$ is equivalent to $\neg H\alpha \vee H\beta \vee \boxed{1} \neg \boxed{1}^i \bot$, and hence to $\neg H\alpha \vee H\beta \vee \boxed{1} \bot$. If A is of form (3), then $\boxed{1} A$ is equivalent to $\neg H\alpha \vee H\beta \vee \boxed{1}(\neg \boxed{1}^i \bot \vee \boxed{1}^j \bot)$, and thus, since $i > j$, equivalent to $\neg H\alpha \vee H\beta \vee \boxed{1}^{j+1} \bot$. In all three cases then, we have found a nice equivalent of $\boxed{1} A$.

GLB is also the joint logic of provability and provability under the ω-rule in analysis

We conclude by stating a theorem about GLB and analysis. For any realization $*$ (now a function from the sentence letters of modal logic into those of analysis) and any bimodal sentence A, define A^* by:

$$p^* = {}^*(p)$$
$$\bot^* = \bot,$$
$$(A \to B)^* = (A^* \to B^*)$$
$$\Box(A)^* = \mathrm{Bew}(\ulcorner A^* \urcorner)$$
$$\boxed{1}(A)^* = \Theta(\ulcorner A^* \urcorner)$$

Here Bew(x) is the standard provability predicate for analysis and $\Theta(x)$ is the formula defined in Chapter 14, naturally expressing provability in analysis under the ω-rule.

By routinely superimposing the appropriate notions from analyis defined in Chapter 14 onto the completeness proofs for GLB and GLSB of Chapter 15 (replacing ω-provability, in particular, by provability in analysis under the ω-rule), the following informative, but by now unsurprising, theorem can be proved.

Theorem. *Let A be a bimodal sentence. Then* GLB$\vdash A$ *iff for all* $*$, A^* *is a theorem of analysis; and* GLSB$\vdash A$ *iff for all* $*$, A^* *is true.*

17

Quantified provability logic

Here and in our final chapter we study quantified (or predicate) provability logic. We consider translations of formulas of quantified modal logic (QML) into the language $\mathscr{L}$ of arithmetic under which the box $\Box$ of modal logic is taken, as in earlier parts of this work, to represent provability in arithmetic. In the "pure" predicate calculus, function signs, the equals-sign $=$, and modal logical symbols such as $\Box$ and $\Diamond$ do not occur. We shall define an expression to be a formula of QML if and only if it can be obtained from a formula of the "pure" predicate calculus, by replacing (zero or more) occurrences of the negation sign $\neg$ with occurrences of $\Box$. Thus $\Box$ and $\neg$ have the same syntax in QML, as was the case in propositional modal logic.

Our results are negative: we show that there are no simple characterizations of the always provable or always true sentences of QML. Apart from the definition of the sentence D and Lemma 7 below, curiously little use is made of the quantificational–modal–logical properties of Bew(x). Indeed, the main definitions, techniques, and theorems that are to follow may seem to come from a branch of logic rather unrelated to the one we have been studying up to now.

We shall suppose that the variables, $v_0, v_1, \ldots$, are common to the languages of QML and of arithmetic. The first n variables are, of course, $v_0, \ldots, v_{n-1}$.

A *realization* is a function $*$ from a set of predicate letters to formulas of $\mathscr{L}$ such that for all n, if π is an n-place predicate letter in the domain of $*$, then $*(\pi)$ is a formula in which exactly the first n variables occur free. A *realization of* a formula F of QML is a realization whose domain contains all predicate letters occurring in F.

We write: π^* instead of: $*(\pi)$.

For every formula F of QML and realization $*$ of F, we define the translation F^* of F under $*$ as follows:

If F is the atomic formula $\pi x_1, \ldots, x_n$, then F^* is the result $\pi^*(x_1, \ldots, x_n)$ of respectively substituting $x_1, \ldots, x_n$ for $v_0, \ldots, v_{n-1}$ in π^*. (As usual, the bound variables of π^* are supposed rewritten, if necessary, so that none of $x_1, \ldots, x_n$ is captured by a quantifier in π^*.)

$(F \to G)^*$ is $(F^* \to G^*)$;
$\bot^*$ is $\bot$;
[and therefore $(\neg F)^*$ is $\neg(F^*)$, $(F \wedge G)^*$ is $(F^* \wedge G^*)$, etc.];
$(\exists x F)^*$ is $\exists x(F^*)$;
[and therefore $(\forall x F)^*$ is $\forall x(F^*)$]; and
$(\Box F)^*$ is Bew$[F^*]$ (cf. Chapter 2).

Let us notice that F^* contains exactly the same variables free as F, that formulas beginning with quantifiers require no special treatment, and that F^* depends only on the formulas that $*$ assigns to predicate letters actually contained in F.

We call a sentence S of QML *always provable* if for all realizations $*$ of S, S^* is a theorem of PA, and *always true* if for all realizations $*$ of S, S^* is true (in the standard model N). We are going to give characterizations of the class of always provable sentences and of the class of always true sentences.

In the present chapter we shall prove that the class of always true sentences cannot be defined by a formula of the language of arithmetic and the class of always provable sentences cannot be axiomatized, i.e., recursively axiomatized. These theorems are due, respectively, to S. N. Artemov and V. A. Vardanyan and were discovered in 1984 and 1985. We shall also prove a refinement of Artemov's result due independently to Vann McGee, Vardanyan, and the author. In the next chapter we prove a remarkable result, also due to Vardanyan, according to which these theorems hold even for the tiny fragment of QML containing only one one-place predicate letter (and in which nesting of boxes is forbidden!).

We shall try to make our treatment of these results almost completely self-contained, and to this end we now give a brief review of some basic concepts and results of recursion theory. There are many easily accessible sources in which a full (and adequate) treatment of these notions may be found. $\dashv$

A brief review of some recursion theory

We begin with the notion of an oracle machine; like that of a Turing machine, the idea is due to Turing.

We say, intuitively, that a function f is computable *in* a set A of natural numbers if there is a machine which computes f, but from time to time interrupts its computation to ask questions of an external source of information, an "oracle". The questions have the form: Is $n \in A$?, where n is the number of 1's on the machine tape at the time the computation is interrupted. To make this idea precise, we need the idea of an *oracle* machine.

An oracle machine is a kind of Turing machine in whose table there may occur instructions of a special kind, *oracle* instructions:

$$\langle (\text{state})i, (\text{symbol})s, (\text{state})j_1, (\text{state})j_2 \rangle$$

The idea is that an oracle machine whose table contains the instruction $\langle i, s, j_1, j_2 \rangle$, when it is in state i scanning a symbol of type s, stops to ask whether the number of 1s then on its tape belongs to a certain set of natural numbers. The machine will resume its computation and enter state j_1 if it receives a "yes" answer from the oracle and enter state j_2 if it receives a "no". Every ordinary Turing machine (trivially) counts as an oracle machine.

A (halting) computation by an oracle machine will be said to be *correct for* a set A of natural numbers if whenever $\langle i, s, j_1, j_2 \rangle$ is a special instruction in its table, then for any moment of the computation at which the machine is in state i scanning a symbol of type s, the machine enters state j_1 at the next moment if the number of 1s on its tape is in A and enters state j_2 at the next moment if not.

We shall assume ourselves to be employing some formulation of the notion of an oracle machine that satisfies the following condition: if k is the Gödel number of any computation by an oracle machine and n is a number about which the oracle is questioned during the computation, then $n \leqslant k$. On all standard accounts, this condition is met.

We let: i abbreviate: $i_1, \ldots, i_n$.

The relativized Kleene T-predicate T_n is the relation that holds among numbers e, i, k, and set A if and only if k is the Gödel number of a halting computation that is correct for A by the oracle machine with Gödel number e when given the inputs i. One writes: $T_n^A(e, \mathrm{i}, k)$, dropping the subscript 'n' when $n = 1$ and omitting the superscript 'A' when A is N.

A total n-place function f is *recursive in* the set A of natural numbers if and only if for some oracle machine M, for all i, $f(\mathrm{i})$ is the number yielded as output in any halting computation of M

that is correct for A, when M is given input i. Intuitively, a function is recursive in A if it can be computed by a machine with the aid of answers from an oracle which responds with answers that are correct with respect to the set A whenever an inquiry is made of it. As ever, a relation is recursive in A if and only if its characteristic function is recursive in A. A function is recursive if and only if it is recursive in N (= recursive in $\varnothing$ = recursive in every set).

For any set A, the relation T^A, $= \{\langle e, \mathrm{i}, k\rangle : T^A(e, \mathrm{i}, k)\}$, is recursive in A: first decide whether k is the Gödel number of a halting computation C for the oracle machine with Gödel number e when given input i. If not, then not: $T^A(e, \mathrm{i}, k)$. But if so, then test (with the aid of an oracle for A) each of the finitely many numbers about which the oracle is questioned during C to determine whether or not k is correct for A. If so, then $T^A(e, \mathrm{i}, k)$; if not, then not: $T^A(e, \mathrm{i}, k)$.

We now inductively define the relations that are Σ^0_m in A and the relations that are Π^0_m in A:

A relation R is Σ^0_0 in A, or Π^0_0 in A, iff R is recursive in A.

An n-place relation R is Σ^0_{m+1} in A if for some $(n+1)$-place relation S that is Π^0_m in A, $R = \{\mathrm{i}: \exists j S(\mathrm{i}, j)\}$.

An n-place relation R is Π^0_{m+1} in A if for some $(n+1)$-place relation S that is Σ^0_m in A, $R = \{\mathrm{i}: \forall j S(\mathrm{i}, j)\}$.

Thus a relation is Π^0_m in A if and only if its complement is Σ^0_m in A.

The relations that are Σ^0_1 in A are often called *recursively enumerable* in A (*r.e.* in A, for short).

Every relation R that is recursive in A is both Σ^0_1 and Π^0_1 in A: $R = \{\mathrm{i}: \exists j(R(\mathrm{i}) \wedge j = j)\} = \{\mathrm{i}: \forall j(R(\mathrm{i}) \wedge j = j)\}$. (Note that $\{\langle \mathrm{i}, j\rangle : R(\mathrm{i}) \wedge j = j\}$ is recursive in A if R is.) By similarly tacking on vacuous quantifiers we see generally that every relation that is either Σ^0_m in A or Π^0_m in A is both Σ^0_{m+1} in A and Π^0_{m+1} in A.

The existence of recursive unpairing functions η_1 and η_2 enables adjacent quantifiers of the same kind, existential or universal, to be "collapsed". For example, $\{\mathrm{i}: \exists j_1 \exists j_2 S(\mathrm{i}, j_1, j_2)\} = \{\mathrm{i}: \exists j S(\mathrm{i}, \eta_1(j), \eta_2(j))\}$. (The relation $\{\langle \mathrm{i}, j\rangle : S(\mathrm{i}, \eta_1(j), \eta_2(j))\}$ will be Σ^0_m in A if S is Σ^0_m in A and Π^0_m in A if S is Π^0_m in A.)

By collapsing adjacent quantifiers we see that the intersection of two r.e. relations is r.e., the union of two r.e. relations is r.e., and that the projection (existential quantification) of an r.e. relation is r.e. A set is *arithmetical* if it is defined by some formula of the language $\mathscr{L}$ of arithmetic. By converting formulas of $\mathscr{L}$ to prenex form and collapsing adjacent quantifiers of the same kind, we see that a set is arithmetical if and only if it is Σ^0_m or Π^0_m, for some m.

The *truth set* V is the set of Gödel numbers of the sentences of $\mathscr{L}$ that are true in the standard model N. By Tarski's theorem, V is not arithmetical. However, for each r, the set V_r of Gödel numbers of sentences of $\mathscr{L}$ that are true and contain $\leqslant r$ occurrences of the logical operators is arithmetical.[1] Every arithmetical set is recursive in V: if $F(x)$ defines A, then $A = \{i$: the Gödel number of $F(\mathbf{i}) \in V\}$.

Kleene's enumeration theorem states that for every relation R recursively enumerable in A, there is an e such that $R = \{\mathrm{i}: \exists k T_n^A(e, \mathrm{i}, k)\}$. [*Proof*: Suppose that $R = \{\mathrm{i}: \exists k R'(\mathrm{i}, k)\}$, with R' recursive in A. Let e be the Gödel number of a machine that, with the aid of an oracle for A, when given any input i, tests each natural number k in turn to determine whether or not $R'(\mathrm{i}, k)$. If and when the machine finds a k such that $R'(\mathrm{i}, k)$, it outputs 0 (arbitrarily) and halts. Then $R = \{\mathrm{i}: \exists k T_n^A(e, \mathrm{i}, k)\}$.]

It follows that if a set S is Σ_m^0 in A, then for some $e, S = \{i: \exists k_1 \forall k_2 \ldots Qk_m \backslash T^A(e, i, k_1, k_2, \ldots, k_m)\}$, where Q is $\forall$ and $\backslash T^A$ is $\neg T^A$ if m is even, and Q is $\exists$ and $\backslash T^A$ is T^A if m is odd. For if S is Σ_m^0 in A, then for some relation R recursive in A, $S = \{i: \exists k_1 \forall k_2 \ldots Qk_m R(i, k_1, k_2, \ldots, k_m)\}$. By Kleene's enumeration theorem, for some e, $\{\langle i, k_1, k_2, \ldots, k_{m-1}\rangle: \exists k_m \backslash R(i, k_1, k_2, \ldots, k_m)\} = \{\langle i, k_1, k_2, \ldots, k_{m-1}\rangle: \exists k_m T^A(e, k_1, k_2, \ldots, k_m)\}$, and therefore $S = \{i: \exists k_1 \forall k_2 \ldots Qk_m \backslash T^A(e, i, k_1, k_2, \ldots, k_m)\}$. (Take complements if m is even.)

Let $K_m^A = \{i: \exists k_1 \forall k_2 \ldots Qk_m \backslash T_m^A(i, i, k_1, k_2, \ldots, k_m)\}$. K_m^A is Σ_m^0 in A. However, $N - K_m^A$ is not Σ_m^0 in A, as the usual Russellian argument shows: Suppose $N - K_m^A$ is Σ_m^0 in A. Then for some $e, N - K_m^A = \{i: \exists k_1 \forall k_2 \ldots Qk_m \backslash T^A(e, i, k_1, k_2, \ldots, k_m)\}$. But then $e \in N - K_m^A$ iff $\exists k_1 \forall k_2 \ldots Qk_m \backslash T^A(e, e, k_1, k_2, \ldots, k_m)$, iff $e \in K_m^A$, contradiction.

A set S is called Π_m^0-complete in A, $m > 0$, if it is Π_m^0 in A and for every set S' that is Π_m^0 in A there is a recursive function f such that $S' = \{i: f(i) \in S\}$. "Σ_m^0-complete in A" is defined analogously. S is Π_m^0-complete in A iff $N - S$ is Σ_m^0-complete in A.

If S is Π_m^0-complete in A, then it is not Σ_m^0 in A. For suppose S is Σ_m^0 in A. Then by Kleene's enumeration theorem as above, for some $e, S = \{i: \exists k_1 \forall k_2 \ldots Qk_m \backslash T^A(e, i, k_1, k_2, \ldots, k_m)\}$. Since $N - K_m^A$ is Π_m^0, if S is also Π_m^0-complete in A, there is a recursive function f such that $N - K_m^A = \{i: f(i) \in S\} = \{i: \exists k_1 \forall k_2 \ldots T^A(e, f(i), k_1, k_2, \ldots)\}$, and then $N - K_m^A$ is Σ_m^0 in A, which is not the case.

Thus if a set S is Π_2^0-complete, then it is not Σ_2^0, hence not Π_1^0, Σ_1^0, or recursive. And if a set S is Π_1^0-complete in V, then S is not Σ_1^0 in V, hence not recursive in V, or arithmetical.

End of the brief review of some recursion theory.

The full statement of Vardanyan's theorem employs the concept of a Π^0_2-complete set; it states that the class of always provable sentences of QML is Π^0_2-complete; the refinement of Artemov's theorem referred to above is that the class of always true sentences is Π^0_1-complete in the truth set V for arithmetic.

The reader who is already somewhat familiar with elementary recursion theory may have noticed that the situation as regards the axiomatizability or decidability of predicate provability logic is worst possible, in a precise technical sense. For since the identity of S^* depends only on S and on what $*$ assigns to predicate letters actually occurring in S, S is always provable if and only if S^* is provable in arithmetic for all $*$ that assign formulas to all *and only* the predicate letters occurring in S. Such finite realizations $*$ can be coded by natural numbers, and the set of Gödel numbers of always provable sentences S will then be Π^0_2 at worst, for it is the set of Gödel numbers of sentences meeting the following condition: *for all* $*$ (that assign formulas to all and only the predicate letters of S) *there is* a proof in PA of the result of substituting π^* for each predicate letter π contained in S. By Vardanyan's theorem and a basic result of recursion theory reviewed above, the class of always provable sentences of QML cannot have a characterization that is simpler than Π^0_2. Since the class of derivable sentences of any given axiomatization is always characterizable, more simply, as a Σ^0_1 (= r.e.) class – a sentence S is a theorem if and only if *there is* a proof of S – the always provable sentences cannot be axiomatized.

Similarly, as regards the always true sentences. Since a sentence S is always true iff S^* is true for all $*$ (that assign formulas to all and only the predicate letters of S), the class of always provable sentences is at worst Π^0_1 in V: *for all* $*$ (that assign $\cdots$), S^* is true. The theorem of McGee, Vardanyan, and the author implies that the always true sentences lack any simpler classification.

The contrast with propositional provability logic and the ordinary, non-modal, predicate calculus is sharp. GL axiomatizes the class of always provable sentences of propositional modal logic; GLS, the class of always true sentences of propositional modal logic. These systems are decidable, as we have seen, and therefore so are the classes they axiomatize. And according to the Hilbert–Bernays extension of the Skolem–Löwenheim theorem, a sentence of the pure predicate calculus that is not valid is false in some model whose domain is the set of natural numbers and in which the predicate letters are assigned *arithmetically definable* relations.[2]

Thus the class of valid sentences of the pure predicate calculus, which, of course, is axiomatized by any standard (Hilbert-style) formalization of logic, coincides with both the class of always provable sentences of the pure predicate calculus and the class of always true sentences of the pure predicate calculus.[3]

Vardanyan's theorem settled a long-standing problem. In the precursor to this work, dated 1979, its author wrote, "One major open question in this area is whether the set of theorems of the relevant system is recursively enumerable,"[4] but the problem had been formulated by Kripke some fifteen years earlier.

The problem of characterizing the always provable and the always true formulas of QML is also a highly natural one. In her pioneering study of quantified modal logic, Ruth Barcan Marcus had investigated the formula $\Diamond \exists x Fx \to \exists x \Diamond Fx$, now known as the Barcan formula. The Barcan formula is not always true, as we may see by taking F^* as Proof $(v_0, \ulcorner \bot \urcorner)$, but its converse $\exists x \Diamond Fx \to \Diamond \exists x Fx$ is always provable, as can be seen by formalizing a proof of the fact that an existential quantification is consistent if one of its instances is. It is entirely natural to try to characterize axiomatically the formulas that, like the converse Barcan formula, exhibit such good behavior.

For a long time, the conjecture went unrefuted that the always provable formulas are axiomatized by the system obtained simply by adjoining ordinary quantificational logic to GL. In 1984, however, Franco Montagna gave an example of an always provable sentence that was not a theorem of this system. And in the following year, Vardanyan's Π^0_2-completeness theorem put an end to the search for axiomatizations of quantified provability logic.

There are well-known difficulties that are thought to attach to quantified modal logic. Quine has argued that, along with the unclarity of the notion of necessity, there is an extra obscurity that arises when one "quantifies in", i.e., when one attaches a quantifier ranging over arbitrary objects to a formula containing a modal operator meaning "it is necessary that". The difficulty, it should be observed, is not so much with the quantifier as with the interpretation of "open sentences" (formulas with free variables) whose principal connective is $\Box$; once the interpretation of a boxed open sentence $\Box \cdots x \cdots$ is determined, there is no further problem in saying what $\forall x \Box \cdots x \cdots$ means. To do so, one may first say: "It means: no matter which object x may be," and then say something U that expresses the meaning of $\Box \cdots x \cdots$. Whatever obscurity this explanation of the meaning of $\forall x \Box \cdots x \cdots$ may possess will lie wholly in U.

Difficulties over the interpretation of boxed formulas with free variables are sidestepped in our present, arithmetical, context, thanks to the notions of the numeral for a number and the operation of substitution. Under the provability interpretation of $\Box$, a formula $\Box A$ containing just the n variables $x_1, \ldots, x_n$ free will be true of the numbers $i_1, \ldots, i_n$ (with each i_j assigned to x_j) if and only if the sentence that results when the numerals $\mathbf{i}_1, \ldots, \mathbf{i}_n$ for $i_1, \ldots, i_n$ are respectively substituted in A for the variables $x_1, \ldots, x_n$ is provable. There is nothing at all in this explanation of the truth-conditions of $\Box A$ to which even the strictest of Quineans could take exception.

Difficulties, however, would apparently confront one attempting to do set-theoretical quantified provability logic. How can one give a definition, even inductively, of what it is for an arbitrary *set* to satisfy a formula *provably*? Only for a language whose symbols were so numerous as not to form a set, it seems, could one give an account of the meaning of formulas $\Box A$ containing free variables ranging over all sets that is parallel to the one we have given for formulas with free variables over all natural numbers.

Let us now put these worries aside and take up the study of quantified provability logic in the arithmetical setting in which it is certainly possible. Our first aim is to develop the techniques needed for a proof of Artemov's theorem that the set of always true sentences of QML is not arithmetical: no formula of the language of arithmetic is true of exactly the Gödel numbers of the always true sentences of QML.

$\mathscr{L}$ is the language $\{\mathbf{0}, \mathbf{s}, +, \times\}$ of arithmetic.

Let G be a one-place predicate letter.

$\mathscr{L}^+$ is $\mathscr{L} \cup \{G\}$.

For each atomic formula F of $\mathscr{L}^+$, let $\hat{F}$ be some standard logical equivalent of F with the same free variables, and built up by conjunction and existential quantification from atomic formulas of one of the six forms $u = v$, $\mathbf{0} = u$, $\mathbf{s}u = v$, $u + v = w$, $u \times v = w$, and Gu. For example, if F is $\mathbf{ss0} + \mathbf{s0} = x$, $\hat{F}$ might be $\exists y \exists z \exists w(\mathbf{0} = y \wedge \mathbf{s}y = z \wedge \mathbf{s}z = w \wedge w + z = x)$. We define $\hat{F}$ for non-atomic formulas of $\mathscr{L}^+$ by letting $\wedge$ commute with truth-functional operators and quantifiers.

Now let Z be a one-place predicate letter other than G, let E and S be two two-place predicate letters, and let A and M be two three-place predicate letters. For each formula F of $\mathscr{L}^+$, let $\{F\}$ be the formula obtained from $\hat{F}$ by replacing each formula $u = v$, $\mathbf{0} = u$,

$\mathbf{s}u = v$, $u + v = w$, $u \times v = w$ by *Euv*, *Zu*, *Suv*, *Auvw*, *Muvw*, respectively. (Formulas *Gu* are left alone.) $\{F\}$ is a formula of the pure predicate calculus with the same free variables as F.

We now introduce a certain sentence T of the language $\mathscr{L}$ of arithmetic. Which sentence T may be taken to be will become clear as we proceed. T should be thought of, for now, as a conjunction of axioms of arithmetic, among whose conjuncts are the equality axioms and identity axioms for $0, s, +$, and $\times$, the logically valid sentence $\exists x\, \mathbf{0} = x \wedge \forall x \forall y(\mathbf{0} = x \wedge \mathbf{0} = y \rightarrow x = y)$, together with similar valid sentences expressing that s, $+$, and $\times$ define functions, the usual recursion axioms for zero, successor, plus and times, and certain other theorems of arithmetic. Thus one of the conjuncts of $\{T\}$ will be the sentence $\exists x Zx \wedge \forall x \forall y(Zx \wedge Zy \rightarrow Exy)$ (which is definitely not *logically* valid).

For any realization $*$ of $\{T\}$, let $^*R(x, y)$, or $R(x, y)$ for short, be the formula of $\mathscr{L}$:

$$\exists s(\text{FinSeq}(s) \wedge \text{lh}(s) = x + 1 \wedge s_x = y \wedge Z^*(s_0) \wedge \forall z < x S^*(s_z, s_{z+1}))$$

We may think of $R(x, y)$ as saying that y represents x in the model determined by the realization $*$. In general, a number x will be represented by many y, but the class of y that represent x will turn out be an E^*-equivalence class, because axioms expressing the reflexivity, symmetry, and transitivity of identity are included among the conjuncts of T.

We now let $*$ be an arbitrary realization.

Lemma 1. $\text{PA} \vdash \{T\}^* \rightarrow \forall x \exists y R(x, y)$.

Proof. Work in PA. Assume that $\{T\}^*$ holds. Now use induction on x. Suppose $x = 0$. Since, as we have assumed, one of the conjuncts of T is the sentence $\exists x\, \mathbf{0} = x$, one of the conjuncts of $\{T\}$ is $\exists x Zx$, and one of the conjuncts of $\{T\}^*$ is $\exists x Z^*(x)$. Thus for some y, $Z^*(y)$. Let s be the finite sequence of length 1 such that $s_0 = y$. Then $R(0, y)$.

For the induction step, suppose as inductive hypothesis that for some y, $R(x, y)$. Let s be a finite sequence as in the definition of R that witnesses the truth of $R(x, y)$. Since, as we may assume, one of the conjuncts of T is $\forall x \exists x'\ \mathbf{s}x = x'$, one of the conjuncts of $\{T\}^*$ is $\forall x \exists x' S^*(x, x')$. Thus for some $y', S^*(y, y')$. Let s' be the finite sequence of length $x + 2$ extending s such that $s'_{x+1} = y'$. Then s' witnesses the truth of $R(x + 1, y')$. $\dashv$

Lemma 2. $\text{PA} \vdash \{T\}^* \wedge R(x, y) \wedge E^*(y, y') \rightarrow R(x, y')$.

Proof. The proof is an induction on x like that of Lemma 1. For the basis step we assume that T contains $\forall x \forall x'(\mathbf{0} = x \wedge x = x' \rightarrow \mathbf{0} = x')$; for the induction step we assume that T contains $\forall x \forall x' \forall x''\ (\mathbf{s}x = x' \wedge x' = x'' \rightarrow \mathbf{s}x = x'')$. ⊣

Lemma 3

(a) $\text{PA} \vdash \{T\}^* \wedge R(x, y) \wedge R(x', y') \rightarrow (x = x' \leftrightarrow E^*(y, y'))$;

(b) $\text{PA} \vdash \{T\}^* \wedge R(x, y) \rightarrow (\mathbf{0} = x \leftrightarrow Z^*(y))$;

(c) $\text{PA} \vdash \{T\}^* \wedge R(x, y) \wedge R(x', y') \rightarrow (\mathbf{s}x = x' \leftrightarrow S^*(y, y'))$;

(d) $\text{PA} \vdash \{T\}^* \wedge R(x, y) \wedge R(x', y') \wedge R(x'', y'') \rightarrow (x + x' = x'' \leftrightarrow A^*(y, y', y''))$;

(e) $\text{PA} \vdash \{T\}^* \wedge R(x, y) \wedge R(x', y') \wedge R(x'', y'') \rightarrow (x \times x' = x'' \leftrightarrow M^*(y, y', y''))$.

Proof. The proof of each of these is similar to that of Lemma 1. One first observes that a certain finite number of simple theorems about the natural numbers can be proved in PA. Since these theorems may be assumed to be conjuncts of T, braced-and-starred versions of them may thus be assumed to follow form $\{T\}^*$. One then appeals to the facts stated in these versions in order to prove the proposition by induction. ⊣

We readopt a convention we adhered to in Chapter 2. 'x' abbreviates '$x_1, \ldots, x_n$' and 'y' abbreviates '$y_1, \ldots, y_n$'. We let '$\mathsf{R}(\mathsf{x}, \mathsf{y})$' abbreviate '$R(x_1, y_1) \wedge \cdots \wedge R(x_n, y_n)$'.

Lemma 4. *Let* $F(\mathsf{x})$ *be any formula of* $\mathscr{L}$. *Then*
$\text{PA} \vdash \{T\}^* \wedge \forall y \exists x R(x, y) \wedge \mathsf{R}(\mathsf{x}, \mathsf{y}) \rightarrow (F(\mathsf{x}) \leftrightarrow \{F\}^*(\mathsf{y}))$.

Proof. Induction on the construction of $F, = F(\mathsf{x})$. We may assume that every atomic formula of F is of one of the forms $u = v$, $\mathbf{0} = u$, $\mathbf{s}u = v$, $u + v = w$, or $u \times v = w$. Lemma 3 takes care of the atomic cases; the truth-functional cases are handled as usual. As for the quantifier case, $\forall x \exists y R(x, y)$, which follows from $\{T\}^*$ by Lemma 1, and $\forall y \exists x R(x, y)$, which is a conjunct of the antecedent, suffice for the deduction of Lemma 4 for $\exists x F$ from Lemma 4 for F. ⊣

We now aim to find a formula D of QML such that D^* may replace the conjunct $\forall y \exists x R(x, y)$ in Lemma 4.

A *bounded* formula of $\mathscr{L}$ is one that is built up from atomic formulas and their negations by truth-functional operations and bounded existential and universal quantification.

Lemma 5. *Let* $F(\mathsf{x})$ *be any bounded formula of* $\mathscr{L}$. *Then* $\mathrm{PA}\vdash\{T\}^* \wedge \mathsf{R}(\mathsf{x},\mathsf{y})\rightarrow(F(\mathsf{x})\leftrightarrow\{F\}^*(\mathsf{y}))$.

Proof. Induction on the construction of $F(\mathsf{x})$. Lemma 3 takes care of the atomic case; the truth-functional cases are as ever. In the bounded quantifier case, suppose that $F(\mathsf{x}, x)$ is $\forall z<xG(\mathsf{x}, z)$ and Lemma 5 holds for $G(\mathsf{x}, z)$. Now proceed by induction in PA on x. Assume $\{T\}^*$, $\mathsf{R}(\mathsf{x},\mathsf{y})$, and $R(x, y)$. Suppose $x=0$. Then certainly $F(\mathsf{x}, x)$. But since $R(0, y)$, $Z^*(y)$. We may assume that $\forall z\neg z<0$ is one of the conjuncts of T. Thus also $\forall z\neg z\{<\}^*y$. But then we have $\forall z\{<\}^*yG(\mathsf{y}, y)$, i.e., $\{F\}^*(\mathsf{y}, y\}$.

Suppose $x=sx'$. Then for some y', $R(x', y')$ and $S^*(y', y)$. And then $F(\mathsf{x}, x)$ iff $F(\mathsf{x}, x')$ and $G(\mathsf{x}, x')$, iff by the i.h. and Lemma 5 for $G(\mathsf{x}, x)$, $\{F\}^*(\mathsf{y}, y')$, and $\{G\}^*(\mathsf{y}, y')$, iff $\forall z\{<\}^*y'\{G)^*(\mathsf{y}, z)$ and $\{G\}^*$ (y, y'). Since $S^*(y', y)$ and $\forall x'\forall z(z<\mathbf{s}x'\leftrightarrow z<x' \vee z=x')$ is a conjunct of T, as we may assume, $z\{<\}^*y$ iff $z\{<\}^*y'$ or $z\{=\}^*y$. The obvious induction on the construction of G shows that if $z\{=\}^*y'$, then $\{G\}^*(\mathsf{y}, y')$ iff $\{G\}^*(\mathsf{y}, z)$. Thus $\forall z\{<\}^*y'\{G\}^*(\mathsf{y}, z)$ and $\{G\}^*(\mathsf{y}, y')$ iff $\forall z\{<\}^*yG(\mathsf{y}, z)$, i.e., $\{F\}^*(\mathsf{y}, y)$. ⊣

Lemma 6. *Let* $F(\mathsf{x})$ *be any* Σ *formula of* $\mathscr{L}$. *Then* $\mathrm{PA}\vdash\{T\}^* \wedge \mathsf{R}(\mathsf{x},\mathsf{y})\rightarrow(F(\mathsf{x})\rightarrow\{F\}^*(\mathsf{y}))$.

Proof. By Lemma 5 it suffices to deduce Lemma 6 for $\exists xF$ from Lemma 6 for $F, = F(\mathsf{x}, x)$. Work in PA. Suppose $\{T\}^*$ and $\mathsf{R}(\mathsf{x},\mathsf{y})$. By Lemma 1, for some $y, R(x, y)$. Thus if $F(\mathsf{x}, x)$, then by Lemma 6 for $F(\mathsf{x}, x)$, $\{F\}^*(\mathsf{y}, y)$, and then also $\exists x\{F\}^*(\mathsf{y}, x)$, i.e., $\{\exists xF\}^*(\mathsf{y})$. ⊣

Let $K(\mathsf{x})$ be a formula of arithmetic. The formula of arithmetic expressing that $K(\mathsf{x})$ *defines a recursive relation* is a formula built up from $K(\mathsf{x})$ stating that there is a Turing machine μ such that for every n-tuple i of natural numbers, μ outputs 0 (yes) if $K(\mathsf{i})$ holds and outputs 1 (no) if $K(\mathsf{i})$ does not hold.

Let D be the following formula of QML:

$$\begin{aligned}
&\Diamond\top \wedge \\
&\forall x(Zx\rightarrow\Box Zx)\wedge\forall x(\neg Zx\rightarrow\Box\neg Zx)\wedge \\
&\forall x\forall y(Exy\rightarrow\Box Exy)\wedge\forall x\forall y(\neg Exy\rightarrow\Box\neg Exy)\wedge \\
&\forall x\forall y(Sxy\rightarrow\Box Sxy)\wedge\forall x\forall y(\neg Sxy\rightarrow\Box\neg Sxy)\wedge \\
&\forall x\forall y\forall z(Axyz\rightarrow\Box Axyz)\wedge\forall x\forall y\forall z(\neg Axyz\rightarrow\Box\neg Axyz)\wedge \\
&\forall x\forall y\forall z(Mxyz\rightarrow\Box Mxyz)\wedge\forall x\forall y\forall z(\neg Mxyz\rightarrow\Box\neg Mxyz)
\end{aligned}$$

Lemma 7. $\mathrm{PA} \vdash D^* \to Z^*$, E^*, S^*, A^*, *and* M^* *define recursive relations.*

Proof. Work in PA. Suppose D^* holds. Then $(\Diamond \top)^*$ holds, i.e., arithmetic is consistent. Consider, e.g., A^*. The following algorithm decides A^*: Given numbers x, y, z, run through all proofs in PA until a proof of $A^*(\mathbf{x}, \mathbf{y}, \mathbf{z})$ or a proof of $\neg A^*(\mathbf{x}, \mathbf{y}, \mathbf{z})$ is found. If a proof of the former is found first, output 0; if a proof of the latter is found first, output 1. By the consistency of arithmetic, it is not the case that both have a proof; by the law of excluded middle, one or the other holds; and by the eighth and ninth conjuncts of D^*, whichever holds has a proof. ⊣

Lemma 8. $\mathrm{PA} \vdash \{T\}^* \wedge D^* \to \forall y \exists x R(x, y)$.

Before we begin the proof of Lemma 8, let us remark on the strategy of Lemmas 7 and 8. Think of $*$ as defining a model of some theory of the natural numbers, in the natural numbers. In this model, the numbers that satisfy Z^* will all represent zero; there may well be more than one of them, but they will all be E^*-equivalent. Lemma 1 assures us that every natural number has a representative in the model defined by *. We would like to arrange matters so that, "modulo" E^*-equivalence, the model is isomorphic to the standard model of arithmetic. Now it is a familiar fact that any model in which a certain small finite number of theorems of PA hold will have an initial segment that is isomorphic to the standard model, and according to Tennenbaum's theorem,[5] such a model will be standard if the relations assigned to $+$ and $\times$ are recursive.

The first use of Tennenbaum's theorem in a similar situation appears to be due to V. E. Plisko, who proved that the set of realizable formulas of the predicate calculus is not arithmetical.[6]

Lemma 7 has just shown us how, with the aid of a formula of QML, to guarantee that the relations assigned by $*$ to A and M are recursive. The consequent in Lemma 8 states that every number *is* a representative: the model is standard. Not surprisingly then, our proof of Lemma 8 recapitulates one of the usual proofs of Tennenbaum's theorem.

Proof of Lemma 8. Let $C(e, x, z)$ be a Σ formula defining the notion "*e* is the Gödel number of a Turing machine that halts on input *i* with output m". Let $C_0(x)$ and $C_1(x)$ be the Σ formulas $C(x, x, \mathbf{0})$ and $C(x, x, \mathbf{1})$. We may assume that T implies the sentence $\forall x \neg (C_0(x) \wedge C_1(x))$.

Let $B_0(a, b, i)$ and $B_1(a, b, i)$ be the formulas

$$\exists q(q \times (\mathbf{1} + (i + \mathbf{1}) \times b) = a)$$

and

$$\exists q((q \times (\mathbf{1} + (i + \mathbf{1}) \times b)) + \mathbf{1} = a)$$

β-function technology (applied to characteristic functions of the set defined by $F(x)$, so that remainders are either 0 or 1) shows that for any formula $F(x)$ of arithmetic, the following sentence is a theorem of PA:

$$\forall k \exists a \exists b \forall j < k((F(j) \leftrightarrow B_0(a, b, j)) \wedge (\neg F(j) \leftrightarrow B_1(a, b, j))$$

In particular, the sentence S

$$\forall k \exists a \exists b \forall j < k((C_0(j) \leftrightarrow B_0(a, b, j)) \wedge (\neg C_0(j) \leftrightarrow B_1(a, b, j))$$

is a theorem of PA. We assume that T implies S.

Now work in PA. Assume $\{T\}^*$ and D^*. Suppose, for reductio, that $\forall y \exists x R(x, y)$ is false. Let k be such that for no $r, R(r, k)$. Since T implies S, $\{T\}^*$ implies $\{S\}^*$, and S^* yields numbers a, b such that for every j, if $j\{<\}^*k$, then $\{C_0\}^*(j)$ iff $\{B_0\}^*(a, b, j)$ and not: $\{C_0\}^*(j)$ iff $\{B_1\}^*(a, b, j)$.

Since D^* holds, by Lemma 7, $Z^* E^*, S^*, A^*, M^*$ define recursive relations. Since Z^*, E^*, S^*, A^*, M^* define recursive relations, $\{B_0\}$ and $\{B_1\}$ are equivalent to formulas built up from Z, E, S, A, M by existential quantification, conjunction, and disjunction, and $\{B_0\}^*$ and $\{B_1\}^*$ therefore define r.e. relations.

It is apparent from the definition of the formula $R(x, y)$ that since Z^* and S^* are recursive, $R(x, y)$ also defines an r.e. relation.

We now describe the action of a certain Turing machine μ. Applied to any number i, μ begins by finding a number j such that $R(i,j)$ holds. According to Lemma 1, some such j will always exist, and since the formula $R(x, y)$ defines an r.e. relation, j can be found effectively. μ then looks for witnesses to the truth either of $\{B_0\}^*(a, b, j)$ or of $\{B_1\}^*(a, b, j)$. If it first finds a witness to the truth of $\{B_0\}^*(a, b, j)$ it outputs 1; if it first finds a witness to the truth of $\{B_1\}^*(a, b, j)$, it outputs 0.

We now show that μ is totally defined, that is, gives an output for every input. It is sufficient to show that if $R(i, j)$, then $j\{<\}^*k$, for if $j\{<\}^*k$, then since $C_0(j)$ either holds or does not hold, a witness to the truth of $\{B_0\}^*(a,b,j)$ or $\{B_1\}^*(a,b,j)$ will exist and so μ will output 1 or 0 on every input i. We may assume that T implies $\forall x\, \mathbf{0} \leqslant x$, $\forall x \forall x'(x < x' \rightarrow \mathrm{s}x \leqslant x')$, and $\forall x \forall x'(x \leqslant x' \wedge x \neq x' \rightarrow x < x')$. If $R(0,j)$, then by $\{T\}^*$, $j\{\leqslant\}^*k$. But $\neg R(0,k)$, and, by Lemma 2, $\neg E^*(j,k)$. Thus $j\{<\}^*k$. For the induction step, suppose that $R(i+1,j)$. Then for some j', $S^*(j',j)$, $R(i,j')$, and by the induction hypothesis, $j'\{<\}^*k$, whence $j\{\leqslant\}^*k$. But, again, since $\neg R(i+1,k)$, $\neg E^*(j,k)$ and so $j\{<\}^*k$. Thus for every i, if $R(i,j)$, $j\{<\}^*k$.

Now let i be an arbitrary number. Let j be the number such that $R(i,j)$ that is found by μ when given input i. By the above, $j\{<\}^*k$. If $C_0(i)$, then by Lemma 6, $\{C_0\}^*(j)$, and therefore $\{B_0\}^*(a,b,j)$ but not $\{B_1\}^*(a,b,j)$, thus μ outputs 1. If $C_1(i)$, by Lemma 6 again, $\{C_1\}^*(j)$, and then since T implies $\forall x \neg(C_0(x) \wedge C_1(x))$, not $\{C_0\}^*(j)$; therefore $\{B_1\}^*(a,b,j)$ but not $\{B_0\}^*(a,b,j)$; thus μ outputs 0.

Thus μ outputs 1 on input i if $C_0(i)$, and μ outputs 0 on input i if $C_1(i)$, for every naural number i.

It is, however, absurd that there should be such a machine μ. Otherwise, let e be its Gödel number. Then if $C_0(e)$ holds, μ outputs 1 on input e, $C(e,e,1)$, $C_1(e)$, and not $C_0(e)$; if not $C_0(e)$, then μ does not output 1 on input e, μ outputs 0 on input e, $C(e,e,0)$, and $C_0(e)$. The contradiction shows that $\forall y \exists x R(x,y)$ holds. ⊣

Artemov's lemma. *Let $F(\mathsf{x})$ be any formula of $\mathscr{L}$. Then* $\mathrm{PA} \vdash \{T\}^* \wedge D^* \wedge \mathsf{R}(\mathsf{x},\mathsf{y}) \rightarrow (F(\mathsf{x}) \leftrightarrow \{F\}^*(\mathsf{y}))$.

Proof. Artemov's lemma immediately follows from Lemmas 4, 7, and 8. ⊣

Theorem 1 (Artemov). *The class of always true sentences is not arithmetical.*

Proof. By Tarski's theorem, V is not arithmetical. To prove the theorem, it will suffice to show that there is a one–one effective function ! that reduces V to the class of sentences of QML that are always true.

For any sentence S of $\mathscr{L}$, let $S!$ be the sentence $\{T\} \wedge D \rightarrow \{S\}$ of QML. We show that S is true if and only if $S!$ is always true.

By specializing Artemov's lemma to the case in which $F(\mathsf{x})$ is a sentence of $\mathscr{L}$, we see that for every realization $*$, the sentence $\{T\}^* \wedge D^* \rightarrow (S \leftrightarrow \{S\}^*)$ is a theorem of PA and therefore true.

Suppose S true. The for every $*$, $\{T\}^* \wedge D^* \rightarrow \{S\}^*$ is true, and therefore $S!$ is always true.

Conversely, suppose $S!$ always true. Then, where $*$ is the realization that assigns $\mathbf{0} = v_0, v_0 = v_1, \mathbf{s}v_0 = v_1, v_0 + v_1 = v_2$, and $v_0 \times v_1 = v_2$ to Z, E, S, A, M, respectively, $\{T\}^* \wedge D^* \to \{S\}^*$ is true. But $\{T\}^*$ is equivalent to T, and hence true, and D^* is also true, by the consistency of arithmetic and provable Σ-completeness. Thus $\{S\}^*$ is true. But $\{S\}^*$ is equivalent to S. ⊣

The set of Gödel numbers of always provable sentences is not r.e.

We turn now to Vardanyan's result that the set of Gödel numbers of always provable sentences is not r.e., and therefore the always provable sentences cannot be axiomatized.

We remarked above that the set of Gödel numbers of always provable sentences is Π^0_2. In full detail: Let $R(i,j,k)$ if and only if (i is the Gödel number of a sentence S of QML and if j is the Gödel number of a realization $*$ that assigns formulas of $\mathscr{L}$ to all and only the predicate letters of S, then k is the Gödel number of a proof in PA of the result of substituting in S for those predicate letters the formulas assigned to them by $*$). Then R is a recursive relation, and i is the Gödel number of an always provable sentence if and only if for every j there is a k such that $R(i, j, k)$.

We want now to prove that the set of Gödel numbers of always provable sentences is Π^0_2-complete. To do so, we need an alternative characterization of the Π^0_2 sets.

Lemma 9. *S is a Π^0_2 set if and only if for some recursive relation P, $S = \{n: \forall i \exists j (j > i \wedge P(n,j))\}$.*

Proof. Suppose that $S = \{n: \forall e \exists m R(n, e, m)\}$, with R recursive. Let $P(n, j)$ iff j is (the Gödel number of) a finite sequence such that for all $e <$ the length of j, j_e is the least m such that $R(n, e, m)$. P is recursive. If $n \in S$, then for every natural number e there will be such a finite sequence with length $e + 1$, and thus there will be infinitely many such finite sequences. And if there are infinitely many such sequences, then since any two of them have the same values for arguments less than their length, there will be at least one such sequence y of length $e + 1$, and then $R(n, e, j_e)$. Thus $S = \{n: \forall i \exists j (j > i \wedge P(n, j))\}$.

Conversely, if P is recursive and $S = \{n: \forall i \exists j (j > i \wedge P(n, j))\}$, then S is visibly Π^0_2. ⊣

Theorem 2 (Vardanyan). *The class of always provable sentences is* Π^0_2*-complete.*

Proof. Suppose that S is Π^0_2. Since the class of always provable sentences is itself Π^0_2, to prove the theorem it suffices to show how to effectively associate with each natural number n, a sentence ϕ_n of QML such that $S = \{n\text{: for all } *,\ \mathrm{PA} \vdash \phi_n^*\}$.

By Lemma 9, let P be a recursive relation such that $S = \{n{:}\ \forall i \exists j (j > i \wedge P(n, j))\}$.

Let Q be a Σ formula that defines P.

Let E be the sentence $\forall z \forall z'(Ezz' \rightarrow (\Box\, Gz \leftrightarrow \Box\, Gz'))$ of QML.

Write $Q(\mathbf{n}, y)$ as $Q_n(y)$.

Let $H(v, z)$ be a Σ formula naturally formalizing "v is the Gödel number of a Turing machine that halts on input z". We may take $H(v, z)$ to be $\exists y C(v, z, y)$, with C as in Lemma 8.

For each n, let ϕ_n be the QML sentence

$$\{T\} \wedge D \wedge E \rightarrow \exists v \exists w (v\{<\}w \wedge \{Q_n\}(w) \wedge \forall z(\Box\, Gz \leftrightarrow \{H\}(v, z)))$$

We are to show that $n \in S$ if and only if for every $*$, $\mathrm{PA} \vdash \phi_n^*$.

Suppose $n \in S$. Let $*$ be arbitrary. We show that $\mathrm{PA} \vdash \phi_n^*$, i.e.,

$$\mathrm{PA} \vdash \{T\}^* \wedge D^* \wedge E^*$$
$$\rightarrow \exists v \exists w (v\{<\}^* w \wedge Q_n\}^*(w) \wedge \forall z(\mathrm{Bew}[G^*(z)] \leftrightarrow \{H\}^*(v, z))).$$

(1) For some natural number x,

$$\mathrm{PA} \vdash D^* \rightarrow ((\exists z(R(z_0, z) \wedge \mathrm{Bew}[G^*(z)]) \leftrightarrow H(\mathbf{x}, z_0))$$

Proof. Work in PA. Suppose D^* holds. Then, by the argument of the proof of Lemma 7, Z^*, E^*, S^*, A^*, and M^* are all equivalent to Σ formulas, for (e.g.) i, j satisfy S^* iff there is a proof of $S^*(\mathbf{i}, \mathbf{j})$ with a smaller Gödel number than any proof of $\neg S^*(\mathbf{i}, \mathbf{j})$, a property of pairs of numbers defined by a Σ formula. Therefore $R(z_0, z)$ is a Σ formula, and since $\mathrm{Bew}[G^*(z)]$ is also Σ, so is the left-hand side of the consequent. It is routine to show by induction on the construction of strict Σ formulas that for every strict Σ formula $F(\mathrm{z})$, there is (a Gödel number of) a Turing machine μ such that it is provable in PA that μ halts on just those numbers that satisfy $F(\mathrm{z})$. But the left side the consequent is a Σ formula, and hence equivalent to some strict Σ formula. $\dashv$

Now fix the number x as in (1).

(2) $\mathrm{PA} \vdash \{T\}^* \wedge D^* \wedge E^* \wedge R(z_0, z) \rightarrow (\mathrm{Bew}[G^*(z)] \leftrightarrow H(\mathbf{x}, z_0)).$

Proof. Work in PA. Assume the antecedent. By (1), if Bew$[G^*(z)]$, $H(\mathbf{x}, z_0)$. Conversely, assume $H(\mathbf{x}, z_0)$. By Lemma 1, for some z', $R(z_0, z')$ and Bew$[G^*(z')]$. By Lemma 3, since $R(z_0, z)$ and $R(z_0, z')$, $E^*(z, z')$. But then by E^*, Bew$[G^*(z)]$. ⊣

(3) $\mathrm{PA} \vdash \{T\}^* \wedge D^* \wedge R(\mathbf{x}, v) \wedge R(z_0, z) \rightarrow (H(\mathbf{x}, z_0) \leftrightarrow \{H\}^*(v, z))$.

Proof. (3) is an instance of Artemov's lemma. ⊣

By (2) and (3),

(4) $\mathrm{PA} \vdash \{T\}^* \wedge D^* \wedge E^* \wedge R(\mathbf{x}, v) \wedge R(z_0, z)$
$\rightarrow (\mathrm{Bew}[G^*(z)] \leftrightarrow \{H\}^*(v, z))$

By Lemma 8, $\mathrm{PA} \vdash \{T\}^* \wedge D^* \rightarrow \forall y \exists x R(x, y)$. Thus from (4), we have

(5) $\mathrm{PA} \vdash \{T\}^* \wedge D^* \wedge E^* \wedge R(\mathbf{x}, v) \rightarrow \forall z(\mathrm{Bew}[G^*(z)] \leftrightarrow \{H\}^*(v, z))$

Now, as we have supposed, $n \in S$. Thus there exists a number y such that $x < y$ and $Q_n(y)$ holds. Another application of Artemov's lemma yields

(6) $\mathrm{PA} \vdash \{T\}^* \wedge D^* \wedge R(\mathbf{x}, v) \wedge R(\mathbf{y}, w)$
$\rightarrow (\mathbf{x} < \mathbf{y} \wedge Q_n(\mathbf{y}) \leftrightarrow (v\{<\}^* w \wedge \{Q_n\}^*(w)))$

Since Q and $x < y$ are Σ,

(7) $\mathrm{PA} \vdash (\mathbf{x} < \mathbf{y} \wedge Q_n(\mathbf{y}))$

Thus from (6) and (7) we have

(8) $\mathrm{PA} \vdash \{T\}^* \wedge D^* \wedge R(\mathbf{x}, v) \wedge R(\mathbf{y}, w) \rightarrow (v\{<\}^* w \wedge \{Q_n\}^*(w))$

Together with (5), (8) yields

(9) $\mathrm{PA} \vdash \{T\}^* \wedge D^* \wedge E^* \wedge R(\mathbf{x}, v) \wedge R(\mathbf{y}, w)$
$\rightarrow ((v\{<\}^* w \wedge \{Q_n\}^*(w)) \wedge \forall z(\mathrm{Bew}[G^*(z)] \leftrightarrow \{H\}^*(v, z)))$

By the predicate calculus,

(10) $\mathrm{PA} \vdash \{T\}^* \wedge D^* \wedge E^* \wedge \exists v R(\mathbf{x}, v) \wedge \exists w R(\mathbf{y}, w)$
$\rightarrow \exists v \exists w((v\{<\}^* w \wedge \{Q_n\}^*(w)) \wedge$
$\forall z(\mathrm{Bew}[G^*(z)] \leftrightarrow \{H\}^*(v, z)))$

Since by Lemma 1, $\mathrm{PA} \vdash \{T\}^* \rightarrow \exists v R(\mathbf{x}, v) \wedge \exists w R(\mathbf{y}, w)$, it follows from (10) that

$$\text{PA} \vdash \{T\}^* \wedge D^* \wedge E^*$$
$$\rightarrow \exists v \exists w (v\{<\}^* w \wedge \{Q_n\}^*(w) \wedge \forall z(\text{Bew}[G^*(z)] \leftrightarrow \{H\}^*(v, z))),$$

which is what we were trying to prove.

Conversely, suppose that for every $*$, $\text{PA} \vdash \phi_n^*$. We shall show that $n \in S$.

We consider a series of realizations $*^i$, differing only in what they assign to G: In $*^i$, Z, E, S, A, M are all standardly interpreted, i.e., A^{*i} is the formula $v_0 + v_1 = v_2$, etc., and G^{*i} is the formula $v_0 = \mathbf{i}$.

Let us observe that every theorem of PA is true and that for every realization $*$ in which Z, E, S, A, M are standardly interpreted, $\{T\}^* \wedge D^* \wedge E^*$ is true. Thus for each i, $\exists v \exists w (v\{<\}w \wedge \{Q_n\}(w) \wedge \forall z(\Box Gz \leftrightarrow \{H\}(v, z)))$ $*^i$ is true. But that is to say – since $*^i$ treats Z, E, S, A, M standardly – that for each i, there exist natural numbers v, w such that $v < w$, $Q_n(w)$ holds, and for all z, $\mathbf{z} = \mathbf{i}$ is provable if and only if the Turing machine with Gödel number v halts on z. By the consistency of arithmetic, $\mathbf{z} = \mathbf{i}$ is provable if and only if $z = i$, and therefore for each i, there exist natural numbers v, w such that $v < w$, $Q_n(w)$ holds, and the Turing machine with Gödel number v halts on i and i alone. Of course, if the Turing machine with Gödel number v halts on i and i alone, the Turing machine with Gödel number v' halts on i' and i' alone, and $i \neq i'$, then $v \neq v'$. Thus for each i, there exist numbers v and w, with different v for different i, such that $v < w$ and $Q_n(w)$. Thus there are infinitely many numbers v such that for some w, $v < w$ and $Q_n(w)$. Thus for every x, for some w, $x < w$ and $Q_n(w)$, i.e., $n \in S$. Theorem 2 is proved.

The class of always true sentences is Π_1^0-complete in V

Our final major result in this chapter is a characterization of the class of always true sentences.

V_0 is the set of Gödel numbers of true atomic sentences of $\mathscr{L}$. V_0 is a recursive set.

Theorem 3 (McGee, Vardanyan, Boolos). *The class of always true sentences is Π_1^0-complete in V.*

The proof will require a number of definitions and lemmas.

Let $F(\mathsf{x})$ be any formula of $\mathscr{L}^+$. We shall say that $F(a_1, \ldots, a_n)$ holds *at* the set A of natural numbers if $F(\mathsf{x})$ is satisfied by numbers $a_1, \ldots, a_n$ when A is assigned to the predicate letter G.

Let $I = \{T\} \wedge D \wedge \forall x \forall x'(Gx' \wedge Exx' \rightarrow Gx)$.

Lemma 10. *Let $F(\mathsf{x})$ be any formula of $\mathscr{L}^+$ and let $*$ be any realization of I. Suppose that I^* is true, $A = \{a$: for some b,*

$R(a,b)$ and $G^*(b)$ hold\}, and $R(a_1,b_1),\ldots,R(a_n,b_n)$ hold. Then $F(a_1,\ldots,a_n)$ holds at A if and only if $\{F\}^*(b_1,\ldots,b_n)$ holds.

Proof. An induction like the one in the proof of Lemma 4. Lemma 3 takes care of all atomic cases except the one in which the formula is of the form Gu.

As for that case, suppose $R(a,b)$ holds. Assume $G(a)$ holds at A. Then for some $b, R(a,b')$ and $G^*(b')$ hold. By Lemma 3(a), $E^*(b,b')$ holds. Since $\forall x\forall y(Gx \wedge Exy \to Gy)^*$ is true, $G^*(b)$ holds. The converse is immediate from the definition of A. Thus if $R(a,b)$ holds, then $G(a)$ holds at A iff $G^*(b)$ holds.

The truth-functional cases are treated as usual, and since $\{T\}^*$ and D^* are true, so are $\forall x\exists yR(x,y)$ and $\forall y\exists xR(x,y)$ (Lemmas 1 and 8), and these suffice to handle the quantifier cases. ⊣

Lemma 11. *Let F be any sentence of $\mathscr{L}^+$ and let $*$ be any realization of I. Suppose that I^* is true and $A = \{a$: for some b, $R(a,b)$ and $G^*(b)$ hold\}. Then F holds at A if and only if $\{F\}^*$ is true.*

Proof. Lemma 11 is the special case of Lemma 10 in which F has no free variables. ⊣

We shall say that sets A and B of natural numbers are *k-equivalent* if for every $m \leqslant k$, $m \in A$ iff $m \in B$.

Lemma 12. *If $T^A(e,i,k)$ and A and B are k-equivalent, then $T^B(e,i,k)$.*

Proof. Any number about which an inquiry is made of an oracle in the course of a computation is less than the Gödel number of that computation. Thus if k is correct for A (see the brief review), k is also correct for B. ⊣

Let us now say that A *m-approximates* V if the following condition holds:

[(m is not (the Gödel number of) a sentence of $\mathscr{L} \to m \notin A$) $\wedge$
(m is a sentence of $\mathscr{L} \to$
$\forall n$(n is a subsentence of the sentence $m \to$
[n is an atomic sentence $\to (n \in A \leftrightarrow n \in V_0)$] $\wedge$
[n is a conditional $F \to F' \to (n \in A \leftrightarrow (F \in A \to F' \in A))$] $\wedge$
[n is a universal quantification $\forall x F \to$
$(n \in A \leftrightarrow$ for all i, $F_x(i) \in A)$])))]

(For each $i, F_x(\mathbf{i})$ counts as a subsentence of $\forall xF$, of course.)

Now let $F(x, y)$, $= F(x, y, G)$, be the formula of $\mathscr{L}^+$ expressing: $\forall m(\forall j < m \neg T^A(e, i, j) \rightarrow A$ m-approximates V). Here x, y, G symbolize e, i, A, respectively.

Lemma 13. *Suppose that A is arithmetical and* $F(\mathbf{e}, \mathbf{i})$ *holds at A. Then for some k,* $T^A(e, i, k)$.

Proof. If for all k, $\neg T^A(e, i, k)$, then for all m, A m-approximates V and hence is identical with V. But V is not arithmetical. ⊣

For each e, i, let $\psi_{e,i}$ be the sentence $I \wedge \{F(\mathbf{e}, \mathbf{i})\}$.

Lemma 14. $\exists k T^V(e, i, k)$ *iff for some* $*$, $\psi^*_{e,i}$ *is true.*

Proof. Suppose $T^V(e, i, k)$. Let r be a number greater than the number of occurrences of logical operators in any sentence of $\mathscr{L}$ with Gödel number $\leqslant k$. Let A be the set of Gödel numbers of true sentences of $\mathscr{L}$ that contain $< r$ occurrences of the logical operators. A is an arithmetical set and is k-equivalent to V (for if $m \leqslant k$ and m is the Gödel number of a sentence S, then the number of logical symbols in S is $< r$, and then $m \in A$ iff $m \in V$; if m is not the Gödel number of a sentence, then m is not in A or V). By Lemma 12, $T^A(e, i. k)$. Moreover, $F(\mathbf{e}, \mathbf{i})$ holds at A, for if $\forall j < m \neg T^A(e, i, j)$, then $m \leqslant k$, and since A is the set of Gödel numbers of true sentences of $\mathscr{L}$ that contain $< r$ occurrences of the logical operators, A m-approximates V.

Now define $*$ as follows. Let $B(v_0)$ be a formula of $\mathscr{L}$ defining the arithmetical set A. Let Z, E, S, A, M receive their standard realizations (M^* is $v_0 \times v_1 = v_2$, etc.), and let G^* be $B(v_0)$. Then D^*, $\{T\}^*$, and $\forall x \forall x'(Gx' \wedge Exx' \rightarrow Gx)^*$ are true; thus I^* is true. Moreover, since $R(a, b)$ holds iff $a = b$, $A = \{a$: for some b, $R(a, b)$ and $G^*(b)$ hold$\}$. By Lemma 11, then, $\{F(\mathbf{e}, \mathbf{i})\}^*$ is true, and therefore so is $\psi^*_{e,i}$.

Conversely, suppose that $\psi^*_{e,i}$ is true.

Let $A = \{a$: for some b, $R(a, b)$ and $G^*(b)$ hold$\}$. Z^* and S^* define arithmetical relations, and therefore so does $R(x, y)$. Since G^* also defines an arithmetical set, A is also arithmetical. Since I^* and $\{F(\mathbf{e}, \mathbf{i})\}^*$ are true, by Lemma 11, $F(\mathbf{e}, \mathbf{i})$ holds at A. By Lemma 13, for some k, $T^A(e, i, k)$. Now suppose $m \leqslant k$. Then $\forall j < m \neg T^A(e, i, j)$, and since $F(\mathbf{e}, \mathbf{i})$ holds at A, A m-approximates V. Thus if m is not the Gödel number of a sentence, m is not in A or V, but if m is the Gödel number of a sentence F, then by induction on subsentences

F' of F, if n is the Gödel number of a subsentence F' of F, then $n \in A$ iff F' is true, iff $n \in V$. Therefore $m \in A$ iff $m \in V$, A is k-equivalent to V, and by Lemma 12, $T^V(e, i, k)$. $\dashv$

We can now prove Theorem 3. The set of Gödel numbers of always true sentences is itself Π^0_1 in V: Let $U(i, j)$ if and only if (i is the Gödel number of a sentence S of QML and if j is the Gödel number of a realization $*$ that assigns formulas of $\mathscr{L}$ to all and only the predicate letters of S, then the result of substituting in S for those predicate letters the formulas assigned to them by $*$ is true). U is recursive in V, and a sentence is always true iff its Gödel number is in $\{i: \forall j U(i, j)\}$.

Now let A be an arbitrary set that is Π^0_1 in V. Then $N-A$ is Σ^0_1 in V, and thus for some e, $N-A = \{i: \exists k T^V(e, i, k)\}$. By Lemma 14, $N-A = \{i$: for some $*$, $\psi^*_{e,i}$ is true$\}$. Therefore $A = \{i: \neg \psi_{e,i}$ is always true$\}$. Theorem 3 is thus proved, for we have shown how to effectively find from an arbitrary i a sentence ϕ_i of QML so that $A = \{i: \phi_i$ is always true$\}$: take $\phi_i = \neg \psi_{e,i}$.

For a change, let us look at an interesting class of quantified modal sentences that is easily seen to be decidable.

Let K= be the system of quantified modal logic in which $=$ is the sole predicate letter and whose rules and axioms are those of quantification theory, the modal system K, and all formulas

(1) $\exists x(x \neq y_1 \wedge \cdots \wedge x \neq y_n) \qquad (n \geqslant 1)$

and the formula

(2) $(x \neq y \rightarrow \Box x \neq y)$

Consideration of K= will enable us to give an effective procedure for deciding the truth-values of sentences of PA built up from identities (formulas $x = y$), $\top$, and $\bot$ by means of truth-functional operators, quantifiers, and the formula Bew(x).

Theorem 4. *Every formula A of* K= *is equivalent (in* K=*) to a truth-functional combination of identities and letterless sentences that contains no free variables not free in A.*

Proof. To prove the theorem it clearly suffices to suppose that A is a truth-functional combination of identities and letterless sentences and to show that $\exists x A$ and $\Box A$ are equivalent to truth-functional combinations of identities and letterless sentences that contain no free variables not free in A.

$\exists xA$ can be treated in routine fashion. Rewrite A as a disjunction $(C_1 \wedge D_1) \vee \cdots \vee (C_n \wedge D_n)$ in which each C_i is a (possibly null) conjunction of identities and negations of identities containing the variable x and D_i is a conjunction of letterless sentences and identities and negations of identities not containing x. Then $\exists xA$ is equivalent to $(\exists xC_1 \wedge D_1) \vee \cdots \vee (\exists xC_n \wedge D_n)$. It is thus enough to show $\exists x_i C_i$ equivalent to $\top$, to $\bot$, or to a (possibly null) conjunction of identities and negations of identities containing no new free variables. If $x \neq x$ is a conjunct of C_i, then $\exists xC_i$ is equivalent to $\bot$. The identity $x = x$ may be deleted from C_i. If x occurs in some identity $x = y$ or $y = x$ in C_i, then $\exists xC_i$ is equivalent to the result of replacing x by y everywhere in C_i, a formula of the requisite sort; otherwise C_i is a conjunction of negations $x \neq y$ and $y \neq x$ of identities. But then by (1), $\exists xC_i$ is equivalent to $\top$.

As for $\Box A$, call a formula an *n-formula*, $n \geqslant 0$, if it is a truth-functional combination of letterless sentences, (any number of) identities, and formulas $\Box B$, where B is a truth-functional combination of letterless sentences and at most n identities. A 0-formula is thus a truth-functional combination of identities and letterless sentences, and $\Box A$ is an m-formula for some m. Thus it suffices to show that any $(n+1)$-formula is equivalent to an n-formula containing the same free variables. Suppose that C is an $(n+1)$-formula. Let $x = y$ be a subformula of some formula B such that $\Box B$ is a truth-functional component of C; let C' (C'') be the result of replacing each occurrence in C of $x = y$ by an occurrence of $\top$ $(\bot)$, and let $C!$ be the formula $(x = y \wedge C') \vee (x \neq y \wedge C'')$. $C!$ is an n-formula containing the same free variables as C. Moreover, $C!$ is equivalent to C: For since $x = y \rightarrow (\Box x = x \rightarrow \Box x = y)$ and $\Box x = x$ are theorems of K=, so is

(3) $(x = y \rightarrow \Box x = y)$

And since no identity in C occurs in the scope of two or more nested $\Box$s,

(4) $(x = y \wedge \Box x = y) \rightarrow (C \leftrightarrow C')$

(5) $(x \neq y \wedge \Box x \neq y) \rightarrow (C \leftrightarrow C'')$

are theorems of K=. But (2), (3), (4), and (5) truth-functionally imply $(C \leftrightarrow C!)$. $\dashv$

It follows from the theorem that every quantified modal sentence containing no predicate letter except = is equivalent in K= to a truth-functional combination of letterless sentences. The standard translation (on which $=*$ is $=$) of any formula (1) is obviously provable in PA, and by provable Σ_1-completeness so is that of (2). Since the translations of the other theorems of K= are also provable in PA, it follows that every sentence of PA built up from identities, $\top$, and $\bot$ by means of truth-functional operators, quantifiers, and Bew(x) is equivalent in PA to a sentence of PA built up from $\top$ and $\bot$ by means of truth-functional operators and Bew(x). The procedure given in Chapter 7 for deciding the truth-values of sentences in the latter class thus provides a decision procedure for deciding those in the wider former class.

A somewhat surprising corollary of Theorem 4, the result with which we shall conclude this chapter, is another theorem due to Vardanyan.

Theorem 5. *The Craig interpolation lemma fails for the class of always provable sentences.*

Proof. Let Z', E', S', A', M' be new predicate letters of the same degrees as Z, E, S, A, M, and for each quantified modal formula X let X' be the result of priming each predicate letter in X. Let 1 Con be the sentence of $\mathscr{L}$ saying that PA is 1-consistent.

We redefine D by deleting its first conjunct $\Diamond\top$.

The conditional $\{T\} \wedge D \wedge \{1\,\text{Con}\} \to (\{T\}' \wedge D' \to (\Box\bot \vee \{1\,\text{Con}\}'))$ is always provable: for if $*$ is any realization, then by Artemov's lemma, $\text{PA} \vdash \{T\}^* \wedge D^* \to (\Box\bot^* \vee (1\,\text{Con} \leftrightarrow \{1\,\text{Con}\}^*))$ and $\text{PA} \vdash \{T\}'^* \wedge D'^* \to (\Box\bot^* \vee (1\,\text{Con} \leftrightarrow \{1\,\text{Con}\}'^*))$, and therefore $\text{PA} \vdash \{T\}^* \wedge D^* \wedge \{1\,\text{Con}\}^* \to (\{T\}'^* \wedge D'^* \to (\Box\bot^* \vee \{1\,\text{Con}\}'^*))$.

Suppose now that B is an interpolation formula for this conditional. There are no predicate letters in the language of B except possibly $=$. Existentially closing, we may suppose that B is a sentence. Let $C = (B \wedge \neg\Box\bot)$. By Theorem 4, C is equivalent in K= to some truth-functional combination of sentences of the form $\Box^n\bot$. Let $*$ be the standard realization, i.e., $A^* = A'^* = v_1 + v_2 = v_3$, etc. By provable Σ_1-completeness, under the new definition of D, $\text{PA} \vdash \{T\}^* \wedge \{T\}'^* \wedge D^* \wedge D'^*$. In addition, $\{1\,\text{Con}\}^* = \{1\,\text{Con}\}'^* =$ 1 Con. Thus $\text{PA} \vdash 1\,\text{Con} \to B^*$ and $\text{PA} \vdash B^* \to (\Box\bot^* \vee 1\,\text{Con})$. Since $\text{PA} \vdash 1\,\text{Con} \to \neg\Box\bot^*$, $\text{PA} \vdash C^* \leftrightarrow 1\,\text{Con}$. But then 1 Con is equivalent to some truth-functional combination of sentences of the form $\Box^n\bot^*$, which by Theorem 6 of Chapter 7 is certainly not the case, since 1 Con is true and implies $\neg\Box^n\bot$ for all n. $\dashv$

18

Quantified provability logic with one one-place predicate letter[1]

Let G be a one-place predicate letter. The aim of the present chapter is to demonstrate the remarkable result of V. A. Vardanyan according to which Theorems 2 and 3 (and hence also Theorem 1) of the previous chapter hold good even for the language $\{G\}$ of quantified modal logic in whose formulas no occurrence of $\Box$ lies within the scope of another occurrence of $\Box$ and in which *no predicate letter other than G occurs.* That is to say, the class of always provable sentences of $\{G\}$ is Π_2^0-complete and the class of always true sentences of $\{G\}$ is Π_1^0-complete in the truth set V. Readers are warned that although the proofs of these results contain much ingenuity and trickery, they are torturously intricate. It is quite possible that simpler proofs exist, but needless to say, none are known to the author.

We begin by defining two one-place relations of natural numbers, Z and Y; three two-place relations; V, A', and M'; and two three-place relations, A'' and M'':

Zi iff $i = 0$;
Yi iff $i = 1$;
Vij iff either $i = j + 1$ or $j = i + 1$;
$A'ij$ iff $i \neq j$ and either $i + i = j$ or $j + j = i$;
$M'ij$ iff $i \neq j$ and either $i \times i = j$ or $j \times j = i$;
$A''ijk$ iff $i \neq j \neq k \neq i$ and either $i + j = k$ or $j + k = i$ or $k + i = j$; and
$M''ijk$ iff $i \neq j \neq k \neq i$ and either $i \times j = k$ or $j \times k = i$ or $k \times i = j$.

Like $\neq$, each of the relations Z, Y, V, A', M', A'', and M'' holds of an n-tuple of numbers only if all coordinates of the n-tuple are distinct and holds of an n-tuple iff it holds of any permutation of that n-tuple. (This is trivially so for Z and Y.)

Lemma 1. *Identity, zero, successor, addition, and multiplication are all definable from $Z, Y, \neq, V, A', M', A'', M''$, and $\leqslant$ by means of $\wedge$ and $\vee$ alone.*

Proof. $i=j$ iff $(i \leqslant j \wedge j \leqslant i)$. $S(i,j)$ iff $(Vij \wedge i \leqslant j)$. $A(i,j,k)$ iff $([(Zi \wedge j=k] \vee [Zj \wedge i=k] \vee [A'ik \wedge i=j] \vee [A''ijk \wedge i \leqslant k \wedge j \leqslant k])$. $M(i,j,k)$ iff $([(Zi \vee Zj) \wedge Zk] \vee [Yi \wedge j=k] \vee [Yj \wedge i=k] \vee [M'ik \wedge i=j] \vee [M''ijk \wedge i \leqslant k \wedge j \leqslant k])$. ⊣

We shall use Z, Y, $\neq$, V, A', M', A'', M'', and $\leqslant$ both as relation letters in a modal language and as denoting the relations of natural numbers just introduced (or, in the case of $\neq$ and $\leqslant$, the relations they standardly denote).

Let $\mathscr{S}$ be the language (of the pure predicate calculus) whose predicate letters are $\leqslant$, Z, Y, $\neq$, V, A', M', A'', and M''.

Let T be the conjunction of the axioms of a sufficiently rich finite theory of arithmetic expressed in $\mathscr{S}$; each of the conjuncts of T is assumed provable in PA under the definitions of the predicate letters of $\mathscr{S}$ given above. As in the previous chapter, the meaning of "sufficiently rich" will emerge as we proceed. But for now we will assume that among the conjuncts of T are certain sentences of a logical character such as $\forall x\, x=x$, i.e., $\forall x(x \leqslant x \wedge x \leqslant x)$ and others expressing the existence and uniqueness of zero and (ordinary) successor, sum, and product, which are not certified as valid in the pure predicate calculus, as well as translations into $\mathscr{S}$ of the first six axioms of PA and other sentences describing elementary properties of zero, successor, sum, product, and less-than. Lemma 1 and the definitions of the relations Z, Y, V, A', M', A'', M'' provide standard translations between the languages $\mathscr{S}$ and $\mathscr{L}$. Where necessary, we tacitly assume standard translations between these languages to have been made.

Let G and N be two new one-place relation letters.

We reserve ten individual variables y_π, one for each of the ten predicate letters π of $\mathscr{S} \cup \{N\}$. We call these the special variables.

We shall consider realizations $*$ of the formulas of the language $\mathscr{S} \cup \{G, N\}$; we now allow the possibility, however, that in addition to $v_0, v_1, \ldots, v_{n-1}$, the formula π^* of PA assigned by $*$ to an n-place predicate letter π of $\mathscr{S} \cup \{N\}$ may also contain its special variable as a free variable.

By a Σ realization, we mean a realization that assigns Σ formulas to the ten predicate letters of $\mathscr{S} \cup \{N\}$. (A Σ realization may assign a formula that is not Σ to G.)

For any formula ρ of $\mathscr{S} \cup \{G\}$, let ρ^N be the result of relativizing all quantifiers in ρ to N. Of course, if ρ contains no quantifiers, e.g., if ρ is $x \neq y$, then ρ^N is ρ. Two of the conjuncts of T^N may thus be assumed to be $\{\exists x Zx\}^N$ and $\{\forall x \exists y S(x,y)\}^N$.

Let $*$ be an arbitrary Σ realization.

Let $*$ $R(x, y)$, or $R(x, y)$ for short, be the formula

$$\exists s(\mathrm{FinSeq}(s) \wedge lh(s) = x + \mathbf{1} \wedge \forall z \leqslant x N^*(s_z) \wedge Z^*(s_0) \\ \wedge \forall z < x(V^*(s_z, s_{z+1}) \wedge s_z \leqslant {}^* s_{z+1}) \wedge s_x = y)$$

$R(x, y)$ says that y is the image of x in the model determined by $*$: there is a finite sequence each of whose values is in the extension of N^*, whose first value is in the extension of Z^*, each of whose values except the first is the $*$-successor of the previous one, and whose last value is y. Since N^*, Z^*, V^* and $\leqslant^*$ are all Σ formulas, $R(x, y)$ is Σ too. It should be borne in mind that $\mathrm{PA} \vdash R(x, y) \rightarrow N^*(y)$.

Our immediate aim is to prove Lemma 10 (below), a version of Artemov's lemma in which D^* is omitted from the antecedent.

Lemma 2. $\mathrm{PA} \vdash T^{N*} \rightarrow \forall x \exists y R(x, y)$.

Proof. Like that of Lemma 17.1. We work in PA, assume T^{N*}, and proceed by induction on x. We need to observe here for the basis of the induction that since $\exists x Z x$ is a conjunct of T, by T^{N*}, for some y such that $N^*(y)$, $Z^*(y)$, and for the induction step, that since $\forall x \exists x' S(x, x')$ is also a conjunct of T, if $N^*(y)$, then for some y', $N^*(y)$ and $S^*(y, y')$. ⊣

Lemma 3. $\mathrm{PA} \vdash T^{N*} \wedge R(x, y) \wedge N^*(y') \wedge E^*(y, y') \rightarrow R(x, y')$.

Proof. Like that of Lemma 17.2 ⊣

Lemma 4

(a) $\mathrm{PA} \vdash T^{N*} \wedge R(x, y) \rightarrow [Zx \leftrightarrow Z^*(y)]$;
(b) $\mathrm{PA} \vdash T^{N*} \wedge R(x, y) \rightarrow [Yx \leftrightarrow Y^*(y)]$;
(c) $\mathrm{PA} \vdash T^{N*} \wedge R(x, y) \wedge R(x', y') \rightarrow [x \leqslant x' \leftrightarrow y \leqslant {}^* y']$;
(d) $\mathrm{PA} \vdash T^{N*} \wedge R(x, y) \wedge R(x', y') \rightarrow [x \neq x' \leftrightarrow y \neq {}^* y']$;
(e) $\mathrm{PA} \vdash T^{N*} \wedge R(x, y) \wedge R(x', y') \rightarrow [Vxx' \leftrightarrow V^*(y, y')]$;
(f) $\mathrm{PA} \vdash T^{N*} \wedge R(x, y) \wedge R(x', y') \rightarrow [A'xx' \leftrightarrow A'^*(y, y')]$;
(g) $\mathrm{PA} \vdash T^{N*} \wedge R(x, y) \wedge R(x', y') \rightarrow [M'xx' \leftrightarrow M'^*(y, y')]$;
(h) $\mathrm{PA} \vdash T^{N*} \wedge R(x, y) \wedge R(x', y') \wedge R(x'', y'') \rightarrow [A''xx'x'' \leftrightarrow A''^*(y, y', y'')]$;
(i) $\mathrm{PA} \vdash T^{N*} \wedge R(x, y) \wedge R(x', y') \wedge R(x'', y'') \rightarrow [M''xx'x'' \leftrightarrow M''^*(y, y', y'')]$.

Proof. Like that of 17.3. ⊣

Lemma 5. *Let $F(\mathrm{x})$ be any formula of $\mathscr{S}$. Then* $\mathrm{PA} \vdash T^{N*} \wedge \forall y(N^*(y) \to \exists x R(x, y)) \wedge R(\mathrm{x}, \mathrm{y}) \to [F(\mathrm{x}) \leftrightarrow F^{N*}(\mathrm{y})]$.

Proof. Like that of 17.4. Note that if $R(x, y)$, $N^*(y)$. ⊣

Lemma 6. *Let $F(\mathrm{x})$ be any bounded formula of $\mathscr{S}$. Then* $\mathrm{PA} \vdash T^{N*} \wedge R(\mathrm{x}, \mathrm{y}) \to [F(\mathrm{x}) \leftrightarrow F^{N*}(\mathrm{y})]$.

Proof. Like that of 17.5. ⊣

Lemma 7. *Let $F(\mathrm{x})$ be any Σ formula of $\mathscr{S}$. Then* $\mathrm{PA} \vdash T^{N*} \wedge R(\mathrm{x}, \mathrm{y}) \to [F(\mathrm{x}) \to F^{N*}(\mathrm{y})]$.

Proof. Like that of 17.6. By Lemma 6 it suffices to deduce Lemma 7 for $F(\mathrm{x})$, $= \exists x F(\mathrm{x}, x)$, from Lemma 7 for $F(\mathrm{x}, x)$. Work in PA. Suppose T^{N*} and $R(\mathrm{x}, \mathrm{y})$ hold. If $F(\mathrm{x}, x)$ holds, then by Lemma 1, for some y, so does $R(x, y)$, whence by Lemma 7 for $F, F^{N*}(\mathrm{y}, y)$ holds, and then, since $N^*(y)$ holds, so does $\exists x(N^*(x) \wedge F^{N*}(\mathrm{y}, x))$, i.e., $F^{N*}(\mathrm{y})$. ⊣

Lemma 8. $\mathrm{PA} \vdash T^{N*} \to \forall y(N^*(y) \to \exists x R(x, y))$.

Proof. Like that of Lemma 17.8. Here, however, the fact that $*$ assigns Σ formulas to predicate letters makes up for the absence of D^*. The formulae B_0 and B_1 are now built up from atomic formulae of $\mathscr{S}$ by $\exists$, $\wedge$, and $\vee$, and Z^*, Y^*, $\leqslant^*$, $\neq^*$, V^*, A'^*, M'^*, A''^*, M''^*, and N^* are all Σ. Thus B_0^{N*} and B_1^{N*} define r.e. relations. Let the formulas C_0 and C_1 and the sentence S be as before. Assume T^{N*} and suppose, for reductio, that $N^*(k)$, but for no r, $R(r, k)$. As before, since Z^*, V^*, $\leqslant^*$, and N^* define r.e. relations, so does the formula $R(x, y)$. Routine modifications to the proof of 17.8 now yield the desired contradiction. ⊣

Lemma 9. *Let $F(\mathrm{x})$ be any formula of $\mathscr{S}$. Then* $\mathrm{PA} \vdash T^{N*} \wedge R(\mathrm{x}, \mathrm{y}) \to [F(\mathrm{x}) \leftrightarrow F^{N*}(\mathrm{y})]$.

Proof. By Lemmas 5 and 8. ⊣

Let $I = T \wedge \forall x \forall x'(Gx \wedge \neg Gx' \to x \neq x')$.

Lemma 10. *Let $F(\mathrm{x})$ be a formula of $\mathscr{S} \cup \{G\}$. Then, where $E(\mathrm{x})$ is the result of substituting $\exists y(R(x, y) \wedge G^*(y))$ for Gx in $F(\mathrm{x})$,* $\mathrm{PA} \vdash I^{N*} \wedge R(\mathrm{x}, \mathrm{y}) \to (E(\mathrm{x}) \leftrightarrow F^{N*}(\mathrm{y}))$.

Proof. An induction like the one in the proof of Lemma 9, except that we must now also consider the case in which $F(\mathrm{x})$ is an atomic formula Gu.

In that case we must show that $\mathrm{PA} \vdash I^{N*} \wedge R(x,y) \to (\exists z(R(x,z) \wedge G^*(z)) \leftrightarrow G^*(y))$. Work in PA. Suppose I^{N*} and $R(x,y)$. Then if $G^*(y)$, $\exists z(R(x,z) \wedge G^*(z))$. Conversely, assume $R(x,z)$ and $G^*(z)$. By Lemma 4(d), $\neg y \neq {}^* z$ and then by the second conjunct of I^{N*}, $G^*(y)$. ⊣

The following lemma will be useful later.

Lemma 11. *Let F be any sentence of* $\mathscr{S} \cup \{G\}$. *Then, where E is the result of substituting* $\exists y(R(x,y) \wedge G^*(y))$ *for Gx in F,* $\mathrm{PA} \vdash I^{N*} \to (E \leftrightarrow F^{N*})$.

Proof. Lemma 11 is the special case of Lemma 10 in which F has no free variables. ⊣

We now introduce a magic formula, O.

By the generalized diagonal lemma, there is a formula O with one free variable such that $\mathrm{PA} \vdash O(y) \leftrightarrow$"$y$ is a number such that there is a proof of the negation of the result of substituting the numeral for y for the free variable of O, and there is no proof with a lower Gödel number of the negation of the result of substituting any numeral for the free variable of O".

It is clear that $O(y)$ is Σ.

Lemma 12. (a) $\mathrm{PA} \vdash O(y) \wedge O(z) \to y = z$;
(b) $\mathrm{PA} \vdash \exists y\, \mathrm{Bew}[\neg O(y)] \to \mathrm{Bew}(\ulcorner \bot \urcorner)$.

Proof. (a) is clear. As for (b), working in PA, suppose that for some i, $\neg O(\mathbf{i})$ is provable. Let j be the number such that the lowest Gödel-numbered proof of any sentence of the form $\neg O(\mathbf{k})$ is a proof of $\neg O(\mathbf{j})$. Then $\neg O(\mathbf{j})$ is provable. But $O(\mathbf{j})$ is true. Since $O(\mathbf{j})$ is Σ, $O(\mathbf{j})$ is provable. Thus $\bot$ is provable. ⊣

Lemma 13. *$O(y)$ is false of every natural number.*

Proof. Suppose $O(y)$ is true of i. Then there is a proof of $\neg O(\mathbf{i})$. But since $O(y)$ is Σ and $O(y)$ is true of i, $O(\mathbf{i})$ is provable, contra the consistency of PA. ⊣

Our next main goal is Lemma 17, which readily follows from the tedious Lemma 14.

Let $D_2, D_3, \ldots, D_9$ be $\{1 + 16i : i \in \omega\}$, $\{3 + 16i : i \in \omega\}, \ldots, \{15 + 16i : i \in \omega\}$. These are disjoint infinite sets of odd numbers.

Let us call $\langle p,q\rangle$ and $\langle p',q'\rangle$ equivalent if $\{p,q\}=\{p',q'\}$; similarly, $\langle p,q,r\rangle$ and $\langle p',q',r'\rangle$ are equivalent if $\{p,q,r\}=\{p',q',r'\}$.

Let f_2 be a one–one Σ map of all natural numbers onto D_2. Let f_3 be a one–one Σ map of all natural numbers onto D_3. Let f_4 be a Σ map of all ordered pairs of natural numbers onto D_4 that takes pairs to the same number if and only if they are equivalent. Similarly for f_5 and D_5, f_6 and D_6, and f_7 and D_7.

Let f_8 be a Σ map of all ordered triples of natural numbers onto D_8 that takes triples to the same number if and only if they are equivalent. Similarly for f_9 and D_9.

Recall that each of the eight predicate letters Z, Y, $\neq$, V, A', M', A'', and M'' is true of a k-tuple of numbers only if all coordinates of the k-tuple are distinct and is true of a k-tuple iff it holds of any permutation of that k-tuple.

Let

$$\begin{aligned}
C(0) &= \{0\}\\
C(1) &= \{0\}\cup\{2,4,6,\ldots\}\\
C(2) &= \{0\}\cup\{f_2(p){:}\neg Zp\}\\
C(3) &= \{0\}\cup\{f_3(p){:}\neg Yp\}\\
C(4) &= \{0\}\cup\{f_4(p,q){:}\neg p\neq q\}\\
C(5) &= \{0\}\cup\{f_5(p,q){:}\neg Vpq\}\\
C(6) &= \{0\}\cup\{f_6(p,q){:}\neg A'pq\}\\
C(7) &= \{0\}\cup\{f_7(p,q){:}\neg M'pq\}\\
C(8) &= \{0\}\cup\{f_8(p,q,r){:}\neg A''pqr\}\\
C(9) &= \{0\}\cup\{f_9(p,q,r){:}\neg M''pqr\}\\
C(j+10) &= \{2+2m{:}\, m\leqslant j\}\cup\{f_3(p){:}j\in\{p\}\}\\
&\quad \cup\cdots\cup\{f_{10}(p,q,r){:}j\in\{p,q,r\}\}
\end{aligned}$$

Let $C(w,x)$ define the relation $\{m,n{:}\, m\in C(n)\}$.
We shall write: $w\in C(x)$ instead of: $C(w,x)$.
Let $B(x)=\forall w(w\in C(x)\rightarrow\neg O(w))$.

Lemma 14
(a) $\mathrm{PA}\vdash x\geqslant 10\rightarrow \mathrm{Bew}[B(0)\vee B(x)]$;
(b) $\mathrm{PA}\vdash\neg x\geqslant 10\rightarrow(\mathrm{Bew}[B(0)\vee B(x)]\rightarrow \mathrm{Bew}(\ulcorner\bot\urcorner))$;
(c) $\mathrm{PA}\vdash x\leqslant y\rightarrow \mathrm{Bew}[B(1)\vee(B(y+10)\rightarrow B(x+10))]$;
(d) $\mathrm{PA}\vdash\neg x\leqslant y\rightarrow(\mathrm{Bew}[B(1)\vee(B(y+10)\rightarrow B(x+10))]\rightarrow \mathrm{Bew}(\ulcorner\bot\urcorner))$;

(e) $\mathrm{PA} \vdash Zx \to \mathrm{Bew}[B(2) \vee B(x+10)]$;

(f) $\mathrm{PA} \vdash \neg Zx \to (\mathrm{Bew}[B(2) \vee B(x+10)] \to \mathrm{Bew}(\ulcorner \bot \urcorner))$;

(g) $\mathrm{PA} \vdash Yx \to \mathrm{Bew}[B(3) \vee B(x+10)]$;

(h) $\mathrm{PA} \vdash \neg Yx \to (\mathrm{Bew}[B(3) \vee B(x+10)] \to \mathrm{Bew}(\ulcorner \bot \urcorner))$;

(i) $\mathrm{PA} \vdash x \neq y \to \mathrm{Bew}[B(4) \vee B(x+10) \vee B(y+10)]$;

(j) $\mathrm{PA} \vdash \neg x \neq y \to (\mathrm{Bew}[B(4) \vee B(x+10) \vee B(y+10)] \to \mathrm{Bew}(\ulcorner \bot \urcorner))$;

(k) $\mathrm{PA} \vdash Vxy \to \mathrm{Bew}[B(5) \vee B(x+10) \vee B(y+10)]$;

(l) $\mathrm{PA} \vdash \neg Vxy \to (\mathrm{Bew}[B(5) \vee B(x+10) \vee B(y+10)] \to \mathrm{Bew}(\ulcorner \bot \urcorner))$;

(m) $\mathrm{PA} \vdash A'xy \to \mathrm{Bew}[B(6) \vee B(x+10) \vee B(y+10)]$;

(n) $\mathrm{PA} \vdash \neg A'xy \to (\mathrm{Bew}[B(6) \vee B(x+10) \vee B(y+10)] \to \mathrm{Bew}(\ulcorner \bot \urcorner))$;

(o) $\mathrm{PA} \vdash M'xy \to \mathrm{Bew}[B(7) \vee B(x+10) \vee B(y+10)]$;

(p) $\mathrm{PA} \vdash \neg M'xy \to (\mathrm{Bew}[B(7) \vee B(x+10) \vee B(y+10)] \to \mathrm{Bew}(\ulcorner \bot \urcorner))$;

(q) $\mathrm{PA} \vdash A''xyz \to \mathrm{Bew}[B(8) \vee B(x+10) \vee B(y+10) \vee B(z+10)]$;

(r) $\mathrm{PA} \vdash \neg A''xyz \to (\mathrm{Bew}[B(8) \vee B(x+10) \vee B(y+10) \vee B(z+10)] \to \mathrm{Bew}(\ulcorner \bot \urcorner))$;

(s) $\mathrm{PA} \vdash M''xyz \to \mathrm{Bew}[B(9) \vee B(x+10) \vee B(y+10) \vee B(z+10)]$;

(t) $\mathrm{PA} \vdash \neg M''xyz \to (\mathrm{Bew}[B(9) \vee B(x+10) \vee B(y+10) \vee B(z+10)] \to \mathrm{Bew}(\ulcorner \bot \urcorner))$;

(We have not boldfaced '+' or the numerals for 0, 1, ..., 10.)

Proof. Note first that the antecedent $F(x)$ of each conditional is a Σ formula and therefore $\mathrm{PA} \vdash F(x) \to \mathrm{Bew}[F(x)]$. In each of (a), (c), (e), ..., (s), it thus suffices to prove the corresponding conditional from which "Bew[···]" is missing. To prove each of (b), (d), (f), ..., (t), which are all of the form $\mathrm{PA} \vdash F(x) \to (\mathrm{Bew}[G(x)] \to \mathrm{Bew}(\ulcorner \bot \urcorner))$, it suffices in each case to find a pterm t such that $\mathrm{PA} \vdash F(x) \wedge G(x) \to \neg O(t)$, for then $\mathrm{PA} \vdash F(x) \wedge G(x) \wedge t = y \to \neg O(y)$, and therefore $\mathrm{PA} \vdash \mathrm{Bew}[F(x)] \wedge \mathrm{Bew}[G(x)] \wedge \mathrm{Bew}[t = y] \to \mathrm{Bew}[\neg O(y)]$, whence $\mathrm{PA} \vdash \mathrm{Bew}[F(x)] \wedge \mathrm{Bew}[G(x)] \wedge \exists y\, \mathrm{Bew}[t = y] \to \exists y\, \mathrm{Bew}[\neg O(y)]$. But $\mathrm{PA} \vdash F(x) \to \mathrm{Bew}[F(x)]$; certainly $\mathrm{PA} \vdash \exists y\, \mathrm{Bew}[t = y]$; and by Lemma 12(b), $\mathrm{PA} \vdash \exists y\, \mathrm{Bew}[\neg O(y)] \to \mathrm{Bew}(\ulcorner \bot \urcorner)$, whence we are done.

We omit the proofs of (g)–(r), since these are not interestingly different from those of (s) and (t). In each case, work in PA.

(a) Suppose $x \geqslant 10$, $\neg B(0)$, and $\neg B(x)$. Then for some w, w', $w \in C(0)$, hence $w = 0$, $w' \in C(x)$, $O(w)$, and $O(w')$; by Lemma 12(a), $w = w'$. Thus $0 \in C(x)$, which is not the case since $x \geqslant 10$.

(b) Suppose $x < 10$. $0 \in C(0) \cap C(x)$. Then if either $B(0)$ or $B(x)$, $\neg O(0)$.

(c) Suppose $x \leqslant y$, $\neg B(1)$ and $\neg B(x+10)$. Then for some w, w', $w \in C(1)$, hence $w \neq 1$, $w' \in C(x+10)$, hence $w' \neq 0$, $O(w)$, $O(w')$, and so $w = w'$; thus w' is an even number $\geqslant 2$. Since $x \leqslant y$, $w' \in C(y+10)$. Thus $\neg B(y+10)$.

(d) Suppose $x > y$. Let $a = 2 + 2x$. Then $a \in C(1) \cap C(x+10)$, but $a \notin C(y+10)$. If either $B(1)$ or $B(x+10)$, $\neg O(a)$. But if $\neg B(y+10)$, then for some z, $O(z)$ and $z \in C(y+10)$, whence $z \neq a$; by Lemma 12(a) $\neg O(a)$.

(e) Suppose Zx, $\neg B(2)$, and $\neg B(x+10)$. Then, for some w, w', $O(w)$, $O(w')$, $w \in C(2)$, $w' \in C(x+10)$, and $w = w'$. Since f_2 is one–one, $w = f_2(p)$, for some p such that $\neg Zp$ and $x \in \{p\}$, impossible.

(f) Suppose $\neg Zx$. Let $a = f_2(x)$. Then $a \in C(2) \cap C(x+10)$, and then if either $B(2)$ or $B(x+10)$, $\neg O(a)$.

(s) Suppose $M''xyz$, $\neg B(9)$, $\neg B(x+10)$, $\neg B(y+10)$, and $\neg B(z+10)$. Then $x \neq y \neq z \neq x$ and for some w, w', w'', w''', $O(w)$, $O(w')$, $O(w'')$, $O(w''')$, whence $w = w' = w'' = w'''$, and $w \in C(9) \cap C(x+10) \cap C(y+10) \cap C(z+10)$. Since $w \in C(9)$ and $0 \notin C(x+10)$, $w = f_9(p, q, r)$ for some p, w, r such that $\neg M''pqr$. And since $w \in C(x+10) \cap C(y+10) \cap C(z+10)$ and f_9 takes inequivalent triples to different numbers, x, y, z are all in $\{p, q, r\}$. Thus $\{p, q, r\} = \{x, y, z\}$, and therefore $M''pqr$ iff $M''xyz$, contradiction.

(t) Suppose $\neg M''xyz$. Let $a = f_9(x, y, z)$. Then $a \in C(9) \cap C(x+10) \cap C(y+10) \cap C(z+10)$, and then if either $B(9)$ or $B(x+10)$ or $B(y+10)$ or $B(z+10)$, $\neg O(a)$. $\dashv$

Lemma 15. *For each i,*
$x \geqslant 10$ *is coextensive (in the standard model) with*
$\mathrm{Bew}[B(0) \vee B(x)]$;
$x \leqslant y$, *with* $\mathrm{Bew}[B(1) \vee (B(y+10) \rightarrow B(x+10))]$;
Zx, *with* $\mathrm{Bew}[B(2) \vee B(x+10)]$;
Yx, *with* $\mathrm{Bew}[B(3) \vee B(x+10)]$;
$x \neq y$, *with* $\mathrm{Bew}[B(4) \vee B(x+10) \vee B(y+10)]$;
Vxy, *with* $\mathrm{Bew}[B(5) \vee B(x+10) \vee B(y+10)]$;
$A'xy$, *with* $\mathrm{Bew}[B(6) \vee B(x+10) \vee B(y+10)]$;
$M'xy$, *with* $\mathrm{Bew}[B(7) \vee B(x+10) \vee B(y+10)]$;
$A''xyz$, *with* $\mathrm{Bew}[B(8) \vee B(x+10) \vee B(y+10) \vee B(z+10)]$;
and

$M''xyz$, with $\text{Bew}[B(9) \vee B(x+10) \vee B(y+10) \vee B(z+10)]$.

Proof. By Lemma 14 and the consistency of arithmetic. ⊣

By Lemma 15, if $x, y, z \geqslant 10$, $x - 10 \leqslant y - 10$ holds iff $\text{Bew}[B(1) \vee (B(y) \to B(x))]$ holds;...; and $M''x - 10$, $y - 10$, $z - 10$ holds iff $\text{Bew}[B(9) \vee B(x) \vee B(y) \vee B(z)]$ holds.

Lemma 16. *Let $D(x)$ be an arbitrary formula. Let $B'(x)$ be the formula*

$$B(x) \wedge (x < 10 \vee \exists y O(y) \vee D(x-10))$$

Then (a)–(t) *of Lemma 14 hold good when B is replaced there with B', and except for numbers <10, $B'(x)$ is coextensive with $D(x-10)$.*

Proof. $O(y)$ is false of every number, by Lemma 13. Therefore $B(x)$ is true of every number, and thus if $n \geqslant 10$, $B'(x)$ is true of n iff $D(x-10)$ is. As for (a)–(t) of Lemma 14, we argue as follows: $\text{PA} \vdash \exists y O(y) \to \forall x(B(x) \leftrightarrow B'(x))$, by the definition of B'. But also $\text{PA} \vdash \neg \exists y O(y) \to \forall x B(x)$, whence for all i and hence for all $i < 10$, $\text{Pa} \vdash \neg \exists x O(y) \to B(\mathbf{i})$. But if $i < 10$, then $\text{PA} \vdash \mathbf{i} < 10$, and therefore also $\text{PA} \vdash \neg \exists x O(y) \to B'(\mathbf{i})$. Thus $\text{PA} \vdash (B(0) \vee B(x)) \leftrightarrow (B'(0) \vee B'(x))$, $\text{PA} \vdash (B(1) \vee (B(y+10) \to B(x+10))) \leftrightarrow (B'(1) \vee (B'(y'+10) \to B'(x+10)))$, ..., and $\text{PA} \vdash (B(9) \vee B(x+10) \vee B(y+10) \vee B(z+10)) \leftrightarrow (B'(9) \vee B'(x+10) \vee B'(y+10) \vee B'(z+10))$, whence the lemma follows by Lemma 14 and the rule: if $\text{PA} \vdash F(x) \leftrightarrow G(x)$, then $\text{PA} \vdash \text{Bew}[F(x)] \leftrightarrow \text{Bew}[G(x)]$. ⊣

Lemma 17. *Let $x, y, z \geqslant 10$. Let $D(x)$ and $B'(x)$ be as in Lemma 16. Then*
$D(x-10)$ holds iff $B'(x)$ holds;
$x \geqslant 10$ holds iff $\text{Bew}[B'(0) \vee B'(x)]$ *holds;*
$x - 10 \leqslant y - 10$ holds iff $\text{Bew}[B'(1) \vee (B'(y) \to B'(x))]$ *holds;*
$Z(x-10)$ holds iff $\text{Bew}[B'(2) \vee B'(x)]$ *holds;*
$Y(x-10)$ holds iff $\text{Bew}[B'(3) \vee B(x)$ *holds;*
$x - 10 \neq y - 10$ holds iff $\text{Bew}[B'(4) \vee B'(x) \vee B'(y)]$ *holds;*
$V(x-10, y-10)$ holds iff $\text{Bew}[B'(5) \vee B'(x) \vee B'(y)]$ *holds;*
$A'(x-10, y-10)$ holds iff $\text{Bew}[B'(6) \vee B'(x) \vee B'(y)]$ *holds;*
$M'(x-10, y-10)$ holds iff $\text{Bew}[B'(7) \vee B'(x) \vee B'(y)$ *holds;*
$A''(x-10, y-10, z-10)$ holds iff
$\text{Bew}[B'(8) \vee B'(x) \vee B'(y) \vee B'(z)]$ *holds;*

$M''(x-10, y-10, z-10)$ *holds iff*
$\quad$ $\text{Bew}[B'(9) \vee B'(x) \vee B'(y) \vee B'(z)]$ *holds.*

Proof. As above, and by Lemma 16. $\dashv$

We now prove Vardanyan's Π^0_2-completeness theorem for the language $\{G\}$.

We recall the definition of *A m-approximates V* from the previous chapter: *A* *m*-approximates *V* iff

$[(m$ is not (the Gödel number of) a sentence of $\mathscr{L} \rightarrow m \notin A) \wedge$
$\quad(m$ is a sentence of $\mathscr{L} \rightarrow$
$\quad\forall n(n$ is a subsentence of the sentence $m \rightarrow$
$\qquad[n$ is an atomic sentence $\rightarrow (n \in A \leftrightarrow n \in V_0)] \wedge$
$\qquad[n$ is a conditional $F \rightarrow F' \rightarrow (n \in A \leftrightarrow (F \in A \rightarrow F' \in A))] \wedge$
$\qquad[n$ is a universal quantification $\forall x F \rightarrow$
$\qquad\quad(n \in A \leftrightarrow$ for all i, $F_x(\mathbf{i}) \in A)]))]$

Let $H(G, v)$ be a formula of the language $\mathscr{S} \cup \{G\}$ that naturally defines: *A m*-approximates *V*.

Let *S* be an arbitrary Π^0_2 set. According to Lemma 9 of Chapter 17, there is a recursive relation *P* such that $S = \{n: \forall i \exists j(j > i \wedge P(n, j))\}$,

We suppose that none of the special variables occurs in the formula χ_n, defined below.

Let Q be a Σ formula that defines *P*; we shall write $Q_n(y)$ instead of $Q(\mathbf{n}, y)$.

For each *n*, let χ_n be the formula

$$I \rightarrow \exists v \exists w(v < w \wedge Q_n(w) \wedge \neg H(G, v))$$

We obtain a formula ϕ_n of quantified modal logic whose only predicate letter is *G* and in which no occurrence of $\Box$ lies in the scope of another occurrence of $\Box$ as follows:

We replace each occurrence of $x \leqslant y$ in χ_n^N by an occurrence of $\Box(G(v_{\leqslant}) \vee (G(y) \rightarrow G(x))$; and for each *m*-place predicate letter π of $\mathscr{S} \cup \{N\}$ other than $\leqslant$, we replace each occurrence of $\pi(x_1, \ldots, x_m)$ in χ_n^N by an occurrence of $\Box(G(v_\pi) \vee G(x_1) \vee \cdots \vee G(x_m))$. (We leave *G* unchanged.) We then universally quantify the result with respect to the special variables to obtain ϕ_n.

We shall show that $n \in S$ if and only if ϕ_n is always provable.

Suppose $n \in S$. Let $^\#$ be an arbitrary realization of ϕ_n. (Of course $^\#$ need do nothing other than assign to *G* a formula containing just the variable v_0 free.)

Let $F(v_0) = G^{\#}$.

We define a Σ realization $*$ of χ_n: Let $\leqslant^*$ be $\mathrm{Bew}[F(v_{\leqslant}) \vee (F(v_1) \rightarrow F(v_0))]$. For each m-place predicate letter π of $\mathscr{S} \cup \{N\}$ other than $\leqslant$, let $\pi^* = \mathrm{Bew}[F(v_\pi) \vee F(v_0) \vee \cdots \vee F(v_{m-1})]$. And let G^* be $G^{\#}$.

Then $\phi_n^{\#}$ is identical with the universal quantification of χ_n^{N*} with respect to the ten special variables. To show that $\mathrm{PA} \vdash \phi_n^{\#}$, it thus suffices to show that $\mathrm{PA} \vdash \chi_n^{N*}$.

Let $H(\{x: \exists y(R(x,y) \wedge G^*(y))\}, v)$ be the result of substituting $\exists y(R(x,y) \wedge G^*(y))$ for Gx throughout $H(G, v)$ (of course relettering variables if necessary).

For each $n \geqslant 1$, let $\mathrm{su}_n(x, \mathsf{u})$ be a Σ pterm for an $(n+1)$-place function f such that for any k, p, if k is the Gödel number of a formula $F(\mathsf{u})$, then $f(k, \mathsf{p})$ is the Gödel number of $F(\mathbf{p})$.

Let $S(x, \mathsf{u})$ be an arbitrary formula.

By the generalized diagonal lemma, there is a formula $F(\mathsf{u})$ such that

$$\mathrm{PA} \vdash F(\mathsf{u}) \leftrightarrow \neg S(\mathrm{su}_n(\ulcorner F(\mathsf{u}) \urcorner, \mathsf{u}), \mathsf{u})$$

Let i be the Gödel number of $\forall u_1 \ldots \forall u_n F(\mathsf{u})$.

Inductively, if $G(v_1, \ldots, v_r)$ is a subformula of $F(\mathsf{u})$,
$\mathrm{PA} \vdash H(\{x: S(x, \mathsf{u})\}, \mathbf{i}) \rightarrow$
$(G(v_1, \ldots, v_r) \leftrightarrow S(\mathrm{su}_r(\ulcorner G(v_1, \ldots, v_r) \urcorner, v_1, \ldots, v_r), \mathsf{u})$. [For, working in PA: if $\{k: k, \mathsf{q}$ satisfy $S(x, \mathsf{u})\}$ m-approximates the truth set V, then a subformula of $F(\mathsf{u})$ will be satisfied by certain numbers if and only if the result of substituting the numerals for those numbers for the appropriate variables in the subformula is in some suitably good approximation to the truth set V; if and only if the Gödel number of that result, together with the q, satisfies S.]

Since $F(\mathsf{u})$ is a subformula of itself, $\mathrm{PA} \vdash H(\{x: S(x, \mathsf{u})\}, \mathbf{i}) \rightarrow (F(\mathsf{u}) \leftrightarrow S(\mathrm{su}_n(\ulcorner F(\mathsf{u}) \urcorner, \mathsf{u}), \mathsf{u})$, and therefore $\mathrm{PA} \vdash \neg H(\{x: S(x, \mathsf{u})\}, \mathbf{i})$.

Now let $S(x, \mathsf{u})$ be $\exists y(R(x,y) \wedge G^*(y))$ and let i be as above. [Note that several of the special variables occur in $R(x, y)$, and hence also in $\exists y(R(x,y) \wedge G^*(y))$.]

Then we have

(1) $\mathrm{PA} \vdash \neg H(\{x: \exists y(R(x,y) \wedge G^*(y))\}, \mathbf{i})$

By Lemma 10, we have

(2) $\mathrm{PA} \vdash I^{N*} \wedge R(\mathbf{i}, v) \rightarrow (H(\{x: \exists y(R(x,y) \wedge G^*(y))\}, \mathbf{i})$
$\leftrightarrow H^{N*}(\{y: G^*(y)\}, v))$

So, by (1),

(3) $\mathrm{PA} \vdash I^{N*} \wedge R(\mathbf{i}, v) \rightarrow \neg H^{N*}(\{y: G^*(y)\}, v)$

Since $n \in S$, for some j, $i<j$ and $Q_n(j)$ holds. Thus $\mathbf{i}<\mathbf{j} \wedge Q_n(\mathbf{j})$ is true and Σ, and therefore

(4) $\mathrm{PA} \vdash \mathbf{i}<\mathbf{j} \wedge Q_n(\mathbf{j})$

By Lemma 9 and (4),

(5) $\mathrm{PA} \vdash T^{N*} \wedge R(\mathbf{i}, v) \wedge R(\mathbf{j}, w) \rightarrow (v <^* w \wedge Q_n^{N*}(w))$

whence

(6) $\mathrm{PA} \vdash I^{N*} \wedge R(\mathbf{i}, v) \wedge R(\mathbf{j}, w) \rightarrow$
$(v <^* w \wedge Q_n^{N*}(w) \wedge \neg H^{N*}(\{y : G^*(y)\}, v))$

By Lemma 2, $\mathrm{PA} \vdash T^{N*} \rightarrow \forall x \exists y R(x, y)$. Since $\mathrm{PA} \vdash R(x, y) \rightarrow N^*(y)$, we have

(7) $\mathrm{PA} \vdash I^{N*} \rightarrow \exists v(N^*(v) \wedge \exists w(N^*(w) \wedge$
$[(v <^* w \wedge Q_n^{N*}(w)) \wedge \neg H^{N*}(\{y : G^*(y)\}, v)]))$

i.e., $\mathrm{PA} \vdash \chi_n^{N*}$.

Thus if $n \in S$, $\mathrm{PA} \vdash \phi_n^{\#}$.

Conversely, suppose that for all realizations $^{\#}$, $\mathrm{PA} \vdash \phi_n^{\#}$. Now fix i. We must find a j such that $i<j$ and $Q_n(j)$. Let $D(x)$ be a formula of arithmetic defining a set that m-approximates V for all $m<i$.

Let $B'(x)$ be obtained from $D(x)$ as in Lemma 16.

Let $G^{\#} = B'(v_0)$. Since $\mathrm{PA} \vdash \phi_n^{\#}$, $\phi_n^{\#}$ is true in the standard model. $\phi_n^{\#}$ begins with a string of universal quantifiers over the special variables. Let ψ be the result of universally instantiating those variables $v_N, v_{\leqslant}, v_Z, v_Y, v_{\neq}, v_V, v_{A'}, v_{M'}, v_{A''}, v_{M''}$ with 0, 1, 2, 3, 4, 5, 6, 7, 8, 9, respectively. Then ψ is also the result of respectively substituting $B'(x)$ for Gx, $\mathrm{Bew}[B(0) \vee B(x)]$ for Nx, $\mathrm{Bew}[B(1) \vee (B(y) \rightarrow (B(x))]$ for $x \leqslant y$, $\mathrm{Bew}[B(2) \vee B(x)]$ for $Zx, \ldots$, and $\mathrm{Bew}[B(9) \vee B(x) \vee B(y) \vee B(z)]$ for $M''xyz$ in χ_n^N. All quantifiers in ψ are relativized to $\mathrm{Bew}[B(0) \vee B(x)]$, and by Lemma 17, ψ has the same truth-value, namely true, as the result of respectively subsituting $B'(x)$ for Gx, $x \geqslant 10$ for Nx, $x-10 \leqslant y-10$ for $x \leqslant y$, $Z(x-10)$ for $Zx, \ldots$, and $M''(x-10, y-10, z-10)$ for $M''xyz$ in χ_n^N, and therefore the same truth-value as the result σ of substituting $D(x)$ for Gx [for $D(x-10)$ is coextensive with $B'(x)$ if $x \geqslant 10$], $x \leqslant y$ for $x \leqslant y$, Zx for $Zx, \ldots$, and $M''xyz$ for $M''xyz$ in χ_n. The antecedent of σ is true, therefore so is the consequent, and thus there exist numbers v and w such that $v<j$, $Q_n(j)$ holds and $\neg H(\{x : D(x)\}, v)$ holds. Since $\neg H(\{x : D(x)\}, v)$ holds, the set of numbers satisfying $D(x)$ does not v-approximate

V. But the set of numbers satisfying $D(x)$ m-approximates V for all $m<i$. Thus $i\leqslant v<j$, and the theorem is proved.

We conclude by showing that, like the class of always true sentences of QML, the class of always true sentences of the fragment $\{G\}$ of QML is Π^0_1-complete in V.

An *assignment* is a function that assigns numbers to the special variables $v_N, v_{\leqslant}, v_Z, \ldots, v_{M''}$.

Let $F(x)$ be any formula of $\mathscr{S}\cup\{G\}$. As in the proof of Theorem 3 of the previous chapter, we say that $F(a_1,\ldots,a_n)$ holds *at* the set A of natural numbers if $F(x)$ is satisfied by numbers $a_1,\ldots,a_n$ when A is assigned to the predicate letter G. Lemma 11 then asserts that if F is a sentence of $\mathscr{S}\cup\{G\}$, $*$ a Σ realization, α an assignment, I^{N*} is true under α and $A=\{a$: for some b, $R(a,b)$ and $G^*(b)$ hold under $\alpha\}$, then F holds at A under α if and only if F^{N*} is true under α.

The definition of "A and B are k-equivalent" is given in the previous chapter. Lemma 17.12 asserts that if $T^A(e,i,k)$ and A and B are k-equivalent, then $T^B(e,i,k)$.

Now let $F(x,y)$, $=F(x,y,G)$, be the formula of $\mathscr{S}\cup\{G\}$ expressing: $\forall m(\forall j<m\neg T^A(e,i,j)\rightarrow A$ m-approximates $V)$. As in Chapter 17, if A is arithmetical and $F(\mathbf{e},\mathbf{i})$ holds at A, then for some k, $T^A(e,\mathbf{i},k)$.

For each e,i, let $\psi_{e,i}$ be the sentence $I\wedge F(e,i)$.

Let $\sigma_{e,i}$ be the formula of $\{G\}$ obtained from $\psi^N_{e,i}$ by making the same substitution of modal formulas defined above, i.e., leaving each occurrence of Gx in $\psi^N_{e,i}$ unchanged, replacing each occurrence of $x\leqslant y$ by an occurrence of $\Box(G(v_{\leqslant})\vee(G(y)\rightarrow G(x)))$, and replacing each occurrence of $\pi(x_1,\ldots,x_m)$, where π is a predicate letter of $\mathscr{S}\cup\{N\}$ other than $\leqslant$, by an occurrence of $\Box(G(v_\pi)\vee G(x_1)\vee\cdots\vee G(x_m))$. Finally, let $\rho_{e,i}$ be the result of existentially quantifying the special variables in $\sigma_{e,i}$.

Lemma 18. $\exists kT^V(e,i,k)$ *iff for some* $^{\#}$, $\rho^{\#}_{e,i}$ *is true.*

Proof. A modification of that of 17.14. Suppose $T^V(e,i,k)$. Let r be a number greater than the number of occurrences of logical operators in any sentence of $\mathscr{S}$ with Gödel number $\leqslant k$. Let A be the set of Gödel numbers of true sentences of $\mathscr{S}$ that contain $<r$ occurrences of the logical operators. As in the proof of 17.14, A is an arithmetical set, $T^A(e,i,k)$, and $F(\mathbf{e},\mathbf{i})$ holds at A.

Let $D(x)$ be a formula of $\mathscr{S}$ defining the arithmetical set A. Let $B'(x)$ be obtained from $D(x)$ as in Lemma 16. Let $G^{\#}$ be $B'(v_0)$.

We define a Σ realization $*$ by also assigning $B'(v_0)$ to G,

$\text{Bew}[B'(v_N) \vee B'(v_0)]$ to N,
$\text{Bew}[B'(v_{\leqslant}) \vee (B'(v_1) \to B'(v_0))]$ to $\leqslant$,
$\text{Bew}[B'(v_Z) \vee B'(v_0)]$ to $Z, \ldots,$ and
$\text{Bew}[B'(v_{M''}) \vee B'(v_0) \vee B'(v_1) \vee B'(v_2)]$ to M''.

Let α assign 0, 1, 2, 3, 4, 5, 6, 7, 8, 9 to the special variables v_N, $v_{\leqslant}, v_Z, v_Y, v_{\neq}, v_V, v_{A'}, v_{M''}, v_{A''}, v_{M''}$, respectively.

$\forall x \forall x'(Gx \wedge \neg Gx' \to x \neq x')^{N*}$ is true under α iff $\forall x(\text{Bew}[B'(0) \vee B'(x)] \to \forall x'(\text{Bew}[B'(0) \vee B'(x')] \to (B'(x) \wedge \neg B'(x') \to \text{Bew}[B'(4) \vee B'(x) \vee B'(x)])$ is true, iff, by Lemma 15, $\forall x(x \geqslant 10 \to \forall x'(x' \geqslant 10 \to (D(x-10) \wedge D(x'-10) \to x-10 \neq x'-10)$, iff $\forall x \forall x'(D(x) \wedge \neg D(x') \to x \neq x')$ is true. Thus $\forall x \forall x'(Gx \wedge \neg Gx' \to x \neq x')^{N*}$ is true under α. And, in like manner, since T is true under the standard realization, T^{N*} is also true under α. Thus I^{N*} is also true under α.

By Lemma 15, $Z^*(y)$ holds iff $y = 10$, $V^*(y, y')$, holds iff $V(y-10, y'-10)$, and $y \neq^* y$ holds iff $y - 10 \neq y' - 10$; therefore $S^*(y, y')$ holds iff $y' - 10 = (y - 10) + 1$. Thus $R(x, y)$ holds iff $y = x + 10$, and $\{a$: for some $b, R(a, b)$ and $G^*(b)$ hold under $\alpha\} = \{a$: for some $b, b = a + 10$ and $B'(b)$ hold$\} = \{a$: for some $b, b = a + 10$ and $D(b-10)$ hold$\} = A$.

By Lemma 11, $F(\mathbf{e}, \mathbf{i})^{N*}$ is true under α, and therefore $\psi_{e,i}^{N*}$ is true under α. But $\sigma_{e,i}^{\#} = \psi_{e,i}^{N*}$. Thus $\sigma_{e,i}^{\#}$ is true under α. But $\rho_{e,i}$ is the result of existentially quantifying the special variables in $\sigma_{e,i}$. Thus $\rho_{e,i}^{\#}$ is true.

Conversely, suppose $\rho_{e,i}^{\#}$ true. Then for some assignment α, $\sigma_{e,i}^{\#}$ is true under α. Let $*$ be the Σ realization that assigns $G^{\#}v_0$ to G, and as before, $\text{Bew}[B'(v_N) \vee B'(v_0)]$ to N, $\text{Bew}[B'(v_{\leqslant}) \vee (B'(v_1) \to B'(v_0))]$ to $\leqslant$, $\text{Bew}[B'(v_Z) \vee B'(v_0)]$ to $Z, \ldots,$ and $\text{Bew}[B'(v_{M''}) \vee B'(v_0) \vee B'(v_1) \vee B'(v_2)]$ to M''. Then $\psi_{e,i}^{N*} = \sigma_{e,i}^{\#}$, and so $\psi_{e,i}^{N*}$ is true under α, i.e., I^{N*} and $F(\mathbf{e}, \mathbf{i})^{N*}$ are true under α. G^*v_0, i.e., $G^{\#}v_0$, defines an arithmetical set. And since Z^* V^*, $\neq^*$, and N^* are all Σ formulas, $R(x, y)$ defines an r.e. relation. Let $A = \{a$: for some b, $R(a, b)$ and $G^*(b)$ hold under $\alpha\}$. By Lemma 17, $F(\mathbf{e}, \mathbf{i})$ holds at A. A is an arithmetical set. By Lemma 17.13, for some k, $T^A(e, i, k)$, and then, as at the end of the proof of Lemma 17.14, for some k, $T^V(e, i, k)$. ⊣

It follows as in Chapter 17 that the class of always true sentences of $\{G\}$ is Π_1^0-complete in V: The class is certainly Π_1^0 in V. Let A be an arbitrary set that is Π_1^0 in V. Then $N{-}A$ is Σ_1^0 in V, and thus for some e, $N{-}A = \{i: \exists k T^V(e, i, k)\}$. By Lemma 18, $N{-}A = \{i$: for some $^{\#}$, $\rho_{e,i}^{\#}$ is true$\}$. Therefore $A = \{i: \neg\rho_{e,i}$ is always true$\}$, and we are done.

Notes

Introduction

1. Lukasiewicz, *Aristotle's Syllogistic*, p. 133
2. Kneale and Kneale, *The Development of Logic*, p. 86.
3. Lewis and Langford, *Symbolic Logic*, p. 155.
4. Ibid., p. 23.
5. Ibid., p. 160.
6. Gödel's own term was *entscheidungsdefinit*.
7. It is assumed that the sentence expressing the consistency of P' is obtained from a standard presentation of the new axioms *as* a primitive recursive set.
8. Since Peano himself formulated mathematical induction as a single (second-order) sentence, the name "Peano arithmetic" is, as Warren Goldfarb has pointed out to me, rather a bad one for a theory whose variables range only over the natural numbers. (Moreover, as everyone ought to know, the "Peano postulates" were formulated earlier by Dedekind.) But the name is unlikely to be changed now.
9. In "On formally undecidable propositions...", Gödel used "Bew(x)" as an open sentence of the language in which *he* studied P.
10. Elsewhere in mathematics, x is called a "fixed point" of a function f if $f(x) = x$.
11. Is any "truth-teller" sentence *really* true?
12. First isolated by Harvey Friedman in "One hundred and two problems in mathematical logic".
13. The relevant theorem is Theorem 1.
14. Done in Boolos, "Omega-consistency and the diamond".

Chapter 1

1. I used to call the system GL 'G', but now prefer the designation 'GL', which slights neither M. H. Löb, whose contributions to this branch of logic were fundamental, nor P. T. Geach, an important contributor to modal logic, after whom a different system was once named 'G'. GL is also known as KW, K4W, and PrL.
2. Kripke, "Semantical analysis of modal logic I: Normal modal propositional calculi".
3. B is named after Brouwer. Cf. the theorem $p \to \neg\neg p$ in intuitionistic

logic. Intuitionists suppose that the negation of a sentence S asserts that a contradiction is derivable from S; replacing intuitionistic "$\neg$" by its approximate definition "$\Box\neg$" yields $p \rightarrow \Box \Diamond p$.

4. I am grateful to Mike Byrd for telling me of this theorem.

Chapter 2

1. Hilbert and Bernays, *Grudlagen der Mathematik*, Vol. II., 2d ed., p. 295.
2. M. H. Löb, "Solution of a problem of Leon Henkin".
3. Raymond M. Smullyan, *First-Order Logic*, p. 7.
4. One particularly attractive formulation of logic, due to Tarski, is found in Monk's *Mathematical Logic*.
5. In detail: if t is a term, v a variable, and t' a term, then $t'_v(t) = t''$ iff there are two finite sequences $h'_0, \ldots, h'_r$ and $h''_0, \ldots, h''_r$ such that (1) $h'_r = t'$; (2) $h''_r = t''$; (3) for every $i < r$, either h'_i is $\mathbf{0}$ or a variable or for some $j, k < i$, h'_i is $\mathbf{s}h'_j$, $(h'_j + h'_k)$ or $(h'_j \times h'_k)$; (4) if h'_i is $\mathbf{0}$ or a variable other than v, then h''_i is h'_i; (5) if h'_i is v, then h''_i is t; and (6) if h'_i is $\mathbf{s}h'_j$, $(h'_j + h'_k)$ or $(h'_j \times h'_k)$ for some $j, k < i$, then h''_i is $\mathbf{s}h''_j$, $(h''_j + h''_k)$ or $(h''_j \times h''_k)$, respectively. [If t or t' is not a term of v not a variable, then t'' is (say) $\mathbf{0}$.]
6. E.g., by a consistency proof of the type first given by Gentzen.
7. For a proof, see Davis and Weyuker, *Computability, Complexity, and Languages*, Chapter 13.
8. Monk, *Mathematical Logic*.
9. We assume that the result of substituting a term in something that is not a formula is 0 and the result of substituting a term in a formula for a variable that does not occur free in that formula is that very formula.

Chapter 3

1. Realizations are sometimes called "interpretations" or "substitutions". But these terms have other uses, and I prefer to stick with "realization".
2. *Journal of Symbolic Logic* 17 (1952), p. 160.
3. Löb, "Solution of a problem of Leon Henkin". Henkin was the referee of Löb's paper and observed that Löb's proof that the answer to his question was yes actually proved the better result now known as Löb's theorem, viz., that any statement implied by its own provability is provable. In Chapter 11 we use K and K4 to compare the strength of Löb's theorem and the statement that any sentence equivalent to its own provability is provable.
4. The restriction to *sentences*, i.e., formulas without free variables, is of course essential. PA is certainly incomplete, but it is not so solely because neither $x = y$ nor $x \neq y$ is a theorem.
5. Thanks to Warren Goldfarb for telling me the arguments contained in the last two paragraphs.
6. Thanks to Vann McGee for a simplification.

Chapter 4

1. Most notably in Kripke, "Semantical analysis of modal logic I".
2. The term *forcing relation* is sometimes used for this notion. But since the clauses for the propositional operators in the definition of '$\models$' are perfectly classical, that piece of terminology is as unfortunate as can be.
3. It follows that the *second*-order sentence $\forall X \forall w(\forall x[wRx \rightarrow (\forall y[xRy \rightarrow Xy] \rightarrow Xx)] \rightarrow \forall x[wRx \rightarrow Xx])$ is true in exactly the transitive converse wellfounded frames.

Chapter 5

1. Repeatedly use the distributive laws and the equivalence of p with $(p \wedge q) \vee (p \wedge \neg q)$.
2. This completeness proof for GL, very much simpler than that given in *The Unprovability of Consistency*, is due to Solovay and Goldfarb. The completeness theorem for GL is due to Krister Segerberg.

Chapter 6

1. Due to Dana Scott, E. J. Lemmon, D. C. Makinson, and M. J. Cresswell.

Chapter 7

1. Following a suggestion of Quine's.
2. Friedman, "One hundred and two problems in mathematical logic." Problem 35 is on p. 117.
3. Two (missing) asterisks have been inserted.
4. First given by the author, with the aid of the normal form theorem, discovered by him in 1973, together with its application to the concept of provability in formal theories. The affirmative answer to Friedman's question was the first use of modal logic to settle a significant question of mathematical logic. Friedman's problem was also solved by Claudio Bernardi and Franco Montagna; the normal form theorem for letterless sentences was also proved by Johan van Benthem.
5. This term is due to Artemov.
6. Due to the author.

Chapter 8

1. 'Niff' means 'iff not:'.
2. The present version is taken from Boolos and Jeffrey, *Computability and Logic*, 3d ed.; it is akin to the proof in Sambin and Valentini, "The modal logic of provability". De Jongh's original proof was never published; a syntactical version of his proof is found on pp. 22–25 of C. Smorynski, "Calculating self-referential statements I".
3. The notion of a character was introduced by Kit Fine, in "Logics containing K4".

4. Commonly so called. "Craig interpolation theorem" would be preferable.
5. The Craig interpolation lemma for GL was independently found by Smorynski and the author. The author's original proof, given in *The Unprovability of Consistency*, resembled his proof of the fixed point theorem.

Chapter 9

1. Artemov: "A country will issue you a visa only if you provide proof that you will not reside there permanently."

Chapter 11

1. The original text of Henkin's problem, received by the *Journal of Symbolic Logic* on February 28, 1952, and published in Vol. 17 (1952), no. 2, on p. 160, reads, "3. *A problem concerning provability.* If S is any standard formal system adequate for recursive number theory, a formula (having a certain integer q as its Gödel number) can be constructed which expresses the proposition that the formula with Gödel number q is provable in S. Is this formula provable or independent in S?" Note that Henkin's problem is apparently a question about one specific formula (which depends on S), whose construction is analogous to that of the Gödel formula. Henkin had presumably observed that by the second incompleteness theorem, the formula could not be refutable in any such standard and hence consistent system S.

Chapter 12

1. This result is due to W. J. Blok and K. E. Pledger. See van Benthem and Blok, "Transitivity follows from Dummett's axiom".
2. The proof given here is a simplification, due to Goldfarb, of the proof of Segerberg's completeness theorem for S4Grz given in *The Unprovability of Consistency*.
3. The equivalence of (3) and (9) was first proved by A. V. Kuznetsov and A. Yu. Muravitsky, "The logic of provability", and independently by R. Goldblatt, "Arithmetical necessity, provability and intuitionistic logic".
4. Due to the author.
5. The proof depends only on the most elementary considerations of Kripke semantics and on no other result of that chapter.
6. McKinsey and Tarski, "Some theorems about the sentential calculi of Lewis and Heyting".
7. Grzegorczyk, "Some relational systems and the associated topological spaces". The axiom Grzegorczyk added in his original paper was

$$\Box((\Box(\Box(F \to \Box G) \to \Box G) \wedge \Box(\Box(\neg F \to \Box G) \to \Box G)) \to \Box G)$$

8. For a fuller account of the connections between intuitionist logic and modal logic, see A. S. Troelstra's introductory note to Gödel's paper in *Kurt Gödel: Collected Works*, Vol. I, pp. 296–299.
9. See Smorynski, "Applications of Kripke models".

Chapter 13

1. Kenneth Kunen, *Set Theory: An Introduction to Independence Proofs.*
2. I am grateful to Tony Dodd for telling me of this theorem.
3. The proof is short enough and hard enough to find that we have decided to include it instead of merely citing it. The proof we give is taken from J. Barwise and E. Fisher, "The Shoenfield absoluteness lemma".
4. I am grateful to McGee for suggesting the material in this section.
5. Frank R. Drake, *Set Theory: An Introduction to Large Cardinals.* The discussion is on pp. 123–124.

Chapter 14

1. Hartley Rogers, *Theory of Recursive Functions and Effective Computability*; Gerald Sacks, *Higher Recursion Theory.*
2. Joel W. Robbin, *Mathematical Logic: A First Course.*
3. For further discussion, see the beginning of Chapter 15.
4. In particular, the reducibility of θ to O, it will be recalled, may be proved by effectively, and uniformly in x, converting the Brouwer–Kleene ordering K derived from θ and x into another linear ordering L with certain desirable properties (e.g., the order type of $L=\omega\cdot\zeta+1$, where ζ is the order type of K; successors and limits in L can be effectively recognized) and using the recursion theorem to define a function f on the field of L such that $x\in\theta$ iff K is a well-ordering, iff f embeds L into $<_O$, iff $g(x)\in O$, $g(x)$ being the image under f of the last element of L. Cf. Rogers, op. cit., pp. 205–212. The formalization in analysis presents no special difficulties.
5. As in Chapter 9, let $A^s=(\bigwedge\{(\Box C\rightarrow C)\text{: }\Box C \text{ is a subsentence of } A\}\rightarrow A)$. It will suffice to show that if $\mathrm{GL}\nvdash A^s$, then for some $*$, A^* is false.

   Thus we may suppose that for some n, W, R, V, $W=\{1,\ldots,n\}$, $1\nvDash A^s$, and so for all subsentences $\Box C$ of A, $1\vDash\Box C\rightarrow C$, and $1\nvDash A$. Without loss of generality, we may assume that if $w\in W$ and $w\neq 1$, then $1Rw$.

   We extend R and define the Solovay sentences $S_0, S_1, \ldots, S_n$ as above. We let $*(p)=\bigvee\{S_w\text{: } wVp \vee (w=0 \wedge 1Vp)\}$. It will suffice to show inductively that for all subsentences B of A, if $1\vDash B$, then $\vdash S_0\rightarrow B^*$ and if $1\nvDash B$, then $\vdash S_0\rightarrow\neg B^*$, for then since $1\nvDash A$ and S_0 is true, A^* is false. (Lemma 14 holds for all subsentences of A^s, hence for all subsentences of A.)

   Suppose $B=p$. If $1\vDash p$, then S_0 is a disjunct of B^*; if $1\nvDash p$, then by Lemma 6, S_0 is incompatible with every disjunct of B^*.

   The cases for the propositional connectives are unproblematic.

Suppose $B = \Box C$. Assume $1 \vDash \Box C$. Then since $1 \vDash \Box C \rightarrow C$, $1 \vDash C$, and by the i.h. $\vdash S_0 \rightarrow C^*$. Since $1 \vDash \Box C$, for every $w \in W$, $w \vDash C$. By Lemma 14, for every $w \in W$, $\vdash S_w \rightarrow C^*$. But since by Lemma 10, $\vdash S_0 \vee S_1 \vee \cdots \vee S_n$, whence $\vdash C^*$, $\vdash \Theta(\ulcorner C^* \urcorner)$, i.e., $\vdash B^*$, and so $\vdash S_0 \rightarrow B^*$.

Assume $1 \nvDash \Box C$. Then for some x, $1Rx$, $x \nvDash C$, whence by Lemma 14, $\vdash S_x \rightarrow \neg C^*$, and so $\vdash \neg \Theta(\ulcorner \neg S_x \urcorner) \rightarrow \neg B^*$. But $\vdash S_0 \rightarrow \neg \Theta(\ulcorner \neg S_x \urcorner)$, by Lemma 11.

Chapter 15

1. The word "simple" is sometimes used to distinguish ordinary consistency or provability from other kinds of consistency or provability, e.g., ω-consistency, ω-provability, or provability under the ω-rule.
2. Ignatiev called the system 'LN', but there was no reason for this choice of letters.

Chapter 17

1. For a proof, see, e.g., Chapter 19 of Boolos and Jeffrey's *Computability and Logic*.
2. Indeed, Δ^0_2, i.e., $\Sigma^0_2 \cap \Pi^0_2$, relations; and further improvements are possible.
3. The restriction to the pure predicate calculus is necessary: $\exists x \exists y \neg x = y$ is not valid but is always provable if $=$ is treated as a logical symbol.
4. Boolos, *The Unprovability of Consistency*, p. viii. The word "system" must be understood rather loosely for this statement to make sense.
5. A proof of Tennenbaum's theorem is given in Chapter 29 of the third edition of Boolos and Jeffrey's *Computability and Logic*.
6. Plisko, "On realizable predicate formulas".

Chapter 18

1. The theorems and techniques of proof in this chapter are due to V. A. Vardanyan and Vann McGee. I am extremely grateful to Warren Goldfarb, Vladimir A. Shavrukov, and McGee for explaining to me important aspects of Vardanyan's argumentation and for correcting errors. I have appropriated some of their terminology and notation.

Bibliography

Artemov, Sergei N., "Arithmetically complete modal theories," *Semiotika i Informatika* (1980), 115–33 (Russian).

"Nonarithmeticity of the truth predicate logics of provability," *Doklady Akademii nauk SSSR*, 284 (1985), 270–1 (Russian).

"Numerically correct logics of provability," *Doklady Akademii nauk SSSR*, 290 (1986), 1289–92 (Russian).

"On logics that have a provability interpretation," in *Questions of Cybernetics: Complexity of Computation and Applied Mathematical Logic*, ed. S. N. Adyan, Scientific Council on the Complexity Problem "Cybernetics," Academy of Sciences of the USSR, 1988, 5–22 (Russian).

Artemov, Sergei N., and Giorgie K. Dzhaparidze, "On effective predicate logics of provability," *Doklady Akademii nauk SSSR*, 297 (1987), 521–3 (Russian).

"Finite Kripke models and predicate logics of provability," *Journal of Symbolic Logic*, 55 (1990), 1090–8.

Avron, Arnon, "On modal systems having arithmetical interpretations," *Journal of Symbolic Logic*, 49 (1984), 935–42.

Barwise, Jon, and Edward Fisher, "The Shoenfield absoluteness lemma," *Israel Journal of Mathematics*, 8 (1970), 329–39.

Beklemishev, L. D., "Provability logics for natural Turing progressions of arithmetical theories," *Studia Logica*, 50 (1991), 107–28.

"On the classification of propositional logics of provability," *Izvestia Akademii nauk SSSR*, ser. math. 53 (1989), 915–43 (Russian).

Bernardi, C., "The fixed-point theorem for diagonalizable algebras," *Studia Logica*, 34 (1975), 239–51.

"On the equational class of diagonalizable algebras," *Studia Logica*, 34 (1975), 321–31.

"The uniqueness of the fixed-point in every diagonalizable algebra," *Studia Logica*, 35 (1976), 335–43.

Boolos, George, *The Unprovability of Consistency: An Essay in Modal Logic*, Cambridge University Press, 1979.

"On deciding the truth of certain statements involving the notion of consistency," *Journal of Symbolic Logic*, 41 (1976), 779–81.

"Reflection principles and iterated consistency assertions," *Journal of Symbolic Logic*, 44 (1979), 33–5.

"Omega-consistency and the diamond," *Studia Logica*, 39 (1980), 237–43.

"Provability, truth, and modal logic," *Journal of Philosophical Logic*, 8 (1980), 1–7.

"Provability in arithmetic and a schema of Grzegorczyk," *Fundamenta Mathematicae*, 96 (1980), 41–5.

"On systems of modal logic with provability interpretations," *Theoria*, 46 (1980), 7–18.

"Extremely undecidable sentences," *Journal of Symbolic Logic*, 47 (1982), 191–6.

"On the nonexistence of certain normal forms in the logic of provability," *Journal of Symbolic Logic*, 47 (1982), 638–40.

"The logic of provability," *American Mathematical Monthly*, 91 (1984), 470–80.

"The analytical completeness of Dzhaparidze's polymodal logics," *Annals of Pure and Applied Logic*, 61 (1993), 95–111.

Boolos, George, and Richard C. Jeffrey, *Computability and Logic*, 3d ed., Cambridge University Press, 1989.

Boolos, George, and Vann McGee, "The degree of the set of sentences of predicate provability logic that are true under every interpretation," *Journal of Symbolic Logic*, 52 (1987), 165–71.

Boolos, George, and Giovanni Sambin, "An incomplete system of modal logic," *Journal of Philosophical Logic*, 14 (1985), 351–8.

"Provability: the emergence of a mathematical modality," *Studia Logica*, 50 (1991), 1–23.

Buss, Samuel R., "The modal logic of pure provability," *Notre Dame Journal of Formal Logic*, 31 (1990), 225–31.

Carnap, Rudolf, *The Logical Syntax of Language*, Routledge and Kegan Paul, 1937.

Chellas, Brian F., *Modal Logic: an Introduction*, Cambridge University Press, 1980.

Cresswell, M. J., "Frames and models in modal logic," in *Algebra and Logic*, ed. J. N. Crossley, Springer-Verlag, 1975.

"Magari's theorem via the recession frame," *Journal of Philosophical Logic*, 16 (1987), 13–15.

Davis, Martin D., and Elaine J. Weyuker, *Computability, Complexity, and Languages: Fundamentals of Theoretical Computer Science*, Academic Press, 1983.

Drake, Frank R, *Set Theory: An Introduction to Large Cardinals*, North-Holland, 1974.

Dummett, Michael, *Elements of Intuitionism*, Oxford University Press, 1977.

Dzhaparidze, Giorgie, "The polymodal logic of provability," in *Intensional Logics and the Logical Structure of Theories: Material from the Fourth Soviet-Finnish Symposium on Logic, Telavi, May 20–24, 1985*, Metsniereba, Tbilisi, 1988 (Russian).

"The arithmetical completeness of the logic of provability with modality quantifiers," *Bulletin of the Academy of Sciences of the Georgian SSR*, 132 (1988), 265–8 (Russian).

"Decidable and enumerable predicate logics of provability," *Studia Logica*, 49 (1990), 7–21.

"Provability logic with modalities for arithmetical complexities," *Bulletin of the Academy of Sciences of the Georgian SSR*, 138 (1990), 481–4.

"Predicate provability logic with non-modalized quantifiers," *Studia Logica*, 50 (1991), 149–60.

Feferman, S., "Arithmetization of metamathematics in a general setting," *Fundamenta Mathematicae*, 49 (1960), 35–92.

"Transfinite recursive progressions of axiomatic theories," *Journal of Symbolic Logic*, 27 (1962), 259–316.

Fine, Kit, "Logics containing K4. Part I," *Journal of Symbolic Logic*, 39 (1974), 31–42.

Friedman, Harvey, "One hundred and two problems in mathematical logic," *Journal of Symbolic Logic*, 40 (1975), 113–29.

Gleit, Zachary, and Warren Goldfarb, "Characters and fixed points in provability logic," *Notre Dame Journal of Formal Logic*, 31 (1990), 26–36.

Gödel, Kurt, *Collected Works, Vol. I*, ed. Solomon Feferman et al., Oxford University Press, 1986.

"Über formal unentscheidbare Sätze der Principia Mathematica und verwandter Systeme I" ["On formally undecidable propositions of *Principia Mathematica* and related systems I"], *Monatshefte für Mathematik und Physik*, 38 (1931), 173–98, translated in Kurt Gödel, *Collected Works, Vol. I*, 145–95.

"Eine Interpretation des intuitionistischen Aussagenkalküls," *Ergebnisse eines mathematischen Kolloquiums*, 4 (1933), 6, translated in Kurt Gödel, *Collected Works, Vol. I*, 300–3.

Goldblatt, R., "Arithmetical necessity, provability and intuitionistic logic," *Theoria*, 44 (1978), 38–46.

Grzegorczyk, Andrzej, "Some relational systems and the associated topological spaces," *Fundamenta Mathematicae*, 60 (1967), 223–31.

Henkin, Leon, "A problem concerning provability," *Journal of Symbolic Logic*, 17 (1952), 160.

Heyting, Arend, *Intuitionism: an Introduction*, North-Holland, 1956.

Hilbert, D., and P. Bernays, *Grundlagen der Mathematik*, Vols. I and II, 2d ed., Springer-Verlag, 1968.

Hodges, Wilfrid, *Logic*, Penguin Books, 1977.

Hughes, G. E., and M. J. Cresswell, *A Companion to Modal Logic*, Methuen, 1984.

An Introduction to Modal Logic, Methuen, 1968.

Ignatiev, Konstantin N., "On strong provability predicates and the associated modal logics," *Journal of Symbolic Logic*, 58 (1993), 249–90.

"The closed fragment of Dzhaparidze's polymodal logic and the logic of Σ_1-conservativity," *ITLI Prepublication Series for Mathematical Logic and Foundations*, X-92-02, University of Amsterdam, 1992.

Jeffrey, Richard C., *Formal Logic: Its Scope and Limits*, 3d. ed. McGraw-Hill, 1991.

Jensen, Ronald, and Carol Karp, "Primitive recursive set functions," in *Axiomatic Set Theory*, Proceedings of Symposia in Pure Mathematics XIII(I), ed. Dana S. Scott, American Mathematical Society, 1971, 143–67.

Jeroslow, R. G., "Redundancies in the Hilbert-Bernays derivability conditions for Gödel's second incompleteness theorem," *Journal of Symbolic Logic*, 38 (1973), 359–67.

Kleene, Stephen Cole, *Introduction to Metamathematics*, Van Nostrand, 1952.

Kneale, William, and Martha Kneale, *The Development of Logic*, Oxford University Press, 1984.

Kreisel, G., "Mathematical logic," in *Lectures on Modern Mathematics III*, ed. T. L. Saaty, John Wiley and Sons, 1965.

Kreisel, G., and A. Lévy, "Reflection principles and their use for establishing the complexity of axiomatic systems," *Zeitschrift für mathematische Logik und Grundlagen der Mathematik*, 14 (1968), 97–142.

Kripke, Saul, "A completeness theorem in modal logic," *Journal of Symbolic Logic*, 24 (1959), 1–14.

"Semantical analysis of modal logic I. Normal modal propositional calculi," *Zeitschrift für mathematische Logik und Grundlagen der Mathematik*, 9 (1963), 67–96.

"Semantical analysis of modal logic II. Non-normal modal propositional calculi," in *The Theory of Models*, ed. J. W. Addison, L. Henkin, and A. Tarski, North-Holland, 1965.

"Semantical considerations on modal logic," *Acta Philosophica Fennica*, 16 (1963), 83–94.

"The undecidability of monadic modal quantification theory," *Zeitschrift für mathematische Logik und Grundlagen der Mathematik*, 8 (1962), 113–16.

Kunen, Kenneth, *Set Theory: An Introduction to Independence Proofs*, North-Holland, 1980.

Kuznetsov, A. V., and A. Yu. Muravitsky, "The logic of provability," *Abstracts of the 4th All-Union Conference on Mathematical Logic* (1976), 73 (Russian).

Lemmon, E. J., in collaboration with Dana Scott, *An Introduction to Modal Logic*, ed. Krister Segerberg, Americal Philosophical Quarterly monograph series, no. 11, 1977.

Lévy, Azriel, "Axiom schemata of strong infinity in axiomatic set theory," *Pacific Journal of Mathematics*, 10 (1960), 223–38.

Lewis, C. I., "Implication and the algebra of logic," *Mind*, 21 N.S. (1912), 522–31.

A Survey of Symbolic Logic, Dover Publications, Inc., 1960.

Lewis, C. I., and C. H. Langford, *Symbolic Logic*, Dover Publications, Inc., 1959.

Lewis, David, "Intensional logics without iterative axioms," *Journal of Philosophical Logic*, 3 (1974), 457–66.

Löb, M. H., "Solution of a problem of Leon Henkin," *Journal of Symbolic Logic*, 20 (1955), 115–18.

Lukasiewicz, Jan, *Aristotle's Syllogistic*, 2d ed., Oxford University Press, 1957.

Macintyre, A., and H. Simmons, "Gödel's diagonalization technique and related properties of theories," *Colloquium Mathematicum*, 28 (1973), 165–80.

Magari, R., "The diagonalizable algebras," *Bollettino della Unione Matematica Italiana*, 4 (1975), 321–31.

"Representation and duality theory for diagonalizable algebra," *Studia Logica*, 34 (1975), 305–13.

"Primi risultati sulla varietà di Boolos," *Bollettino della Unione Matematica Italiana*, 6, 1-B (1982), 359–67.

Makinson, D., "On some completeness theorems in modal logic," *Zeitschrift für mathematische Logik und Grundlagen der Mathematik*, 12 (1966), 379–84.

Maksimova, Larisa L., "Definability theorems in normal extensions of the provability logic," *Studia Logica*, 48 (1989), 495–507.

Marcus, Ruth Barcan, "A functional calculus of first order based on strict implication," *Journal of Symbolic Logic*, 11 (1946), 1–16.

"The identity of individuals in a strict functional calculus of first order," *Journal of Symbolic Logic*, 12 (1947), 12–15.

"Strict implication, deducibility, and the deduction theorem," *Journal of Symbolic Logic*, 18 (1953), 234–6.

"Modalities and intensional languages," *Synthese*, 13 (1961), 303–22.

McGee, Vann, *Truth, Vagueness, and Paradox: An Essay on the Logic of Truth*, Hackett Publishing Company, 1991.

"How truthlike can a predicate be? A negative result," *Journal of Philosophical Logic*, 14 (1985), 399–410.

McKinsey, John C. C., and Alfred Tarski, "Some theorems about the sentential calculi of Lewis and Heyting," *Journal of Symbolic Logic*, 13 (1948) 1–15.

Mendelson, Elliott, *Introduction to Mathematical Logic*, 3d ed., Wadsworth & Brooks/Cole, 1987.

Monk, J. Donald, *Mathematical Logic*, Springer-Verlag, 1976.

Montagna, Franco, "On the diagonalizable algebra of Peano arithmetic," *Bollettino della Unione Matematica Italiana*, 5, 16-B (1979), 795–812.

"The predicate modal logic of provability," *Notre Dame Journal of Formal Logic*, 25 (1984), 179–89.

Montague, R., "Syntactical treatments of modality, with corollaries on reflexion principles and finite axiomatizability," in R. Montague, *Formal Philosophy*, ed. Richmond H. Thomason, Yale University Press, 1974.

Moschovakis, Yiannis N., *Elementary Induction on Abstract Structures*, North-Holland, 1974.

Plisko, V. E., "On realizable predicate formulas," *Doklady Akademii nauk SSSR*, 212 (1973), 553–6 (Russian).

Quine, W. V., *Word and Object*, MIT Press and John Wiley and Sons, 1960.

"The ways of paradox," in W. V. Quine, *The Ways of Paradox and Other Essays*, revised and enlarged edition, Harvard University Press, 1976, 1–18.

"Necessary truth," in W. V. Quine, *The Ways of Paradox and Other Essays*, revised and enlarged edition, Harvard University Press, 1976, 68–76.

Rautenberg, Wolfgang, *Klassische und nichtklassische Aussagenlogik: Logik und Grundlagen der Mathematik*, Vieweg, 1979.

Reidhaar-Olson, Lisa, "A new proof of the fixed-point theorem of provability logic," *Notre Dame Journal of Formal Logic*, 31 (1990), 37–43.

Robbin, Joel W., *Mathematical Logic: A First Course*, W. A. Benjamin, 1969.

Rogers, Hartley, *Theory of Recursive Functions and Effective Computability*, McGraw-Hill, 1967.

Rosser, J. Barkley, "Extensions of some theorems of Gödel and Church," *Journal of Symbolic Logic*, 1 (1936), 87–91.

"Gödel theorems for non-constructive logics," *Journal of Symbolic Logic*, 2 (1937), 129–37.

Sacks, Gerald, *Higher Recursion Theory*, Springer-Verlag, 1990.

Sambin, Giovanni, "Un estensione del teorema di Löb," *Rendiconti del Seminario Matematico della Università di Padova*, 52 (1975), 193–9.

"An effective fixed point theorem in intuitionistic diagonalizable algebras," *Studia Logica*, 35 (1976), 345–61.

Sambin, Giovanni, and Silvio Valentini, "The modal logic of provability: The sequential approach," *Journal of Philosophical Logic*, 11 (1982), 311–42.

Schütte, Kurt, *Vollständige Systeme modaler und intuitionistischer Logik*, Springer-Verlag, 1968.

Segerberg, Krister, *An Essay in Classical Modal Logic*, Filosofiska Föreningen och Filosofiska Institutionen vid Uppsala Universitet, 1971.

Shavrukov, V. Yu., "The Lindenbaum fixed point algebra is undecidable," *Studia Logica*, 50 (1991), 143–7.

"A note on the diagonalizable algebras of PA and ZF," *ITLI Prepublication Series for Mathematical Logic and Foundations*, ML-91-09, University of Amsterdam, 1991.

Shoenfield, Joseph R., *Mathematical Logic*, Addison-Wesley, 1967.

Smiley, T. J., "The logical basis of ethics," *Acta Philosophica Fennica*, 16 (1963), 237–46.

Smorynski, C., *Self-reference and Modal Logic*, Springer-Verlag, 1985.

"Applications of Kripke models," in A. S. Troelstra, *Metamathematical Investigation of Intuitionistic Arithmetic and Analysis*, Springer-Verlag, 1973, 324–91.

"Consistency and related metamathematical properties," University of Amsterdam, Report 75-02, Department of Mathematics, 1975.

"The incompleteness theorems," in *Handbook of Mathematical Logic*, ed. Jon Barwise, North-Holland, 1977, 821–65.

"Beth's theorem and self-referential sentences," in *Logic Colloquium '77*, ed. A. Macintyre, L. Pacholski, and J. Paris, North-Holland, 1978, 253–61.

"Calculating self-referential statements I: Explicit calculations," *Studia Logica*, 38 (1979), 17–36.

"Fifty years of self-reference in arithmetic," *Notre Dame Journal of Formal Logic*, 22 (1981), 357–74.

"The development of self-reference: Löb's theorem," in *Perspectives on the History of Mathematical Logic*, ed. Thomas Drucker, Birkhäuser, 1991, 110–33.

Smullyan, Raymond M., *First-Order Logic*, Springer-Verlag, 1968.

"Languages in which self-reference is possible," *Journal of Symbolic Logic*, 22 (1957), 55–67.

Gödel's Incompleteness Theorems, Oxford University Press, 1992.

Sobocinski, B., "Family $\mathscr{K}$ of the non-Lewis systems," *Notre Dame Journal of Formal Logic*, 5 (1964), 313–18.

Solovay, Robert, "Provability interpretations of modal logic," *Israel Journal of Mathematics*, 25 (1976), 287–304.

Letter to George Boolos, Dated June 6, 1979.

Tarski, Alfred, "On the concept of logical consequence," in Alfred Tarski, *Logic, Semantics, Metamathematics*, Oxford University Press, 1956, 409–20.

Tarski, Alfred, in collaboration with Andrzej Mostowski and Raphael M. Robinson, *Undecidable Theories*, North-Holland, 1953.

Valentini, Silvio, "The modal logic of provability," *Journal of Philosophical Logic*, 12 (1983), 471–6.

van Benthem, J. F. A. K., Ph.D. Thesis, Department of Mathematics, University of Amsterdam, 1974.

van Benthem, J. F. A. K., and W. J. Blok, "Transitivity follows from Dummett's axiom," *Theoria*, 44 (1978), 117–18.

van Heijenoort, J., ed., *From Frege to Gödel: A Source Book in Mathematical Logic, 1879–1931*, Harvard University Press, 1967.

van Maaren, H., "Volledigheid v.d. modale logica L," Thesis, Mathematical Institute of the University of Utrecht, 1974.

Vardanyan, V. A., "On the predicate logic of provability," preprint of the Scientific Council on the Complexity Problem "Cybernetics," Academy of Sciences of the USSR, 1985 (Russian).

"Lower bounds on arithmetical complexity of predicate logics of provability and their fragments," preprint of the Scientific Council on the Complexity Problem "Cybernetics," Academy of Sciences of the USSR, 1985 (Russian).

"Arithmetical complexity of predicate logics of provability and their fragments," *Doklady Akademii nauk SSSR*, 288 (1986), 11–14 (Russian).

"Bounds on arithmetical complexity of predicate logics of provability," in *Questions of Cybernetics: Complexity of Computation and Applied Mathematical Logic*, ed. S. N. Adyan, Scientific Council on the Complexity Problem "Cybernetics," Academy of Sciences of the USSR, 1988, 46–72 (Russian).

Letter to George Boolos, dated May 5, 1988.

Letter to George Boolos, dated January 7, 1989.

Visser, Albert, *Aspects of Diagonalization and Provability*, Thesis, Department of Philosophy, University of Utrecht, 1981.

"The provability logics of recursively enumerable theories extending Peano Arithmetic at arbitrary theories extending Peano Arithmetic," *Journal of Philosophical Logic*, 13 (1984), 97–113.

"Peano's smart children: A provability logical study of systems with built-in consistency," *Notre Dame Journal of Formal Logic*, 30 (1989), 161–96.

"The formalization of interpretability," *Studia Logica*, 50 (1991), 81–105.

"An inside view of EXP," *Journal of Symbolic Logic*, 57 (1992), 131–65.

Whitehead, Alfred North, and Bertrand Russell, *Principia Mathematica*, 2d ed., Cambridge University Press, 1927.

Index

Notation and symbols